W. Somerset Maugham
and the Quest for Freedom

2

Robert Lorin Calder

3

W. Somerset Maugham
and the Quest for Freedom

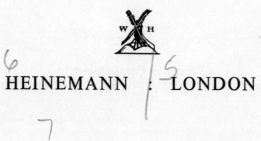

6
5

HEINEMANN : LONDON

7
1972
9

William Heinemann Ltd
15 Queen Street, Mayfair, London W1X 8BE

LONDON · MELBOURNE · TORONTO
JOHANNESBURG · AUCKLAND

First published 1972

© Robert Lorin Calder 1972

434 10504 x

Printed in Great Britain by
Richard Clay (The Chaucer Press) Ltd, Bungay, Suffolk

For Mother and Ernie

Contents

		page
	PREFACE	ix

Chapter

I	Biographical Introduction	1
II	*Liza of Lambeth* and the Novels of Misery	39
III	Seven Early Novels: Experiments and Potboilers	52
IV	*Of Human Bondage* and the Novels of Apprenticeship	78
V	*The Moon and Sixpence* and the Artist-Hero Novels	131
VI	Marriage: A Condition of Bondage	152
VII	*Cakes and Ale*	172
VIII	The Cosmopolitan: Aspects of the Maugham *Persona*	200
IX	*The Razor's Edge* and the New Vedanta	224
X	Conclusion	254

Appendices

| A | 'Rosie' | 267 |
| B | Maugham's Role in Allied Espionage in Russia in 1917 | 273 |

C Five Fictional Portraits of Somerset
   Maugham   290
D Images of Bondage and Freedom   298

NOTES   301

A SELECT BIBLIOGRAPHY   317

INDEX   322

Preface

'Willie' Maugham, the man, was an enigma; W. Somerset Maugham, the literary artist, remains a mystery. Although he has always had a following of responsible critics, the majority is still prone to dismiss him as a superficial commercial author. For a great many reasons his writing has disturbed the critical fraternity, and he has been largely ignored in the important studies of twentieth-century literature.

The number of comprehensive critical studies of Maugham's writing available to the student and to the interested ordinary reader is depressingly small. Paul Dottin's *W. Somerset Maugham et ses Romans* (1928), Suzanne Guéry's *La Philosophie de Somerset Maugham* (1933), and Richard Heron Ward's *W. Somerset Maugham* (1937), valuable as they are, were written too early to examine more than a part of his work. Karl G. Pfeiffer's *Somerset Maugham* (1959) is superficial; John Brophy's pamphlet, *Somerset Maugham* (1958) is necessarily brief; and Laurence Brander's *Somerset Maugham: A Guide* (1963) is limited. M. K. Naik's *W. Somerset Maugham* (1966) is an interesting survey of Maugham's career, but tends to reduce his writing to a struggle between cynicism and humanitarianism. Ronald E. Barnes' *The Dramatic Comedy of William Somerset Maugham* (1968) is perceptive, but necessarily restricted to one area of his body of work.

Since these books were written before 1965, there has been in effect no serious lengthy examination of Maugham's career produced since his death. Ivor Brown's *W. Somerset Maugham* (1970) is a penetrating analysis of Maugham's character, but one wishes that it were longer than seventy-six pages. The one satisfactory monograph on the man and his writing, Richard Cordell's *W. Somerset Maugham: A Biographical and Critical Study*, was published in 1961, with a new concluding chapter added in 1969. This is surely insufficient for a career as lengthy as that of Somerset Maugham.

The absence of serious consideration of Maugham's writing seems strange when one considers his achievements. Had he written nothing

but plays, *The Circle* and *The Constant Wife* would have assured him
a prominent position in the history of English dramatic comedy. Had
he written nothing but novels, *Of Human Bondage* and *Cakes and Ale*
would have guaranteed him a place among the best English novelists.
Had he written nothing but short stories, he would be remembered as
the greatest English exponent of that genre in the twentieth century.
In addition, he wrote some of the best travel books, some charming
and perceptive essays, and one of the most distinguished literary
autobiographies of this century. Although he may not have achieved
greatness in any one form, there are few modern English writers who
have achieved so much in so many fields.

It would be foolish to claim greatness for Maugham, and he
would have been embarrassed by the use of that word. He is nevertheless a very good writer, a superb craftsman who is far better than
his current reputation in academic circles, who misses greatness
because of a number of inherent weaknesses. It is therefore worth
examining Maugham's career as a whole to discover why he was able,
for five decades, to maintain an immense popularity with a great
many common readers and a minority of intellectual ones, and to
determine why he will not stand among the greatest English writers.

This study examines Maugham's career from two separate, yet
interacting, points of view. First, it shows that the most cherished
value in his life was personal freedom, and that this became the
central theme running throughout his writing. His concern with the
manifestations of freedom and dependence has been frequently
analysed in criticism of *Of Human Bondage*, but the extent to which
this theme dominates the remainder of his work has not previously
been recognised.

Physical and spiritual freedom is, in some form, the guiding spirit
behind most writers and artists, and it is in no way exclusive to
Maugham. A condition or attitude sought by most people of any
period, the concept of freedom has no boundaries and can assimilate
all other ideas, hopes, responses, arguments, and actions into its
framework. Thus, the struggling artist can be seen to be seeking the
freedom to express his creative instincts, and the tyrant can be
viewed as searching for the liberty to commit any act. In this study,
however, the idea of freedom, independence, liberty, and liberation,
is restricted to the individual's ability to realise the strongest elements
in his character without subjugating the lives and personalities of
others. Maugham's various expressions of true independence, however, mean a sacrifice of human involvement and of human life itself,
and thus one must determine whether his studies of freedom are
ultimately a negative rejection of life or a positive search for the

state of liberty in which the human personality can realise its potential to the fullest measure.

The second consideration is that of Maugham as a dedicated professional author. More than many writers, he was astute at sensing the literary climate at any particular time and therefore able to produce fiction which could be expected to have an appeal. This explains why his writing, more than that of almost any other writer, rarely seemed dated at the time of publication. It can be seen, ultimately, that Maugham's central theme was the forms which freedom and bondage take, and that this recurs again and again in new expressions as literary fashions change.

Since he was conservative in his approach to experiments in form, there is little relation between Maugham and the great innovators of English literature in this century—James Joyce, Virginia Woolf, D. H. Lawrence, and others. Instead, he must be considered in connection with writers such as Samuel Butler, Arthur Morrison, Henry Handel Richardson, Arnold Bennett, and many others from whose examples he profited. A careful examination shows that, while he avoided the innovations in form in the literature of his time, he was influenced by various genres and themes—such as slum literature, the novel of adolescence, the artist-hero novel, and the novel of mysticism —which enjoyed popularity at various times during his life.

This study will by no means explain fully the enigma of Somerset Maugham, but hopefully it will contribute to a proper and objective evaluation of a writer who has been too much ignored.

I wish to express my gratitude to Mr J. R. B. Horden, Director of the Institute of Bibliography and Textual Criticism at the University of Leeds, whose advice, criticism, encouragement, and many kindnesses, made my research a source of immense pleasure. Among many others who assisted me, I am especially grateful to the late Sir Gerald Kelly, who, although sceptical of academic investigation into the lives of 'Willie' and his friends, treated my enquiries with patience and generosity; I am indebted to him for numerous insights into Maugham. Sir Ronald Howe was also kind enough to talk to me about Maugham and to offer unqualified assistance in my research. I am also indebted to Lord Clark, Lord Maugham, and Mr Richard A. Cordell for their consideration in answering my queries and bringing their knowledge to bear on my hypotheses. I am grateful to Mr R. N. Pittman and The King's School, Canterbury, who without hesitation gave me access to the Maugham Library and to the Maugham manuscripts. Others who assisted in some measure include Mr Alan Searle, Mr R. D. Chambers, Mr Garson Kanin, and Mrs John Nesfield. I am indebted as well to my brother, Dr Kenneth J.

Calder, who brought to my attention a number of important documents concerning Maugham which I would not otherwise have discovered. I acknowledge the skill of Mr Geoffrey V. Wilkins, who read my proofs and compiled the index. Finally I must acknowledge the assistance of my wife, Barbara, whose patience, criticism and encouragement were a source of strength.

R.L.C.

University of Saskatchewan,
Saskatoon, Canada.
July 1972

I

Biographical Introduction

"The main thing I've always asked from life is freedom. Outer and inner freedom, both in my way of living and my way of writing."[1]

IN THIS STATEMENT Somerset Maugham summed up his life and revealed the guiding purpose in it: the quest for freedom. Examined in its many fascinating stages, the course of his life can indeed be seen to be a succession of attempts to discover complete freedom—not merely physical liberty, but true independence of spirit. What this freedom involved was not merely escape from physical ties, financial dependence, or the restraints of time and place. These were only the external aspects of a search for a deeper liberation—intellectual freedom and emotional detachment. In one way or another, almost everything Maugham willingly did was motivated by this vision.

Somerset Maugham was a man of great complexity, whose life spanned almost ninety-one years. He remained in many ways mysterious, even to his friends, during his lifetime, and he was determined that nothing should be told which did not fit into the pattern he had designed for his career. Thus in 1957 he published a request that all his friends destroy any correspondence from him, and in 1958 he burned practically all his papers, notes, letters, fragments, and unpublished material. There were many who wanted to tell his story, but he always discouraged potential biographers. An accurate rendering of Maugham's life is therefore a very elusive matter; it will not come about without a great amount of diligent research, and it will have to be a massive study. So the interpretation of Maugham, the man, presented here is in no way intended to be a complete portrait. It concentrates, rather, on some of the most important aspects of his personality, particularly those which explain much about the course taken by his literary career.

The key to the complexities and paradoxes of Maugham, the man, must surely lie in the miseries of his youth. In a letter to this author, Maugham's nephew, Robin (Robert Cecil Romer Maugham, 2nd Viscount Maugham of Hartfield), wrote:

> I find your general idea about my uncle's "concern for his independence" extremely interesting and I am sure it is valid.
>
> But I think essentially he was a person who was crippled by his emotional experiences as a child and from which he never recovered, for all his success.[2]

Indeed, Maugham's youth is almost a psychological textbook example of the deprived childhood, and it is here that many of the sources of later obsessions can be found, particularly the seeds of his intense desire for physical and emotional independence.

The first important factor in Maugham's life was his birth in France. Born in the British Embassy in Paris to the wife of an English solicitor on 25 January 1874, Maugham spent his first ten years in France and in many respects was raised as a native. His first language was therefore French, not English, and when he was sent to live in England after the death of his father it was as if he had entered a foreign country. He had only begun to learn English two years earlier when he had been taken out of the French school he attended and was taught by an English clergyman attached to the embassy. On disembarking at Dover, all he could say was: 'Porteur! Cabriolet!', and many years later he wrote in *The Summing Up* of the humiliation he felt when at school he pronounced the phrase 'unstable as water' as if 'unstable' rhymed with 'Dunstable'.

The effect of Maugham's French background on his literary career is obvious; it accounts a great deal for his love of French literature and is responsible for many of the French characteristics of his writing. Nevertheless, while Maugham later acknowledged that his years in Paris were an intellectually liberating experience, he attributed to them a serious emotional handicap:

> The accident of my birth in France, which enabled me to learn French and English simultaneously and thus instilled into me two modes of life, two liberties, two points of view, has prevented me from ever identifying myself completely with the instincts and prejudices of one people or the other, and it is in instinct and prejudice that sympathy is most deeply rooted.[3]

It is easy to see that, for a ten-year-old French-speaking boy, life in an English village in the late nineteenth century could present difficulties. They are, of course, problems which could be overcome, but Maugham at least felt that language represented a barrier between himself and his fellows. It has also been suggested, with some plausibility, that the change of primary language in his youth contributed to his lifelong stammer.

The most traumatic episode of Maugham's life occurred in these early years—the death of his mother on 31 January 1882, when he was eight years old. When he was four years of age his three older brothers were sent to a boarding school in England and in the following years his mother's love was lavished almost exclusively on him. A woman of beauty, charm and wit, Edith Maugham provided her son with an environment of love, protection and security. Young Willie shared a bedroom with his French nurse, but he was allowed to spend the mornings in the seclusion of his mother's room while she rested in bed. In the afternoons he would be taken in to tea, at which he met his mother's friends, many of whom were prominent in Parisian society. Edith Maugham, however, had long suffered from tuber- culosis, and her early death from this disease was a shock from which Maugham never fully recovered. Robin Maugham explains:

I suppose that this was one of the most important periods in his long life, for though he was to write only a little about it in his reminiscences, his early boyhood and his mother's illness and her death had a profound effect on his character which endured to his own death. Her love, her protection, her physical beauty, her comfortable apartment, and her elegant pattern of living—all were suddenly torn away from him and replaced soon by an environment so alien and bleak and so lacking in affection that it scarred his mind forever.[4]

The strength of Maugham's life-long affection for his mother's memory was demonstrated in a number of ways. For a great many years, his bedside bureau contained three pictures of her, at least one of which was there the day he died. A vivid revelation of the psycho- logical scars borne by Maugham from that time occurred when, in 1945, he was asked to record for a series of 'Talking Books' for the blind the section of *Of Human Bondage* in which he describes the death of Philip's mother. Although it was then more than fifty years after the event, Maugham broke down and wept when he came to Philip's last meeting with his mother, and he could not continue. Similarly, in *Somerset and All the Maughams* Robin Maugham tells of dining with his uncle late in his life, when the old man suddenly inter- jected: 'I shall never get over her death. I shall never get over it.'

The death of Maugham's mother may also have had a lasting effect on the future portrayal of his fictional heroines. When his mother died he was at the age when, according to psychologists, boys tend to develop a type of romantic attachment to their mother. Most boys grow out of it, but Maugham was perhaps prevented from reaching this natural maturity by her death. Certainly, the heroines of his fiction, whether it be Liza, Norah, Ata, or Rosie, all have a strong maternal element in their characters. Rosie is Maugham's most fully developed female character and her maternal treatment of 'Willie Ashenden' is a clear attraction in their relationship. Maugham may have unconsciously invested his heroines with this quality which he had seen disappear with his mother's death.

Another formative element in Maugham's early life in Paris was the class into which he was born and the social milieu in which his parents lived. His father, Robert Ormond Maugham (1823–84), had followed the family profession by becoming a solicitor. Having established a flourishing partnership with William Dixon, Robert Maugham managed the Paris office, and around 1850 he became solicitor to the British Embassy. This meant that Maugham's parents became part of the society which surrounded the embassy, and their mode of living was stylish, glamorous and comfortable. Their apartment in the Avenue d'Antin was large, and they employed a number of servants. Young Willie thus grew up with the impression that his parents possessed great wealth.

According to Maugham's nephew, however, Robert Maugham had been forced in later years to work very hard to sustain the family's style of living, and when he died of cancer in 1884 it was discovered that each son was left only one hundred and fifty pounds a year. In that age, when the pound was worth much more than it is today, this may have been a healthy sum; however, in contrast to the apparent wealth of the Maughams in Paris it looked small. Although he was only ten years old at the time, the boy's relatively meagre income was something which he never forgot, and the realisation of his financial vulnerability distressed him. For the remainder of his life he would pursue economic security almost as an obsession.

Upon the death of his father Willie was sent to Whitstable in Kent to live with his uncle, the Reverend Henry MacDonald Maugham, and his German-born wife, and these years were the most miserable of his life. They have been recorded with fidelity in the early sections of *Of Human Bondage*, and the manner in which Philip's character is warped by the wretchedness of his youth reflects Maugham's interpretation of his own childhood. A visit to the vicarage in Whitstable today yields much evidence of the autobiographical nature of that picture.

In addition to the economic factor, the difference between life in the diplomatic circles of Paris and that in a clergyman's home in Kent was a shock to the young boy. Whereas in Paris every comfort had been readily available, in Whitstable Maugham's aunt and uncle had constantly to scrutinise the spending of money. One of their economies—that of sharing *The Times* with a neighbour—later appeared in *Of Human Bondage*. Maugham, moreover, accustomed to the titled and cultured people with whom his parents associated in Paris, was humiliated by the way in which his uncle deferred to the local figures of Kentish society. Robin Maugham writes:

"My uncle toadied to the local squire," Willie told me. "And the man was just a vulgar lout. He'd *never* have been tolerated in my mother's drawing room. My uncle was a cracking snob. I was never allowed even to speak to the local tradesmen."[5]

The shame of seeing his uncle 'toadying' to the local squire was, according to Maugham's nephew, the reason that he later relished friendship with the titled and the affluent.

Maugham's portraits of his uncle, bitter in *Of Human Bondage* and softened in *Cakes and Ale*, are not generous, but then the Rev. Mr Maugham was not a pleasant or admirable man. According to those who knew him, he was narrow-minded, unintelligent, pedantic, lazy, snobbish, and severe. His wife, it seems, was affectionate but prim and straitlaced. When Willie arrived from France, they were in their fifties and childless, and a small shy young boy was almost an intrusion on their well-ordered household. Although Maugham grew in time to have some sort of affectionate relationship with his aunt, his uncle seems to have been constitutionally incapable of understanding the young boy, and he remained distant and austere. Deprived of his parents' love, and separated from his three brothers, young Willie must indeed have spent many unhappy hours at the vicarage. The cost to him in emotional terms is perhaps revealed in a passage written years later in *A Writer's Notebook*:

He had had so little love when he was small that later it embarrassed him to be loved. It made him feel shy and awkward when someone told him that his nose was good and his eyes mysterious. He did not know what to say when someone paid him a compliment and a manifestation of affection made him feel a fool.[6]

Added to the unhappy life at the vicarage, Maugham suffered from a physical disability which was to plague him all his life—his stammer. Already a sensitive and sheltered boy, in some ways more French than English, his speech impediment further handicapped him in making friends. This affected him to such a degree that he once prayed for a miracle to transform him, just as Philip Carey in *Of Human Bondage* prays for his club-foot to be made normal. Considering the natural thoughtlessness of children, it is not hard to imagine the amount of ridicule and humiliation to which Maugham must have been subjected. Cruelty, however, is not exclusive to children, and Maugham remembered suffering from the impatience of adults. He has described how the schoolmasters in Canterbury seized on his stammer as a point of vulnerability, and his frustration is vividly expressed in another incident. Having been to London, Maugham went to get a train ticket. After some time in a long queue, his turn came, but to his horror he could not get the words out. 'Whitstable' would not come, and finally two men pushed him aside:

" 'We can't wait all night for you,' they said; 'stop wasting our time.' So I had to go to the back of the queue and start all over again. I'll never forget the humiliation of that moment – with everyone staring at me.''[7]

There is no doubt that Maugham's affliction very much helped to shape his belief that the nature of the soul is determined by one's physical being, and it certainly moulded his own personality. His description of Arnold Bennett's stammer reveals much about his attitude to his own impediment:

Arnold was afflicted with a very bad stammer; it was painful to watch the struggle he sometimes had to get the words out. It was torture to him. Few realised the exhaustion it caused him to speak. What to most men is as easy as breathing was to him a constant strain. It tore his nerves to pieces. Few knew the humiliations it exposed him to, the ridicule it excited in many, the impatience it aroused, the awkwardness of feeling that it made people find him tiresome, the minor exasperation of thinking of a good, amusing or apt remark and not venturing to say it in case the stammer ruined it. Few knew the distressing sense it gave rise to of a bar to complete contact with other men. It may be that except for the stammer which forced him to introspection Arnold would never have become a writer. But I think it is no small proof of his strong and sane character that, notwithstanding this impediment, he was able to retain his splendid balance and regard the normal life of man from a normal point of view.[8]

The final sentence of this passage carries a special emphasis, because Maugham certainly was convinced that *his* stammer had affected his life and had prevented him from ever having 'a normal point of view'. He believed that his stammer had isolated him in his youth to such a degree that he could never thereafter respond normally to emotional intimacy. In his introduction to *A Traveller's Library*, he tells how his impediment, and more important the nervousness that accompanied it, separated him from the common life of his fellows. He has never, he says, been able to lose himself in a crowd, so that his emotions have become merged with the rest; he remains always an outsider. When on New Year's Eve people join hands to sing 'Auld Lang Syne', he always feels exceedingly embarrassed. Lord Clark, a friend of Maugham for over thirty years, corroborates this emotional reticence: 'He disliked open expressions of heartiness and shrank from the well-meaning greetings of "good guys".'[9]

Maugham's stammer, like that of Arnold Bennett, contributed to making him introspective and detached. It made it impossible for him to go into the family profession of law, and it hindered him socially. There can be little doubt that some of the detachment of the narrator of his fiction owes its origin to this physical impediment.

In addition to his stammer, Maugham was throughout his life plagued with an obsession about his short stature. According to Sir Ronald Howe, who knew him from the nineteen-thirties until his death, Maugham had a deeply felt inferiority complex about his height. He would frequently complain that he was too short and that things would be much different if he were taller. Whether or not a few inches would have essentially changed anything, Maugham remained convinced throughout his life that this was important. In 1930 he wrote in his notebook: 'The world is an entirely different place to the man of five foot seven from what it is to the man of six foot two.'

At the age of ten Maugham was sent to King's School, Canterbury, and his wretchedness there has been vividly recreated in the early part of *Of Human Bondage*. The bullying and ridicule to which he was subjected is the familiar story of many sensitive boys at English public schools—the tale has been told many times by writers such as Hugh Walpole, E. M. Forster, Osbert Sitwell, George Orwell and Cyril Connolly. It is clear, moreover, that Maugham intensely disliked the restraints imposed on him by a school whose masters did nothing which drew his admiration. His longing for freedom reached its apex on the occasion when he was bullied for his stammering. Having been asked to construe a passage in Latin, he began to stammer, and soon the whole class was laughing. Finally, says Maugham, the master called him a fool and ordered him to sit down.[10]

The most vivid aspect of this episode, although written over seventy years after it happened, is the frustration of the small boy who has no control over events around him. Unable to speak easily, unable to prevent himself from becoming an object of ridicule, and unable to gain revenge on his tormentors, he longs for the time when he will be master of the situation, when he will associate with people on his own terms. That day being a long way in the future, Maugham soon achieved the next best thing and escaped by going to the Continent to study for a year.

When the various elements in Maugham's childhood are considered, it is obvious that his early life contained little happiness, and he once summed up this period by saying: 'I shall never forget the misery of those next few years.'[11] In his maturity he was to have an almost inordinate affection for children, and he most deeply sympathised with those who had suffered in childhood. He was, for example, careful to point out the unhappy childhoods of Jules Renard (in the preface to *A Writer's Notebook*) and Augustus Hare (in 'Augustus', *The Vagrant Mood*). The most significant result of his misery, however, was the drive to achieve independence, to be free from his tormentors. He sought to escape from the austere régime of an uncle whom he despised yet upon whom he was dependent, and he wished to be free from the restrictions of public school. Perhaps most deeply of all, he wished to reach a position where he would be liberated from the hindrance of his stammer. Whatever the reasons, the young man rejoiced when he was finally able to break away from the dull conventional life in Kent and find independence in Germany and London.

Maugham's first taste of real liberty came when, at seventeen, he spent a year in Heidelberg, and it was an experience which he always recalled with fondness. Here he was his own master, and he was able for the first time to experience real intellectual freedom, leading finally to his rejection of religious belief. He revelled in his liberty.

Upon his return to England his uncle pressed him to go into the Church, but, as Maugham later said in his autobiography, 'I had for the first time tasted freedom and I could not bear the thought of going to Cambridge and being subjected once more to restraint.' It was finally decided that he would study to be a doctor. Medicine did not especially appeal to Maugham, but the opportunity of living in London outweighed the disadvantages. He had his own lodgings, some free time, and solitude. The classes might be dull, 'But I had the freedom I yearned for.'

Some time during his days as a medical student Maugham began the practice of keeping a notebook, a habit which endured until very late in his life. His later comment on many of the early exaggerated and immature entries reveals just how much he felt he had been emancipated upon leaving Whitstable:

They are the expression of a very young man's reaction to real life, or what he thought was such, and to liberty, after the sheltered and confined existence, perverted by fond fancies and the reading of novels, which was natural to a boy in the class in which I was born; and they are the expression of his revolt from the ideas and conventions of the environment in which he had been brought up.[12]

Liberating as it seemed, life in London was merely a stage in Maugham's quest. He had tasted a measure of independence and he wanted more. Five years of medical studies, and of struggling to live on his relatively meagre income, began to seem like years of drudgery. He had for a long time wanted to be a writer but, because of the feeling still prevalent even at the turn of the century that professional authorship was 'common', he had been discouraged by his family.

When his brother, Henry Neville Maugham, himself a writer (a gentleman author, however, not a professional), read *Liza of Lambeth*, he advised Willie to forget any ideas he had of a literary career. Nevertheless, when *Liza of Lambeth* was published in 1897, Maugham believed that his literary reputation was assured, and he saw his way out of medicine. He went to Spain to write, and eight years later he described what the country represented for him:

So to myself Seville means ten times more than it can mean to others. I came to it after weary years in London, heartsick with much hoping, my mind dull with drudgery; and it seemed a land of freedom. There I became at last conscious of my youth, and it seemed a *belvedere* upon a new life. How can I forget the delight of wandering in the Sierpes, released at length from all imprisoning ties, watching the various movement as though it were a stage-play, yet half afraid that the falling curtain would bring back reality.[13]

Maugham soon discovered, however, that his literary career had not been established, and he returned to London for a period of struggle and, if we are to believe his account, economic hardship. His novels evoked only lukewarm public response, and his plays were rejected. After the appearance of *Liza of Lambeth* he had been invited to luncheons, dinners, dances and parties, but as his reputation flagged the invitations came less frequently. In 1904 he therefore sought once more to break out of the routine into which he had fallen, and he went to Paris. A preface written in 1955 for the revised edition of *Mrs Craddock*, in which he discusses the influence of France on the young man he was, tells a great deal about what he was seeking: 'The only excuse I can make for his attitude, besides his youth, is that for him England signified constraint and convention, whereas France signified freedom and adventure.'[14]

After three more years of struggle, Maugham suddenly achieved brilliant success as a dramatist. In October 1907 the Court Theatre in London produced *Lady Frederick*, and the following year *Mrs Dot* played at the Comedy, *Jack Straw* at the Vaudeville, and *The Explorer* at the Lyric. Thus almost instantaneously the writer who had previously been able to see only one of his plays in production had achieved what no other dramatist had ever done—having four plays running simultaneously in London. His commercial popularity was established, and from this point on his financial security was never endangered.

Until recent years, when the advertising and selling of books has become super-efficient and when film rights have greatly inflated their value, Maugham was probably the highest-paid writer in history. In the first three decades of the twentieth century, when the artist had become most alienated from his audience, a great many critics irrationally used this to belittle Maugham's intentions, assuming that any contemporary who writes books which appeal to a great many people must be prostituting his art. Until his popularity as a dramatist, Maugham was indeed guilty of writing a few 'pot-boilers', but he has always maintained that the greatest value of his financial success was its liberation from economic dependence. In 1908 he observed in his notebook:

Success. I don't believe it has had any effect on me. For one thing I always expected it, and when it came I accepted it as so natural that I didn't see anything to make a fuss about. Its only net value to me is that it has freed me from financial uncertainties that were never quite absent from my thoughts. I hated poverty. I hated having to scrape and save so as to make both ends meet.[15]

Maugham's idea of poverty seems hardly to have been what is generally meant by the word. He may have had to exercise restraint on spending, but he never suffered the extreme penury of many other struggling artists. Sir Gerald Kelly, who knew Maugham in the latter half of this period, does not recall him being in great financial need. Richard Cordell has pointed out that he always had his hundred and fifty pounds from his father's estate and an average yearly income of a hundred pounds from his writing.[16] Nevertheless, these years gave Maugham a desire for the security of money which lasted to the end of his life.

In *Remembering Mr Maugham* Garson Kanin tells a fascinating story which illustrates Maugham's concern for money even in his eighties. Kanin and his wife, Ruth Gordon, are travelling with Maugham to Paris in 1954, and when the conversation turns to currency, Maugham instructs his secretary to show them his funds:

Alan picks up one of the attache cases, unlocks it, and opens it. I damn near fall out because there, neatly stacked and packed, are huge piles of American currency. I see nothing but $100 bills in fat stacks.

"Holy God!" I exclaim.

Ruth says practically, "Is it safe to carry that much around?"

Maugham: "Certainly not. It's most . . . dangerous. There's over a hundred thousand dollars there. It might easily be lost or stolen. The train might be . . . derailed, or the Channel boat might sink."

I ask the logical, dumb question, "Why do you do it then?"

"Because," says Maugham, "I was once trapped in the . . . fall of France without sufficient currency in my possession, and vowed at that time that, should I . . . come through, I would never again permit myself to be caught in a similar situation. Experience has . . . taught me that American currency is usually the best coin. Had I had some at that time, I might have saved myself and my friends a good deal of . . . difficulty and discomfort."

He reaches out and touches the money with his fingertips, reassuringly.[17]

The importance to Maugham of his success was the spiritual liberation that it gave him. As he was to demonstrate in *Of Human Bondage*, he never believed that penury and struggle are ennobling; they tend to degrade the character, to force it into meanness and pettiness. Financial security, on the other hand, gives the individual a measure of emotional stability, and he argued that this improved his character. As he was to claim later, it is the poor who are obsessed with wealth; those who have it know its advantages and disadvantages and can view it with detachment.

From the artist's point of view, however, Maugham's financial security gave him something else—freedom of action—and with this came a large degree of artistic freedom. Much later he wrote:

I was glad to earn a great deal of money as a dramatist. It gave me liberty. I was careful with it because I did not want ever again to be in a position when for want of it I could not do anything I had really a mind to.[18]

Maugham was grateful because 'I now had the liberty I had always desired and could tell any publisher or theatrical manager to go to hell—as, at times, I have.'[19] His newly acquired freedom of action was indeed exercised in questions of artistic integrity more frequently than his critics like to admit. His independence enabled him to resist the pleas of Charles Frohman to lighten the second act of *The Land of Promise* in order to satisfy the demands of the box office. When he was invited to Hollywood in 1920—along with other writers such as Maurice Maeterlinck, Edward Knoblock, Gouverneur Morris, Gertrude Atherton and Sir Gilbert Parker—to be in effect window-dressing for the film studio, he was able to turn his back on this charade without even watching the shooting of his script. Similarly, Maugham wrote to his American literary agent, Charles Hanson Towne, to protect his artistic independence: 'I will not conceal from you that I am extremely vexed at your having signed an agreement with Doran which gives me nothing that I wanted but on the contrary takes away what I value most dearly, my freedom of action.'[20] George H. Doran himself testified to Maugham's artistic integrity:

I have been with him on two occasions when he gave emphatic evidence of his freedom. One was when he returned a cheque for $25,000 offered to him if he would write a brief scenario for one of the earliest talking picture producers. The other was when he returned a contract which involved the payment within twelve months of not less a sum than $150,000 if he would write talking-picture scenarios. He was totally unwilling to risk the hazard of any misrepresentation of his art.[21]

The most tangible literary result of his financial independence was, of course, that he could afford to devote several years to writing *Of Human Bondage*.

Wealth, however, seems to have meant something more to Maugham than mere luxury or the power to control his artistic career. From all accounts, he was not a self-indulgent man, and his tastes, despite the impression given by his first-person narrator, were relatively simple. Yet he was surrounded by the trappings of wealth. Both Cyril Connolly[22] and Malcolm Muggeridge argue that money represented for him a defence from the world. Emotionally damaged by a childhood of loneliness, lovelessness and physical impediment, Maugham used wealth to create a wall between himself and those from whom he wished to be defended. Muggeridge writes:

> Like all timid, lonely people, money seemed to him a protection. It set up a buffer between him and a largely alien and hostile world. To this end he sought it, first diligently and ardently, and finally as an addiction.[23]

Maugham's financial success enabled him in 1928 to buy the Villa Mauresque, in St-Jean Cap Ferrat. This beautiful and spacious home along the Riviera provided him with an ideal fortress; from here he could travel to all parts of the world and return to its seclusion and protection. Here, too, he could entertain many of the greatest names in literature, art, politics and society—it might be H. G. Wells, Winston Churchill, Michael Arlen, Kenneth Clark, or Noël Coward —and he could meet them on his own terms. In his own microcosmic world he could set the scenes, arrange the people, and make his entrances and exits when he wished (his schedule, for example, included the morning spent writing, and no one was ever permitted to disturb this). In this regard, his old friend Sir Gerald Kelly, in a conversation with this author in September 1969, said that at the Villa one did as Maugham expected or one knew that the invitation might not be extended again. It was not that Maugham acted in an authoritarian manner; it was, rather, that the situations in a setting of his own design were never likely to threaten his essential self.

Despite Maugham's gratification at his sudden popularity in 1908, he later looked back upon his success with a realisation of some of its drawbacks. Success, he claimed in *The Summing Up*, is the most difficult thing with which the writer has to cope: 'When after a long and bitter struggle he has at last achieved it he finds that it spreads a snare to entangle and destroy him.' Recognition, he discovered, places the writer in a new world and it carries its own restrictions and barriers. He finds it difficult to remain close to the world in which he formerly moved, the way of life which has given him his material. His old friends can no longer associate with him with ease, and the new world may never be fully open to him. The successful author suddenly finds that there are new responsibilities, new claims on him.

In Maugham's case, he soon grew tired of the life into which his fame as a playwright took him. Although he was pleased to associate with the high-born and the affluent, he always retained an essential disdain for them and a special abhorrence of social dictates and taboos. He soon grew bored with the role which was expected of him as a popular dramatist, and he became disenchanted with the narrow spectrum of artistic and literary people with whom he came in contact in London. As he later wrote in *The Summing Up*, 'It was stifling me.'

It has been pointed out that on at least three occasions in his early life Maugham sought to escape through travel—to Germany, Spain, and France. Once again, through travel he was able to escape from the conventions of London life, and it became one of his greatest pleasures. Indeed, Maugham was one of the most widely travelled authors of any age. At any time, he might be found in Capri, or Spain, or South America, or Tahiti, or China, or Russia, or Bermuda. Even when he was eighty-five years old he was visiting a judo academy in Tokyo, and when he created the Somerset Maugham literary award a stipulation was that the winner must use the money to travel.

There is no doubt that Maugham travelled in order to find fresh material for his writing, and his short stories and travel books are filled with his impressions of the worlds he explored. Nevertheless, the language which he used to describe his love of travel is repeatedly that of escape:

I am attached to England, but I have never felt myself very much at home there. I have always been shy with English people. To me England has been a country where I had obligations that I did not want to fulfil and responsibilities that irked me. I have never felt entirely myself till I had put at least the Channel between my native country and me. Some fortunate persons find freedom in their own minds; I, with less spiritual power than they, find it in travel.[24]

Similarly, in the introduction to the Collected Edition of *On a Chinese Screen* Maugham writes that he likes to travel because of 'the sensation it gives you of freedom from all responsibility'.

Travel to foreign ports and exotic lands offered Maugham the means of preventing himself from being too closely drawn into cliques and societies, and it enabled him to avoid becoming a social institution (although ironically he could not prevent himself becoming, like Edward Driffield in *Cakes and Ale*, the Grand Old Man of English Letters). By departing for distant shores whenever he felt the urge to travel, he was able to remain elusive. This became particularly obvious in the years following his unfortunate marriage in 1916 and coinciding with his friendship with Gerald Haxton. If Maugham's accounts are to be believed, his marriage was the worst mistake of his life, and his voyages became more frequent after it than before. He had met Haxton during the war, and the young man became his secretary. Charming, friendly and boisterous, his gregarious nature facilitated Maugham's travel and access to the raw material for his stories. According to Beverley Nichols's version of this relationship, Haxton gave the older man a means of escape denied him by his own reticent nature:

To Gerald – and therefore, vicariously, to Willie – life had been an eternal escape from life, an escape to far places and distant kingdoms, to curious corners of the world where no questions were asked, to remoter, rickety stages where voices could be joined in a bawdy song that would have been highly unsuitable for American serialization.[25]

One of the most striking aspects of Somerset Maugham in maturity is that, even to those who knew him intimately, he remained an enigma. Lord Clark, for example, writes:

We knew Mr. Maugham well for over thirty years and stayed with him for a week or two every winter after the war until he became an invalid. We were both very fond of him and he talked to us freely about his life and work. Nevertheless he remains an extremely mysterious character. He was obviously a very sensitive and vulnerable man and this made him rather suspicious.[26]

Another long-standing friend, Sir Noël Coward, writing in the Foreword to Kanin's *Remembering Mr Maugham*, says: 'I myself am indebted to him for nearly fifty years of kindness and hospitality, but I cannot truthfully say that I really knew him intimately.' Similarly, John Colton, who with Clemence Randolph converted 'Rain' into a highly successful play, found Maugham an elusive character:

"I cannot imagine anyone really knowing him. . . . He lives behind a wall of gentlemanliness, a wall of exquisite good manners. No one has ever broached these defences. I am sure that Maugham knows I like him, and I think that he likes me, but I've never been able to penetrate the barriers he has erected between himself and the world. I doubt, furthermore, if anyone else has."[27]

Yet another old acquaintance talks of the caution with which Maugham approached social intercourse:

"I always have the feeling that Willie is wearing a mask. . . . And not once, in all the years that I've known him, have I seen the mask drop. He's on guard all the time, alert as a hawk, watching everything he does and says."[28]

Much of Maugham's reticence can, of course, be attributed to his innate shyness and to his speech impediment; however, this does not explain everything. In his mature years, he was well known as an excellent, if succinct, conversationalist and, according to Sir Gerald Kelly, Garson Kanin and Robin Maugham, his stammer rarely stood between himself and his friends. He even became very skilled at using it to heighten the effect of the stories he told.

The origin of the 'mask' to which so many people refer must surely have a psychological basis. The mask, whether in literary usage or in real life, is nearly always adopted as a protective device. Behind a deceptive façade the individual is able to operate with a greater flexibility and mobility than would otherwise be possible. He can choose his personal commitments with caution and he can maintain a buffer between his real self and the risks of human involvement. In *The Summing Up* Maugham discusses the way in which the famous show the world a mask and learn to play the role expected of them. However, he adds: 'You are stupid if you think that this public performance of theirs corresponds with the man within.'

Although Maugham participated in public developments on several occasions, his preference was always to avoid becoming involved in movements or organisations. It is true that he was active in the redevelopment of King's School, that he established a literary award, and that he served as a vice-president of the Royal Literary Fund (which assists aged writers in distress). These, however, were rare occasions and, as he said in *The Summing Up*, 'My natural inclination has been to keep aloof from every kind of public activity and it has been with the greatest reluctance that I have even served on committees formed to effect some aim of passing interest.'

On several occasions Maugham has said that he wished that he could pass through the world unnoticed and that he had kept to his plan of writing under a pseudonym. Indeed, his wish at one time to write anonymously is proved by the manuscript of *Liza of Lambeth*, in which the author is identified as 'William Somerset'. The observer unobserved was clearly a situation which appealed to him.

In Maugham's case the mask protected a sensitive and vulnerable spirit. The pain he suffered when his mother died, the misery of his childhood, and the self-inflicted torture of the super-sensitive nature, determined him to adopt a defensive attitude. In an equally significant way, a number of what he considered to be unrequited love affairs—with the originals of Mildred in *Of Human Bondage* and Rosie in *Cakes and Ale*—contributed to his reluctance ever again to risk himself emotionally. In this regard, it is perhaps revealing that Maugham noted this aphorism in his copy of Logan Pearsall Smith's *Afterthoughts*: 'If we shake hands with icy fingers, it is because we have burnt them so horribly before.'[29]

Like Swift, Maugham adopted a mask of cynicism and irony to

protect a sensitive, and often sentimental, nature from the hardness of
the world. In his days as a medical student, he had seen enough of the
suffering which is inflicted on man by circumstances over which he has
no control, and he had learned to accept this as part of the pattern of
life. What he found difficult to tolerate, however, was the pain which
man needlessly inflicts on himself. Because he felt genuine pity for
people, and because this could be an agonising emotion, he tended to
adopt the protective device of being harshly critical of people.
Through blaming people's suffering on their own follies and vices, he
could shield himself from having to endure the pain which he felt for
them.

This mask of cynicism and irony accounts for the great disparity
which exists in the regard with which Maugham is held by those who
knew him. Those who saw only the public face condemn him for being
cold, ruthless and decadent; on the other hand, those who managed,
in varying degrees, to reach the man within defend him with intense
loyalty. Sir Gerald Kelly, who knew Maugham longer than anyone,
remembered him as a deep personal friend:

I knew Willie in some ways as well as anybody. I was not shocked by what
he did. I was devoted to him because he made me laugh.[30]

According to Kelly, they became friends in 1904 when they were both
struggling to establish reputations. Success came to Maugham much
earlier than to Kelly, yet, said Sir Gerald, Maugham never let this
stand as a barrier to their friendship. Eager to advance Kelly's career,
Maugham held dinners and parties where Kelly was able to meet a
number of the influential people who could help him. The friendship
of these two men never dissolved. To Kelly Maugham revealed something of the inner man: 'Very few people, you know, have any idea
of how happy and interesting a life I live behind a rather sedate
exterior.'[31]

To the world in general, however, the essential Maugham remained elusive behind the veneer of gentlemanliness, cosmopolitanism and worldliness. Moss Hart, whom Maugham admired,
talked of his guarded personality:

"I always feel . . . that I am not quite getting over with him. There's a glass
wall between us. I wouldn't call him unyielding, but he does hold you at
arm's length, doesn't he?"[32]

It seems that at some stage in his life Maugham opted for a life of
detachment and solitude instead of one of commitment and friendship. He was far from being a misanthropist—although he echoed
Swift's statement that he loved individuals but never much cared for
people in the mass—and he enjoyed the company of others. A stream

of guests visited the Villa Mauresque in the 'thirties and after the Second World War, and Maugham had many acquaintances throughout the world. He remained, nevertheless, cautious and guarded in the degree of intimacy that he would allow, and this led to the feeling of unpredictability which he often gave to his friends. As he said in *The Summing Up*, 'For my part I chiefly wanted to be let alone, but I had discovered that not many wanted that, and if I let them alone they thought me unkind, indifferent and selfish.' What many people who did not really understand Maugham's personality took for slights and insults were very likely to be manifestations of his desire to withdraw, rather than become involved. Maugham's attitude to the obligations of friendship is perhaps revealed by his comment used by Doubleday, Doran (his American publishers) on a Christmas card in 1936: 'The danger of making friends is that you may not be able to drop them when you want to; the advantage of reading a book is that if it bores you, you can put it aside without compunction.'[33] It should be remembered that he also once wrote in *Books and You*, that 'to acquire the habit of reading is to construct for yourself a refuge from almost all the miseries of life'.

One of the central conflicts in Maugham's life, like that of many other artists, was that between involvement and detachment. Throughout his career, he maintained that it was not enough for him merely to observe and record life; he meant to experience it to the fullest. He had decided as a young man that life had no meaning beyond the existential plane, and this led to a form of hedonism, a striving to live every moment intensely. Thus when he had finished his medical studies, he left for Spain, feeling that through his struggles he had been cheated of his youth (a loss which, whether real or imagined, he never forgot). Later, he left for the South Seas because he felt that real life was passing him by in London, where his life had become routine. Always he argued that the writer must fully experience life before he can adequately recreate it in words.

Despite this deeply felt philosophy, Maugham appears to have never been able to become fully involved in the experiences he had. He joined an artistic community in bohemian Paris, became a secret agent during the First World War, and traced the foot-steps of Gauguin in Tahiti. He trekked through Burma, visited Indian yogis and shrines, and lived briefly in the fantasy world of Hollywood. In all these ventures, however, exciting and interesting as they were, Maugham seems to have remained essentially uninvolved. In the case of his South Seas and Far East journeys, he has readily admitted that it was the participation of Haxton which gave him the really intimate access to the lives of the people, which became the raw material for his stories. Similarly, despite the charm and detail of *On a Chinese Screen* and other works, a friend who knew the author in the Far East, Harold Acton, believes that Maugham never really got inside Chinese culture. For Maugham, he says, China was 'Cathay', not China, and he was not particularly interested in the Chinese language, drama, or religion.[34]

It seems, therefore, that despite his strong desire to experience life to the fullest, Maugham ultimately chose, or was forced to accept, the position of the detached observer moving within, but never entirely with, events around him. He may in fact have opted for an unusual position of detached involvement, so that he neither denied life nor became overwhelmed by it. Frank Swinnerton, writing in 1936, argued that Maugham's stance was adopted by choice:

> He has a faculty which some will never be able to relish, the power to be interested without becoming attached. He prizes his cool independence more than the applause of a thousand devotees.[35]

The conflict within Maugham between his belief in the writer's need to experience and his desire for detachment may eventually have been resolved. The effect on his writing, however, of his 'cool independence' is considerable. Although he treats a wide variety of experiences and situations and although he is extremely skilful at giving them credibility, there is very often a feeling that he has not really found the essence of the experience. In a number of places, his writing has the appearance of journalist's 'copy'—assiduously collected information which, when arranged around the framework of a story, gives it a ring of authenticity. A passage in the manuscript of *The Summing Up*, deleted from the published version, frankly reveals this professional approach:

> Because I once wrote two or three things about China, people are constantly sending me, or advising me to read, books on that wonderful country. How they bore me! I have written all I want to about China & while I was doing it read as many books about it as I could get hold of, histories, travels, translations from its literature, novels; but now I am as little interested in it as I am in the ritualistic quarrels of the Byzantine Empire. It is an experience I have passed through. It has nothing to do with me any more. Other subjects claim my attention.[36]

It is extremely difficult to believe that a writer could fully grasp the essential character and meaning of an experience without being permanently affected to some degree. Maugham, however, seems to have remained untouched.

Maugham's reluctance fully to involve himself in an experience is largely responsible for the lack of intensity in much of his writing. When he describes a penal colony, the view is that of a warden or prison officer, not that of the prisoner who endures his private hell. When he talks of taking opium, it is not as one who has experimented to the point of real understanding, but rather as a curious observer. When he writes of Indian mysticism, it is as a student of philosophy, not as an enraptured devotee. This lack of real involvement in what he is writing about can be found in many parts of his work. Maugham no doubt cherished his amused detachment more than intense participation, and he would probably have replied to criticism by arguing that the professional writer uses as wide a spectrum of material as possible, regardless of a real understanding of it. Nevertheless, the lack of deep penetration into experience is a serious weakness of his writing.

A further paradox of Maugham's adult life was the conflict between the abhorrence of convention which had been left from his youth and his tendency to enjoy the company of conventional society. From what he wrote about social manners and customs in works such as *Our Betters* and *Of Human Bondage*, there can be no doubt that he regarded the codes which society imposed on the individual as stifling and artificial. It must be remembered, as well, that when he decided to become a professional writer he was in effect rejecting the class in which his family belonged. *Liza of Lambeth*, in fact, shocked his relations, and for many years Maugham bitterly resented his brother Frederick's[37] opinion that he had disgraced himself.

In spite of these opinions of society, Maugham in his later life certainly enjoyed associating with the rich and famous. His nephew discusses this conflict:

There was, indeed, a strong desire in him to break away from conventional society—and yet he lived in a form of smart society on the Riviera and in London and New York until the very day he died.
His break with convention was never complete.[38]

Maugham was undoubtedly impressed with some of the trappings of affluence and privilege. He was pleased, for example, that after his daughter, Liza, married Lord John Hope (now Lord Glendevon) she could visit the Royal Family at Balmoral. Similarly, he was gratified to be made a Companion of Honour in 1954, and he enjoyed entertaining the royalty (albeit exiled and impoverished) which lived along the Riviera.

In Maugham's defence, however, it should be noted that his attitude toward the aristocracy was not hypocritical; he intensely disliked snobbery and class prejudice wherever he recognised them. He was fond of stating that, if the Battle of Waterloo was won on the playing fields of Eton, then it may be that the historians of the future will say that India was lost in the public schools of England. He frequently took the opportunity of pointing out that narrow, stupid colonial administrators had left behind in country after country a deep hatred of Englishmen. Apart from his many portrayals of this phenomenon in his short stories, his most sustained attack can be found in his foreword to *The Memoirs of the Aga Khan* (1954). There is, as well, the occasion of the opening of the Maugham Library at King's School, Canterbury, when the theme of his address was that it would be a good thing if the public school system, the cause of much of the detestation of Englishmen in the world, were to die out. It made no difference that King's School is the oldest public school in the English-speaking world.

It would appear that Maugham approached 'smart' society as he did everything else—with restraint and caution. Malcolm Muggeridge, always quick to detect hypocrisy, argues that Maugham remained detached although moving in a world of glamour and titles:

The impression of Maugham which nothing will efface is of an outsider. Of the many who have claimed that honorific title of our time, he unquestionably deserved it. He had many acquaintances among what he would call, with a deprecating smile, the great; Churchill and Beaverbrook, for instance. Visitors were frequent at the Villa Mauresque, and included a variety of notabilities. Yet Maugham was never, as it were, fully integrated into this world of the eminent and successful, even though he ostensibly upheld its credentials. . . . It was this side of his character which appealed to me and made me feel always affectionately disposed to him; a sort of fastidiousness, an essential integrity which held him aloof. At the end of a long life full of fame and wealth and distinction, he remained triumphantly an outsider.[39]

In many ways Maugham was indeed an outsider, and his writing is nearly always concerned with the individual who seeks to remain detached from society or from complete surrender to a person or situation.

The title of Maugham's most autobiographical novel was taken from Spinoza's *Ethics*—'Of Human Bondage, or the Strength of the Emotions'—and in Maugham's life it was the passions which he regarded as the greatest threat to his independence. He was aware that, because of the emotional starvation of his youth, he was especially vulnerable to difficult entanglements in his adult life. He claimed that, as a young man, he experienced a number of painful unrequited love affairs, and the importance lies not in whether this was literally true, but in that in his mind they seemed to have happened. Mildred in *Of Human Bondage* is too well-drawn a character not to have some basis in reality, and it is known that Maugham had an eight-year affair with the woman he portrayed as Rosie in *Cakes and*

Ale, which ended with her rejecting his proposal of marriage. There are, in addition to these occasions, a number of hints in his auto-biographical fragments of other painful romantic attachments. In *The Summing Up* he even goes so far as to claim that 'though I have been in love a good many times I have never experienced the bliss of requited love'.

There are few young men who do not at some time suffer the anguish of love rejected, and most of them regain their emotional equilibrium. In Maugham's case, however, the craving for love and affection which resulted from his emotionally bleak childhood made him extremely sensitive to rejection, and he seems to have been unable to come to terms with the situation. Because of in part his innate shyness and in part his reluctance to allow himself to be emotionally hurt ever again, Maugham appears in his adult years to have been cautious about the degree of intimacy which he would allow himself with women. With very few exceptions, he valued his detachment more than the complications of love:

I have tried, with gentleness when possible, and if not, with irritation, to escape from the trammels with which their love bound me. I have been jealous of my independence. I am incapable of complete surrender.[40]

Maugham has frequently been accused of being a misogynist, but, as in the case of Swift, this conclusion is too simple and too super-ficial. Maugham, in fact, enjoyed the companionship of beautiful, intelligent or witty females, and the list of women who found him charming and attractive is long. It includes, among others: Billie Burke, Marie Lohr, Ruth Gordon, Barbara Back, Christabel, Lady Aberconway and Mrs Ian Fleming. If there was a vein of misogyny in Maugham it was, like his attitude to mankind as a whole, directed at women in general; he never lost interest in women as individuals. His reticence to commit himself emotionally to any degree was clearly part of his intention to remain aloof.

Maugham, nevertheless, married Syrie Wellcome (*née* Barnardo) in 1916, and the explanation which he later gave for this is charac-teristic. In *The Summing Up*, he wrote that the condition of marriage attracted him as a means of obtaining peace—peace from the dis-turbance of love affairs, and peace which would enable him to write all he wanted without loss of time or mental unrest: 'I sought freedom and thought I could find it in marriage.' One result of this wish was the idealised picture of marriage at the end of *Of Human Bondage*, written two years before.

Three years before his death, however, Maugham gave a much different and more lengthy interpretation of his marriage, in the

B

notorious series of articles, 'Looking Back', published first in the
United States by *Show* magazine in June, July and August 1962, and
then in Britain in serial form in the *Sunday Express* in September and
October of the same year. According to this account, Syrie had been
the mistress of a number of prominent men and, while separated from
Henry Wellcome, had developed a relationship with Maugham. She
had a child by Maugham, and Wellcome sued for divorce. Since this
would have left Syrie with a relatively small income and the child
without a father, Maugham reluctantly accepted marriage. He writes
that when Sir George Lewis, a lawyer, asked if he wanted to marry
Syrie, he replied: 'No, . . . but if I don't I shall regret it all my life.'

'Looking Back' is the bitter and vengeful outpouring of an old
man approaching senility, and therefore the account of his marriage
must be regarded with suspicion. Certainly Syrie is not treated fairly
in this version. Nevertheless, considering Maugham's memories of
his own childhood virtually as an orphan, it would not be surprising
for him to have very much wanted the child to have a father. If it is
true that he married out of a feeling of obligation, there is a great
irony in this behaviour from the man who had written *A Man of
Honour* and *The Merry-Go-Round*, both works which vividly portray
the self-inflicted miseries of a young man who marries out of conscience. Maugham, after all, was not a young man blinded by the
idealism of a social conscience; he was in his forties and knew the
risks of a marriage of honour.

The marriage, needless to say, was not a success. Willie and Syrie
were temperamentally unsuited to one another, and they belonged to
different worlds. The rhythms of their lives were too disparate and
they seem to have been unable to reconcile their separate interests.
Moreover, Maugham was on the move and frequently away from
England. In 'Looking Back' he published what he claimed was a
rough copy of a letter which he sent to Syrie outlining his position.
It is essentially a plea for liberty, for his freedom to come and go as
he pleases, to give what he can without having much more demanded
of him which he cannot. He argues that no one has ever complained
of him, nagged him and harangued him as she has. How can she
expect him to preserve his affection for her when she has terrorised
him with her demands? Because she has few resources she places an
intolerable burden on him. He wants, he says, his freedom from her
demands, or they must separate.[41] The independence which Maugham
expected, however, was not possible within the framework of
marriage. Much later he told Wilmon Menard:

"A marriage, at the best, is the most abnormal of relationships between man
and woman. I refuse to believe that it was ever intended for man and

woman to be bound together by a legal contract under one roof. It constitutes an invasion of privacy, an encroachment on individuality, the
shattering of peace-of-mind, the interruption of independent thought and
action, and the engulfment of an innocent human into the bog of boredom.'"[42]

If Maugham has been accurately quoted here by Menard, his
attitude toward marriage seems remarkably narrow. The argument
that the marriage contract is an unnatural state is tenable and can be
defended on a number of grounds. His complaints about the 'invasion
of privacy', 'encroachment on individuality', 'shattering of peace-of-
mind' and 'interruption of independent thought and action', however,
seem surprisingly naïve. Cohabitation assuredly involves these disadvantages in some degree, but to stress them as essential drawbacks
betrays a dictating egoism. It reveals an inability to yield any part of
the self to another and to recognise any possibility that two people
can exist together with anything but conflict between their characters.
One hardly needs to point out that a great many artists and writers
have maintained a fierce individuality and independence of thought
even though they are committed to a deeply involved relationship.

It would seem obvious that Maugham's marriage proved to be
unworkable because it was not compatible with the personal freedom
which was so essential to him. There is, however, another important
element which must be considered—Gerald Haxton. It may well be
that Maugham did not reject marriage out of a desire for freedom
but that he was drawn from it by a different and greater bondage.

There is little doubt that Maugham had strong homosexual
tendencies. Throughout his life, he associated with a large number of
known homosexuals—for example, John Ellingham Brooks, E. F.
Benson,[43] Ronald Firbank, Reggie Turner and Norman Douglas—
and in his later years, when he was 'The Master' to many, he often
took a great interest in the careers of struggling young bachelor
authors. *Time* magazine, in October 1930, took careful note of
Maugham's 'effeminate men friends', and in April 1931 expressed
some surprise that the vicious attack on him in *Gin and Bitters* (see
Chapter VII) did not include some salacious material of this nature.

Frederick Gerald Haxton (1892–1944) was an American whom
Maugham met during the First World War. Energetic, charming and
attractive, he appealed to Maugham, and became his friend and
secretary. In addition to his sophistication and amiability, however,
the young man was also a heavy drinker, and his conduct became
increasingly reckless. Beverley Nichols has written of him: 'He had
about him an aura of corruption.'[44] In 1915 he was arrested in London
on a charge of gross indecency and, although he was acquitted by
the jury, the result was that a few years later he was declared an

undesirable alien and barred from ever again entering England. According to Robin Maugham, this was the most important consideration in Maugham's decision to live abroad permanently.

One of Maugham's oldest friends has stated that 'Willie was in love with Haxton for many years', and another has said, somewhat circumspectly, that 'Willie was very, very fond of Gerald'. Certainly the tone of Maugham's dedication to him in *A Writer's Notebook*— 'In Loving Memory of My Friend Frederick Gerald Haxton'—lacks the characteristic reserve found in his other dedications. It appears that, ironically, the writer who so fully expounded the dangers of emotion and the safety of restraint and moderation allowed himself to be dominated by this unusual relationship.

Homosexuality is a matter of degree, and it is impossible to know to what extent, if any, Maugham was a practising homosexual. Perhaps Haxton was merely an immense help to him in his travels and in his pursuit of raw material. Perhaps Maugham simply preferred male companionship, the demands of which are necessarily of a different and perhaps less engulfing nature than those of female companionship. Perhaps, in the young man's vitality, gregariousness and exuberant masculinity, Maugham vicariously experienced the life denied him by his shyness and reticence.

Whatever the nature of Haxton's attraction for Maugham, it seems to have meant enslavement for the Master. Two of his young protégés of the nineteen-twenties and nineteen-thirties, Godfrey Winn and Beverley Nichols, have remarkably similar impressions of the relationship. Winn, describing an occasion when Haxton brashly rebuked Maugham, writes:

Whereupon the man who was my literary god, instead of silencing the rebellion from his throne, where he sat wearing for the evening the black silk mandarin trousers that he had brought back from China, was himself silent and seemed – or was it my own literary imagination taking over? – to gaze back in fear.[45]

The playboy's losses at the various casinos he patronized were paid up grimly by the patron over whom, as the weeks passed, I began to suspect he had the kind of hold which a blackmailer exerts. Was this what was really meant by the expression "your evil genius"? I baulked from recognizing the full implications of a situation that I realize now had its roots in the past rather than the present.[46]

Beverley Nichols, whose stated intentions it should be noted are to defend the reputation of Maugham's wife, writes rather more melodramatically:

There was something akin to black magic in Gerald's domination, something uncanny in the way in which he caused the Master to dance to his tune – sometimes, quite literally, with a flick of his fingers, summoning him across a crowded room to replenish his cocktail glass, when he knew, and I knew, and everybody else knew, that by obeying him the Master was performing an act of public humiliation, even as he tipped the cocktail shaker. There they were, the two of them. The handsome young man, lolling in his armchair, with one bare leg thrown over the arm, holding up his glass, demanding his poison. The ageing genius, standing before him, pouring out the libation, as if he were making a sacrifice to a young god whom, in his heart of hearts, he despised even while he loved him, whom he feared, even while the whip was in his hands.[47]

Even allowing for the natural jealousy that these two young admirers would feel for the man who held first place in the Master's affections, these two independent accounts, for all their melodrama, cannot be ignored. They reveal a form of human bondage which Maugham never in any way touched upon in his writing, a form of aberration which he never publicly acknowledged. The dictates of conventional behaviour were perhaps stronger in him than he would have liked to admit, and thus he attempted to deny his homosexual streak. Late in his life he admitted to his nephew that his greatest mistake was that 'I tried to persuade myself that I was three-quarters normal and that only a quarter of me was queer—whereas really it was the other way round.'[48]

It is a questionable practice, of course, to speculate about what a writer might have produced had he written other than he did, but it is interesting to consider what Maugham could possibly have accomplished by treating the theme of homosexuality as a form of human bondage. A few authors—Jean Genet being the best example —have expressed their homosexuality in literary terms, and their candour has contributed to a general increase in the public tolerance of deviation from the normal. With his readership, Maugham had a great opportunity to enlighten a large segment of the public about the nature of homosexuality and liberate it from the myths and prejudices which surround it.

The laws concerning homosexuality during most of Maugham's life and his concern for his public reputation, however, prevented him from ever treating the subject. His attitude is reflected in the advice which he gave his nephew about the publication of Robin's homosexual book, *The Wrong People*:

My uncle said, "I'm going to pour you a particularly large martini, because you're going to need it. Yours is the only book I've taken to bed and had to read right through to the end. But I think it will kill you stone dead as a writer. They will murder you." Then my uncle said that various details would imply that at some stage in my life I must have had some experience of homosexuality, and that would be bad for my public.[49]

In psychological terms, the cost to Maugham of repressing this knowledge over the years must have been great.

Whatever the entanglements of Maugham's adult life, he greeted the approach of middle and old age, with all their physical handicaps, as a form of liberation. Surprisingly, what he emphasised was the freedom from pressures to conform brought by advancing years. In spite of his frequent protestations of aloofness from the demands of others and despite his determination to follow a life pattern of his own design, it becomes obvious that he paid more heed to the opinions of others than he admitted. Discussing the compensations of middle age, he writes:

Youth is bound hand and foot with the shackles of public opinion. Middle age enjoys freedom. I remember that when I left school I said to myself: "henceforward I can get up when I like and go to bed when I like." That of course was an exaggeration, and I soon found that the trammelled life of the civilised man only permits of a modified independence. Whenever you have an aim you must sacrifice something of freedom to achieve it. But by the time you have reached middle age you have discovered how much freedom it is worth while to sacrifice in order to achieve any aim that you have in view.[50]

What Maugham claims to have found in middle age was a freedom from being expected to perform in a prescribed manner. He argues that, although he was not physically strong, he felt obliged in his youth to emulate the feats of others—in games, walking, or diving. Now, no one expects a man of his years to do these things, and he is free to be reconciled with himself. This passage, written in 1933, is remarkable for what it reveals in retrospect of Maugham's real concern for the opinions of others.

Three years later, the description of what he saw for himself in old age carries the same emphasis:

The philosophers have always told us that we are the slaves of our passions, and is it so small a thing to be liberated from their sway? . . . It is something to be free from the pangs of unrequited love and the torment of jealousy. . . . free at last, the soul delights in the passing moment, but it does not bid it stay.[51]

In 1944, the message is repeated:

When later I came to think it over, it occurred to me that the greatest compensation of old age is its freedom of spirit. I suppose that is accompanied by a certain indifference to many of the things that men in their prime think important. Another compensation is that it liberates you from envy, hatred and malice.[52]

As Maugham approached old age, he realised, and accepted without bitterness, that he was becoming increasingly divorced from the changing world. He had always claimed that the writer should immerse himself in life so that he can give his writing the immediacy and credibility which come through personal experience, and he recognised that more and more he was becoming a stranger to the mainstream of mid-twentieth-century life. It was, nevertheless, one of his greatest achievements that he maintained his contemporaneity well into his seventies.

As one who could well remember the Boer War and the First World War, Maugham turned his attention to the dilemma of the Second World War. In the early stage, he toured France as a reporter and described his findings in *France at War* (1940), a reading of the situation which unfortunately soon proved to be far from accurate. In 1941, however, he wrote *Strictly Personal*, in which in retrospect he could more carefully diagnose the reasons for the fall of France. His opinion that it was a question of values is contained in one of his most famous lines: 'If a nation values anything more than freedom, it will lose its freedom; and the irony of it is that if it is comfort or money that it values more, it will lose that too.'[53]

In the post-war period, Maugham remained an astute observer of social customs and manners and, as a man who had lived as a late Victorian, an Edwardian, and a Georgian, his comments on contemporary life carry considerable authority. Earlier, in 1936, he had looked ahead and found the prospect interesting. 'The young', he wrote in *The Summing Up*, 'enter upon life now with advantages that were denied to the young of my generation. They are hampered by fewer conventions and they have learnt how great is the value of youth.' The theme of his talk on BBC radio in 1954 on the occasion of his eightieth birthday was the same:

It is true that as a nation we are sadly impoverished, but in compensation as individuals we are freer. We have rid ourselves of many stupid prejudices. Relations between the sexes are more unconstrained. We are less formal in our dress and far more comfortable. We are less class-conscious. We are less prudish. We are less arrogant.[54]

Remembering the narrow provincial life of Whitstable and the rigid decorum of London life at the turn of the century, Maugham envied the new liberties he saw the younger generations claiming. Socially and sexually there were fewer taboos, and the individual had greater mobility than he had been allowed in the Victorian and Edwardian eras. This admiration for, and sympathetic understanding of, the new forms of freedom found expression in his last major work —*The Razor's Edge* (1944).

Despite this degree of optimism, a number of aspects of contemporary life disturbed Maugham, and he felt some relief at becoming more an observer and less a participant. Although he had recognised as early as 1940 that a socialist government would be elected in England after the war and that the post-war world would be much changed, he was distressed by his feeling that politically the individual was losing his independence. In the preface to *The Partial View* (1954), he wrote:

I did not realise that peace would bring us not a return to the old life we had known, but a future of anxiety and apprehension. The state is assuming ever greater power over the individual and it seems inevitable that his liberty will continue to be encroached upon. For my part I rejoice that I shall not have to cope with the regimented life that I see approaching.[55]

In spite of the emotional and spiritual liberation which Maugham envisaged in old age, his medical knowledge did not let him forget the threats which accompany physical decline and senility. He had at least once before been an invalid for some length of time, when his tuberculosis forced him to spend a few months in a sanatorium in Scotland. Strange as it might at first seem, Maugham's reaction to his confinement, as recorded in *The Summing Up*, was one of pleasure: 'It gave me a delicious sense of security, aloofness and freedom.' The toll of age, however, was a different matter and, because the prospect that he might become an invalid, dependent upon others for everything, was abhorrent, he was determined to prevent it. Despite having concluded *A Writer's Notebook* in 1949 by stating that he was prepared to die—'I am on the wing'—he undertook in the last twelve years of his life a series of rejuvenation treatments involving life-preserving injections at a clinic in Switzerland. These treatments may have extended Maugham's physical life beyond its normal length, but it is the opinion of some—Alan Searle and Garson Kanin, for example—that they contributed to the mental deterioration of his final years. There is probably a good deal of truth in the suggestion that the injections gave his body a vigour which his failing mind could not match. Certainly, when the accounts of his last years given in *Somerset and All the Maughams* and *Remembering Mr Maugham* are considered, there can be no doubt that his final five years seem hardly to have been worth the living. Noël Coward, visiting the old man near the end, describes him best: 'He was infinitely pathetic.'[56]

What Maugham most feared about old age was the helplessness of senility. He had once intended to commit suicide at sixty-five, but when he reached that age his interest in people and places stayed his hand. He later claimed that the mistake in procrastination in this is that when one becomes much older the will is weakened and one is left with no courage for any positive action. The individual is rendered helpless.

Maugham, however, was extremely fortunate to have had a kind and devoted companion, Alan Searle, to protect him in his vulnerable old age. From 1945 until the author's death Searle acted as his secretary, but his services extended far beyond this capacity. Maugham had a fear of becoming an invalid and losing his independence to nurses, doctors and servants, and Searle's total dedication to the Master's comfort enabled the old man to retain a measure of freedom and dignity which he would not have otherwise had. His lifelong dread of physical contact with strangers increased in old age, and so Searle had to take the place of a nurse. In Robin Maugham's opinion, without the devotion of his secretary Maugham would have either gone mad or killed himself. The old man was himself well aware of what this friendship meant for him and in 1962 he paid warm tribute to the man who had willingly given up his own life to ease Maugham's loneliness and attend to his needs.[57]

One of Maugham's most cherished wishes of his final years was that he should die at his beloved Villa Mauresque. On 10 December 1965 he suffered a severe stroke and was taken to a hospital in Nice. Nevertheless, when he died six days later he was in the Villa. In his autobiography he had characteristically written of death: 'It seems to me then to offer me the final and absolute freedom.'

When one attempts to interpret the life of a man born in 1874 and who was still publishing in 1962, it cannot but seem a distortion to claim that everything he did emanated from an obsessive search for physical and spiritual liberty. Maugham was a man of complexity, a figure who played many parts, and a writer who in millions of words has said much about a great many things. Nevertheless, from his earliest notebook entries to his final article, the language in which he wrote of his literary career, and of the world in general, is consistently that of freedom and restraint. It may be that what Maugham really wanted was power, wealth, admiration, friendship, or love, but when his writing is examined as a whole, the framework in which he most often discusses matters is that of liberty or bondage.

Consider first the way in which he writes about his career. Although he liked to call himself a professional author, his theory of the motivation of the artist is psychological and romantic. Art is, he says, essentially a form of release or catharsis. The writer, painter or musician experiences life's joys and sorrows more sensitively than other men, and these experiences obsess his mind for a period of time until he must give them creative expression in order to be free of them. 'The artist', he writes in *The Summing Up*, 'produces for the liberation of his soul.' The pains of artistic creation are like the pains of childbirth, and the creative vision is like an organic thing which develops in the brain, heart, nerves and viscera, and becomes a burden so oppressive that it must be thrown off. The writer is liberated, says Maugham, not when the work is completed—and here his professionalism becomes obvious—but when it is published.

A number of Maugham's books quite clearly are the products of the need for this type of catharsis. His childhood and adolescence so haunted him that he twice worked it out in literature—first in the unpublished 'The Artistic Temperament of Stephen Carey' and later in *Of Human Bondage*. Of the latter, he wrote in *The Summing Up*: 'The book did for me what I wanted, and when it was issued to the world . . . I found myself free forever from those pains and unhappy recollections.' Similarly, when he collected his theories of art, literature, drama and philosophy, in the same book, it was so that 'when they are written down I shall have finished with them and my mind will be free to occupy itself with other things'.

When Maugham describes his movements from one form of literature to another, his language is again that of liberation. He does not talk about the richness or opportunity of one form as opposed to another; he speaks rather of the sense of liberty he felt when he turned to another area. When success as a dramatist came to him in 1908, for example, he decided never to write another novel; the realisation that he would never again have to describe in prose what could be represented by a stage scene gave him a great feeling of freedom. Many years later, however, he grew tired of the constraints he had discovered in writing for the theatre—having to soften a statement for the audience's sensibilities, having to tailor conversation to the stage, and having to follow the necessary conventions of the drama. He explains:

"To every literary man who is honest with himself, the theatre is a prison. He has to submit his work to all sorts of limitations imposed by the producer and the cast. He has to say all he wishes to say between twenty minutes to nine and five minutes past eleven. It has always seemed to me that literature can only find its fullest and freest expression in the essay or short story."[58]

As he wrote in *The Summing Up*, 'I sighed for the liberty of fiction.' When, after travelling through the narrow mountain passes, you come out onto the plain, 'you have a wonderful sense of freedom. So I felt when I had done with my last play.'

The same sense of liberation is apparent when Maugham talks of coming to the end of his lengthy writing career. Having many years before envisaged a pattern which his body of work should take, he seems to have been determined to see it completed according to his vision. This desire to see his pattern fulfilled was the motivation behind *Then and Now* (1946) and *Catalina* (1948), neither of which enhanced his reputation. Thus, despite the catharsis which he claimed to experience and despite having developed a sixty-six-year habit of writing, he looked upon the publication of his final book— *Points of View* (1958)—as relief from a self-imposed burden: 'It's a wonderful thought—after 62 years I shall be free.'[59] To William Hickey he said:

"Writing with me has been like a disease . . . I am looking forward to being free. To be free" – he sighed – "In the autumn when this book of essays is finished, then I shall be free from work."[60]

Even allowing for the natural feeling of relief which Maugham would feel at being free from the actual task of writing, his comments carry a great emphasis on liberation. It is almost as if the years of rigid self-discipline had taken such a hold on him that its relaxation came as an emancipation.

When Maugham's description of his progression from one literary form to another, from writing to liberate the soul to freedom from the burden of creation, are analysed, there is clearly an insatiable desire to rise above the technical restraints of writing—insatiable because he found restrictions in each genre. There is throughout a feeling of spiritual restlessness, of movement and change, of fear of becoming settled in a position which becomes imprisoning. There is a distinct impression of a continual wish to escape, to find a new condition in which there is more flexibility and fewer constraints.

Consider, also, the direction of his discussions of philosophy, morality and aesthetics in *The Summing Up*. When he reveals how, as a young man in Heidelberg, he ceased to believe in God, he does not stress peace, serenity or knowledge; rather, 'I felt the exhilaration of a new freedom.' Later, he tells how he began to read Kant, who he claims forced him to abandon the materialism and psychological determinism of his youth. Unaware of the weaknesses in Kant's philosophy, he found an emotional satisfaction in this system, and that emotion was 'a peculiar sense of liberation'.

In the final chapters of *The Summing Up* Maugham discusses the triad of values which he believes gives man's life meaning above mere biological existence—Truth, Beauty and Goodness. Truth, he says, is theoretically objective and independent, but in practice nearly always is subject to the idealism of man. The effect of beauty on him is

an excitement that gives me a sense of exhilaration, intellectual but suffused with sensuality, a feeling of well-being in which I seem to discern a sense of power and of liberation from human ties; . . . I feel rested, at peace and yet spiritually aloof.[61]

The greatest value for Maugham, however, is goodness, a concept which increasingly occupied his interest in the latter half of his life. Although he only encountered true goodness on a few occasions, he was awed by it. In his essentially utilitarian outlook, it should logically follow that a man is good because it is painful to be otherwise. Thus, the good man is such simply because it is the easier course to take and because he hopes to be accorded treatment consistent with the values by which he lives.

For Maugham, however, the significance of goodness lies in metaphysics. In a world which seems unreal, a mirage, what Albert Camus called 'absurd', goodness stands out as something real, an expression of basic human freedom:

It may be that in goodness we may see, not a reason for life nor an explanation of it, but an extenuation. In this indifferent universe, with its inevitable evils that surround us from the cradle to the grave, it may serve, not as a challenge or a reply, but as an affirmation of our own independence.[62]

Despite his belief in man's essential lack of free will, of his dependence on the accidents of birth, environment and history, Maugham sees in unalloyed and unqualified goodness a form of freedom from these restraints. The good man's goodness is an affirmation of independence because it exists in spite of the pressures to act as a passive instrument of fate, to always take the path of least resistance. The good man, like the rebel, the artist and the rogue, interests Maugham because he represents a defiance of determinism. Thus he writes with admiration of Sheppey (*Sheppey*) and Larry Darrell (*The Razor's Edge*) because they alter the course of their lives in a direction which, according to their background and environment, is against all expectation.

Maugham's attitude to rebellion has much the same motivation behind it. Although he could never be considered a rebel himself—his attitude was one of 'amused tolerance'—he was attracted by the positive act of rebellion because it defied circumstance. 'Resignation', he once recorded in *A Writer's Notebook*, 'is a surrender to the hostile whims of chance', a passive yielding to forces outside one. It may be that a man is doomed to lose his battle against circumstance, but the important thing is that his act of defiance is an act of freedom:

And even though the fetters that bind a man cannot be broken, let him remain a rebel still: though he suffers from cold and hunger, illness and poverty and lack of friends, though he knows that the road *is* uphill all the way and that the night has no morning, let him refuse ever to acknowledge that cold and hunger, illness and poverty are good; though he has not the strength to continue the hopeless battle, let him keep that one last spark of freedom in his heart which enables him to say that pain is bad.[63]

It would be a fairly simple matter to point out inconsistencies and basic flaws in Maugham's arguments about goodness and rebellion. The significance of these passages, however, lies in his way of viewing these philosophical conditions—that is, that they are expressions of freedom.

If Maugham's life was a long search for physical and spiritual freedom, did he in fact find the liberation for which he had sacrificed so much? In so far as it is possible for man to be truly independent, he achieved a high degree of personal freedom. He found success in the profession of his choice, in spite of a considerable amount of discouragement. After an unfortunate experiment with marriage, he maintained his freedom of movement by remaining unattached. Established in his comfortable villa in France, he was able to travel the world yet find seclusion when he wished. On a spiritual level, he developed an attitude of 'amused tolerance' which enabled him to remain relatively free from prejudices and snobberies, and his lifelong agnosticism, both in religious terms and more generally, gave him a freedom of intellect which permitted him to appreciate a wide range of experiences and beliefs. Thus in 1936 he could write with considerable justification that 'I have sought freedom, material and spiritual, and now on the threshold of old age, I am not disinclined to think that I have at last achieved it.'[64]

In some ways, however, Maugham unfortunately never escaped from human bondage. The effects of his childhood unhappiness—the loss of his mother, his stammer, and his life at the vicarage—were diminished in the course of time, but they were never eliminated. He thought he had expunged them through *Of Human Bondage* but they returned to haunt him in old age. His homosexuality, as well, held him against his will, and the conflict between his inclinations and his wish to be normal was anguishing.

By the cruellest sort of irony, Maugham was betrayed by one of the strongest of human emotions—that of wanting to hang on to life for as long as possible—and it revealed in the most pathetic manner just how little his spirit was detached and free. There is no doubt that he lived at least five years longer than he should have done, and these were years of self-condemnation and vengeful retribution on others for imagined injuries supposedly committed long in the past. In 1962 he auctioned his collection of paintings at Sotheby's, and was sued for part of the proceeds by his daughter. In the following year he attempted to disinherit her and adopt his secretary but, like

Shakespeare's Lear, he found himself powerless even to control the future of his wealth.

In earlier, more lucid, times Maugham had written in *Points of View* regretfully of 'the burden of one's memories', and in his final years this burden became unbearable. Unable to free himself from his memories of wounds inflicted many years before, he abandoned his retirement from writing (thus destroying the pattern he had set), and published the shocking autobiographical fragment, 'Looking Back'. Savage and spiteful, these articles were an attempt to justify his past actions, particularly regarding his marriage, to give him the kind of catharsis that he had always believed came through the publication of one's obsessions. Brilliant though they were in parts, they only served to damage Maugham's reputation and to destroy a number of his oldest friendships.

To a large extent it is unfair to judge Maugham's life on the basis of his last years. Just as it is an error to consider that Swift was insane because he died in a coma in old age, it is unfair to point to Maugham's senility as proof that his life was one of bondage. There is more justice in looking at the man in his prime, when his detached interest, calm rationality and moderate temperament were dominant. What the sorrows of old age do perhaps reveal is that beneath his cool exterior he was never quite able to find the true spiritual independence which he had made his life's quest.

Maugham's lifelong concern with freedom, or at least his tendency to see life's problems within the framework of freedom or bondage, is paralleled by his examination of the manifestations of human bondage and freedom in his fiction. Although the situations may differ, and the forms may vary, the essential theme which runs throughout his writing, from first to last, is that of freedom and enslavement. Critics have frequently acknowledged this in studies of *Of Human Bondage*, but it has not been recognised that his many other volumes are equally about the individual and liberation. Many of the titles—for example, *The Merry-Go-Round*, *The Painted Veil*, *The Narrow Corner*, *Cakes and Ale* and *The Razor's Edge*—carry the connotation that man is in some way faced with narrowness and restraint on all sides. Although Maugham's writing contains many themes—man's paradoxical nature, the importance of rhythm in men's lives, the attitude of the empire builders to the native population—the central one is freedom and bondage. It is the same motif, whether it is Liza in the slum, Bertha Craddock among the landed gentry, Philip Carey tormented by Mildred Rogers, Charles Strickland driven to paint, Rosie Driffield defying puritanical convention, Dr Saunders on his voyage of liberation, or Larry Darrell seeking to escape American materialism. Maugham's vision remains basically the same throughout; what changes is the form in which he dramatises that vision.

One of the most amazing aspects of Maugham's career is that there are few writers of any age who have been able to move so successfully with the times. In some respects, he is a literary chameleon *par excellence*. He began writing, it should be remembered, when Kipling, Moore, Gissing, Barrie, Hardy and James were still active, and he was still publishing in the age of Osborne, Golding and Salinger. His achievement was that, unlike Galsworthy, Wells, Shaw and many others, he almost never had the appearance of an anachronism. Just as his first novel—*Liza of Lambeth* (1897)—reflected the literary currents at the turn of the century, *The Razor's Edge* (1944) over forty years later caught the spirit of its age. The reason for this remarkable ability to maintain his contemporaneity lies in Maugham's dedicated professionalism.

Despite all that Maugham has written about creating because one has an inner need to express oneself, fine writing did not come naturally or easily to him. He always wanted to be a writer, and he approached authorship with a determined, workmanlike attitude. It was through unceasing application that Maugham developed his ability to write good English. He has described how, as a young man, he recorded the names of various jewels, their colours, and the Byzantine relics in the British Museum in an attempt to improve (as he then thought) his sparse vocabulary. He has also talked of studying the Authorised Version of the Bible, under the impression that it contained the greatest prose in the English language, and of copying passages from Taylor's *Holy Dying*. Fortunately his inclinations took him elsewhere, and he began to assimilate the style of the Augustans. As he had done with Taylor, he copied large extracts of Swift, and this made a lasting impression on his style.

Throughout his career, Maugham never lost interest in improving his literary ability. Although he was never associated with a literary clique or school, he was well aware of the currents which were flowing at any time in the literary world. His reading, as he says in the introduction to his anthology *The Traveller's Library* (1933), was for more than mere enjoyment: 'I have read a great deal, sometimes for instruction and sometimes for pleasure, but never since I was a small boy without an inward eye on the relation between what I was reading and my professional interests.'

In addition, although Maugham professed to be indifferent to criticism, he was in fact sensitive to it and could be influenced by the judgements of others. The origin of the title of *The Mixture as Before* is evidence of his awareness of criticism. In its review of *Cosmo-politans*, *The Times* (London) had written deprecatingly of 'the mixture as before', and Maugham, arguing in the preface that consistency is a virtue, used the phrase for the title of his next volume of short stories.

Because of his perception of developments around him, Maugham was adept at sensing trends and movements in literature and drama. Writing in 1920, Desmond MacCarthy discussed this ability:

Possessing a remarkable aptitude for carrying out in a workmanlike fashion any literary task he sets himself, and being also undominated by temperament, he is always free to look about him for subjects and therefore to choose one which is already "in the air" and likely to prove interesting simultaneously to a large number of people.[65]

This analysis of Maugham's skills is more than usually interesting because it was MacCarthy to whom Maugham later referred in *The Summing Up* when he described how he had intimately discussed his strengths and weaknesses with a distinguished critic during the First World War. He was subsequently surprised, he says, to find his acute self-analysis reproduced in an article by the critic in 'an important paper'. What the above passage then amounts to is almost a statement of purpose by the author.

David Paul ascribes to Maugham a related ability to perceive changes in public attitudes and interests in a more general way:

I can only describe it as a sensitivity to current mythology as it is in the process of formation, an intuitive feeling for the drifts and fashions in contemporary impulse and aspiration as they take place. It is this which makes him, in spite of the consciousness of age which he does not conceal, and the worn Edwardian quality of his style, so surprisingly up to date.[66]

MacCarthy and Paul undoubtedly pinpoint the strength of Maugham's professional approach. Because he could adapt to changes in literary fashion and to new forms, he was able to maintain a remarkable level of consistency. It may surprise a great many, but, although Maugham made a great deal of money through his pen, he never appeared on the 'best-seller' lists until his final novel—*Catalina*. The remainder of his books never sold in monumental numbers; neither did they ever fail to achieve some success. Maugham's books, on the whole, have tended to reach high average sales and to maintain a selling power years after publication.

Maugham's adaptability is further demonstrated by his willingness to see his stories presented as plays, radio and television dramas and films. There have been few writers who have so readily and easily adjusted to new ways of presenting their stories, and no serious author of this century has been so frequently adapted for other media. Val Gielgud, who came in contact with Maugham through his productions for the BBC, writes of Maugham's flexible attitude to adaptation:

Most established authors, especially in the early days of broadcasting, were the reverse of forthcoming in the face of requests that their works might be adapted to the new medium. Some declined to have a phrase or comma cut. Some demanded fees far outside the BBC's capacity to pay. Others hedged hypothetical consent about with stipulations regarding casting or times of performance both impractical and exaggerated. . . . Mr. Maugham was not among those who imagined that to make his works familiar to the largest possible public was likely to diminish the number of his readers or the size of his theatre audiences.[67]

While it is true that Maugham's professional attitude made him acutely conscious of trends and fashions in literature, it would be wrong to assume that he simply mirrors what is popular. Although he manages to be repeatedly in the mainstream of current styles, he does not write merely what the age demands. On the contrary, Maugham is skilful in adapting his own themes to the kinds of literature or the mythology which is popular at various times. Thus his writing is basically a tailoring of the theme of freedom and bondage to the demands of the time. When the slum novel is in vogue, he treats the situation of an intensely vital girl in the narrow life of a slum street. When the public becomes interested in the problems of class, he writes about the stifling life of an emancipated woman as the wife of a newly arrived landed gentleman. When he turns to the novel of adolescence, it becomes a study in depth of a young man's search for independence. When he writes his portrait of the artist, he treats his hero as a man enslaved by the urge to create. When he turns to the East and writes a novel of mysticism, it become the story of a young man's search for spiritual liberation.

In *The Razor's Edge* Maugham writes: 'Art is triumphant when it can use convention as an instrument of its own purpose.' This, more than anything else, describes his literary technique. Rarely an innovator, he is content to adapt what other writers have made into some sort of convention and use it as a means of expressing his own ideas. It is the method of many of the greatest writers—Shakespeare being the best example—but of course it is not one which excites literary critics.

In *The Summing Up* Maugham discusses the problems of the literary innovator, and includes a passage which sheds a great deal of light on his own approach to writing:

In this perpetually changing world people are suspicious of novelty and it takes them some time before they can accustom themselves to it. A writer with an idiosyncrasy has to find little by little the people to whom it appeals. Not only does it take him time to be himself, for the young are themselves only with timidity, but it takes him time to convince that body of persons, whom he will eventually rather pompously call his public, that he has something to give them that they want. The more individual he is the harder will he find it to achieve this and the longer will it take him to earn his living. Nor can he be sure that the result will be lasting, for it may be that with all his individuality he has but one or two things to give and then he will soon sink back into the obscurity from which he with difficulty emerged.[68]

While no one could with justice accuse Maugham of lacking individuality, he seems to have been very much concerned with taking the cautious step of grafting his own ideas to what he recognised that the public was ready to accept. This practice is defensible if it succeeds in presenting the author's sincere beliefs in a form which preserves their integrity and which gains for them a much greater attention than they would otherwise attract. The danger, however, is that the author will so completely adapt to the conventions that his originality, that part of him which is unique, will become indiscernible. There is, in Maugham's case, a definite possibility that some of his works would have been very much better had they not been shaped and cut to suit a particular mould. This may, in the end, explain why, with the exception of *Of Human Bondage*, *Cakes and Ale* and some of the short stories, Maugham's works seem to lack real distinction.

II

Liza of Lambeth
and the Novels of Misery

MAUGHAM'S FIRST NOVEL, *Liza of Lambeth*, was published in 1897. With its composition he began the pattern which, for the most part, he was to repeat throughout his literary career. This pattern involves the adaptation to a current fashionable genre, and the development within this framework of an individual and personal expression. The genre which provided the model for this, Maugham's first published work, was the English variation of the French naturalist *roman*, the realistic slum novel.

The influence of French Naturalism on English literature is apparent in the number of slum novels written after 1880. George Gissing treated naturalistic subjects in *Workers in the Dawn* (1880), *The Unclassed* (1884), *Demos* (1886), *Thyrza* (1887) and *The Nether World* (1889). George Moore, deeply influenced by Flaubert, Huysmans, the Goncourts and particularly by Zola's *L'Assommoir*, adopted the 'scientific' method of the Naturalists and produced *A Mummer's Wife* (1885), *A Drama in Muslin* (1886) and *Esther Waters* (1894). Traces of naturalism can be found in Hubert Crackanthorpe's *Wreckage* (1893) and in Kipling's short story, 'The Record of Badalia Herodsfoot' (in *Many Inventions*, 1893). Its best English exponent, however, was Arthur Morrison, whose short stories, *Tales of Mean Streets* (1894), and novels, *A Child of the Jago* (1896) and *A Hole in the Wall* (1902), dramatised without sentiment the lives of the people in London's slums. Forms of the slum novel continued with Edwin Pugh's *A Street in Suburbia* (1895), *The Man of Straw* (1896), *Tony Drum* (1898), *Mother-Sister* (1900) and *The Stumbling Block* (1903), St John Adcock's *East-End Idylls* (1897), William Pett Ridge's *Mord Em'ly* (1898), Richard Whiteing's *No. 5 John Street* (1899) and Frank Swinnerton's *Nocturne* (1917).

It is in this particular stream of English literature that Maugham made his first attempt in the novel form. In a note written in 1931 at the end of the manuscript of *Liza of Lambeth*, now at King's School, Canterbury, he states that 'this novel, my first, was written in 1895 at 11 Vincent Square, Westminster'. However, *Liza* may in fact have been written any time between 1895 and 1897, when it was published by Fisher Unwin. In *The Summing Up* Maugham explains how, in a letter rejecting two short stories, Unwin asked for a novel. This was so great an encouragement for him that he 'immediately sat down and wrote one'. It is understandable that the young writer would choose a form which would best utilise his own experience, and, as Maugham has acknowledged in *The Summing Up*, his choice was fortunate: 'Any merit it may have is due to the luck I had in being, by my work as a medical student, thrown into contact with a side of life that at that time had been little exploited by novelists.'

Maugham was doubly lucky in the circumstances in which *Liza of Lambeth* was written. First, his duties as a medical student in the out-patient department at St Thomas's Hospital in London provided him with first-hand knowledge of material suitable for a slum novel. He describes the type of environment to which he was exposed:

The messenger led you through the dark and silent streets of Lambeth, up stinking alleys and into sinister courts where the police hesitated to penetrate, but where your black bag protected you from harm. You were taken to grim houses, on each floor of which a couple of families lived, and shown into a stuffy room, ill-lit with a paraffin lamp, in which two or three women, the midwife, the mother, the "lady as lives on the floor below", were standing round the bed on which the patient lay.[1]

Like Zola, Moore and other naturalists, Maugham made notes of his experiences, and these not only provided the bulk of *Liza of Lambeth*, they gave him material he was to use in 'A Bad Example' (in *Orientations*, 1899), *The Merry-Go-Round* and *Of Human Bondage*. *A Writer's Notebook* bears evidence of his care in recording cockney sayings and speech, and, although he claimed to have omitted material that had been used elsewhere, the following maxim, attributed to his cockney landlady, was utilised in *Liza of Lambeth*: 'Oh, it'll all come right in the end when we get four balls of worsted for a penny.'

A second, and perhaps more important, circumstance which greatly benefited Maugham was the objective, detached nature of his medical studies. This admirably equipped him with a point of view suitable to a realistic novel. His years at St Thomas's Hospital gave him a diagnostic approach to life that remained with him in some form throughout his writing career. This becomes obvious when one considers how often Maugham writes in anatomical terms or examines a character with the practised eye of a physician.

Moreover, the objectivity which a doctor develops in order to treat his patients without causing an unbearable emotional strain on himself was combined with Maugham's natural reticence to give him a detachment which he retained throughout his career. Frequently in his life he adopted this point of view as a protective device against the pain of sympathetic anguish. In part, at least, the aloof character of the Maugham *persona* owes its origin to this professional characteristic. In the case of *Liza of Lambeth*, the discipline inherent in his studies helped him to avoid the moralising or sentimentalising that mar so many slum novels.

Examined against the background of late-Victorian literature, there can be little doubt that the young Maugham imitated contemporary slum writers. There is, however, little external evidence which reveals the source of his influences. In *The Summing Up* he states that 'Arthur Morrison with his *Tales of Mean Streets* and *A Child of the Jago* had drawn the attention of the public to what were then known as the lower classes and I profited by the interest he had aroused'. Maugham has frequently admitted the great influence on his writing of Guy de Maupassant, and critics have discussed his debt at considerable length. A deleted comment from the manuscript of *The Summing Up* testifies to Maugham's reverence for the French writer when he wrote *Liza of Lambeth*: 'Though I was not aware of it at the time I know that when I came to write *Liza of Lambeth* I wrote it as I thought Maupassant would have written it.'[2] Maugham, however, acknowledges no further debt.

Of the English writers who treated the slums, George Gissing probably least influenced the young Maugham. Although his choice of subjects is similar to that in *Liza of Lambeth*, his approach to them —personal, moral and propagandistic—bears little resemblance to Maugham's. Unable to view the poor as anything but degraded animals, Gissing fails to convey any of their vitality and exuberance, and his inhibition about recording the speech of the East End prevents him rendering credible dialogue.

George Moore, far more strongly influenced by the French Naturalists, was able to treat his material with greater objectivity, and his *Esther Waters* (1894) is one of the best examples of the Naturalistic novel in English literature. Maugham was familiar with *Esther Waters*, but his statement in *The Summing Up* that 'no one could attach so great a value to that work who had an intimate knowledge of the French novel during the nineteenth century' makes it unlikely that he found it a profitable guide.

In 1893, Rudyard Kipling wrote 'The Record of Badalia Herodsfoot', a short story included in *Many Inventions*. In this story Kipling took the reader even lower into the depths of the East End and achieved greater realism by reproducing as accurately as possible the speech of the slum dwellers. It is this kind of phonetic reproduction which led to the dialogue of Morrison and Maugham:

"Arsk about!" said Badalia indignantly, drawing herself together. " 'Oo sez anythink ag'in me 'ere?"
" 'Oo sez? W'y everybody. I ain't come back more'n a minute fore I finds you've been with the curick Gawd knows where. Wot curick was 'e?"[3]

Arthur Morrison continued this type of realism in *Tales of Mean Streets* (1894) and *A Child of the Jago* (1896). It is in this period, between 1895 and 1897, that Maugham wrote *Liza of Lambeth*, and an examination of naturalistic characteristics common to these works will illustrate how closely he followed his immediate predecessors.

The first notable quality found in these works is a sharp and constant focus on the confines of the slum. Unlike Gissing and Moore, whose slum novels frequently move out of the slum or treat middle-class characters, Kipling, Morrison and Maugham keep within narrow geographical limits. Thus there is a feeling in their stories of the restriction of the ghetto or the 'street'. This is intensified in each case by a skilfully constructed picture of a colourful, squalid and cramped lower-class milieu, the impression of the communal nature of each being made more powerful by their supposedly notorious names. Kipling's tale is set in 'Gunnison Street'; Morrison's begins with a description of the 'Jago'; and Maugham's opens with a picture of 'Vere Street, Lambeth'. Thus each environment becomes almost an entity in itself, with overwhelming power to influence events, and in all three stories the street is viewed as a trap, a force which plays a great part in the course of the action.

The effect of environment on the individual is dramatically revealed in these stories. Badalia temporarily rises above her situation by managing some of the charitable attempts of the curate, but she is eventually brought down when her wayward husband returns and beats her to death. In *A Child of the Jago* Dicky Perrott attempts to escape the slum through an honest job, but this attempt is easily ruined by Mr Weech, a type of Fagin for whom Dicky has previously stolen. As 'old Beveridge' says, 'So do your devilment, or God help you, Dicky Perrott—though he won't: for the Jago's got you!'[4] In Maugham's story Liza attempts to defy Vere Street by having an illicit affair with a married man, and she is beaten and reduced to drunken carousing with her alcoholic mother.

Second, these stories vividly dramatise the violence inherent in a life which is close to an animal existence, and they especially stress the suffering of the women in the slum. Kipling describes the beating that Badalia's husband gives his mistress, and he observes that 'the bruises furnished material for discussion on doorsteps among such women as had been treated in like manner by their husbands. They were not few.'[5] Similarly, Morrison describes with detailed realism the feud between the Ranns and the Learys, the fight between Josh Perrott and Billy Leary, and the savagery of women like Sally Green. In *Liza of Lambeth* Maugham emphasises the suffering of women through the beatings of Mrs Stanley and Liza's friend, Sally. With a succinctness more characteristic of his later career, he writes: 'It was Saturday night, the time when women in Vere Street weep.'

A third characteristic common to these works is the cheapness of life in the slum conditions. Babies are born in great numbers and they die in great numbers. Badalia's child dies of croup, and Lascar Loo's mother calls the names of children 'long since slain by dirt and neglect'. In *A Child of the Jago* Dicky Perrott's young sister dies, a victim of exposure and neglect. In *Liza* Maugham effectively shows the midwife's familiarity with death:

"I've been very unfortunate of lite," remarked Mrs. Hodges, as she licked her lips; "this mikes the second death I've 'ad in the last ten days – women, I mean, of course I don't count bibies."[6]

Fourth, these writers stress the callousness and lack of affection for their children of degenerate parents, with the implication that this is a result of the tough struggle for survival. Kipling shows Lascar Loo's mother intercepting and keeping the 'custids' intended for her daughter. In *A Child of the Jago* Josh Perrott has little time to be concerned with his children, and Mrs Perrott leaves her sick child to go to the pub. Similarly, in *Liza*, there is little love for Liza shown by her mother, who, as her daughter lies dying, drinks with a friend and discusses the expense of funerals.

Fifth, the central figure in all these stories dies at the end. Badalia suffers a fearful beating from her husband, Dicky Perrott is stabbed during a street brawl, and Liza dies as a result of a miscarriage. All these deaths are in the naturalistic tradition.

Finally, there is great similarity in the use of dialogue by these writers. As mentioned previously, Kipling added the dimension of realistic dialogue not found in the novels of Gissing and Moore, and Morrison and Maugham followed his lead. While Maugham gained much of his language from personal observation, it is likely that he profited by a study of Kipling and Morrison. The manuscript of *Liza of Lambeth* indicates that he took great care in reproducing cockney speech; he appears to have gone through the completed work,

changing what came naturally from his pen to a closer representation
of East End speech. 'Without' became 'withaht', 'that' became
'thet', 'you' became 'yer'; 'be cross' was changed to 'tike on', 'say' to
'sy', 'stay' to 'sty' and 'waiting' to 'witin''. Thus Maugham, like
Kipling and Morrison, was able to convey the vitality of East End
life, and this quality of *Liza of Lambeth* was one that was to serve him
well in his career as a dramatist. Indeed, on the basis of this first
novel, Henry Arthur Jones predicted that Maugham would be one of
the most successful dramatists of the time.

The influence of Morrison was probably greater than Maugham
acknowledges in *The Summing Up*. That he could remember those
works which have become obscured by time probably indicates a
close knowledge of, or interest in, them in the past. In any case,
Maugham's admiration for Morrison was such that he included
'Without Visible Means' (from *Tales of Mean Streets*) in *Tellers of
Tales* (1939). In his study of the English naturalistic writers William C.
Frierson rightly concludes: 'Mais pour la majeure partie l'influence
de M. Morrison est si fortement marquée que l'on n'est pas incité à
chercher plus loin.'[7]

The greatest similarity between Morrison's writing and *Liza of
Lambeth* lies in their objectivity, and it is not surprising, therefore,
that, of all the slum writers, Morrison and Maugham have been the
most strongly attacked as being callous and sensational. Morrison,
however, had carefully considered the problems of demonstrating the
horrors of ghetto life, and his technique was designed to expose the
reader to these miseries without giving him the protection of emotional catharsis. Reacting to the sentimental treatment of the slums
by other writers, he aimed to spare the reader nothing:

In my East End stories I determined that they must be written in a different
way from the ordinary slum story. They must be done with austerity and
frankness, and there must be no sentimentalism, no glossing over. I felt that
the writer must never interpose himself between his subject and his reader.
I could best bring in real life by keeping myself and my . . . moralizing out
of it. For this I have been abused as hard and unsympathetic, but I can
assure you it is far more painful for me to write stories than for you to
read them.[8]

Morrison's reasons for complete objectivity are as psychological as
aesthetic:

Their [his critics'] wish is not that I shall weep, but that I shall weep
obscenely in the public gaze. In other words, that I shall make public
parade of my sympathy in their behalf, so that they may keep their own
sympathy for themselves, and gain comfort from the belief that they are
eased of their just responsibility by vicarious snivelling.[9]

In *Liza of Lambeth* Maugham's point of view is very close to Morrison's. With the exception of a few lapses, he lets the facts of the story convey the misery of slum life. In such potentially sentimental or melodramatic situations as Liza's seduction (where he reverses the usual Victorian formula by making Liza very happy in her 'fall'), the beatings of Mrs Stanley and Sally, the alcoholism of Mrs Kemp, and the death of Liza, he writes with considerable restraint. Maugham, therefore, like Morrison, was subsequently accused of lack of conviction. *The Bookman* reflected the opinion of many when it wrote: 'It is all very hopeless, and unrelieved by any sense of strong feeling working in the writer.'[10]

It is clear that Maugham's first novel was written with particular naturalistic models as guides. Nevertheless, despite artistic inexperience and intellectual immaturity, he was capable of using the conventions of the slum novel to communicate his youthful vision of the world. *Liza of Lambeth* therefore contains a number of elements which are the young writer's personal expression, and it is largely these things which make it such a remarkable first novel.

Liza of Lambeth represents a departure from previous slum novels or 'novels of misery' in that Maugham is not directly concerned with economic matters. Money plays a major role in all of Gissing's slum novels, and Moore, Kipling and Morrison show their characters in an unending struggle to live from day to day. In Maugham's story, however, there is no hard struggle for survival. This is strikingly obvious when one compares *Liza* to *Of Human Bondage*, where the horrors of poverty are much more strongly felt through the reactions of Philip Carey, a middle-class young man, when he wanders through the streets of London unable to pay his landlady. Furthermore, in *Liza of Lambeth* there is none of this kind of explicit attack on poverty which can be found in the later novel:

Philip could not get out of his eyes the dead girl lying on the bed, wan and white, and the boy who stood at the end of it like a stricken beast. The bareness of the squalid room made the pain of it more poignant. It was cruel that a stupid chance should have cut off her life when she was just entering upon it; but in the very moment of saying this to himself, Philip thought of the life which had been in store for her, the bearing of children, the dreary fight with poverty, the youth broken by toil and deprivation into a slatternly middle age – he saw the pretty face grow thin and white, the hair grow scanty, the pretty hands, worn down brutally by work, become like the claws of an old animal – then, when the man was past his prime, the difficulty of getting jobs, the small wages he had to take; and the inevitable, abject penury of the end: she might be energetic, thrifty, industrious, it would not have saved her; in the end was the workhouse or subsistence on the charity of her children. Who could pity her because she had died when life offered so little?[11]

In *Liza of Lambeth*, however, the characters live in relative comfort. Liza's mother receives a pension and can supplement this with odd jobs, and Liza seems to make a reasonable living by working in a factory. If, therefore, economics play a part in *Liza*, it is indirectly, through particular manifestations of slum life which are the result of poverty.

Maugham's real concern is with the stifling and restricting nature of ghetto society. He views this life as an intensely tribal existence, with all of the pressures and unwritten laws which accompany it. *Liza of Lambeth* shares with *A Child of the Jago* a subtle understanding of how slum life operates as a society to maintain its own particular taboos and customs. Liza's story is that of a strong individualist who attempts to defy the laws of the tribe and soon suffers its punishment.

Like Kipling's 'Gunnison Street' and Morrison's 'Jago', Vere Street is treated almost as a character, and it is a powerful force. Maugham is careful to establish the social nature of the street at the beginning of the story:

The number of babies was prodigious; they sprawled about everywhere, on the pavement, round the doors, and about their mothers' skirts. The grown-ups were gathered round the open doors; there were usually two women squatting on the doorstep, and two or three more seated on either side on chairs; they were invariably nursing babies, and most of them showed clear signs that the present object of the maternal care would be soon ousted by a new arrival. Men were less numerous but such as there were leant against the walls, smoking, or sat on the sills of the ground-floor windows. It was the dead season in Vere Street as much as in Belgravia, and really if it had not been for babies just come or just about to come, and an opportune murder in a neighbouring doss-house, there would have been nothing whatever to talk about. As it was, the little groups talked quietly discussing the atrocity or the merits of the local mid-wives, comparing the circumstances of their various confinements.[12]

The scene continues with what has been called the 'choral voice'[13] of the women discussing matters in cockney dialect. An organ grinder appears, and a feeling of close-knit social existence is communicated in the ensuing dancing. In this kind of environment, the life of the people is in the street.

Unlike many other slum novelists, Maugham invests his Lambeth with a strong code of righteousness, which, more often than not, is merely made up of gestures of respectability copied from other sections of Victorian society. Sally's husband, for example, makes her give up her job because 'a woman's plice is 'er 'ome an' if 'er old man can't afford ter keep 'er without 'er workin' in a factory—well, all I can say is thet 'e'd better go an' git single'. Similarly, Liza, on

seeing a 'New Woman' cycling in Battersea Park, 'with
fashioned prejudice of her class, would look after the rider a
some remark about her, not seldom more forcible than ladyli
Maugham, the particularly abhorrent characteristic of Vere
respectability is its hypocrisy. Like other segments of society, .
only think of virtue in sexual terms. Drunkenness and wife-be
are tolerated, but love is strictly regulated. Liza's mother is a personification of Vere Street hypocrisy; she is lazy, corrupt, and
drunken, but she claims respectability: 'I was lawfully married in
church, an' I've got my marriage lines now ter show I was, an' thet
one of my daughters should 'ave gone wrong in this way—well, I
can't understand it.' Not only does she claim respectability, she
sincerely believes she is worthy of it, and at the end she can abandon
Liza to her death because she has proved to be 'very bad'.

For an inexperienced young writer, Maugham is remarkably
skilful at using subtle literary techniques to reinforce the feeling of the
strength of the communal pressures in Lambeth. A great deal of the
action takes place in the street, and Maugham repeatedly shows Liza
escaping to the relative privacy of her own corner, usually with a
sense of relief. For example, he often ends his chapters with his
characters in some kind of retreat:[14]

She blushed to the very roots of her hair, quickly extricated herself from
his arms, amid the jeers and laughter of everyone, slid into the door of the
nearest house and was lost to view. (Chapter I)

And quickly drawing back, she slammed the window to, and moved into
the further part of the room. (Chapter II)

At last she tore herself from him, and opening the door slid away into the
house. (Chapter V)

And together they slid down into the darkness of the passage. (Chapter
VII)

Immediately a great shout of laughter broke from the group, and she heard
them positively screaming till she got into her own house. (Chapter X)

The repetition of the word 'slid' creates the impression of rats returning to their holes. This technique is similar to Morrison's in *A Child
of the Jago*, where the slum is treated as a rat-trap and the streets and
alleys as rat runs.

Into this atmosphere of close communal living, Maugham places a
character whose spirits are too strong and exuberant to be forced
into the expected course of events. It is interesting that on the back
page of the manuscript there is a title—'The Pagan'—crossed out. It is
likely that this was a title that Maugham considered for his story; in
any case, it aptly describes Liza's character.

As soon as Liza is introduced into the story, the author establishes her vitality and energy. She is dressed in 'brilliant violet', with 'great lappets of velvet', and she wears 'an enormous black hat covered with feathers'. She is shown in a great many scenes, up to the decay in the relationship with Blakeston, which illustrate her exuberant high spirits. She dances in the street, wrestles with neighbourhood boys, plays cricket, and enjoys playful banter with others in the street. Maugham portrays her with affection and sympathy, and she remains one of his most delightful female creations.

Because of her high-spirited nature, Liza is not satisfied with Tom, the pleasant young man she is expected to marry. In his proposal Tom argues that 'you've come aht walkin' with me ever since Whitsun', and it is clear that Liza, like her friend, Sally, is expected to settle down with the nearest sufficient young man. She needs someone, however, with vitality and sensuousness to match her own, and her tragedy is that she finds it in Jim Blakeston, a married man.

Liza's relationship with Blakeston means defiance of the social mores of Vere Street. The community may accept that it is natural for a man to beat his wife and squander his meagre earnings on beer, but it does not tolerate the woman who becomes involved with a married man. Like any other social group with a strong tribal cohesion, it regards this as a disruptive action. The affair between Liza and Jim must therefore be conducted outside the social life of Vere Street, and Maugham treats the pair always as fugitives. Their first meeting as lovers is at night, when the communal life of the street is suspended:

The street was perfectly silent, and the lamp-posts, far apart, threw a dim light which only served to make Liza realise her solitude. There was such a difference between the street at midday, with its swarms of people, and now, when there was neither sound nor soul besides herself, that even she was struck by it. The regular line of houses on either side, with the even pavements and straight, cemented road, seemed to her like some desert place, as if everyone were dead, or a fire had raged and left it all desolate.[15]

On other occasions the lovers meet outside the confines of Vere Street—at the theatre, in the private bar of a pub, or in the waiting-room at Waterloo or Charing Cross. Maugham effectively conveys the claustrophobic narrowness of the slum and the ease and freedom the lovers feel when they emerge from it:

She walked close along the sides of the houses like a thief, and the police-man as she passed him turned round and looked at her, wondering whether she was meditating some illegal deed. She breathed freely on coming into the open road, and seeing Jim skulking behind a tree, ran up to him, and in the shadows they kissed again.[16]

In the close society of Vere Street, however, it is impossible to preserve one's privacy for long. The community soon becomes aware of Liza's affair with Blakeston, and it reacts with considerable authority. Maugham is careful to illustrate that Liza, at the beginning when she has the approval of her society, is the darling of Vere Street:

"Oo, Liza!" they shouted; the whole street joined in, and they gave long, shrill, ear-piercing shrieks and strange calls, that rung down the street and echoed back again.[17]

You felt there could be no questioning her right to the tyranny of Vere Street.[18]

Liza at this point is the favourite, and the approval of the community is expressed by the friendly nature of the jokes and banter in which she is involved. When, however, the affair becomes known (and there is always the feeling that it is impossible to hide anything in Vere Street), the atmosphere quickly changes. The jokes become harsh and are directed at Liza rather than in celebration with her:

"Tike care yer don't get into trouble, that's all," said one of the men, with burlesque gravity.

"Yer might give us a chanst, Liza; you come aht with me one evenin'. You oughter give us all a turn, jist ter show there's no ill-feelin'."[19]

The joking has changed from warmth to cruelty, and it is significant that Liza loses her composure and cannot defend herself as she was able to do so capably before.

The culminating point in the communal judgement of Liza comes in the scene where she fights Mrs Blakeston. It takes place in the street and the crowd is unwilling to interfere; it appoints a referee and keeps time, and the fight becomes a trial by combat for Liza, a duel fought according to certain rules and conditions in the presence of the tribe.

As the fight progresses, the comments of the crowd become a chorus, reflecting in a fashion on sin and retribution:

"She deserves all she gets, an' a damn sight more inter the bargain."

"Quite right," put in a third; "a woman's got no right ter tike someone's 'usbind from 'er. An' if she does she's bloomin' lucky if she gits off with a 'idin' – thet's wot I think."

"So do I. But I wouldn't 'ave thought it of Liza. I never thought she was a wrong 'un."

"Pretty specimen she is!" said a little dark woman, who looked like a Jewess. "If she messed abaht with my old man, I'd stick 'er – I swear I would!"

"Now she's been carryin' on with one, she'll try an' git others – you see if she don't."

"She'd better not come round my 'ouse; I'll soon give 'er wot for."[20]

Although the fight is stopped before a decision is reached, the judgement of Vere Street has been given. Liza has taken the worst of the beating, and thus begins the process which leads to her death. Street 'justice' has been administered.

In the final chapters of the novel, Maugham emphasises the failure of Liza's attempt to defy Vere Street, and he displays the naturalist's belief in the effect of environment. In the fight with Mrs Blakeston, fear, rage and pain make Liza lose her timidity and attack her antagonist viciously. Liza, who had listened with horror to Sally's account of her beating, is forced into the violence and degradation of street fighting.

Liza's fall is further illustrated by her drunken carouse with her alcoholic mother. Having previously been critical of her mother, she now joins her in heavy drinking and vulgar singing. Maugham's picture of Liza at this point, so different from the attractive portrait at the beginning, is not pretty:

Her dress was all disarranged; her face covered with the scars of scratches, and clots of blood had fixed under her nose; her eye had swollen up so that it was nearly closed, and red; her hair was hanging over her face and shoulders, and she laughed stupidly and leered with heavy, sodden ugliness.[21]

Mrs Kemp's observation that 'you're a chip of the old block' is a perceptive comment on Liza's potential future. Just as the 'Jago' has Dicky Perrott, Vere Street has Liza Kemp.

Finally, Liza dies. The causes are her savage beating in the street, exposure in the night when both she and her mother are in a drunken stupor, and, following this, her miscarriage. Maugham, like Kipling and Morrison, ends his story with the death of the central figure, and his treatment is the same—detached and objective.

Although *Liza of Lambeth* is in many ways a conventional slum novel, there are many ideas and themes in it which reappear in Maugham's later, more mature, work. With the possible exception of Tom, the characters are typically Maughamian—paradoxical mixtures of good and bad. Adultery is used as a catalyst to introduce conflict and action, and, as in his later stories, it is not expressly condemned. The unrequited love theme which appears so often in Maugham's writing is present in the form of Tom's plight. Finally, the central idea of rebellion against social pressures anticipates the kinds of revolt that motivate so many Maugham characters—artists, seekers, adulterers and criminals. *Liza of Lambeth* is, then, not so much a novel of the slums as a story of an individual's attempt to be free from the pressures to conform to the rules of a particular society.

Maugham could have placed it in Mayfair; circumstances, however, were more propitious for seeing his theme in the slum environment of Lambeth.

As a first novel, *Liza of Lambeth* is a considerable achievement, and readers in 1897 might have expected Maugham's career to advance spectacularly. He demonstrates a skilful use of dialogue and an ability to create a vivid scene with a minimum of carefully selected details. The characters of Liza, Mrs Kemp and Jim, although not fully developed, are memorable, and, like Morrison and Maupassant, Maugham tells a story of brutality and death without falling into sentimentality. *Liza* has been reprinted numerous times without extensive revision and it is readable today. In addition to being a vivid picture of a form of London life which has almost disappeared, it is a moving story.

III

Seven Early Novels:
Experiments and Potboilers

MAUGHAM'S FIRST NOVEL had been in many ways a happy accident, the result of a combination of fortunate circumstances; it was not, as he later readily admitted, an accurate gauge of his writing skill. That *Liza of Lambeth* is to a certain extent a special case in the Maugham canon is obvious when one realises that, with the possible exception of *Mrs Craddock*, he did not write as good a novel until *Of Human Bondage*, almost twenty years later. In the interim, Maugham produced seven novels—*The Making of a Saint* (1898), *The Hero* (1901), *Mrs Craddock* (1902), *The Merry-Go-Round* (1904), *The Bishop's Apron* (1906), *The Explorer* (1907) and *The Magician* (1908). Three of these—*The Merry-Go-Round, The Explorer* and *The Bishop's Apron*—are merely unproduced plays fashioned into novels, and some were written simply out of immediate financial need.

These novels represent, on the whole, an attempt by Maugham to repeat the success of *Liza of Lambeth* by following current trends in fiction. *The Making of a Saint* was written because the author was led to believe that a young writer should attempt only historical novels. *The Hero* reflected contemporary interest in the Boer War; *The Merry-Go-Round* was influenced by the aesthetes; and *The Explorer* was a poor imitation of Kipling's imperialistic fiction. Similarly, *The Magician* was a straightforward bid to benefit from the current interest in magic and the occult. These, together with *Mrs Craddock* and *The Bishop's Apron*, were the experiments of an immature writer, and if they accomplished anything it was to show Maugham his limitations.

Maugham has frequently been accused of pandering to public literary tastes, of being more interested in commercial popularity than artistic achievement. This charge, the curse of the financially successful author, is really only applicable to Maugham in the period between 1904 and 1913. His earlier writings, while constructed with an eye on contemporary vogues, were not the kind of fiction to capture a wide readership. In the case of *Liza of Lambeth*, for example, it must be remembered that, while the slum novel had prestige in literary circles, it was far from a popular form of literature.

Maugham's early fiction was a sincere attempt to produce significant and uncompromising writing. *Liza of Lambeth* did not pander to the public taste for a sentimental treatment of the slums. *Schiffbruechig* (*Marriages are Made in Heaven*), his first published play (produced in 1902), and *A Man of Honour* (1903) gave the English audience a realism which at that time they were unwilling to accept. 'A Bad Example' and 'Daisy' (in *Orientations*) were fairly astringent attacks on conventional morality and hypocrisy. Finally, it should be remembered that Maugham was co-editor, with Laurence Housman, of the short-lived periodical, *The Venture: An Annual of Art and Literature*, in 1903. The contributors included John Masefield, G. K. Chesterton, Thomas Hardy, Richard Garnett, Havelock Ellis, Edmund Gosse, Alfred Noyes, Arthur Symons and James Joyce.

Maugham's novels of this very early period—*The Making of a Saint, The Hero, Mrs Craddock* and *The Merry-Go-Round*—are not great literature, but their failure is not due to a lack of sincerity. *The Making of a Saint*, while an attempt in a popular form, meant a departure from a proven subject which had brought a degree of success. *The Hero* was an examination of a serious problem—the alienation of a young soldier returning to the narrow life of a small English village. *Mrs Craddock* was a rather daring study of the female temperament and of class differences. *The Merry-Go-Round* was an experiment in structure, and it incorporated the realistic, uncompromising plot of *A Man of Honour*. Thus, while these novels fail for various reasons, it would be unfair to say that Maugham wrote them merely to satisfy public taste. They are therefore worth examining in relation to his development as a serious and skilled writer.

According to Maugham, he had already written *The Making of a Saint* when Unwin asked for another slum novel. Feeling that he had exhausted the material gained from his experiences in Lambeth, he turned, under the influence of some articles by Andrew Lang, to the historical novel. Lang had written, says Maugham:

... that it was absurd for the young writer to try to write about his own day and the life about him. What could he know about them? The only novel he could hope to write that might have merit was a historical one. Here his lack of worldly wisdom, his vernal innocence, could be no hindrance.[1]

Following this advice, Maugham wrote a historical romance based on a story from Machiavelli's *History of Florence*, the account of

C

Caterina Sforza and the siege of Forli. After diligently researching the subject in the British Museum, he spent the summer writing in Capri.

As Maugham later recognised, Lang's advice was faulty, and the achievement of *Liza of Lambeth* was not repeated. Whereas the first novel had been a product of his own experience and a success, *The Making of a Saint* was an imaginative fabrication and a failure. Indeed, the qualities which had so admirably suited the slum novel— understatement, irony, realism and detachment—were damaging in historical romance. The detail, which in the first novel had added to an understanding of the characters, merely smothered the story in facts. Finally, and most important, Maugham's temperament was not suited to historical romance:

In *The Making of a Saint* his cynical and youthfully brash observations on "the people", the mob, the rulers, and the general frailty of mankind were violently out of place in the romantic historical novel of the time. Equally exceptionable was the bitter ending, dark with disillusion and pessimism.[2]

Maugham himself recognised the weaknesses of his second novel, and did not choose to have it included in the Collected Edition of his works. In his nephew's copy he wrote: 'A very poor novel by W. Somerset Maugham'.[3]

In this otherwise superficial novel, critics have noted a number of themes and devices which Maugham later developed with more maturity. Appearance and reality, so prominent a theme in the short stories, is present in the false Giulia, and the torment of a passion that one cannot conquer appears in Filippo's dilemma. His friend, Matteo, is a prototype of the character of the *raissoneur* common to so many of Maugham's novels and plays. The dialogue, which is occasionally witty, anticipates the lines of the drawing-room comedies, and, finally, *The Making of a Saint* is Maugham's initial use of one of his most characteristic devices—the first person narrator.

The Making of a Saint is interesting also because it is one of the few works in which Maugham touches on politics. He was emphatic in his belief that a writer should avoid such subjects, but here the core of the story is political. The novel is constructed around the rebellion by a group of citizens of Forli against the tyranny of Girolamo Riario. The leader, Checco d'Orsi, having assisted Girolamo to gain power, chafes at the thought of being his servant.

In an atmosphere of machination and treachery, Checco is persuaded to murder Girolamo in the name of liberty. The parallels between this story and that of Shakespeare's *Julius Caesar* are so numerous as to suggest that Maugham borrowed rather liberally. Checco, like Brutus, has been a close friend of the ruler and, like

Brutus, he becomes involved in the plot for the sake of the country's freedom:

"Is it necessary that birth and life here should be the birth and life of slaves? Our glorious ancestors never submitted to this terrible misfortune. They were free, and in their freedom they found life. But this is a living death.

"You all know the grievous wrongs I have suffered at the hands of the man whom I helped to place on the throne. But these wrongs I freely forgive. I am filled only with devotion to my country and love to my fellow men. If you others have private grievances, I implore you to put them aside, and think only that you are the liberators from oppression of all those you love and cherish. Gather up to your hearts the spirit of Brutus, when, for the sake of Freedom, he killed the man whom above all others he loved."[4]

When the assassination has taken place, Checco cries: 'Give me my dagger, Matteo; it is sacred, now. It has been christened in blood with the name of Liberty. Liberty, my friends, Liberty!'

As in Shakespeare's play, Checco is hailed as a hero and offered the authority of ruler. Similarly, the mob proves to be fickle and, when a counter-revolution appears to be imminent, it turns on Checco's faction and drives it out of the city. The revolution fails, and the 'liberators' end their lives in bitterness.

As a discussion of political tyranny and freedom, *The Making of a Saint* is superficial. The plot too closely imitates Shakespeare's and there is never any real analysis of the problems of political freedom and their corollaries. Checco is a cardboard character, and liberty becomes merely platitudinous in his mouth. The author is, of course, restricted because he has chosen to dramatise a historical fact; nevertheless, much that could be said about the relationship between individual liberty and the powers of the state never appears. It is not, in fact, until *Of Human Bondage* that Maugham discusses the social contract, and not until *Christmas Holiday*, forty years later, that he treats the problems of freedom in revolution in any kind of depth.

With *The Hero*, Maugham again reveals a sensitivity to literary influences and public tastes. Mildred C. Kuner has suggested that in this novel he was attempting the theme of the loss of faith, for which such works as Mrs Humphry Ward's *Robert Elsmere* (1888) and Henry Arthur Jones' *Michael and his Lost Angel* had created a vogue.[5] Other critics point to the timely subject of the Boer War, and in this regard Maugham admitted in the preface to *Liza of Lambeth* that 'it was suggested by the Boer War and influenced by my study of the French novelists'.

It would nevertheless be a serious mistake to view *The Hero* as

merely an attempt to satisfy public taste. It is hard to imagine the
general reading public at the turn of the century endorsing a novel
which attacked patriotism, home, family, church and honour.
Furthermore, the bleak suicidal ending, with its expression of despair
and loneliness, is hardly likely to have appealed to a great many
people.

Of all Maugham's early novels, *The Hero* is the most directly concerned with the question of individual freedom. Although his intention was to portray the conflict created by the loss of faith in one
member of an engaged couple, the novel became a picture of a young
man fighting to preserve a newly discovered liberty. Most of the story
is concerned with the hero's struggle to free himself from the smother-
ing effect of ignorance, prejudice and illusion, as represented by the
demands of his parents and the pressures of public opinion. In this
scheme, the conflict with his fiancée becomes merely a part of his
effort to escape.

The hero, James Parsons, is a young soldier who returns from the
Boer War, where he has distinguished himself by an act of bravery.
He has been away for five years and is coming back to the girl, Mary
Clibborn, who has patiently waited. Like James's parents, Mary
assumes that her fiancé will be content to settle in 'Little Primpton'
(Maugham strains to use a suggestive name), and resume living as
before. Like Larry Darrell in *The Razor's Edge* forty years later,
however, the war has transformed James, making him psychologically
and intellectually unfit to live in the narrow, stifling atmosphere of a
small village. He can never return to being the person he was before,
and so the story becomes one of attempted escape.

Maugham's choice of a returning soldier as protagonist is astute.
Because James is a product of village life and morality who has
experienced an enforced enlightenment by his years abroad, his
return to this environment takes on added sharpness. Through his
recognition of what he was and what he has become, the provin-
cialism and inadequacy of this kind of life for a sensitive person is
presented with clarity and emphasis.

One of the major problems in James's relationship with Mary
derives from the great transformation in his attitudes toward women
which he has undergone since his proposal of marriage five years
earlier. Prior to his service in the Boer War he was stationed in India,
where a passionate affair taught him how puritanical were his ideas
about women. Nevertheless, Maugham does not underestimate the
power of conditioning through upbringing and background:

And when at last he fell passionately in love, it meant to him ten times
more than to most men; it was a sudden freedom from himself. He was

like a prisoner who sees for the first time in his life the trees and the hurrying clouds, and all the various movement of the world. For a little while James had known a wonderful liberty, an ineffable bliss which coloured the whole universe with new, strange colours. But then he learnt that the happiness was only sin, and he returned voluntarily to his cold prison.[6]

As a result of this sexual awakening and realisation, James now finds unpleasant those qualities in Mary which had previously attracted him. She seems dull and plain and almost masculine; above all, she lacks sexual warmth. Thus it quickly becomes clear to James that they are no longer compatible.

Maugham gives Mary an additional quality to which James reacts with aversion—a desire to dominate and control others—and this becomes a trait shared by most of Maugham's unpleasant female characters. In a damning scene, Mary is shown going on her rounds of charitable deeds, imposing her will on her patients. She quarrels with the doctor on a matter of treatment, and then insists on altering one man's pillows to her liking even though they then cause considerable discomfort. Finally, she complains to James that the girls to whom she teaches sewing live in unpleasant surroundings and are happy:

"I can't get them to see that they ought to be utterly miserable."
"Oh, I know," sighed the curate; "it makes me sad to think of it."
"Surely, if they're happy, you can want nothing better," said James, rather impatiently.
"But I do. They have no right to be happy under such circumstances. I want to make them feel their wretchedness."
"What a brutal thing to do!" cried James.
"It's the only way to improve them. I want them to see things as I see them."[7]

Needless to say, a wife with this kind of desire for domination is totally incompatible with James' vision of independence.

Maugham's hero, however, is bound to his fiancée by his proposal five years earlier, and there are considerable forces working to ensure that he lives up to the conventional idea of duty. The strength of public pressure to do the 'honourable' thing, for better or for worse, shown in its early destructive stages, is similar to the sense of duty which causes so much grief in *A Man of Honour* and *The Merry-Go-Round*.

The major instruments of public pressure on James are his parents. They represent narrow provincial morality, and they utilise every claim on their son's fidelity to enforce their will. They attempt to live their lives through that of their son, and they cannot visualise his wanting to be anything but what they have tried to make him. James therefore sees his home as a 'hot-house', where he is put on a 'leading-string', merely a puppet in their hands:

> Throughout, they had been unwilling to let him live his own life, but desirous rather that he should live theirs. They loved him tyrannically, on the condition that he should conform to all their prejudices. Though full of affectionate kindness, they wished him always to dance to their piping – a marionette of which they pulled the strings.[8]

The young man is nevertheless unwilling to sacrifice his liberty in order to retain their devotion:

> They wished to exercise over him the most intolerable of all tyrannies, the tyranny of love. It was a heavy return they demanded for their affection if he must abandon his freedom, body and soul; he earnestly wished to make them happy, but that was too hard a price to pay.[9]

Added to the censure of the parents is the great pressure exerted by the village community, and the oppressive closeness of this society is similar to the communal life in *Liza of Lambeth*. As in his first novel, Maugham initially shows his protagonist as the favourite of the people; James is welcomed home as a hero in an effusive public ceremony. Later, however, when he breaks off his engagement, the village turns against him and shows its displeasure.

The greatest conflict between James and the life he is expected to lead in Little Primpton is on the intellectual level, and here Maugham launches a savage, if somewhat immature, attack on conventional and dogmatic society. The Parsonses, its best representatives, are unthinking, accepting believers in conventional morality, and to the agnostic and critical James this is abhorrent:

> The Parsons had lived their whole lives in an artificial state. . . . They walked round and round in a narrow circle, hemmed in by false ideals and by ugly prejudices, putting for the love of God unnecessary obstacles in their path, and convinced that theirs was the only possible way, while all others led to damnation. . . . They were not living creatures, but dogmatic machines.[10]

During the period in which he was abroad, James went through an intellectual awakening and discovered that life is more complex than he had been taught to believe. The ideas of his parents were too simple, too narrow; every question had more aspects than they were willing to admit. In this recognition lay a liberation:

> James found in existence new beauties, new interests, new complexities; and he gained a lighter heart and, above all, an exquisite sense of freedom. At length he looked back with something like horror at that old life in which the fetters of ignorance had weighed so terribly upon him.[11]

James' entire philosophy is in antipathy to that of his parents and the village. He attempts to point out that they are living in a world of illusion, that their lives are conducted according to narrow and unattractive ideals. In the end, however, he sees that his efforts are futile, and the enlightenment which he has undergone has made him unable to accept 'a rule of life which governed every action with an iron tyranny'.

The Hero is one of Maugham's strongest expressions of determinism. By the end of the novel, James' position has become impossible, and his dilemma cannot be resolved; he has become homeless wherever he may be. It seems that, although his years abroad brought illumination and intellectual awareness, they have not given him emotional strength or a viable independence. The doors have been opened for him, but he does not have the power to walk through them. His position has become cruel: on the one hand, he has nothing but contempt for his background; on the other, he needs the solidity of his roots. At one point, he goes to London and briefly revels in his escape; however, this life is somehow unsatisfactory and he returns to the village.

James discovers that, although he can recognise and combat the oppressive forces outside him, he cannot escape his inhibitions. However much he tries, he cannot avoid being a product of his background; its effect on his life is inescapable. In a gloomy passage leading to his hero's suicide Maugham defines the problem in strong deterministic terms:

James was like a foolish bird, a bird born in a cage, without power to attain its freedom. His lust for a free life was futile; he acknowledged with cruel self-contempt that he was weaker than a woman – ineffectual. He could not lead the life of his little circle, purposeless and untrue; and yet he had not power to lead a life of his own. Uncertain, vacillating, torn between the old and the new, his reason led him; his conscience drew him back. But the ties of his birth and ancestry were too strong; he had not the energy even of the poor tramp, who carries with him his whole fortune, and leaves in the lap of the gods the uncertain future. James envied with all his heart the beggar boy, wandering and homeless and penniless, but free. He, at least, had not these inhuman fetters which it was death to suffer and death to cast off; he, indeed, could make the whole world his servant. Freedom, freedom! If one were only unconscious of captivity, what would it matter? It is the knowledge that kills. And James walked again by the neat iron railing which enclosed the fields, his head aching with the rigidity and decorum, wishing vainly for just one piece of barren unkept land to remind him that all the world was not a prison.[12]

The world, however, *is* a prison for James, and its bars are 'lovingkindness and trust, tears, silent distress, bitter disillusion and old age'. Characteristically, his suicide is motivated by one thought: 'It is the beginning of my freedom.'

The Hero is not a great novel; it is not even a good one. It is not, however, the simple money-maker that some critics believe, nor is it uninteresting. It is, as Maugham has claimed in the preface to *Liza of Lambeth*, 'an honest piece of work', and, however immature, an attempt at serious social criticism.

From a stylistic point of view there is an interesting attempt by Maugham to adapt a borrowed practice to his own purpose. He has admitted that he was influenced by his study of French novelists and that his admiration for Flaubert led him to write long descriptions of scenery. *The Hero* does, in fact, contain a number of these pastoral descriptions, but they are very often employed as a device to re-inforce the central theme of imprisonment. When James feels the restraints tightening on him he thinks of the sense of freedom he experienced in the vastness of Africa. Later, he interprets the domes-ticated Kentish countryside in terms of custom and convention:

Nature herself was under the power of the formal influence, and flourished with a certain rigidity and decorum. After a while the impression became singularly irksome; it seemed to emphasise man's lack of freedom, remind-ing one of the iron conventions with which he is inevitably bound. . . . The primness of the scene then was insufferable; the sombre, well-ordered elms, the meadows so carefully kept, seemed the garden of some great voluptuous prison, and the air was close with servitude.[13]

Finally, the hopelessness of his attempt to escape is reflected in the surroundings:

On every inch of it the hand of man was apparent. It was a prison, and his hands and feet were chained with heavy iron. . . . All round, the hills were dark and drear; and that very fertility, that fat Kentish luxuriance, added to the oppression. It was a task impossible to escape from that iron circle. All power of flight abandoned him.[14]

Maugham's use of background description is neither skilful nor subtle, and it tends to be excessively romantic. Nevertheless, it anticipates the mature writer's effective treatment of environmental influence in later writings such as 'Rain' and the Far East stories.

Maugham's next novel, *Mrs Craddock*, published in 1902, is one of the best that he produced until *Of Human Bondage*. St John Adcock called it 'a subtle and even masterly study of a certain female temperament that is probably not so uncommon as we would like to believe'.[15] Richard Cordell considers it excellent, and rates it as one of Maugham's best novels. It remains one of the most readable of the early novels, and it would not, perhaps, be extravagant to claim for it a certain degree of influence on D. H. Lawrence and other later students of female psychology.

There was a number of possible influences working on Maugham when he wrote *Mrs Craddock*. There are many affinities with *Madame Bovary*, and it has been suggested that there are similarities to Meredith's *Diana of the Crossways*. Certainly this story of class conflicts in marriage was suited to an age in which, as the popularity of much of Wells, Bennett and Galsworthy shows, there was considerable interest in studies of middle-class relationships.

While it is likely that Maugham owes some debts to other studies of marriage and class problems, *Mrs Craddock* was a fairly daring extension of what had been written before. Bertha's passionate nature and her ruthless pursuit of Edward Craddock were examined with a frankness and thoroughness that shocked readers. Uneasy about its straightforward examination of sexual attraction, and particularly its story of the determined pursuit of a man by a passionate woman, every London publisher of consequence refused it. Only after Maugham had removed some offensive passages did William Heinemann accept it. Adcock, writing in 1904, considered the public attitude when he wrote that 'good as it is, the times were not ripe for such frank handling of sex mysteries',[16] and J. P. Collins claimed that the heroine was 'fully a decade ahead of her time'.[17] The accusation, so often levelled at Maugham, that he failed to extend the limits of understanding of a subject, is hardly appropriate to *Mrs Craddock*.

The novel concerns Bertha Ley, a well-educated middle-class woman who, to the astonishment of her friends and relatives, marries out of her class—her husband is an ordinary farmer, Edward Craddock. Problems soon develop in the marriage, and the sources of difficulty are numerous. To a certain extent, hardships are caused by its being a marriage between classes—not because of external social pressures, but because Bertha and Edward, products of their respective backgrounds, have no common interests. Bertha is well-educated, well-travelled, and has been influenced by the Continent. Edward, on the other hand, has had little education, has never travelled extensively, and is extremely insular in outlook. The result is that, although the man soon adapts well to the landed squire's life, he remains nouveau-riche and his wife is always beyond him in sophistication. There is, therefore, understandable conflict at every approach to art, music, drama, literature and politics.

Critical opinion, generally, defines the basic problem in *Mrs Craddock* as a conflict in temperaments. Bertha is intellectual, imaginative and sensitive; she can enjoy an ironic comment, and she sees through much of the stupidity and hypocrisy of her class. Edward however, is the complete reverse, and Cordell is right when he says:

Edward is a completely realised character, who just misses being a caricature of the middle-class Anglo-Saxon – unimaginative, narrowly patriotic, energetically a good fellow, conservative, virtuous. He is a stupid and a happy man. He has no doubts, no struggles, no self-criticisms.[18]

In addition to this schism on the intellectual plane, there is a more important contrast in emotional temperament. Bertha is passionate and sensual; Edward is cold, inhibited and unemotional. Bertha has a need to feel that she is loved, and when Edward fails to demonstrate or proclaim his love she suffers. Thus a marriage which cannot survive on intellectual attraction fails also to find an emotional or sexual basis.

Mrs Craddock, however, is not simply a study of incompatibility in marriage. It must be remembered that, in spite of the attention given to Edward's character, the novel is nevertheless a portrait of Bertha—an individual, not a representative woman—and there is considerable evidence to show that most of the sources of unhappiness can be found within Bertha herself. Edward, after all, is a fairly static personality; most of his apparent changes are only in the eyes of his wife. The factors which strongly influence Bertha and her vision of Craddock are themes which Maugham turns to so often— bondage to passion, bondage to illusion and bondage to an unsatisfactory mate.

Bertha's passionate nature, like that of so many of Maugham's female characters, initiates the unfortunate marriage. Attracted to Craddock because of his rough masculinity, his 'firmness of character' and 'his masterfulness', Bertha imagines herself in his arms and feels that 'he could not dream how intense was her desire'. Characteristically, Maugham describes passion as something painful, disabling and imprisoning:

But her legs would scarcely carry her, she had a sensation that was entirely novel; never before had she experienced that utter weakness of the knees so that she feared to fall; her breathing was strangely oppressive, and her heart beat almost painfully.[19]

This passion grips Bertha, and in the first part of the novel it completely blots out her judgement and rational thought. Much later, she regards the destruction of this feverish emotion with relief.

Bertha's overwhelming desire leads to another form of imprisonment common to many of Maugham's characters—slavery to illusion. As she is attracted to Craddock physically, she weaves about him a number of impressions which blind her to his real character. Succumbing to the romantic's temptation to see the Noble Savage's qualities as a delightful change from jaded sophistication, Bertha actually considers Edward's ignorance, inexperience, and lack of taste to be attractive. Thus her marriage is to the illusion of a man, and her discovery that Edward is dull, unimaginative and unresponsive, is disillusionment; there is no transformation of character in her husband. It is only in Bertha's eyes that he changes.

When Bertha's passion dies and her illusions are shattered, it becomes obvious that one of the major reasons for the failure of the marriage is that Bertha is psychologically and temperamentally unsuited to it. Free from infatuation and imagination, she returns to being the person she was before she met Craddock, and she longs for her independence.

Very early in the novel Maugham establishes that his heroine is a very independent young woman. Having lost her remaining parent when she was eighteen, she went to live with her aunt, Miss Ley. Since the latter is a woman who jealously guards her own freedom, Bertha becomes accustomed to an atmosphere free of restrictions and conformity. When she came to her aunt, she was 'of too independent character to accept a stranger's authority', and they live with mutual respect for each other's freedom.

When she becomes infatuated with Craddock, Bertha seeks a way to prove her love, and she imagines that she would like to sacrifice her freedom and be his slave. Consistent with her romantic illusions, she pictures him as a conqueror and herself as his handmaiden. When Bertha consequently yields to her husband in a dispute, Miss Ley notes her surprising transformation:

A month ago opposition would have made Bertha traverse seas and scale precipices rather than abandon an idea that she had got into her head. Verily, love is a prestidigitator who can change the lion into the lamb as easily as a handkerchief into a flower-pot![20]

When life with Craddock destroys her passion and illusions, however, Bertha longs for her former independence. She discovers that the mastery which her husband has assumed so capably is abhorrent; he ignores her wishes and frustrates her hopes. His philosophy concerning his wife is neatly summed up in his often-repeated maxim: 'Women are like chickens . . . Give 'em a good run, properly closed in with stout wire netting, so that they can't get into mischief, and when they cluck and cackle just sit tight and take no notice.' After the freedom of life on the Continent, life in 'stout wire netting' as the wife of a country squire becomes intolerable, and she is humiliated by her lack of power to change this.

It is significant that, when she becomes pregnant, Bertha looks upon the child, not as a means of bringing her closer to her husband, but as a way of gaining a measure of independence:

She felt that the infantine hands of her son were already breaking, one by one, the links that bound her to her husband. When she divined her pregnancy, she gave a cry not only of joy and pride, but also of exultation in her approaching freedom.[21]

When Bertha's love for Edward finally dies completely, she sees him only with disdain. Life then becomes at least bearable because she has recaptured her emotional independence. Returning now to the self-possessed young woman she was before she met Craddock, she is humiliated by her previous self-abasement:

It was inexplicable that she had been subject to a man so paltry in mind, so despicable in character. It made her blush with shame to think how servile had been her love.[22]

At this point it is not so much Edward's cold and unresponsive nature which distresses her, but rather the manner in which she had surrendered herself to his mastery. It is one thing to be the servant of a master one admires, and another to be the slave of a dictator one despises.

Bertha now only wants to be completely free of her husband. As she says to Dr Ramsay, 'Oh, when I think that I'm shackled to him for the rest of my life, I feel I could kill myself.' She succeeds in a temporary escape when she accompanies her aunt to Rome, where she enjoys an idyllic period of complete liberty. Whereas life at Court Leys[23] is narrow, restricted and dull, Italy is joyous, vital and unrestrained. Maugham describes his heroine as being like 'a prisoner so long immured that freedom dazes him, and he looks for his chains, and cannot understand that he is free'. Even back in London, she exults 'like a captive free from chains'.

After an unhappy love affair with a young cousin in London, from which she learns how easily she can again be enslaved by passion, Bertha returns to Court Leys, not to be with Edward, but to find solace in quiet and solitude. She manages to live a comfortable, if unexciting and unfulfilling, existence with her husband. She now finds her freedom in small things, in wild flowers, in a solitary swim in the sea, or in the realms of literature.

The novel ends with the accidental death of Edward. Horrified at her own lack of grief, Bertha can only think of one thing, a point so important that it is italicised: '*She was free!*' Edward's death means liberation, but not before Bertha escapes a dangerous snare. She begins to remember her husband, not as the man she despised in marriage, but as the attractive young man she thought him in the beginning. Thus she runs the risk of finding herself imprisoned by an illusion for the rest of her life. To avoid this danger, she conducts a soul-shattering purge of all reminders of the young Edward. In a final gesture, she studies his corpse and exorcises her vision of him as a young man. She then decides to leave Court Leys and its memories, and return to the Italy which draws her, 'for now she had no ties on earth, and at last, at last she was free'.

Mrs Craddock ends with a pessimistic comment on the limitations of love and communication with others, but there is also a note of optimism for Bertha. Having made a terrible and costly error, she is once again master of her own physical and emotional life. Like Miss Ley, she will retire into herself and build her world within, living with few intimate personal attachments. When one contrasts this to her life at Court Leys, which Maugham described in the preface to the revised edition as 'narrow, stupid and intolerant; prudish, formal and punctilious', one cannot help feeling that, however inadequate, it is what is best for her. Like Kitty in *The Painted Veil*, and Julia in *Theatre*, Bertha has achieved a kind of contentment in her freedom.

The Merry-Go-Round is interesting today because it is one of Maugham's rare experiments and because two of the three stories that comprise the novel appear in other forms in his career. Also, many of the characters are prototypes of figures who later populate his comedies of manners. The account of the tragic marriage of Basil Kent and Jenny Bush (a forerunner of the Philip–Mildred relationship in *Of Human Bondage*) is the same story told in *A Man of Honour*, and the section dealing with Mrs Castillyon and Reginald Barlow-Bassett reappears in *Landed Gentry*.

The Merry-Go-Round represents the young Maugham's attempt at experimentation, an activity in which he has rarely been successful. He had already tried his hand at minor innovations: in *Liza of Lambeth* he attempted a mock-pastoral treatment of Lambeth revellers;[24] in the unpublished 'The Artistic Temperament of Stephen Carey', he inserted a section in dramatic form showing a flirtatious discussion between a bar-maid and a young man; and in *Mrs Craddock* he interrupted his narrative to dramatise an imaginary conversation about Thackeray's Becky Sharp and Amelia.

In *The Merry-Go-Round* Maugham presents a trio of stories intended to be fused together by the presence of a few link characters. It is, he writes in the preface to *Liza of Lambeth*, an attempt, through portraying a wide spectrum of life, to convey the impression of the complexity of social interaction: 'I saw my novel like one of those huge frescoes in an Italian cloister in which all manner of people are engaged in all manner of activities, but which the eye embraces in a single look.'

The novel, then, is composed of three stories, all connected by the common interest of Miss Ley, the spinster from *Mrs Craddock*, and Frank Hurrell, a young medical student with many affinities with the author. One story concerns the daughter of the Dean of Tercanbury, who falls in love with a young poet. When it is discovered that he is dying, she marries him and they live happily for a brief time. The second story is that of Basil Kent, a young solicitor and aspiring author, who becomes infatuated with a cockney bar-maid. When she becomes pregnant by him, he marries her to satisfy honour and the result is tragic. The third story is one of adultery and repentance. Mrs Grace Castillyon, a prisoner of her passion for a young rogue, commits adultery, but later redeems herself by becoming a more sympathetic person and a better wife.

The Merry-Go-Round is also interesting as a period piece, and Maugham has admitted the strong *fin-de-siècle* flavour:

The book suffered also from the pernicious influence on me at the time of the writings of the aesthetes. The men were inanely handsome and the women peerlessly lovely. I wrote with affectation. My attitude was precious. I was afraid to let myself go.[25]

It is that type of affectation that makes *The Merry-Go-Round* far less readable today than other early novels such as *Liza of Lambeth* and *Mrs Craddock*. It becomes particularly damaging to the Basil Kent–Jenny Bush episode, which demands realistic treatment, not artificiality. Laurence Brander points out, for example, the difference in treatment of Jenny and that of Mildred in *Of Human Bondage*. Jenny is 'an Aubrey Beardsley barmaid from the Strand', a Pre-Raphaelite cockney dream; Mildred, on the other hand, is 'a very real Cockney slut'.[26]

The story of Basil and Jenny is the most significant of the three because it is an expression of the same kind of criticism of social convention that Maugham demonstrated in *The Hero*. Society is once again shown to be able to exert a great and damaging pressure on the individual, and the person finds himself with seemingly little control over his own life. Like many of Maugham's characters who follow the dictates of others instead of his own instincts, Basil undergoes considerable suffering.

The suitably ironic title of the dramatic version of this story, *A Man of Honour*, is indicative of one of Maugham's favourite ideas —that any virtue taken to the extreme will become a vice. This theme is the basis of many of his short stories, two of the best examples being 'The Judgement Seat' and 'Virtue'. In these stories, as in many other of his works, Maugham demonstrates the destructive possibilities of a morality which exists, not as a means to a better and more organised life, but as an end in itself. 'Sin' becomes a minor concern compared to the wretchedness and waste caused by the 'moral' action.

This thesis is developed in *The Merry-Go-Round* in Basil Kent's story. Although he is in love with a beautiful widow, Mrs Murray, Basil is sexually attracted to a bar-maid, Jenny Bush. When she becomes pregnant, his social conscience tells him that he must sacrifice himself to do the honourable thing. The pressure to marry Jenny does not come directly from others, but through what Basil has been conditioned to believe, and for Maugham this is a powerful form of bondage: 'He realized that he was manacled hand and foot with fetters that were only more intolerable because they consisted of nothing more substantial than the dread of causing pain.'[27]

Thinking that he is saving Jenny from suffering, Basil marries her, hoping that somehow they will be happy. However, it soon becomes clear that, although there is genuine affection, they are completely unsuited for one another. Jenny cannot appreciate Basil's interests and she does not understand his desire to be a writer. Basil, on the other hand, is revolted by Jenny's family, especially in contrast to his own circle. Life soon becomes intolerable for them both, but society has dictated that they must live together even though they can only cause each other pain. Convention, as Maugham says through a character, is a vindictive force:

"Society is a grim monster, somnolent apparently, so that you think you can take every kind of liberty; but all the time he watches you, he watches slily, and when you least expect it puts out an iron hand to crush you. . . . Society has made its own decalogue; a code just fit for middling people, who are neither very good nor very bad; but the odd thing is it punishes you as severely if you act above its codes as if you act below."[28]

The marriage continues to deteriorate, and Jenny finally ends her suffering by committing suicide. For Basil, this is the opening of his 'prison door', but he cannot accept his freedom without feeling remorse. In a letter to Miss Ley, he writes:

I ought to go on posing decently to the end – in this world we're made to act and think things because others have thought them good; we never have a chance of going our own way; we're bound down by the prejudices and the morals of all and sundry. For God's sake let us be free. Let us do this and that because we want to and because we must, not because other people think we ought.[29]

Like *The Hero*, this portion of *The Merry-Go-Round* is an expression of Maugham's determinism. Basil, like James Parsons, feels the control of his life slipping from him, and here the author repeats the image of the puppet:

And then it appeared to him as though, after all, he had never had a choice in the matter; he felt himself powerless in the hand of a greater might, and Fate, for once grown ghastly visible, directed each step as though he were a puppet.[30]

Finally, the bleakest comment comes from Frank Hurrell, who is largely a vehicle for Maugham's own views. At Jenny's grave-side, on the day of the wedding of Basil and Mrs Murray, he attempts to find a rational explanation for the course of events:

"The only excuse I can see for them is that they're blind instruments of fate: Nature was working through them, obscurely, working to join them together for her own purposes, and because Jenny came between she crushed her ruthlessly."[31]

Thus, Jenny, like Liza and James Parsons, cannot defy circumstance and fate. It is not until *Of Human Bondage* that Maugham shows a character who, however painfully, can impose his own pattern of living on the world around him.

With *The Bishop's Apron* Maugham began a period of his career in which he abandoned his ideals in favour of striving for financial success. Having written with integrity, he had attracted a following among the intelligentsia; commercial success, however, had eluded him, so he turned to satisfying the popular tastes. In none of the three novels of this period—*The Bishop's Apron*, *The Explorer* and *The Magician*—is there a serious attempt to convey a theme of significance. The first two were, as Maugham has confessed, blatant attempts to earn quick cash, and the third was, as he says in the preface to *Liza of Lambeth*, merely a 'game'. It is not surprising that, after *The Magician*, he abandoned novels altogether to devote himself to the light comedies which brought him success, wealth and the scorn of the intellectuals.

The Bishop's Apron is an adaptation of an unproduced play, *Loaves and Fishes*, written about 1902. It relates the attempts of Canon Theodore Spratte to get a bishopric, and his diplomatic manœuvring is treated with light humour and the slightest touch of satire. In addition, Maugham describes the Canon's campaign to marry the daughter of a wealthy beer baron, after extricating himself from a promise of marriage to a widow, and his simultaneous efforts to dissuade his daughter from marrying a young socialist from the East End. Through all these dealings runs a strong feeling of the Canon's love of power, but this is prevented from becoming a serious theme by the consistent epigrammatic and farcical tone.

Maugham's determinism, so strong in *The Hero* and *The Merry-Go-Round*, is present in the relationship between Winnie and the young socialist, Bertram Railing, but it appears in a dilute form.

Winnie shocks her father by refusing to marry a proper young gentleman of his choice because she is a 'new woman' and wants to be more
than the conventional wife. Having concluded that 'for a wife he
wants a slave, a plaything when he's tired or bored', she looks for
equality in marriage to Railing.

To counteract this wish, Canon Spratte devises a meeting between
Winnie and the young man's family, and the result is similar to that
in *The Merry-Go-Round* where Basil is revolted by Jenny's cockney
family. Winnie soon discovers that, because of her background and
upbringing, she cannot live the kind of life that Railing does. She
quickly decides that the happiest course is to marry a young man
from her own class. This section of the book could have presented
serious criticism, but there is no depth to the arguments and the
characters lack complexity. The episode therefore becomes merely
another means of showing the Canon's talent for manipulating
people.

The Bishop's Apron achieved the popular success which Maugham
had intended for it. The *Athenaeum* praised its epigrams and 'life-like
social sketches',[32] while *The Bookman* spoke of its 'easy and brilliant
success' in glowing terms: 'The whole book is an admirable blend of
cynical gaiety and broadly farcical comedy; it is the smartest and most
genuinely humorous novel that the season has yet given us.'[33]
Laurence Brander goes even further:

It is all told with splendid cynicism and good humour. *The Bishop's Apron*
is the most ebullient farce Maugham wrote in his young days. Its success
was deserved and it would give pleasure today in reprint.[34]

Despite this enthusiasm, *The Bishop's Apron* is nevertheless too
insipid and too much a period-piece, without the redeeming in-
gredients of many sparkling epigrams. Maugham never considered it
worthy of reissue and, although it has been successfully adapted for
radio, its reprinting will add little to his reputation.

The Explorer, a trivial novel, was simply an attempt to make some
quick money by appealing to the public appetite for jingoistic
literature of the kind made popular by Kipling. Like *The Bishop's
Apron*, it was an adaptation of a play, and Maugham has admitted
that he produced it in a month of tedious work. His own insincerity
in this haunted him for some time after:

I have a great dislike for it and if it were possible would willingly suppress
it. At one time it irked my conscience like the recollection of a discreditable
action.[35]

Raymond Toole Stott, in his *Somerset Maugham: A Bibliography*, quotes a letter from the writer accompanying the manuscript to his agent:

Here is the book. I have come to the conclusion it is very dull and stupid: and I wish I were an outside Broker, or – – – – – – – (naming a best-seller novelist), or something equally despicable![36]

According to Susanne Howe's *Novels of Empire*, imperialistic fiction became immensely popular at the end of the nineteenth century because it appealed to the desire for romantic escapism. Readers, tired of the gloom and pessimism of realistic slum literature, looked for something hopeful and optimistic. Problems in 'Darkest London' might be unsolvable, but in 'Darkest Africa' there was a way: 'Personal courage and endeavour were still valid. Stanley had proved it in real life, and many a good vigorous novelist came thundering cheerfully after him.'[37]

In *The Explorer*, Maugham easily falls into the Kipling-inspired class of empire-builders. He celebrates all the imperialistic ideals, the narrow patriotism, and belief in racial superiority, that marked the most enthusiastic jingoists. That Maugham is adopting an attitude for the sake of commercial success can be seen when one remembers that these same qualities in Edward Craddock made him a figure of scorn. Similarly, the real Maugham is apparent in a quip from *The Land of the Blessed Virgin*, written just three years before: 'Liquor is a word for heroes, for the British tar who has built up British glory—Imperialism is quite the fashion now.'

In Alec MacKenzie, the hero of *The Explorer*, however, Maugham closely follows the stereotype of the rugged patriotic explorer carrying the white man's burden into the wilderness. In the preface to *Liza of Lambeth* he explains that 'the chief character was suggested by H. M. Stanley, whose exploits had long fascinated my young fancy, and the strong silent man, owing to Mr Kipling's vogue, was then very much the fashion.'

To the modern reader, MacKenzie is practically a caricature, comic in his exaggerated courage, wisdom, honour, silence and pride. With him, there is no hint of ruthlessness, corruption, personal motive or possibility of succumbing, like Conrad's Kurtz, to the savagery of Africa.[38] Maugham knew his readers, however, and to them MacKenzie typified everything heroic, admirable and British. The *Athenaeum* wrote that 'the hero represents what is, perhaps, the finest type of man that these islands produce'.[39] Even *The Saturday Review* found MacKenzie admirable and lifelike, and a model patriot:

Alec is a true type of the patriotic adventurer; self-confident, not with conceit, but with the steady certainty of his own power, mental and

physical, and the conviction of the nobility of his ambition. A man whom
natives trust and obey (for the native instinct is sure), and whom white men
follow to the death.[40]

As much as Alec MacKenzie is a cardboard figure, it is nevertheless possible to grant Maugham a degree of sincerity in his interest in
the explorer as a hero. It could be argued that he saw in the man who
carved out his own section of the world a figure of individuality and
independence. Howe places considerable emphasis on the part that
the concept of freedom plays in colonial literature:

On the surface, imperialism could be seen as a race full of high endeavour,
a great adventure. It did actually call for and develop some of the greatest
human virtues – courage, self-denial, physical and moral endurance, and,
paradoxically enough, a passion for freedom. In the last analysis this
paradox is not puzzling but merely human. Until very recent times, freedom
of enterprise and of personal endeavour was what the novelists emphasized,
because they valued it as their contemporaries did. "Of old sat Freedom on
the heights," intoned Tennyson, and in the case of the forefathers of empire
a true respect for freedom and a fairly disinterested desire for as much of
it for as many people as possible are justifiably assumed by the novelists
who write lyrically about the early days of expansion.[41]

An integral part of the vision of freedom of personal action of the
empire builders was a reverence for geographical size, especially for
the vastness of Africa. There, it was believed, the individual could
prove his worth unfettered and unhampered by the restrictions of the
mother country.

Maugham's hero fits this pattern very well. He is a strong-willed
individualist, a man who spent two years mastering a subject he
hated simply because someone told him that he was incapable of
doing it. His parents died when he was young, so he has no family
ties, and a considerable inherited income maintains his financial
independence. On a chance expedition into Africa, the vastness of the
country engulfs him:

Alec suddenly found himself at home in the immense distances of Africa.
He felt a singular exhilaration when the desert was spread out before his
eyes, and capacities which he had not suspected in himself awoke in him.[42]

Back in England, 'he felt himself cribbed and confined. He could not
breathe the air of cities.'

When MacKenzie returns to Africa, Maugham makes it clear that
he is drawn there because in that environment he must rely on his
own resources for success or failure. Through the imagination of his
fiancée, Lucy, the reader is supposed to feel the 'thrill of independence' that motivates the explorer to leave England. MacKenzie

himself attempts to communicate the African mystique to the very insular and 'civilised' Dick Lomas:

"Already I can hardly bear my impatience when I think of the boundless country and the enchanting freedom. Here everyone grows so small, so mean; but in Africa everything is built to a nobler standard. There the man is really a man. There one knows what are will and strength and courage. You don't know what it is to stand on the edge of some great plain and breathe the pure keen air after the terrors of the forest."[43]

In addition to manifesting these traditional longings for freedom in the colonial setting, MacKenzie is a kind of privateer, a man who values his independence of spirit. He is, after all, in Africa to halt the slave trade and preserve liberty for the natives. When the British government refuses to sponsor his expedition, he accepts the responsibility himself, free from 'the hindrance of official restraints'. He even sacrifices much of his estate in order to pursue his crusade. Later, when the press and public opinion are against him, demanding that he defend himself against a spurious accusation, he refuses; he feels responsible only to himself. It matters little what the rest of the world demands, 'for, after all, his conscience was free'.

The central issue of the novel, the vow of silence that MacKenzie makes and keeps, is supposed to gain added tension because it is a fetter on such a strong individualist. He knows the price he is paying when he makes the bargain with George Allerton, but, for his love of Lucy, he is willing to give up even this measure of freedom. Back in England, with even his beloved doubting his integrity, he bears his sacrifice nobly. In spite of this conflict, the novel fails miserably on the implausibility of this central idea. As Maugham later recognised, readers and audiences could not believe in MacKenzie's refusal to exonerate himself.

The contrast between *The Explorer* and the colonial stories of Maugham's mature period reflects the changing public attitudes toward imperialism and the colonial administrators. Whereas *The Explorer* expresses unquestioning acceptance of the popular vision of the empire-builder as a figure of nobility, the later stories examine the European in the Far East with a critical eye and he is found to be a complex mixture of weaknesses and strengths, of nobility and shabbiness. The white man's burden has become his wife's adultery, and V. S. Pritchett can rightly claim in 1940: 'Maugham is Kipling turned inside out, discovering alcohol, beachcombing and middle-class sex, where Kipling portrayed the Roman overlord and evoked the secret, savage hierarchy of the jungle.'[44]

The final novel of this period of Maugham's career, *The Magician*, was a straightforward attempt to benefit from the popularity of the horror novel. Reviewing it, *The Nation* noted Maugham's 'quickness to seize the theme of the moment, and facility in turning it to account',[45] and pointed out the similarity to E. F. Benson's *Image in the Sand. The Saturday Review* unfavourably compared Maugham's treatment of the idea of 'homunculi' with a similar idea of W. B. Yeats.[46] The *Athenaeum* saw Maugham playing the part of the Balzac of the 'Peau de Chagrin', the Du Maurier who created Svengali, and the H. G. Wells of the science-fiction fantasies.[47] Finally, Kuner suggests that Maugham may have been influenced by Arthur Machen's *The Inmost Light* (1895).[48]

Maugham has readily admitted that he was well aware of a fashion when he wrote *The Magician*. In the preface to *Liza of Lambeth*, he wrote that the book would never have been written 'except for the great regard I had for Joris Karl Huysmans who was then at the height of his vogue'. Later, in 'A Fragment of Autobiography', he described Aleister Crowley,[49] the model for the central figure of his novel, as a product of the popularity of occultism at the turn of the century:

At the time I knew him he was dabbling in Satanism, magic and the occult. There was just then something of a vogue in Paris for that sort of thing, occasioned, I surmise, by the interest that was still taken in a book of Huysmans's, *Là-bas*.[50]

Maugham was probably also aware of what *The Nation* called 'the curious wave of occultism which has so lately overrun "smart" English society'.[51]

The central figure of the novel, Oliver Haddo, was suggested, according to Maugham, by a portrait of Alessandro del Borro in a museum in Berlin, and by Crowley, an English poet and mystic. Crowley, along with Auguste Rodin, Marcel Schwob, Arnold Bennett, W. E. Henley, Eugene Carriers and Clive Bell, was a frequenter of a small restaurant in Paris called 'Le Chat Blanc' (which becomes 'Le Chien Noir' in *The Magician*), and Maugham was introduced to this group by Gerald Kelly. Crowley, having inherited a considerable income, devoted his time to writing, mountain-climbing, drugs, sex and the occult. In later years the British press waged a prolonged campaign against him, charging that he was 'the wickedest man in the world'. Edward Marsh describes encountering him in later life at a dinner in a Soho restaurant:

To one such occasion, Harold Monro imported a strange and baleful apparition, in conjurer's evening-dress, and sporting in the middle of his shirt-front a large diamond which perhaps looked bogus only because of the frayed and gaping stud-hole in which it wobbled – a singular contrast

with the wholesome and innocent and tweed-clad personalities of Rupert
Brooke, Wilfrid Gibson and the others. He talked wittily, cruelly, diabolic-
ally, and we quaked and cowered like Tweedledum and Tweedledee under
the shadow of the Monstrous Crow. It was the Satanist Alistair [sic]
Crowley; and for once in my life I felt I had been in the presence of Evil
with a capital E.[52]

Although there are a number of differences, the character of
Haddo is largely a transcript, with exaggerations, of Aleister Crowley.
Both Haddo and Crowley were mountaineers, although Maugham
added to his creation considerable skill as a big game hunter. To
Haddo Maugham also gave Crowley's ostentation and verbosity, and
the magical powers that Crowley at least claimed to possess. Finally,
the fictional character is a skilful hypnotist, and the story of his
domination of Margaret Dauncey is consistent with similar powers
possessed by Crowley, who was known to exert a powerful influence
over women, sometimes forcing them to madness or death.

With the exception of Oliver Haddo and the bohemian scenes in
'Le Chien Noir', *The Magician* was almost completely a fabrication.
Much later, Maugham professed to be baffled by much of the material
about magic:

As I read *The Magician*, I wondered how on earth I could have come by
all the material concerning the black arts which I wrote of. I must have
spent days and days reading in the library of the British Museum.[53]

Crowley provided his own explanation for the source of the occult
material. Although his comments must, under the circumstances, be
regarded with considerable scepticism, there is an element of plausibility in them:

Late in 1908 I picked up a book. The title attracted me strongly, *The
Magician*. The author, bless my soul! No other than my old and valued
friend, William Somerset Maugham, my nice young doctor whom I remembered so well from the dear old days of the Chat Blanc. So he had
really written a book – who would have believed it! . . . The Magician,
Oliver Haddo, was Aleister Crowley; his house 'Skene' was Boleskine. The
hero's witty remarks were, many of them, my own. He had, like Arnold
Bennett, not spared his shirt cuff.

But I had jumped too hastily to conclusions when I said, 'Maugham has
written a book'. I found phrase after phrase, paragraph after paragraph,
page after page, bewilderingly familiar; and then I remembered that in my
early days of the G.[olden] D.[awn] I had introduced Gerald Kelly to the
Order and reflected that Maugham had become a great friend of Kelly's,
and stayed with him at Camberwell Vicarage. Maugham had taken some
of the most private and personal incidents of my life, my marriage, my
explorations, my adventures with big game, my magical opinions, ambitions and exploits and so on. He had added a number of the many absurd
legends of which I was the central figure. He had patched all these together
by innumerable strips of paper clipped from the books which I had told

Gerald to buy. I had never supposed that plagiarism could have been so varied, extensive, and shameless.[54]

Crowley left no doubt that Maugham had concocted his novel by borrowing heavily from other writers. Reviewing *The Magician* in *Vanity Fair*[55] under the name of 'Oliver Haddo', Crowley proved conclusively that large segments were little more than transcripts of material from books about the occult. Maugham had used, among others, the introduction to MacGregor Mathers' *Kabbalah Unveiled* (1897), Franz Hartmann's *The Life of Paracelsus* (1896), A. E. Waite's translation of Eliphaz Levi's *Rituel et Dogme de la Haute Magie*, Mabel Collins' *The Blossom and the Fruit* (1888), Dumas' *Memoirs of a Physician* and Wells' *The Island of Dr Moreau* (1896).

Crowley's version of the origins of *The Magician* was largely corroborated by Sir Gerald Kelly in a conversation with this author in September 1969. Crowley indeed had a remarkable influence over women, and he married Kelly's sister, Rose, within two weeks of first meeting her. *The Magician*, said Sir Gerald, was basically the story of this marriage (much altered to suit the occult tale, of course) and of the strange domination of Crowley over his future wife. Furthermore, the story of Maugham borrowing Kelly's books about the occult to provide the background for the novel was true.

Because of the circumstances in which *The Magician* was written, the novel was without sincerity and honesty. It lacked any serious intention and failed even to establish the atmosphere of horror necessary for that particular type of literature. Maugham has characteristically provided his own candid critical assessment:

To me it was all moonshine. I did not believe a word of it. It was a game I was playing. A book written under these conditions can have no life in it.[56]

There is little in *The Magician* which deserves analysis except the treatment of bondage in the form of hypnotic slavery. According to Woodburn O. Ross, 'it is the same old story, except that this time the tie that binds the victim is magic, whereas previously it has been the character's own passions'.[57] Indeed, the basis of the story is the capture of the will of Margaret Dauncey.

Oliver Haddo, seeking revenge on Margaret's fiancé for an injury, uses hypnosis to lure her away from her friends. Through his magic he manages to gain a control over her which, as much as she tries, she is never able to break. To convey the kind of infection which seems to have overtaken her, Maugham uses several images:

It was as if a rank weed were planted in her heart and slid long poisonous tentacles down every artery, so that each part of her body was enmeshed.[58]

Her will had been taken from her, and she was an automaton. She struggled, like a bird in the fowler's net with useless beating of the wings.[59]

Like a bird at its last gasp beating frantically against the bars of a cage, Margaret made a desperate effort to regain her freedom.[60]

While there is a certain amount of interest in Haddo's domination of Margaret, the novel degenerates from this point to the end, and the last half is simply an account of Margaret's death and the revelation of Haddo's experiments with 'homunculi'. A theme which had serious possibilities became merely sensational in the worst manner.

The Magician marks the end of a period of Maugham's career as a novelist. More and more, his interest had been drawn to the theatre and when success came in 1908 he decided to abandon completely the writing of novels. In *The Summing Up* he describes the determination with which he turned from prose fiction:

I was walking along Panton Street one evening. Passing the Comedy Theatre I happened to look up and saw the clouds lit by the setting sun. I paused to look at the lovely sight and I thought to myself: Thank God, I can look at a sunset now without having to think how to describe it. I meant then never to write another book, but to devote myself for the rest of my life to the drama.[61]

The eight novels from *Liza of Lambeth* to *The Magician* are a progression from sincerity and integrity to insincerity and dishonesty. They are the record of a struggling young writer's attempt to establish his reputation, first among the intellectuals, and then with the general reading public. They are also unfortunately the source of the disenchantment of the intelligentsia with Maugham.

These novels are also the experiments of the immature young Maugham, the efforts of an apprentice author to discover his most effective means of expression. If this meant attempting naturalistic, historical, imperialistic or occult fiction, they at least gave him an idea of his own limitations. If it involved imitating the prose of the aesthetes and the styles of contemporary French writers, or the modest innovations of the young novelist himself, they provided a means of evolving a personal expression. Most of these novels were failures and later embarrassments to Maugham, but they were in no small way a proving ground for themes and techniques which he was to use with skill and effect in the novels of his maturity.

Examined as a whole, these early novels provide an important insight into the strength of much of Maugham's writing. Consistently, the high points of these works are those which are based on the author's own experiences. *Liza of Lambeth*, perhaps the best of the early novels, is practically a transcript of the life into which

Maugham was thrust as a young medical student, and the Basil–
Jenny episode, the most interesting in *The Merry-Go-Round*, owes its
material to the same source. The narrow provincial life exposed so
ruthlessly in *The Hero* and *Mrs Craddock*, and the authentic pictures
of the Kentish countryside in a number of the early novels, derive
from Maugham's memories of his boyhood in Whitstable. The verbal
dexterity of the banter between Dick Lomas and Mrs Crowley in *The
Explorer*, which brightens an otherwise dull novel, is a product of the
author's experiences in London society. Finally, in a story as artificial
and contrived as *The Magician*, there is a refreshing air of authenticity
in the descriptions of life in 'Le Chien Noir', and these are thinly
disguised accounts of the author's days in Paris among the art
students at 'Le Chat Blanc'.

There is in Maugham's writing more than a touch of journalism,
and the importance of this quality should not be underestimated. It
is, in fact, almost axiomatic that whenever he writes out of his own
knowledge he is successful, and whenever he attempts to fabricate he
fails. Practically all of his fiction from *Of Human Bondage* onward is
founded upon personal experience, or at least a thorough knowledge
of, and feeling for, the background, environment and atmosphere.
The whole of *Of Human Bondage*, the Paris scenes of *The Moon and
Sixpence*, the South Seas settings of the same novel, *The Narrow
Corner* and many of the short stories, the Far East environment of
The Painted Veil and the colonial stories, the literary milieu and the
Kentish scenes of *Cakes and Ale*, the world of espionage of *Ashenden*,
and the theatrical life of *Theatre*, all owe their authenticity to
Maugham's personal experience. In these works, although often
written with an eye on a particular genre or fashion, Maugham
succeeds in making the reader believe in his world because he has
seen, heard and felt the things he describes. Only rarely after *The
Magician* does he write without a solid basis of personal knowledge.
These novels—*The Hour Before the Dawn, Up at the Villa, Then and
Now* and *Catalina*—are, not surprisingly, failures.

IV

Of Human Bondage and the Novels of Apprenticeship

A LTHOUGH HE HAD decided, after *The Magician*, to devote the remainder of his career to the writing of plays, Maugham soon found that he could not escape an autobiographical novel which was forcing itself upon him:

I was but just firmly established as a popular playwright when I began to be obsessed by the teeming memories of my past life. The loss of my mother and then the break-up of my home, the wretchedness of my first years at school for which my French childhood had so ill-prepared me and which my stammering made so difficult, the delight of those easy, monotonous and exciting days in Heidelberg, when I first entered upon the intellectual life, the irksomeness of my few years at the hospital and the thrill of London; it all came back to me so pressingly, in my sleep, on my walks, when I was rehearsing plays, when I was at a party, it became such a burden to me that I made up my mind that I could only regain my peace by writing it all down in the form of a novel.[1]

The most autobiographic of all Maugham's fiction, *Of Human Bondage*, thus became a catharsis, a means of freeing him from the burden of unhappy memories and the obsession with past mistakes and sorrows. In this respect, his novel served the same function as that of a multitude of autobiographical writings, epitomised by a prototype of this genre—Goethe's *The Sorrows of Young Werther*. Goethe's motivation, as described by Maurice Beebe, is remarkably similar to Maugham's:

Finding that he could not plunge the dagger into his heart, he wrote *Werther* as a means of killing a previous self. It is apparent that he could not have cured himself in this way if he had not attained sufficient detachment from that earlier self to laugh at his own folly. There are two Goethes in *Werther* – the Goethe of the past in the character of Werther, and the Goethe of the present in the editor and interpreter of Werther's letters.[2]

Maugham's purgation in *Of Human Bondage* parallels Goethe's in *Werther* in that it is also an attempt to kill a previous self and there are also two Maughams present—one in the form of the sensitive and lonely Philip and another in the form of the author who examines Philip's development with a critical and unflinching eye.

The chronological position of *Of Human Bondage* in his works is rather unusual. In discussing the genre of which this novel is an excellent example, William York Tindall notes that 'from 1903 onwards almost every first novel by a serious novelist was a novel of adolescence'.[3] *Of Human Bondage*, however, was Maugham's ninth novel, written when he was thirty-eight years old. It is the type of book one would expect the author to have written years earlier.

Maugham did, in fact, attempt an autobiographical novel of adolescence early in his writing career. Some time in 1897, following the qualified success of *Liza of Lambeth* and after having taken his medical degree, he moved to Seville, determined to be a professional writer. Here he wrote a novel of youth called first 'An Artistic Temperament' and then 'The Artistic Temperament of Stephen Carey'. He submitted his manuscript to Fisher Unwin, who, according to Maugham, refused to pay even a hundred pounds for it, and none of the other publishers were interested at any price. These rejections, as he later admitted, were a blessing because they preserved his material for a time when he could treat it with maturity and detachment. More important, this unpublished version failed to provide a purgation of the events and memories which plagued the young writer, and it is the working out of them in painful and honest detail in *Of Human Bondage* which gives it the personal commitment that critics find lacking in his other writing.

'The Artistic Temperament of Stephen Carey' is often referred to as a first draft of the later novel. In reality, while there is a number o similar characters and episodes, there are enough differences, especially in tone and philosophy, to make it a very distant ancestor.

Stephen Carey, like the later Philip, is orphaned at an early age, and he goes to live with his Uncle John and Aunt Nellie. These characters bear no relation to the Vicar and Aunt Louisa in *Of Human Bondage*; although his occupation is never mentioned, the uncle is not a clergyman, and the aunt is far more warm and outgoing than her counterpart in the later novel. In addition, they have a daughter, May, four years younger than Stephen, and this creates a much different atmosphere in the early part of the novel. There is little of the intense feeling of loneliness which so pervades the youth of Philip.

Notably absent from the early version is the club-foot which plays such an essential part in shaping Philip's life and philosophy. Stephen has no such disability, and thus, when he is made an outcast

at school and jeered by his fellows, the lack of motivation makes this
ostracism unconvincing. Similarly, when Stephen puts God to the
same kind of test that Philip does over his club-foot, it appears
ludicrous: he prays for God to make him happy by transforming
him into a better cricket player.

Unlike Philip, Stephen is quite successful at school and wins many
prizes, although like Philip he is bullied and made an outcast. His
uncle nevertheless takes him out of school and sends him to Rouen.
Here he encounters an American, a 'Mr House', with whom he
has many discussions about patriotism and religion. Stephen, as a
result, has many of his beliefs shattered and he too quickly loses his
faith.

After several years in France, Stephen returns to England and goes
to London as an articled clerk. There he associates with a Stanley
Parsons (who becomes Watson in *Of Human Bondage*), his idea of the
perfect gentleman and man of the world. Under Parsons's influence,
Stephen becomes absorbed in the problems of clothes, fashion and
worldliness, something largely absent from the hero of *Of Human
Bondage*. He even moves to the suburbs because it is more fashionable. Class consciousness, which Maugham makes part of Philip's
character, is far stronger in Stephen. For the most part, Philip grows
out of it, but Stephen retains his snobbery to the end.

The early version contains the episode of Stephen's affair with
Miss Wilkinson and it is, with a few minor differences, much the
same as Philip's encounter. Miss Wilkinson is May's governess and,
after having begun the affair, Stephen agrees to live with her in
London. They even have a brief period together in the city, but when
the family goes to Nice for a holiday the affair gradually dies.

Stephen continues to work in London as an articled clerk and,
under Parsons' tutelage, becomes a man-about-town. However, when
Parsons leaves the firm and is replaced by Greene, a bohemian
intellectual, Stephen follows a new lead and soon scorns his previous
role as a man of the world. Stephen and Greene live together in cheap
rooms and have many discussions about art and literature.

At a tea shop frequented by Stephen and Greene they meet a
waitress, Rose Cameron, the counterpart of Mildred in *Of Human
Bondage*. Although she is thin like Mildred, Maugham makes her
more attractive; there is none of the emphasis on physical repulsive-
ness found in his treatment of Mildred. In addition, although her
character is not nearly as well-developed, Rose has a much warmer
personality than Mildred.

Stephen falls madly in love with Rose, and before long they spend
a week-end together in a country hotel. He soon discovers, however,

that she is going to marry a regular visitor to the tea shop, a man called Todd. In this respect Rose comes out better than Mildred because, since her doctor has told her that her health will not permit her to work, she is forced into this marriage by economic necessity. Mildred is given no such excuse.

Like Mildred, Rose finds that Todd does not intend to marry her, and she is soon left pregnant. Stephen is revolted but, unlike Philip, he confronts Todd in his office and, in an absurdly melodramatic scene, he administers a beating to the seducer, with suitable Victorian dramatic exclamations of 'you cad' and 'you cur'. Stephen's sensibilities, nevertheless, do not permit him to accept Rose's offer to live with him.

After a dangerous illness, Stephen returns to his relatives' home in Woodlake to recuperate. There he discovers that May has grown into a very attractive young woman (the equivalent of Sally in *Of Human Bondage*). She nurses him in his recovery, and when he discovers that she loves him he asks her to marry him. He does not love her passionately, but he finds her pleasant and he likes the idea of the wealth he will inherit through her.

Before the marriage, however, Stephen is called back to London by Rose, and he is unable to resist spending a night with her in a hotel. Although stricken by remorse (he takes a symbolic cleansing in the Baths), he returns to Woodlake and marries May. The book ends with Stephen dreaming of his future as landowner, social figure and a member of Parliament.

'The Artistic Temperament of Stephen Carey' is an extremely adolescent piece of literature, and it is easy to understand why no publisher was interested. It is loosely constructed, sloppily written, and badly exaggerated. The little touches and details which bring the characters in *Of Human Bondage* to life are absent, and the people are shallow and lifeless. There are a great many superfluous passages and figures, and there is none of the simplicity or craftsmanship of the later novel. The style, so unlike *Of Human Bondage*, is in many places inflated and grossly romantic. Finally, and most important, the early version lacks a recognisable thematic purpose; there is no philosophical progression, no resolution to a particular vision of life. The effect is so embarrassingly immature and crude that it is hard to believe that it came from the same pen that wrote *Liza of Lambeth* and *Mrs Craddock*. It is not surprising that, when Maugham donated this manuscript to The Library of Congress in Washington, in 1950, he stipulated that no sections or excerpts ever be permitted to be published.

Since 'The Artistic Temperament of Stephen Carey' and *Of Human*

Bondage were written fifteen years apart, they provide valuable evidence of how Maugham reacted to the changing literary climate. Although both are basically novels of adolescence, their treatment of the subject is as much a reflection of their times as of the maturity of the author.

Garson Kanin, having once criticised the title of *Of Human Bondage*, recorded Maugham's defence:

"Perhaps", he says, "you would have . . . preferred the original title –
The Artistic Temperament of Stephen Carey."
"Hardly."
"Strange what fashion is. When the . . . book was written, that first title was thought to be ideal, but when I revised it, I decided to give it a fresh . . . name as well."[4]

The titles provide a key to the differences in intention between the two versions; in 1897 Maugham was attempting to portray the development of an artistic temperament, and in 1913 he was concerned with revealing the spiritual progress of a rather unartistic young man. 'The Artistic Temperament of Stephen Carey' was obviously written under the influence of the aesthetic school at the turn of the century. The style, like that of some of his other early novels, is modelled on the lush and florid writing of the time. As well, Stephen is in many ways the hero of the times, a young man in search of the perfection of his sensibilities and artistic taste. This goal is strongly epitomised in his reaction to the sobering news that his mistress, Miss Wilkinson, is forty years old: 'What a situation for a young man with an artistic temperament.'[5]

Maugham's change of attitude about his hero's goals is indicated by his giving to Hayward, in *Of Human Bondage*, many of the ideas of Stephen, and the author makes it clear that Hayward lives a futile life, deceiving himself and succeeding in nothing. One of the few references to an 'artistic temperament' in *Of Human Bondage* comes when Hayward is described as confusing 'his vacillation for the artistic temperament'.

There are a number of indications that Maugham was influenced to a considerable degree by the myth of Byronism when he wrote this early version. Stephen, at one point, imagines himself as Childe Harold and believes that he has a Byronic soul. Later, he plays the piano and naturally prefers Wagner, especially *Tannhäuser*. When he becomes ill, it is because he has been meditating in the rain! In the tradition of excessive Romanticism, he lies dying, wasting away with gaunt cheeks, and he has a tearful deathbed farewell with Rose. Unlike many of the romantic poets and musicians, however, he rises and lives. Throughout the novel there are numerous references such as 'his Byronic soul' and 'a little Byronic laugh', or to women as Greek goddesses.

Of Human Bondage has been frequently labelled an 'artist novel', 'a novel of adolescence' or a *'bildungsroman'*—the novel of all-round development and self-culture. While it does contain elements of the artist novel, it falls more accurately into one of the two latter categories. In *Wilhelm Meister and His English Kinsmen* Susanne Howe calls it a 'novel of apprenticeship', and her definition is accurate. Although Philip is an intelligent and sensitive young man, he is certainly not an artist (in this respect he is not an accurate picture of Maugham). In addition, unlike other young heroes such as Jean-Christophe Krafft (*Jean-Christophe*), Paul Morel (*Sons and Lovers*), Michael Fane (*Sinister Street*) or Stephen Dedalus (*A Portrait of the Artist as a Young Man*), Philip deliberately chooses an ordinary life, and here Maugham's novel differs from most autobiographical fiction of the early twentieth century. Critics have frequently expressed dissatisfaction with the concluding chapters of *Of Human Bondage* and it is possible that this arises from their attempt to see the story as something that it is not intended to be.

In *Wilhelm Meister and His English Kinsmen* Susanne Howe traces the development of the apprentice novel, begun by Goethe's *The Sorrows of Young Werther*, with its world-weariness, supersensitivity and introspection, and especially by his *The Apprenticeship of Wilhelm Meister*, the prototype of this genre. In Goethe's story of a young man's search for maturity and 'mastery' can be found the basis for a school of literature which affected fiction in many cultures.

Susanne Howe describes *Of Human Bondage* as one of the closest parallels in English literature to the tradition established by *Wilhelm Meister*, and there is considerable evidence to substantiate this claim. She points out that, not unexpectedly, the apprentice pattern is most clearly developed by those English writers who spent some time in Germany or who were familiar with German literature. Maugham, it will be remembered, spent an enlightening year in Heidelberg and was fairly well-read in German writing.

It is certain that Maugham knew Goethe's novel well. In *The Bishop's Apron* he writes: 'Like Wilhelm Meister, he cried that America was here and now.' In addition, the echo of *Wilhelm Meister* is obvious in the early part of 'The Artistic Temperament of Stephen Carey'. Maugham begins his novel with an almost exact parallel of Goethe's story by describing in great length the young boy amusing himself with a toy theatre. Like Wilhelm, Stephen likes acting out plays because it gives free range to his imagination and it is a means of appearing to assume power over events. Finally, the influence of *Wilhelm Meister* is strong in the concluding chapter of *Of Human Bondage*. In what is almost a paraphrase, Philip reaches the same conclusion about the price of liberty as Wilhelm, and the phrase 'America was here and now' is repeated.

When examined closely, it becomes apparent that *Of Human Bondage* is indeed a very good example of the apprentice novel. Howe defines the basic formula of this genre:

The adolescent hero of the typical "apprentice" novel sets out on his way through the world, meets with reverses usually due to his own temperament, falls in with various guides and counsellors, makes many false starts in choosing his friends, his wife, and his life work, and finally adjusts himself in some way to the demands of his time and environment by finding a sphere of action in which he may work effectively.[6]

The apprentice novel is not, however, simply a tale of a pilgrim's progress through the world; its fascination lies in the exceptional nature of the 'apprentice'—sensitive, intelligent and emotional:

For these heroes are, after all, the elect – a little feeble, impressionable, vacillating, perhaps, but endowed with exceptional powers of mind and spirit, though it takes them a long while to find it out. They are more sensitive and more gifted than the average young man; their perceptions are sharper, their failures more heartbreaking, their struggles for adjustment to the world more desperate than those of their fellows, but their ultimate victory is assured.[7]

The degree to which, in spite of being largely autobiographical, Philip Carey resembles this description of the conventional hero is remarkable. He, too, is impressionable, vacillating and a little feeble, and he, too, is more sensitive and perceptive than the average young man. Almost to a fault, his failures hurt him more than others, and his struggle for adjustment is of a greater magnitude than that of any of his fellows.

Philip's course through the novel is largely that of the conventional 'apprentice'. Through people like Parsons, Hayward, Weeks, Lawson, Fanny Price, Cronshaw, Griffiths, Mildred and Athelny, he encounters many guides and influences, and he must choose the true from the false. His own temperament, so warped by his loneliness and deformity, often makes him bring unnecessary suffering upon himself. Finally, like most of the heroes of this genre, he arrives at a philosophy that is tenable in the world he sees, and he finds his own niche. His choice at the end—to live an ordinary unromantic life—is in fact closer to the Goetheian model than those in the majority of apprentice novels.

Of Human Bondage is one of the best examples of Maugham's ability to see his raw material in terms of a particular formula or

genre. In *The Summing Up* he called it 'an autobiographical novel'
and he frequently admitted the factual basis of the story:

"Decent people often say to me, 'Why don't you write another *Of Human
Bondage*?' and I reply, 'Because I've only lived one life. It took me thirty
years of living to possess the material for that one work.'"[8]

"It was the kind of effort that one can only make once in a lifetime. I put
everything into it, everything I knew, everything I experienced."[9]

Yet, in spite of so much of Philip Carey's life and thought being a
thinly disguised version of Maugham's own, *Of Human Bondage*
remains one of the best examples of a conventional genre.

As well as its debt to *Wilhelm Meister* and its tradition, *Of Human
Bondage* shows the effect of late nineteenth- and early twentieth-
century influences. The years between 1897 and 1913, especially,
produced a number of important developments, and these account
for some of the differences between 'The Artistic Temperament of
Stephen Carey' and *Of Human Bondage*. This period saw the publi-
cation of Butler's *The Way of All Flesh* in 1903, Richardson's
Maurice Guest in 1908, Bennett's *The Old Wives' Tale* in 1908 and
Clayhanger in 1910 and Gilbert Cannan's translation of Romain
Rolland's mammoth *Jean-Christophe* from 1910 to 1913.

The impact of *The Way of All Flesh* on early twentieth-century
literature cannot be over-estimated; *Clayhanger, Sons and Lovers*
and *Of Human Bondage* particularly owe much to Butler's achievement. In 1950 Maugham acknowledged its importance:

At the time *Of Human Bondage* was written many novelists, possibly in-
cited by the deep impression made on them by Samuel Butler's *The Way of
All Flesh*, were impelled to write semi-autobiographical novels. . . . Such a
book was *Of Human Bondage*.[10]

As critics have frequently recognised, there is a marked similarity
in flavour between Butler's novel and Maugham's. There is the same
emphasis on the powerful influence of heredity and environment, and
both novelists attempt to show the hero triumphing through strength
of will. Both writers launch strong attacks on the restrictions of
family, school, religion, caste and convention. There is also a similar
respect for money and the power which accompanies it (both Ernest
Pontifex and Philip Carey go through a bleak period because of
stock-market setbacks caused by supposedly knowledgeable friends).

The Way of All Flesh is most notable, of course, for its savage
assault on the figure of the clergyman, and Maugham's portrait of
Philip's uncle, the Reverend William Carey, owes its inspiration to
Butler's lead. It is significant that the uncle of Stephen Carey in the

D

early version is not a cleric; there is no exposure of the domestic life of the clergyman as in the later novel. Maugham's uncle, the Reverend Henry MacDonald Maugham, had died on 18 September 1897, so there was no reason why the young writer should hesitate to portray his life at the vicarage, unless of course he found the events too recent to be able to use them properly. Although attacks on the clergy can be found in much of his early writing, most of them are minor or, as in *The Bishop's Apron*, tinged with a good deal of light humour. It is likely that, upon the publication of *The Way of All Flesh*, Maugham recognised the likeness of his own life under the régime of his uncle to that of the young Ernest. With memories of the vanity and self-centredness of his uncle, he must have delighted in the delineation of the weaknesses and foibles of Theobald Pontifex.

One of the interesting parallels to *The Way of All Flesh* in *Of Human Bondage* is the episode where Philip is required to memorise the collect. Because he is unable to make any sense of the meaning, he develops a mental block which prevents him from learning the passage in the time his uncle has given him. Mrs Carey, coming to see how he has managed, finds him alone, weeping in desperation. This childhood crisis bears a good deal of similarity to that in Butler's novel where the young Ernest begins to sing a hymn but cannot pronounce the consonants 'c' or 'k'. To Theobald's chagrin, he says 'tum' instead of 'come', and despite threats and an ultimatum, Ernest fails to say 'come'. The scene ends with Ernest, like Philip, in tears, although this is brought about largely by the anticipation of the beating that is to follow.

In spite of the many parallels between the two portrayals of clergymen, there are naturally some essential differences. Butler seems to have been motivated by pure hatred for his father and the resulting picture is so one-sided, so much of a caricature, that the author defeats himself and actually enlists sympathy for Theobald. Maugham's picture of the Vicar, although highly critical, is much more sympathetic and understanding. This difference in treatment is obvious in the above-mentioned episode. Butler ends Ernest's trial with Theobald dragging him off in an almost inhuman fashion to be beaten and sent to bed. After Philip's disgrace, however, even though Mr Carey fails to understand the boy, he allows his wife to take Philip some books to amuse him. Thus Maugham manages to show the insensitivity of the uncle without making him an unbelievable tyrant and bully. While Butler exaggerates and caricatures to be certain of destruction, Maugham tries to present an accurate representation of a force in Philip's development.

Because *The Way of All Flesh* is primarily a propagandistic novel, it suffers artistically in a way that *Of Human Bondage* does not. Since he is determined to slaughter so many sacred Victorian cows, Butler tends to make his volleys overshadow the development of his hero's character. In Maugham's novel, however, although the author presents strong attacks on religion, family, school and conventional morality, they are more closely integrated with the story. Maugham is able to make his criticisms, but they are always closely involved in Philip's spiritual development. Thus, unlike in Butler's novel, one rarely encounters a passage which is an obvious dissertation and which halts the narrative.

It is difficult to estimate the extent to which Maugham was influenced by *The Old Wives' Tale* and *Clayhanger*. Both Maugham and Bennett spent some of their formative years in Paris at the same time, and they became friends. Bennett has written in his *Journals* of his amiable jealousy of Maugham's dramatic success, and Maugham wrote warmly of Bennett on a number of occasions. His admiration for *The Old Wives' Tale* was immediate and heartfelt. Sir Gerald Kelly told this author how, on his (Kelly's) return from a voyage to the Far East, Maugham greeted him on the quay with the words: 'Arnold has written a masterpiece!' Clearly, he was very much impressed by Bennett's achievement, and his admiration remained years later when he described his enthusiastic reaction to *The Old Wives' Tale*:

I began reading it with misgiving, but this quickly changed to astonishment. . . . I was deeply impressed. I thought it a great book. I have read many appreciations of it, and I think everything has been said but one thing, which is that it is eminently readable.[11]

Maugham goes on to discuss Bennett's characters—not brilliant, but interesting and sympathetic. Their motives are plausible and their behaviour consistent with their characters. Commenting on Bennett's claim that *The Old Wives' Tale* will survive, he emphasises the importance of fashions in literary taste:

It may be that he was right. That depends on the whirligig of taste. Realism is a fashion that comes and goes. When readers ask their novels to give them fantasy, romance, excitement, suspense, surprise, they will find Arnold's masterpiece pedestrian and rather dull. When the pendulum swings back and they want homely truth, verisimilitude, good sense and sympathetic delineation of character they will find it in *The Old Wives' Tale*.[12]

That this description could equally be applied to *Of Human Bondage* indicates that Maugham probably was well aware which way the pendulum had swung.

The similarities between *The Old Wives' Tale* and *Clayhanger* and *Of Human Bondage* are largely stylistic (although there are parallels between Edwin Clayhanger's development and that of Philip Carey), and there is a danger of crediting Bennett with an influence which may have come from other sources. Both writers were influenced by the French Naturalistic school, and the strongest link between them is their realism. Except that he travels more than Bennett's characters and is a less universal figure than Edwin Clayhanger (because, for example, of his lameness), Philip lives an ordinary life. The ending, with Philip choosing a comfortable, but unexciting, career as a country doctor, is consistent with Bennett's. In addition, Maugham treats his material with the same kind of detail and concern for small events that one finds in the Bennett novels. Every aspect of Philip's development, and every episode which touches him in any way is dissected—to the impatience of many reviewers, who compared the method to explorative surgery, where the scalpel probes every obscure part of the organism, or likened it to a series of unretouched photographs.

Realism, and the naturalist's emphasis on detailed descriptions of heredity and environment, were not, however, new to Maugham in 1912. He had displayed these characteristics in *Liza of Lambeth*, *A Man of Honour* and some short stories, before the appearance of either of Bennett's novels. Nevertheless, it is likely that Maugham learned from Bennett and saw the possibilities of the extended story of the ordinary man.

In 1908, Henry Handel Richardson published *Maurice Guest*, a novel with a number of affinities with *Of Human Bondage*. Richardson's story is of a young English musician who goes to Germany to study. Here he becomes involved with the musical community and meets a young woman for whom he develops a great obsession. After prolonged effort, he is unable to possess her, and the novel ends with his suicide.

Not only is the theme of uncontrollable destructive passion parallel to that in Philip's relationship with Mildred, but the student scenes in Germany are quite similar to the Paris section of *Of Human Bondage*. Richardson creates a vivid and memorable group of young musicians, each with his own ideas and problems, and she shows their discussions and arguments as they attempt to sort out their philosophy of art. In the same manner, Maugham's picture of the bohemian life in Paris, the debates between the writers and artists who frequent the cafés, the affairs between them, the failure of pathetic figures like Fanny Price, is full of vitality and interest. He had used some of his Paris material in *The Magician* and, in an otherwise undistinguished novel, this was favourably noted by the critics. The success of a portrayal of the same type of life in *Maurice Guest* may have persuaded Maugham that his own experiences could be profitably amplified and extended.

If the artistic milieu in *Maurice Guest* influenced Maugham, the appearance of Cannan's translation of *Jean-Christophe* in 1910 would have acted as a strong reinforcement. Rolland's novel is an immense (ten volumes in the original) fictional biography of a musician, based on the lives of Mozart, Beethoven and Wagner. It traces Jean-Christophe Krafft's career from his birth in Germany to his death in old age in Paris. Although there is a strong narrative thread throughout, a great deal of the novel is composed of discussions, soliloquies, essays and tracts about philosophy, politics and art. His years in Paris, particularly, are concerned with the world of musicians, writers and artists, and again Maugham may have been reminded of his own experiences among the artistic community.

There is another essential part of *Of Human Bondage* which perhaps owes more to contemporary influences than is generally recognised. This is the prolonged and agonising affair between Philip and the vulgar, despicable Mildred. Because this relationship stretches over much of the latter half of the novel, and because it is written with great intensity and vividness, critics have assumed that it comes entirely from the author's own experience. Literary sleuths have searched for the woman who was the basis for Mildred, but there have so far been no startling revelations.

Maugham had used the same kind of character in his early writing —Giulia in *The Making of a Saint* and Jenny Bush in *A Man of Honour* and *The Merry-Go-Round*—and his later stories contain versions of the destructive female. However, although it is almost certain that Maugham underwent some of the unfortunate experiences which provided the basis for Philip's suffering, Mildred is probably largely a fictional creation.

In the literature of the late nineteenth and early twentieth centuries there are certainly enough examples of the *femme fatale*, the woman who tortures and destroys her men. There are affinities between Mildred and the recurring type of destructive woman in the novels of George Gissing. H. T. Webster suggests that there are particularly strong parallels between Gissing's treatment of Arthur Golding's marriage to Carrie Mitchell in *Workers in the Dawn* and Philip's affair with Mildred:

In each book, a sensitive and refined man is drawn against his better judgment into an alliance with an uneducated and utterly worthless

woman. Carrie and Mildred alike represent a mental and moral superficiality so great that it becomes the essence of evil. In each book, the
woman reappears in the man's life after several betrayals and separations
so that she remains a permanent blight on it. Carrie and Mildred similarly
degenerate in character from tawdry respectability to prostitution and the
extremes of degradation.[13]

In one form or another a Mildred-type figure appears in most
novels of adolescence in the early twentieth century. It is usually
part of a young man's apprenticeship that he becomes ensnared by a
woman who is vulgar, insensitive and unintelligent. In most cases the
hero finally frees himself and, although emotionally scarred, is more
mature because of his experience. Ernest Pontifex marries an alcoholic servant girl because he feels that honour demands it and, after a
miserable period, is saved by the fortunate discovery that she is
already married. George Ponderevo, in Wells's *Tono-Bungay*, makes
a hasty and unfortunate marriage to a woman whose mentality and
outlook are too remote from his own. Although not as fortunate as
Ernest, he escapes through a divorce. Edwin Clayhanger is made
miserable by his pursuit of the mysterious Hilda Lessways throughout
most of the novel, and it is not until the end that he is rewarded for his
suffering. Michael Fane, in Mackenzie's *Sinister Street*, experiences
an unhappy affair similar to Philip's. He falls in love with Lily Haden
when they both are young, and a few years later, upon hearing that
Lily is in danger of being corrupted, believes that it is his duty to save
her. Although forced to recognise her recent loose living, he retains
his faith in her essential purity, and he plans to marry her. This
prospect, however, is shattered by his discovery of her continued
promiscuity.

The best example of the female destroyer, however, and one which
bears a strong resemblance to Maugham's creation, is Louise
Dufrayer in *Maurice Guest*. Worshipping her from a distance,
Richardson's young hero is unable to do much more. When Louise's
unscrupulous lover, Schilsky, abandons her suddenly, however,
Maurice is able to approach her. Although Schilsky is gone, Louise
still loves him and, as much as she acquiesces in her misery to
Maurice's advances, he is never able to possess her entirely. After
increasingly agonised conflict between them, the novel ends with the
defeated Maurice committing suicide. The final picture is that of
Louise successful in having regained and married Schilsky while
Maurice lies in his grave.

Maugham's admiration for *Maurice Guest* seems to have been considerable. In discussing *The Old Wives' Tale* in *The Vagrant Mood*,
he wrote that 'for a time it looked as though it would have no more

than the sort of *succès d'estime* that *Maurice Guest* had', and when an interviewer once questioned him about Richardson's novel, he replied: 'Ah! There's a novel. One of the great novels, great in the way the novels of Tolstoi are great.'[14]

In several important ways, the relationship between Maurice and Louise resembles that of Philip and Mildred. Louise and Mildred are similar in their callous and insensitive treatment of the young men; neither seems capable of sympathetic realisation of the pain they inflict. As well, both are promiscuous and are themselves prisoners of their passions. Louise cannot free herself of her desire for Schilsky, and she betrays Maurice by sleeping with a former lover. Mildred, too, is almost obscenely promiscuous, and she is unable to resist the advances of men like Miller and Griffiths.

The essential parallel between the two novels, however, lies in the nature of the obsession that each young man has for the woman. Both Maurice and Philip, unlike other apprentice heroes, recognise the unworthiness of the beloved, but neither is able to abandon his desire. Maurice, more than Philip, struggles to retain his illusions about his woman; for some time he refuses to believe what is told to him and what soon becomes obvious. He never regains his emotional independence and, when Louise's betrayal makes it clear that she will never be completely his, he kills himself. Like Maurice, Philip is never free of his obsession, but, where Richardson's hero commits suicide, Maugham's protagonist is able to regain enough balance to be happy with someone else.

One can only conjecture as to the influence *Maurice Guest* may have had on *Of Human Bondage*. As critics have frequently pointed out, the theme of obsessive love for an unworthy person appears in Maugham's early work, and thus it is not a new idea. There is nevertheless a good possibility that Richardson's novel showed Maugham the depth to which this thesis could be explored.

Of Human Bondage remains Maugham's most important novel, though perhaps not artistically his best. *Cakes and Ale* is more skilfully written, with adept changes in time and place, beautifully controlled satire, and more natural and expressive language; however, *Of Human Bondage* examines much more universal and important themes. It is also the best example of the skill with which Maugham was able to transmute personal experience into fiction. His achievement is a novel which is one of the best in the apprentice genre, yet one which finds its power in absolute sincerity and honesty. Maugham has managed consummately to use an artificial framework, yet convey real life.

As well as presenting a rich and varied picture of human life, *Of*

Human Bondage is Maugham's most thorough and comprehensive expression of his concern for the freedom of the individual. Its theme is the development within Philip of a spiritual independence, a freedom from what Maugham called the many 'strange and ruthless forces that are beyond our control'.[15] It is a record, not simply of physical events and actions, but of a philosophical quest, and Philip's victory comes, not as it does for many conventional heroes, but when he can face reality with a tenable belief in life.

Although it is an immense novel, there is little in Of Human Bondage which is not an integral part of the central theme, and it is a serious, and often-repeated, error to concentrate critical attention on one section—the affair with Mildred, for example—to the detriment of others. Each part, scene, or character, is present to demonstrate the mistakes, falsehoods and delusions that Philip must escape before he can evolve a desirable and feasible pattern for his life. Thus critical analysis must be applied to the whole of the novel if the author's intentions are to be fully understood.

The course of Philip's pilgrimage involves almost all the manifestations of human bondage that concerned Maugham. There is, as in Liza of Lambeth, The Hero, Mrs Craddock and The Merry-Go-Round, considerable emphasis on the pressures of the community and the strength of its morality. As in The Hero and Mrs Craddock, religious belief is an intolerable burden which must be shed before one can be free, and, like James Parsons, Philip finds family life an uncomfortable restriction. The power of heredity and accidental physical make-up to dominate the life and thoughts of the individual are given powerful expression in Philip's deformity and the terrible sensitivity and feeling of inferiority it gives him. Maugham's hero, too, is the victim of another form of enslavement common to his writing—that of living in a world of illusion, of not seeing life as it actually is and therefore frequently suffering the pain of disillusionment. Economic dependence plays an important part in Philip's search for liberty, and freedom from economic obligations is an absolute necessity for Maugham. There is, too, the introduction of a new bondage, one which he was to develop more fully in his next novel, that of slavery to the obsession to paint. In Philip's affair with Mildred, Maugham vividly portrays the debilitating and entrapping power of passion. Finally, the most important shackle from which Philip must free himself is the natural human desire to discover a meaning in a meaningless universe. His liberation comes when he is able to recognise that life has no meaning, that the meaning comes from the individual, not from anything eternal or absolute.

Kingsley Amis has written of Of Human Bondage:

The novel shows how one barrier, in the shape of lameness, loneliness, puritanism or stupidity, will set up others: suspicion, over-exclusive affection, vindictiveness, exhibitionism, obstinacy, intolerance, self-torture – the state of what a later generation has learnt to call the injustice collector.[16]

This is a perceptive comment on the novel because it pinpoints the basic problems of Maugham's hero, particularly the process by which they are internalised to become much more serious mental barriers. Maugham is concerned with the physical handicaps of physiological disability, pressures to conform, economic hardship and domestic tyranny. These, however, are recognisable and relatively easily removed. The real danger, and Maugham demonstrates this throughout the novel, is that these restraints create within Philip a host of psychological handicaps, much less easy to recognise and much more difficult to eliminate. Philip's club-foot, for example, makes him the object of ridicule when he first enters school. By the time that this has naturally dissipated, he has been conditioned to feel that he is different and that this is a barrier between himself and others. In the latter part of the novel, one of the logical results of this obsession is his desperate need to be loved, especially his need to endure the miseries of his relationship with Mildred. His sensitivity about his foot remains even in the final pages, when he decides to marry Sally. In this way, an accident of birth, which becomes a physical handicap, is transmuted into a serious psychological bondage.

In the early chapters of *Of Human Bondage*, when the orphaned Philip is sent to live with his uncle, the Reverend William Carey, and his wife, Louisa, Maugham is showing the boy, in his words, 'deprived of the only love in the world that is quite unselfish'. There is no doubt that he took special pains to demonstrate the lack of affection and understanding between Philip and his uncle. There are many places in the early part of the manuscript which reveal that, having first written 'Aunt Louisa' and 'William Carey', he later replaced them with 'Mrs Carey' and 'the Vicar'. As the novel progresses, 'Mrs Carey' becomes 'Aunt Louisa', but the uncle remains the cold and distant 'Reverend Carey'.

This manner of describing the Careys exactly represents Maugham's feelings for his aunt and uncle. Robin Maugham, for example, tells of seeing a copy of *Liza of Lambeth* dedicated 'To the Vicar & Aunt Ellen with the Author's love. Sep. 2nd 1897'.[17] Although it was given to his uncle on his deathbed (he died sixteen days later), it was not inscribed to 'Uncle Henry'.

The particular humiliation which Philip endures at the vicarage is that of the child who is placed under the jurisdiction of someone other than a parent. Vain, parsimonious and petty, the Vicar demands a special place in his household, and the presence of a small boy is an intrusion. The manner in which Philip is made to feel his unimportance is neatly epitomised in an early episode. After his arrival from London, he is placed on a pile of books to have tea:

> Philip perched himself on the books, and the Vicar, having said grace, cut the top off his egg.
> "There," he said, handing it to Philip, "you can eat my top if you like."
> Philip would have liked an egg to himself, but he was not offered one, so took what he could.
> "How have the chickens been laying since I went away?" asked the Vicar.
> "Oh, they've been dreadful, only one or two a day."
> "How did you like that top, Philip?" asked his uncle.
> "Very much, thank you."
> "You shall have another one on Sunday afternoon."[18]

This episode is autobiographical and one which forcibly struck young Willie. Robert Van Gelder tells of Maugham's reply to a suggestion that the manuscript indicates that this passage was written with directness and speed:

> "Good God, I was 10 years old when it happened, and it is almost as sharp now as it was then. In my short life no one ever treated me that way before." The episode still moves him. That was evident by his voice, which sounded a trifle choked.[19]

The passage is indicative of the relationship between Philip and his uncle throughout the novel. The Vicar is always concerned with his own comfort, and his nephew is always humiliated at having to accept anything from his hands. The top of the egg, held out as a reward for good behaviour, becomes symbolic of the dependence from which the young boy wants to be free.

A number of episodes demonstrate that Philip chafes under the regimen that he is expected to follow in the Carey household. Because his aunt dislikes disorder, he must play with his toys in the kitchen; if he fidgets too much, the Vicar becomes annoyed and suggests that he should be at school; and when a castle of bricks tumbles down with a greater clatter, Philip's uncle chastises him for playing on Sunday and attempts to shame him by invoking the memory of his mother. When Philip enquires what he should do instead of playing, he is told that he can 'sit still for once and be quiet'. When he balks at this, he is ordered to memorise the collect.

The most serious effect of the environment of the vicarage and of Philip's childhood is the creation within him of a great hunger for affection and love, to compensate for the lack of it in his childhood.

This hunger frequently leads him desperately to seek friendships and to suffer when these friendships break up, and it gives Philip a hyper-sensitivity to the actions of others toward him.

Another result of the inadequacies of childhood at the vicarage is the development within Philip of a love of literature. Literature, at this stage, is a compensation for his unhappy environment, and it is not surprising that his love of reading begins when he is given some picture-books as a consolation for his frustration at failing to learn the collect. While Maugham makes it clear that there is a great comfort in reading, he also points out that this initiates a problem which haunts Philip for most of the novel—a weakness for idealism and illusion:

Insensibly he formed the most delightful habit in the world, the habit of reading: he did not know that thus he was providing himself with a refuge from all the distress of life; he did not know either that he was creating for himself an unreal world which would make the real world of every day a source of bitter disappointment.[20]

For Maugham, the great struggle for youth coming to maturity is the search for reality. Children, he argues, are filled with illusions and ideals by their parents and teachers, and they cannot understand and accept life as it really is until they have thrown off these burdens. The process of disillusionment, furthermore, involves pain:

He did not know how wide a country, arid and precipitous, must be crossed before the traveller through life comes to an acceptance of reality. It is an illusion that youth is happy, an illusion of those who have lost it; but the young know they are wretched, for they are full of the truthless ideals which have been instilled into them, and each time they come into contact with the real they are bruised and wounded. It looks as if they were victims of a conspiracy; for the books they read, ideal by the necessity of selection, and the conversations of their elders, who look back upon the past through a rosy haze of forgetfulness, prepare them for an unreal life. They must discover for themselves that all they have read and all they have been told are lies, lies, lies; and each discovery is another nail driven into the body on the cross of life.[21]

Maugham clearly demonstrates that Philip endures a great deal of anguish every time one of his illusions is destroyed, but he argues that these disillusionments are necessary if the individual is to achieve intellectual and emotional independence. The course of Philip's development is one of stripping away of his false, ideal visions of the world—his romantic picture of love is destroyed by the reality of Miss Wilkinson, and his conception of *la vie de bohème* by Fanny Price—until he is able to see, and accept, life as it really is.

In Philip's experiences at King's School, in 'Tercanbury' (an anagram of Canterbury), Maugham paints a damning picture of

English public schools of the time, with their communal atmosphere, stagnant education, and streak of sadism. It is here that many of Philip's neuroses are developed, and he has few happy moments until he leaves the school to go to Germany.

Maugham sets the tone of Philip's schooldays by his description of the young boy's first reaction to the sight of King's School:

The high brick wall in front of the school gave it the look of a prison. There was a little door in it, which opened on their ringing; and a clumsy, untidy man came out and fetched Philip's tin trunk and his play-box. They were shown into the drawing-room; it was filled with massive ugly furniture, and the chairs of the suite were placed round the walls with a forbidding rigidity.[22]

During his years at school, Philip is the victim of a considerable amount of bullying by his fellows, but it is probably not a great deal more than that undergone by any small and sensitive boy. What is particularly cruel in his case is the manner in which the boys, and a number of the school-masters, use his club-foot as a means of attacking him. It is, as a result, in this segment of the novel that the groundwork is laid for Philip's obsession with his deformity, an obsession which so much dictates his reactions in later life. As he becomes more aware of himself and his entity, it is consistently emphasised to him that he is somehow different from the others and, by implication, inadequate.

When Philip first arrives at school, his club-foot causes considerable interest, and he is made a figure of ridicule. When he is made to play a game which involves running, he fails miserably and is a source of amusement. At bed-time, he is subjected to an examination by his room-mates and, under torture, he yields. Significantly, it is not so much the display of his foot which hurts him but, rather, the subjection into which he is forced:

He was not crying for the pain they had caused him, nor for the humiliation he had suffered when they looked at his foot, but with rage at himself because, unable to stand the torture, he had put out his foot of his own accord.[23]

For most of the novel, Philip envisages personal independence as the power to make one's will dominant over that of others, and a great many episodes of his youth concern questions of strength of will. Thus, this surrender under duress to his fellows is painful to him because it seems to mean a weakness of character. Similarly, when Philip finally persuades his aunt and uncle to permit him to go to Germany, he exults because his will has triumphed over those of the Careys and the headmaster of the school. Later, much of his obses-

sion with Mildred springs from his determination to prove himself
dominant over her.

With the passage of time, Philip becomes more and more sensitive
about his foot, and this fear of being different and inferior makes him
withdrawn and introspective:

As time went on Philip's deformity ceased to interest. It was accepted
like one boy's red hair and another's unreasonable corpulence. But meanwhile he had grown horribly sensitive. He never ran if he could help it,
because he knew it made his limp more conspicuous, and he adopted a
peculiar walk. He stood still as much as he could, with his club-foot behind
the other, so that it should not attract notice, and he was constantly on the
look-out for any reference to it. . . . He was left a good deal to himself. He
had been inclined to talkativeness, but gradually he became silent. He
began to think of the difference between himself and others.[24]

Because of the recognition that somehow he is different from the
other boys, Philip develops a consciousness of himself at an early age.
Because ordinary rules and criteria do not seem to apply to him, he
must think for himself and formulate his own ideas of conduct. A
result of this is that he never really loses the feeling that there is a
distance between himself and other people.

The effect on Philip's mental outlook of his physical disability
illustrates Maugham's belief in the interaction between the body and
the mind. In *The Summing Up*, he writes that the chills, fevers, aches,
pains and nausea which strike a writer during a composition influence
the nature of his writing, and he points to Flaubert's suffering from
the symptoms of arsenical poisoning while writing of Emma Bovary's
suicide. As we have seen, in discussing Arnold Bennett's stammer in
The Vagrant Mood he suggests that this barrier to complete communication with others may have forced his friend into introspection
and finally authorship. Analysing his own personality, Maugham is
quite emphatic about the importance of his physical being:

I think many people shrink from the notion that the accidents of the body
can have an effect on the constitution of the soul. There is nothing of which
for my own part I am more assured. My soul would have been quite
different if I had not stammered or if I had been four or five inches taller;
I am slightly prognathous; in my childhood they did not know that this
could be remedied by a gold band worn while the jaw is still malleable;
if they had, my countenance would have borne a different cast, the reaction
toward me of my fellows would have been different and therefore my disposition, my attitude to them, would have been different too. But what sort
of thing is this soul that can be modified by a dental apparatus? We all
know how greatly changed our lives would have been if we had not by
what seems mere chance met such and such a person or if we had not been
at a particular moment at a particular place; and so our character, and so
our soul, would have been other than they are.[25]

Maugham's insistence in *The Summing Up* on what he calls 'the body-mind' is reflected in his attitude to love. Pure sexual love—that is, love that is not based on habit, affection, need, comfort or other emotions—depends simply on 'certain secretions of the sexual glands'. His opinion is reflected also in his discussion of mysticism in *Don Fernando*. Here, he writes about the mystical experiences being an awareness of a greater significance in the universe, a sense of union with God, an ecstasy. 'But', he reminds the reader, 'you can get it, if you are that way inclined, from a glass of cold beer.'

This emphasis on the interaction of the body and mind parallels the direction taken by modern psychiatric treatment, where the mentally disturbed patient is treated by controlling his chemical balance. This school of psychiatry argues that many psychological problems are created by disruptions in the normal body chemistry, rather than by emotional or intellectual developments. Similarly, Yoga philosophy is based on the premise that physical positions and exertions, particularly diet and breathing, can induce psychological states.

In *Of Human Bondage*, Philip's club-foot, like Bennett's and Maugham's stammers, profoundly affects the development of his personality and the course of his life. To a great extent, his introspection, his shyness, his feeling of inferiority, and even his obsession with Mildred, can be attributed to this influence.

Life at school soon becomes endless drudgery; the teachers are not capable of inspiring Philip with enthusiasm for their classes and his ambition flags. Suffering under 'that despotism which never vouchsafed a reason for the most tyrannous act', the only thing that seems to be important is his liberty:[26]

He was tired of having to do things because he was told; and the restrictions irked him, not because they were unreasonable, but because they were restrictions. He yearned for freedom. He was weary of repeating things he knew already and of the hammering away, for the sake of a thick-witted fellow, at something he understood from the beginning.[27]

Philip, after the example of a fellow student, conceives the idea of leaving King's School to go to Germany to study. When he confronts the Careys with the plan, however, he encounters the same kind of emotional pressure that the Parsons exerted on their son in *The Hero*. The Careys have already organised their nephew's future—he is to become his uncle's curate—and when it appears that they may be frustrated, Philip feels the restricting force of love:

Philip shivered. He was seized with panic. His heart beat like a pigeon in a trap beating with its wings. His aunt wept softly, her head upon his shoulder.[28]

Philip triumphs, nevertheless, and he is soon permitted to leave school to go to Heidelberg. Thus this part of his life ends with the gain of a liberty, or at least the illusion of a liberty. Philip walks out of the school grounds and feels free. Freedom, however, does not bring immediate happiness since he has gone through with his plans, not from a purely independent choice, but because he has not wanted to admit that he was wrong about school. This is the first of many occasions when the hero rejoices in his freedom only to discover later that he has not actually gained a liberty.

Maugham has often written about the three values—'Truth, Beauty and Goodness'. They are the basis for the final three chapters of *The Summing Up*, where he claims that 'they have superficially an appearance of disinterestedness which gives man the illusion that through them he escapes from human bondage', and it is around this triad that *Of Human Bondage* is constructed. Truth is analysed in Philip's year in Heidelberg, in his discussions with Cronshaw, in his philosophical searching, and in his revelation in the British Museum. Beauty is introduced in his period in Paris, and it becomes an integral part of his philosophy and pattern for living. Goodness is the central issue in the latter half of the novel, with a deliberate contrast created between Mildred and the Athelny family. These three concepts are often intricately involved with each other, and ultimately Philip's view of life incorporates all three.

The Heidelberg section is the first major encounter Philip has with truth, or at least with the recognition that his own beliefs deserve to be examined. When he takes mathematics lessons from an Englishman, Wharton, who thrives on the freedom of the German university, he also receives a lecture on the narrowness of English life:

"You know, there are two good things in life, freedom of thought and freedom of action. In France you get freedom of action: you can do what you like and nobody bothers, but you must think like everybody else. In Germany you must do what everybody else does, but you may think as you choose. They're both very good things. I personally prefer freedom of thought. But in England you get neither: you're ground down by convention. You can't think as you like and you can't act as you like."[29]

Philip, as well, studies Latin and German under Professor Erlin and through him encounters a number of influential books, culminating in his discovery of Goethe's *Faust*. He learns of *The Doll's House*, and sees a number of Ibsen's plays; he hears Wagner and particularly *Lohengrin*; he views Sudermann's *Die Ehre*; and he listens with fascination to Kuno Fischer's lectures on Schopenhauer.

Philip's French teacher, M. Ducroz, is a strange figure, a revolutionary who has fought with Garibaldi, but who left Italy when it became clear that his fight for liberty had really only meant a transfer of yokes. His life, like that of so many of the characters in *Of Human Bondage*, has been futile, and Philip tries to imagine the course of his search for liberty:

One might fancy him, passionate with theories of human equality and human rights, discussing, arguing, fighting behind barricades in Paris, flying before the Austrian cavalry in Milan, imprisoned here, exiled from there, hoping on and upborne ever with the word which seemed so magical, the word Liberty; till at last, broken with disease and starvation, old, without means to keep body and soul together but by such lessons as he could pick up from poor students, he found himself in that little neat town under the heel of a personal tyranny greater than any in Europe. Perhaps his taciturnity hid a contempt for the human race which had abandoned the great dreams of his youth and now wallowed in sluggish ease; or perhaps these thirty years of revolution had taught him that men are unfit for liberty, and he thought that he had spent his life in the pursuit of that which was not worth finding. Or maybe he was tired out and waited only with indifference for the release of death.[30]

Much of Philip's intellectual awakening comes, however, through two young men living at the same boarding-house—Hayward, a young Englishman, and Weeks, an American student. Both of these characters are taken in modified form from Maugham's own Heidelberg experience. In *The Summing Up*, he describes the young man who was the basis for Hayward, calling him 'Brown'; in *A Writer's Notebook* there is a lengthy description of him, here called 'Brooks'; finally, in 'Looking Back' Maugham identifies him as 'Ellingham Brooks'. In this last passage the American is described as a New Englander who taught Greek at Harvard. Maugham in retrospect attributes their interest in him to homosexuality.

Through Hayward, Philip discovers *Richard Feverel, Madame Bovary*, Verlaine, Dante, Matthew Arnold and Fitzgerald's translation of *The Rubáiyát of Omar Khayyám*. Although he has a weak character, Hayward does possess a real feeling for literature, and he becomes a reliable guide for Philip's reading.

The influence of Hayward's aesthetic interests is fortunately balanced by the logic of Weeks, and Philip's understanding is broadened considerably by his own observation of their frequent debates. The most significant result of these discussions, and the climactic point of the Heidelberg section, is Philip's recognition of his loss of faith.

Philip's examination of his religious beliefs is initiated when, after a discussion about religion with Hayward, Weeks suggests that he read Renan's *Vie de Jésus*. Up to this time, religious faith has not been a matter to be questioned, and it has never occurred to Philip to seek a solid intellectual basis for his belief. He has never varied from the narrow Church of England faith of his uncle.

Maugham places considerable emphasis on the role played by environment and conditioning in the formation of Philip's religious faith. Philip has never, he says, had the 'religious temperament', and belief has therefore been forced upon him from the outside. A real core of faith has never existed within him, and when the new environment allows his mind free play he discovers what he really believes. 'He put off the faith of his childhood quite simply, like a cloak that he no longer needed.'

This passage, although early in the novel, is one of the important points in Philip's spiritual development in that it marks the destruction of a false belief, thus opening the way for the evolution of a more sincere, solid and viable philosophy. It is important to note that at this point Philip has simply rid himself of a burden; he has not replaced one belief with another. His reaction, therefore, is characteristic; his predominant feeling is one of liberation, of freedom from a restraint which has hung over him:

He felt like a man who has leaned on a stick and finds himself forced suddenly to walk without assistance. . . . But he was upheld by the excitement; it seemed to make life a more thrilling adventure; and in a little while the stick which he had thrown aside, the cloak which had fallen from his shoulders, seemed an intolerable burden of which he had been eased.[31]

He was free from degrading fears and free from prejudice. He could go his way without the intolerable dread of hellfire. Suddenly he realised that he had lost also that burden of responsibility which had made every action of his life a matter of urgent consequence. He could breathe more freely in a lighter air. He was responsible only to himself for the things he did. Freedom! He was his own master at last.[32]

Thus Philip's attempts to believe quickly come to an end. His reasoning may be simple and adolescent (admitting the autobiographical nature of this episode, Maugham wrote in *The Summing Up* that the reasons were 'of the heart rather than the head'), but it is an essential step in the process of developing a philosophy which will enable him to accept life. It is the destruction necessary to clear the way for more substantial construction.

The discovery of an affair of passion in the boarding-house in Heidelberg, which has a considerable effect on Philip, prepares the way for his first sexual encounter, the tragicomic affair with Miss Wilkinson. Maugham's concern in this episode is with demonstrating his hero's adolescent confusion about appearance and reality, and he therefore emphasises the contrast between Philip's illusion of what the beloved ought to be and the reality of Miss

Wilkinson. The young man, in the beginning, is dazzled and deceived by Miss Wilkinson's conversation and her descriptions of her life in Paris. His imagination transforms her accounts into romantic mysteries, and she cultivates this with deliberate vagueness. When Philip contrasts this imaginary view of life in Paris with his own uneventful days in Heidelberg, he feels that he is missing something.

Throughout the episode, Philip is motivated by the idea that it is his duty to seduce Miss Wilkinson, that it is what every man would do, that it is expected of him. Unlike so many of Maugham's characters, he is not here a slave to sexual passion. Always sensitive to the actions and opinions of others, he reacts to what he thinks Hayward would do, and to what he thinks that Miss Wilkinson expects:

Here at last was his chance of an adventure, and he would be a fool not to take it; but it was a little ordinary, and he had expected more glamour. He had read many descriptions of love, and he felt in himself none of that uprush of emotion which novelists described; he was not carried off his feet in wave upon wave of passion; nor was Miss Wilkinson the ideal: he had often pictured to himself the great violet eyes and the alabaster skin of some lovely girl, and he had thought of himself burying his face in the rippling masses of her auburn hair. He could not imagine himself burying his face in Miss Wilkinson's hair, it always struck him as a little sticky. All the same it would be very satisfactory to have an intrigue, and he thrilled with the legitimate pride he would enjoy in his conquest. He owed it to himself to seduce her.[33]

After a period of time in which Philip acts what he believes to be the part of the lover, he finds the opportunity for seduction when he remains at home one evening with Miss Wilkinson while the others are at church. When the moment arrives, he wishes to back out, but he goes through with his plans because 'what would Miss Wilkinson think of him if he did not!' The consummation is a shattering of Philip's romantic illusions:

She looked grotesque. Philip's heart sank as he stared at her; she had never seemed so unattractive; but it was too late now. He closed the door behind him and locked it.[34]

After the seduction, Philip is continually disturbed by Miss Wilkinson's age and plainness, and he cannot help feeling ridiculous. He is embarrassed by her protestations of love and exasperated by the demands which she is now able to make of him. His discomfort is heightened by his romantic, idealised account of the affair in a letter to Hayward and by his friend's gushing reply. Once again, Philip's imagination has brought him pain, and 'as he put the letter in his pocket, he felt a queer little pang of bitterness because reality seemed so different from the ideal'.

Through Miss Wilkinson, Philip is introduced to Murger's *La Vie de Bohème*, and it is this romanticised picture of Paris life which persuades him to attempt the career of an art student. Throughout the Paris section there is a deliberate contrasting of the bohemian life as presented by Murger with what the reality involves. Before showing what Philip learns in Paris, Maugham sets the illusion before the reader in Philip's first enchantment with *La Vie de Bohème*:

His soul danced with joy at that picture of starvation which is so good-humoured, of squalor which is so picturesque, of sordid love which is so romantic, of bathos which is so moving. Rodolphe and Mimi, Musette and Schaunard! They wander through the gray streets of the Latin Quarter, finding refuge now in one attic, now in another, in their quaint costumes of Louis Philippe, with their tears and their smiles, happy-go-lucky and reckless.[35]

When Philip arrives in Paris, it is with this vision in his mind, and he sees romance everywhere. His room, five flights up, seems quaint and charming; his excursions onto the boulevard and into cafés thrill him; and when he encounters several Americans playing the bohemian role he finds them picturesque. Eager to do something 'characteristic', he orders absinthe: 'He drank with nausea and satisfaction. He found the taste disgusting, but the moral effect magnificent; he felt every inch an art-student.'

The height of Philip's enthusiasm for the bohemian life comes when he meets the notorious degenerate poet, Cronshaw,[36] in a café. Cronshaw talks of art, literature and life, and gives a virtuoso display of oratory. Although the others listen dubiously, Philip is enthralled, and thoroughly overcome by the romance of the artist's life. He is, in the author's words, drunk on 'a more dangerous intoxicant than alcohol'.

Throughout the Paris section, nevertheless, there is a gradual awakening in Philip of a realisation of the reality of the bohemian life. The greatest instrument of destroying his illusions is the pathetic suicide of the untalented painter, Fanny Price. Through his association with her, Philip discovers the falseness of the idea in *La Vie de Bohème* of joyous and carefree poverty. In Fanny Price, he learns that, to the contrary, economic deprivation and struggle are destructive and dehumanising; they make her miserable, petty and resentful. At lunch, she resembles an animal in her hunger:

Philip was squeamish, and the way in which Miss Price ate took his appetite away. She ate noisily, greedily, like a wild beast in a menagerie, and after she had finished each course rubbed the plate with pieces of bread till it was white and shining, as if she did not wish to lose a single drop of gravy. They had Camembert cheese, and it disgusted Philip to see that she ate rind and all of the portion that was given her. She could not have eaten more ravenously if she were starving.[37]

Finally, when Miss Price's money runs out and she can no longer eke out even a meagre existence, she hangs herself. Philip, when investigating her death, learns the hard facts about poverty:

The *concierge* told him what her food had consisted of. A bottle of milk was left for her every day and she brought in her own loaf of bread; she ate half the loaf and drank half the milk at mid-day when she came back from the school, and consumed the rest in the evening. It was the same day after day. Philip thought with anguish what she must have endured . . . he thought of the emaciated body, in the brown dress, hanging from the nail in the ceiling, and he shuddered.[38]

In addition to this shock, after the initial flush of romantic enthusiasm wears off, Philip begins to see life around him differently. He recognises the charlatans, the dilettantes and the *poseurs* among his fellow artists, and he sees the quarrels, jealousies and the failures which are part of their lives. Even Cronshaw loses his mystique and becomes merely an interesting, but degenerate, figure.

Finally, Maugham underlines the distance between fiction and reality through contrasting pictures of music-hall life. At the beginning of Philip's life in Paris, Maugham describes the current vogue for impressions of lower-class life:

Philip, influenced by Hayward, looked upon music-halls with scornful eyes, but he reached Paris at a time when their artistic possibilities were just discovered. . . . Men of letters, following in the painters' wake, conspired suddenly to find artistic value in the turns; and red-nosed comedians were lauded to the skies for their sense of character; fat female singers, who had bawled obscurely for twenty years, were discovered to possess inimitable drollery; there were those who found an aesthetic delight in performing dogs; while others exhausted their vocabulary to extol the distinction of conjurers and trick cyclists. The crowd too, under another influence, was becoming an object of sympathetic interest.[39]

Philip, for a while, falls under this spell. Near the end of his Paris studies, however, his opinion of the mass of people has altered considerably. His vision of the Bal Bullier is distorted to such an extent that it becomes as false in the extreme as the romantic picture. It is, for him, an animal scene:

The room was hot, and their faces shone with sweat. It seemed to Philip that they had thrown off the guard which people wear on their expression, the homage to convention, and he saw them now as they really were. In that moment of abandon they were strangely animal: some were foxy and some were wolf-like; and others had the long, foolish face of sheep. Their skins were sallow from the unhealthy life they led and the poor food they ate. Their features were blunted by mean interests, and their little eyes were shifty and cunning. There was nothing of nobility in their bearing, and you felt that for all of them life was a long succession of petty concerns and sordid thoughts. The air was heavy with the musty smell of humanity.[40]

Philip, at this point in his life, is still a prisoner of his own imagination, of his own illusions. The recurring pattern for him is of a vision of the ideal followed by pain of discovery of the hard facts of reality. In this instance, he has accepted the impression created by an artistic vogue; the subsequent realisation of life as it actually is comes as a traumatic shock. It is not until the climactic scene in the British Museum, when Philip is able to free himself from his own mental chains, that he is able to accept people for what they are.

In spite of Philip's disenchantment, the Paris experience plays an important part in his spiritual development. The process of intellectual extension begun in Germany is continued by the passionate discussions in the cafés and studios and by the ramblings of Cronshaw. It is through Cronshaw's philosophical discourse that many key questions about the individual, freedom and life are raised, questions that remain unanswered until the British Museum episode.

The Paris section is also Maugham's treatment of the theme of beauty and its importance to the individual. Although Philip discovers that he has no creative ability, his own aesthetic sensibility is sharpened by his contact with the artistic community, and this remains with him. The feeling for beauty is shown ultimately to be the most important result of his Paris experience.

In his portrayal of Philip's efforts to find out whether he is an artist, Maugham introduces a theme which he treats in much more depth in his next novel, *The Moon and Sixpence*—the artistic genius and the bondage it entails. Through his natural tendency to introspection, Philip discovers that there is a basic difference between himself and the other art students. Not only do they appear to have more talent, their artistic temperament is a feeling, not an intellectual reaction:

He could not help seeing that art affected him differently from others. A fine picture gave Lawson an immediate thrill. His appreciation was instinctive. Even Flanagan felt certain things that Philip was obliged to think out. His own appreciation was intellectual.[41]

The feelings of his fellow art students seem to be instincts which come from deep within, with an almost autonomous force. Observing Clutton, Philip recognises that 'there seemed to be a mysterious force in him . . . which was struggling obscurely to find an outlet'. As Clutton says, 'The only reason that one paints is that one can't help it.' The story of Gauguin's sacrifice of everything—comfort, home, money, love, honour, duty—for his art leads Philip to recognise the artistic temperament as a form of bondage:

It seemed to Philip, brooding over these matters, that in the true painters, writers, musicians, there was a power which drove them to such complete absorption in their work as to make it inevitable for them to subordinate life to art. Succumbing to an influence they never realised, they were merely dupes of the instinct that possessed them, and life slipped through their fingers unlived.[42]

Philip therefore abandons his art studies, not just because he realises that he has no genius, but because he wishes to retain his spiritual independence, to be able to experience life rather than merely portray it. He has been struck by the futility and waste of the lives of people like Fanny Price and Miguel Ajuria who, with no talent, sacrifice everything in a quest for the unattainable. Even the sacrifice of his successful fellows and the example of Gauguin is, for him, too much. Recognising a bondage as strong as any, he rejects art for life.

Even though he abandons the artist's life, Philip retains from his studies a sensitivity to beauty, and the importance of this sense is demonstrated several times in the remainder of the novel. He discovers on a number of occasions the power of beauty to alleviate frustration and pain. When, for example, Mildred announces that she is going to marry Miller, Philip is crushed. The next day, however, he accompanies Hayward to the National Gallery and then to St James's Park, where he becomes aware of the cathartic effect of beauty:

Philip's heart was filled with lightness. He realised, what he had only read before, that art (for there was art in the manner in which he looked upon nature) might liberate the soul from pain.[43]

When Hayward glibly suggests that Philip has wasted two years in Paris, his friend replies:

"Waste? Look at the movement of that child, look at the pattern which the sun makes on the ground, shining through the trees, look at that sky – why, I should never have seen that sky if I hadn't been to Paris."[44]

Philip later discovers a different, but equally important, value of the perception of beauty. Through Thorpe Athelny's enthusiasm for Spain and Spanish art, Philip is brought into contact with the paintings of El Greco; in these he discovers a power of the artist to communicate a subtle truth. Previously, in Paris, he had divided art into the pretty (idealised) or the realistic (truthful), and he had scrupulously sought the real—to the extent of painting an advertisement of 'Chocolat Menier' in a landscape to avoid prettiness. With El Greco, however, he senses something which fits neither category; the idealism is not cowardly and the realism is something more than simply an acceptance of life as it is. Life is represented realistically, but made more significant by the vividness of art. Not only does this new view of life contribute to the creation within Philip of tolerance and acceptance, the meaning which reaches him from El Greco's painting is an affirmation of the strength of the human will:

He seemed to see that a man need not leave his life to chance, but that his will was powerful; he seemed to see that self-control might be as passionate and as active as the surrender to passion; he seemed to see that the inward life might be as manifold, as varied, as rich with experience, as the life of one who conquered realms and explored unknown lands.[45]

The major theme of the second half of *Of Human Bondage* is concerned with the third of Maugham's triad of values—goodness. The themes of truth and beauty, introduced in the first half, continue to their resolution near the end, but the real interest of the author is with goodness. The essential part of this concept is the contrast between Philip's anguished affair with Mildred and his relationship with Sally. There is a deliberate attempt to present good and evil in the form of the Athelny family as opposed to Mildred and Griffiths.

For the majority of readers, the affair between Philip and Mildred is the central issue of the novel. This relationship, in fact, occupies only about a quarter of the book. What it does represent, however, is a very important and dramatic step in the development of Philip's emotional independence; it is Maugham's treatment of the strength of the emotions and the dangers of their overwhelming one's reason. The agonising entanglement with Mildred is thus merely another trial which the hero must undergo before he can achieve true liberty.

Philip's involvement with Mildred exists in four stages, each one having different emotional character and conducted in a different manner. It is not true, as critics have frequently claimed, that his attraction to her is simply that of sexual passion. It is the manifestation of complex psychological needs arising from deeply rooted problems.

When Philip first encounters Mildred, he is not attracted by physical beauty; he is never, in fact, drawn to her for aesthetic reasons. Their relationship is initiated by his reaction to her insolent and indifferent treatment of him in the tea shop where she works. Something in his personality demands that Mildred be humbled in revenge:

He could not get her out of his mind. He laughed angrily at his own foolishness: it was absurd to care what an anaemic little waitress said to him; but he was strangely humiliated. Though no one knew of the humiliation but Dunsford, and he had certainly forgotten, Philip felt that he could have no peace till he had wiped it out.[46]

Philip unfortunately is never really able to expunge this initial feeling of humiliation. Although he soon gets to know Mildred better, it is not until much later, when he does not care for her, that he is able to dominate or affect her in any way. She remains indifferent and unconcerned, and thus the desire to regain his dignity is increased.

As the relationship progresses, Philip is moved by paradoxical feelings of affection and hatred for Mildred, the hatred as a result of his disgust for her and of his desire to revenge himself. At one point, he imagines killing her, and Maugham effectively conveys his strange complex emotion:

He looked at her neck and thought how he would like to jab it with the knife he had for his muffin. He knew enough anatomy to make pretty certain of getting the carotid artery. And at the same time he wanted to cover her pale, thin face with kisses.[47]

Later, when he contemplates marriage, the element of revenge is again prominent, and he cries: 'By George, if I marry her I'll make her pay for all the suffering I've endured.'

Philip's love involves as much pain as happiness, and the dilemma is that he is as unhappy with her as he is away from her. The situation that Maugham creates here is that of the lover who is emotionally enslaved by one whom he rejects rationally. Rather than making the emotions warp the reason, the author demonstrates the power of the emotions by making them separate from the reason, yet dominant. Philip's agony is the impotence of his reason to kill a feeling which is poisoning his life.

The portrait Maugham presents of Mildred is not a pleasant one. She is thin, anaemic and unattractively coloured. She is unintelligent, insensitive and vulgar, and she is obsessed with class snobbery. Lacking generosity, cold and completely selfish, she has almost no redeeming qualities.

What makes Philip different from most young men in fiction who suffer at the hands of a *femme fatale* is that he is aware of precisely what Mildred is and yet he still loves her:

It seemed impossible that he should be in love with Mildred Rogers. Her name was grotesque. He did not think her pretty; he hated the thinness of her, only that evening he had noticed how the bones of her chest stood out in evening-dress; he went over her features one by one; he did not like her mouth, and the unhealthiness of her colour vaguely repelled him. She was common. Her phrases, so bald and few, constantly repeated, showed the emptiness of her mind; he recalled her vulgar little laugh at the jokes of the musical comedy; and he remembered the little finger carefully extended when she held her glass to her mouth; her manners, like her conversation, were odiously genteel.[48]

Once again, Philip's illusions accentuate the pain he suffers in coming to terms with reality. When he had made love to Miss Wilkinson, the difference between her and his romantic ideal made him suffer. In France, the desire to make love to Ruth Chalice was extinguished by the disparity between his vision of her and her real self:

It was very curious. Away from her he thought her beautiful, remembering only her magnificent eyes and the creamy pallor of her face; but when he was with her he saw only that she was flat-chested and that her teeth were slightly decayed; he could not forget the corns on her toes. He could not understand himself. Would he always love only in absence and be prevented from enjoying anything when he had the chance by that deformity of vision which seemed to exaggerate the revolting?[49]

A similar process of disillusionment helps to emphasise Mildred's inadequacies. When the realisation that he loves her strikes Philip, it is undermined by his vision of what love ought to be. He has always pictured himself coming into a ballroom, an arresting figure, over-whelming the most beautiful woman there with his dancing, and escaping into the night with her. This scene, more suitable as a plot for a romantic story in a cheap woman's magazine, contrasts vividly with his first meeting with the waitress in a common tea shop. While this illusion is only one aspect of his complex attitude toward Mildred, it is nonetheless a significant factor.

Another important part of the suffering Philip undergoes with Mildred is the humiliation of being the slave of a woman he so despises. The constant awareness that he cannot master the situation becomes an obsession with him:

Love was like a parasite in his heart. . . . This love was a torment, and he resented bitterly the subjugation in which it held him; he was a prisoner and he longed for his freedom.[50]

Philip decides that his obsession with Mildred must be sexual hunger, and he assumes that if he can satisfy this he can free himself from 'the intolerable chains' that bind him. He is, in his mind, a mediaeval knight, metamorphosed by magic, seeking the means to regain his proper form. The only way that he can regain his integrity and dignity is to subjugate Mildred.

Before Philip is able to effect Mildred's surrender, however, she announces that she is getting married to a frequenter of the tea shop, a man named Miller. This is the worst possible development for Philip because it means that, although Mildred is taken from him, he is not rid of his obsession. Even though he soon recovers from the loss of her physical presence, the feeling of unrequited passion lies dormant, to be reawakened later with greater force.

Philip's emotional bondage reaches its most critical point in the second stage of his involvement with Mildred. When she returns to him after her abandonment by Miller, all of his passion and obsessions return with greater power than before. Almost instantaneously, he is enslaved again. This is not, however, a sexual passion, because Philip's fastidiousness and active imagination prevent him from desiring Mildred after she has been cast off; neither has he ceased to see her as she really is.

What seems to motivate Maugham's protagonist at this point is pride. Although he feels a certain satisfaction in the domesticity brought about by Mildred's return, he is not particularly happy in her presence. He appears to care about the relationship only when it seems that Griffiths is winning the woman away from him. His 'love' for her is directly affected by the degree to which he cannot have her. When, with considerable assistance and prompting from Philip, Mildred spends a weekend with Griffiths, Philip suffers his worst tortures. Now, while he did not want her when she lived with him, his desire for her is strongest—when she is the possession of another man. Philip here receives a kind of pleasure in masochism and self-pity. He also retains his ability to examine himself and his feelings, but this does not prevent his longings: 'He *felt* that he would never overcome his passion, but he *knew* that after all it was only a matter of time.'

In the solitude and peace of Blackstable, Philip examines critically his emotional weaknesses and attempts to account for his failure with Mildred. He concludes that love is some sort of force 'that passed from a man to a woman, from a woman to a man, and made one of them a slave'. Assessing his ability to retain a mastery over himself, he decides that he is in fact powerless to act with free will:

It seemed to him rather that he was swayed by some power alien to and yet within himself, which urged him like that great wind of Hell which drove Paolo and Francesca ceaselessly on. He thought of what he was going to do and, when the time came to act, he was powerless in the grasp of instincts, emotions, he knew not what. He acted as though he were a machine driven by the two forces of his environment and his personality; his reason was someone looking on, observing the facts but powerless to interfere; it was like those gods of Epicurus, who saw the doings of men from their empyrean heights and had no might to alter one smallest particle of what occurred.[51]

With the end of this second period with Mildred, Philip's enslavement to a passion for her is for the most part terminated. While he becomes entangled with her twice more before the end, both occasions involve far less dangerous emotional demands. It is true that Mildred continues to cause trouble for Philip, but she is never again capable of holding him in emotional subjection.

When Philip next encounters Mildred, it is in Piccadilly Circus, where he discovers that she has become a prostitute. Out of generosity, and perhaps from a desire for self-sacrifice, he allows her and her child to share his rooms. This time Philip is in control of himself, and he feels nothing for her but 'infinite pity'.

Maugham, at this point, when Philip has found emotional freedom, turns his attention to Mildred and reveals in her a slavery to sexual passion far stronger than anything previously seen in the novel. Earlier, when she had left with Griffiths, Philip had been forced to realise the intensity of her physical desires. She appeared to be sexually frigid, yet she twice risked a great deal in order to satisfy her desires.

Now, when Philip takes Mildred back for the second time, his coldness toward her efforts to seduce him frustrate and enrage her. When she suggests that she is willing to sleep with him, he calmly refuses; when they take a holiday at Brighton, he insists on their having separate bedrooms. As well as being sexually frustrated, Mildred is disturbed because her mastery of Philip is gone; she remembers the subservience which marked their previous affairs and is bitterly conscious of his new independence. Finally, in a climactic scene, she forces the issue by using all her charms in an effort to persuade him to make love to her. When this fails, she explodes and directs a torrent of abuse and obscenities at him, culminating in her use of the only effective weapon she has left:

She seized the handle of the door and flung it open. Then she turned round and hurled at him the injury which she knew was the only one that really touched him. She threw into the word all the malice and all the venom of which she was capable. She flung it at him as though it was a blow. "Cripple!"[52]

Mildred is the greater slave to her emotions because, unlike Philip, she does not have the intellectual ability to analyse her situation. Philip, though long unable to assert reason over emotion, is ultimately capable of freeing himself from his obsession. Mildred is never able to, and she remains a prisoner of her narrow mentality.

When Philip encounters Mildred for the last time, it is with no emotion except horror at the venereal disease she has contracted and pity for her predicament. His interest is little more than that of a sociologically minded medical student. He attempts to assist her and prevent her from continuing as a prostitute, but when he fails, and she passes out of his life, he feels no great pain.

To contrast the pettiness, vulgarity and evil of Mildred and many of the other characters Philip encounters in London, Maugham creates the Athelny family, and it is here that he presents many of his positive values. Philip is charmed by the Athelnys, and their influence on his development, spiritually and intellectually, is considerable.

Although he is a somewhat idealised character, Thorpe Athelny is one of the most attractive figures in Maugham's writing. Philip is initially intrigued by him because he is intelligent, witty and well-travelled. When Philip becomes more intimate with him, however, he discovers that he is what no one else that Philip knows has been—a truly free man. Athelny, in his independence of spirit, stands distinctly apart from the rest of the characters in the novel.

Class consciousness and snobbery are prominent in *Of Human Bondage*, and the list of characters whose attitudes and actions are dictated by class awareness is long: the Reverend William Carey and his concern for his position of authority; Hayward and his aesthetic snobbery; the office clerk, Thompson, and his disdain for 'gentlemen'; Mildred with her desire to do what is genteel; and Philip with his own kind of intellectual snobbery and conditioned class consciousness. The narrowness of this concern for position and public respect is, as Brander notes, yet another form of slavery:

Mildred is repulsive, the shop assistants are as bound up in prejudice and formality as a tribe of savages. They are right down on bedrock reality and they survive by escaping into preposterous and pathetic little pretences. Their bondage is not only economic but snobbery and social pretence as well.[53]

Thorpe Athelny is a refreshing change from the multitude of characters whose actions are to a large degree merely reactions based on social conventions and mores. He works in a rather ordinary job as a press representative for a hosiery firm, and he has few pretensions about his importance. When he suffers from jaundice, he enters the hospital as a charity patient, and he does not assume a false sense of humiliation. His plans for the future of his children are modest; he is concerned, not that they occupy a prominent position, but that they will be happy. Because his first wife would not divorce him, he has raised a family of illegitimate children, and he is not ashamed. When he takes his family on a holiday, it is in the form of hop-picking in Kent because this life offers them freedom from the pressures of the city. Athelny is a man who reacts to things naturally, without affectation and without thought of external pressures. Kuner rightly associates him with other literary figures who achieve a measure of freedom:

Athelny, it may be observed, is satisfied because he has followed his own instincts; he is always true to himself and not to the strictures of convention. Though he is pleasant where Strickland (*The Moon and Sixpence*) and Simon (*Christmas Holiday*) are not, he is equally contemptuous of "correct" attitudes. . . . But by his refusal to conform he has fulfilled himself completely; Ernest Pontifex, Stephen Dedalus, Gide's Lafcadio (*Les Caves du Vatican*), Schnitzler's Leonilda (*Der Gang zum Weiher*) all pursue the same vision: self-realization through freedom.[54]

Athelny belongs to that large group of Maugham characters—artists, outcasts, bohemians, rogues, criminals and prostitutes—who are treated sympathetically because they defy convention and social codes. This group includes many of Maugham's most interesting figures—Strickland (*The Moon and Sixpence*), Waddington (*The Painted Veil*), Rosie (*Cakes and Ale*), Captain Nichols and Dr Saunders (*The Narrow Corner*), Larry Darrell and Suzanne Rouvier (*The Razor's Edge*) and Edward Barnard ('The Fall of Edward Barnard'). Athelny, like these characters, is an admirable figure because he ignores social pressures and rules to make his own way in the world.

More than freedom from conventionality and conformity, the Athelny family represents goodness, simple and unqualified. Their interest in Philip is unselfish from the beginning, and he is moved by the ease with which he becomes accepted as a member of the family. When, without money or friends, he is sheltered by them, it is done naturally and without reservation. The influence of their goodness on his philosophy is substantial:

There was one quality which they had that he did not remember to have noticed in people before, and that was goodness. It had not occurred to him till now, but it was evidently the beauty of their goodness which attracted him. In theory he did not believe in it: if morality were no more than a matter of convenience good and evil had no meaning. He did not like to be illogical, but here was simple goodness, natural and without effort, and he thought it beautiful.[55]

An important step in Philip's progress toward independence which is presented in the latter section of the novel concerns the economic factor. Just as Maugham feels that an individual's physical constitution can influence his mental and spiritual outlook, he treats economic deprivation as an external force which can lead to spiritual degradation. When he later discussed Louis Marlow's novel, *Two Made Their Bed*, he approved of such an emphasis on economic matters:

The point is the great, the insinuating, and the overwhelming significance of money in the affairs of life. It is the string with which a sardonic destiny directs the motions of its puppets. It is like the monotonous, enervating, and tremulous music to which, in their coloured and splendid dresses, move the Javanese dancers. With their arms and their long, slim hands they make quick and sudden gestures, as though they sought to escape into freedom, but it is merely the fluttering of leaves on the branches of a tree, and the music, insistent and menacing, chains them to its relentless rhythm.[56]

The part played by money in Maugham's stories is considerable. The decisions of Penelope (*Penelope*) and Constance (*The Constant Wife*) are tempered by economic considerations. In *A Writer's Notebook* and 'A Man With a Conscience', he claims that almost all crimes, including murder, are motivated by the money factor, and in *Of Human Bondage* a casualty ward nurse tells Philip: 'People don't commit suicide for love, as you'd expect, that's just a fancy of novelists; they commit suicide because they haven't got any money.'

The hospital scenes in *Of Human Bondage* illustrate the degree to which the patients there are trapped by lack of money, in some cases condemned to death because they cannot afford a holiday in a warm climate or merely rest from hard labour. Theirs is 'the death which was inevitable because the man was a little wheel in the great machine of a complex civilisation, and had as little power of changing the circumstances as an automaton'.

The importance of economic security to the free man has never been underestimated by Maugham. Whereas other writers might assume that financial hardship and struggle will strengthen and ennoble a person, he has always treated it as a force which can drive a man to humiliation and degradation. As early as 1904, Miss Ley (*The Merry-Go-Round*) says:

"Poverty is a more exacting master than all the conventions of society put together. . . .
"I assure you that no one can be free who isn't delivered from the care of getting money. For myself, I have always thought the philosophers talk sheer silliness when they praise the freedom of a man contented with little; a man with no ear for music will willingly go without his stall at the opera, but an obtuseness of sense is no proof of wisdom. No one can be really free, no one can even begin to get the full value out of life, on a smaller income than five hundred a year."[57]

Although this is a somewhat flippant observation, it represents a deeply felt belief of Maugham—that money is important, not as a value in itself or as a symbol of prestige, but as a means to independence. Not only does it ensure mobility and flexibility of action, it enables the individual to retain his integrity and be free from subservience. In *Up at the Villa* (1941), Maugham tells of a struggling young Austrian who finds that poverty has destroyed the pleasures of youth: 'I live in a prison and there's no escape from it.' This philosophy is presented with greater seriousness and precision in *Of Human Bondage* through the attempts of the Paris art teacher, Foinet, to dissuade Philip from continuing his studies:

"There is nothing so degrading as the constant anxiety about one's means of livelihood. I have nothing but contempt for the people who despise money. They are hypocrites or fools. Money is like a sixth sense without which you cannot make complete use of the other five. Without an adequate income half the possibilities of life are shut off. The only thing to be careful about is that you do not pay more than a shilling for the shilling you earn. You will hear people say that poverty is the best spur to the artist. They have never felt the iron of it in their flesh. They do not know how mean it makes you. It exposes you to endless humiliation, it cuts your wings, it eats into your soul like a cancer. It is not wealth one asks for, but just enough to preserve one's dignity, to work unhampered, to be generous, frank, and independent."[58]

The extent to which economic hardship can force a man into meanness is powerfully illustrated in Philip late in the novel. Although he has calculated that he will just have enough money to last him through his medical studies, he gambles on the stock market in order to earn some extra cash. When the Boer War drags on, however, his stocks fall, and he loses practically all his capital. Having few friends, and prevented by pride from borrowing from these, he soon finds himself bankrupt and homeless. After days of unsuccessful job-hunting and nights spent in the open air, he is taken in by the Athelnys. Having to abandon his medical studies because of his insolvency, he works at the humiliating task of floor-walker at a hosiery store. Although he hates this job, the sight of the many men queuing for employment for only a few shillings frightens him.

Eventually Philip's financial straits create in him the obsessive desire for the death of his uncle. Studying his uncle with a medical student's eye, looking for signs of infirmity, he calculates the old man's age, consults his medical textbooks on chronic bronchitis, and hopes for cold and rainy weather:

His whole desire now was set on his uncle's death. He kept on dreaming the same dream: a telegram was handed to him one morning, early, which announced the Vicar's sudden demise, and freedom was in his grasp. When he awoke and found it was nothing but a dream he was filled with a sombre rage.[59]

Finally, Philip reaches the point where he actually contemplates murder. He considers how easy it would be to give his uncle an over-dose of drugs, and he is prevented only by the thought that he would be forever haunted by remorse. This is the least attractive part of Philip's character, as he is later able to recognise:

> He had heard people speak contemptuously of money: he wondered if they had ever tried to do without it. He knew that the lack made a man petty, mean, grasping; it distorted his character and caused him to view the world from a vulgar angle; when you had to consider every penny, money became of grotesque importance.[60]

It is not until the death of Mr Carey gives Philip economic security that he is free to turn his interests outside himself. The inherited wealth means that he can quit his job at Lynn and Sedley's and resume his medical studies. It means also that he can gain his personal independence and mastery of his own life. What was an inhibition of spiritual freedom and contentment has been removed.

All of these thematic strands—heredity and environment, religious belief, illusion and reality, goodness and evil, passion and economic freedom—are woven into the core of the novel: the evolution within the hero of a philosophy with which he can face life. His reactions to the incidents in his life involving these factors are part of a continuous process and they contribute to the philosophical development. Because Philip is by nature introspective, each episode is carefully analysed and weighed, and then assimilated into his beliefs. Much of the greatness of *Of Human Bondage* lies in the care with which Maugham describes the cumulative events leading to Philip's discovery of the suitable pattern for his life.

One of Philip's greatest forms of bondage is his natural human desire to find meaning in man's existence. This search begins early in the novel and remains an ever-present concern until its resolution near the end. One manifestation of this quest is his repeated impression of the futility and waste of the lives of many people he knows. His aunt lives a life with no significance, faithfully attending an egotistic and selfish husband. Monsieur Ducroz, his French teacher in Heidelberg, seems to have spent his life 'in the pursuit of that which was not worth the finding'. The Spaniard, Miguel Ajuria, is passionately devoted to writing, but his mind is trivial and he sees nothing in the world but the obvious. With much greater force, the futility of life is conveyed to Philip through the suicide of Fanny Price. She has struggled, sacrificed everything for artistic success, and achieved nothing. Having fallen in love with Philip, she cannot even make him aware of her feelings. She dies wretchedly and leaves no impression on the world, just as if she had never existed.

When Cronshaw, who has considerably shaped Philip's impression of the world, dies, the young man sees only the insignificance of his existence:

What troubled him was the absolute futility of the life which had just ended. It did not matter if Cronshaw was alive or dead. It would have been just as well if he had never lived.[61]

Similarly, when Hayward dies in South Africa, Philip is struck by the feeling that his friend has counted for nothing. He had come and gone, without influencing the world at all:

His death had been as futile as his life. He died ingloriously, of a stupid disease, failing once more, even at the end, to accomplish anything. It was just the same now as if he had never lived.[62]

With the recognition that so many lives with which he has had contact have been meaningless and wasted, there is an intense drive within Philip to ensure that his own life has significance. Having lost the pattern of Christian belief dictated from without, he must evolve a more personal pattern from within, and this is the truth which he pursues for most of the novel.

Philip's search for the meaning of existence and the best pattern for his life is inhibited by the determinism which he is repeatedly forced to acknowledge as he looks around him. Over and over again, he strives to find a rational cause for the actions of people, and repeatedly he is struck by their inability to control their lives. The most common image in *Of Human Bondage* is that of the individual acting like a puppet or robot, driven by a force completely divorced from his will.

After the shock of the suicide of Fanny Price, destroyed by a force within her, Philip observes the people at the Bal Bullier seeking pleasure. To him, they seem to be the victims of an uncontrollable influence:

But they danced furiously as though impelled by some strange power within them, and it seemed to Philip that they were driven forward by a rage for enjoyment. . . . They were hurried on by a great wind, helplessly, they knew not why and they knew not whither. Fate seemed to tower above them, and they danced as though everlasting darkness were beneath their feet.[63]

Later, after the death of Cronshaw, Philip considers the life of his friend and concludes that, in spite of his rule of following his instincts with due regard for the policeman around the corner, Cronshaw's existence had no meaning:

Philip was puzzled, and he asked himself what rule of life was there, if that one was useless, and why people acted in one way rather than in another. They acted according to their emotions, but their emotions might be good or bad; it seemed just a chance whether they led to triumph or disaster. Life seemed an inextricable confusion. Men hurried hither and thither, urged by forces they knew not; and the purpose of it all escaped them; they seemed to hurry just for hurrying's sake.[64]

E

When Hayward, long scornful of patriotism and long a man of inaction, joins the army to fight in the Boer War, Philip wonders what kind of power within him is moving him to this inexplicable and uncharacteristic action:

It looked as though men were puppets in the hands of an unknown force, which drove them to do this and that; and sometimes they used their reason to justify their actions; and when this was impossible they did the actions in despite of reason.[65]

Finally, late in the novel, when Philip finds compassion and tolerance, it is through a realisation that people do what they do because they cannot do otherwise. He can forgive Griffiths and Mildred because they are 'the helpless instruments of blind chance' and cannot help themselves.

The question of free will and determinism is essential to Maugham's concept of the free man, and it is an important issue in *Of Human Bondage*. It is, of course, a very complex philosophical problem and one which Maugham has attempted throughout his career to answer satisfactorily. As he later admitted, his conclusion about the possibility of free will can only be tentative. At this stage of his life, in *Of Human Bondage*, it takes the form of a compromise.

The question of free will and determinism first arises in Paris when Philip discusses philosophy with Cronshaw. When he asks the poet whether he has ever regretted any of his actions, Cronshaw replies with a pronouncement which is an acceptance of fatalism, but a kind of fatalism which permits the illusion of free choice:

"The illusion which man has that his will is free is so deeply rooted that I am ready to accept it. I act as though I were a free agent. But when an action is performed it is clear that all the forces of the universe from all eternity conspired to cause it, and nothing I could do could have prevented it. It was inevitable. If it was good I can claim no merit; if it was bad I can accept no censure."[66]

Cronshaw's philosophy is largely Maugham's own, which can be seen by comparing Cronshaw's statements with Maugham's pronouncements in *A Writer's Notebook* and *The Summing Up*. An attempt to discover a working solution to the question of free will, it tries to avoid the tendency of the fatalist to deny responsibility, to take the course of action involving the least resistance or pain, physically or psychologically. It recognises, nevertheless, the magnitude of the forces which act on the individual when he makes his choice, and it admits the difficulty of the decision made in absolute freedom. The credo is tenable because of its acceptance that the belief that the choice is made in freedom may be an illusion, but an illusion which does not inhibit the chooser. Maugham illustrates this point in *The Summing Up* with a metaphor from chess:

The pieces were provided and I had to accept the mode of action that was characteristic of each one; I had to accept the moves of the persons I played with; but it has seemed to me that I had the power to make on my side, in accordance perhaps with my likes and dislikes and the ideal that I set before me, moves that I freely willed. It has seemed to me that I have now and then been able to put forth an effort that was not wholly determined. If it was an illusion it was an illusion that had its own efficacy.[67]

Cronshaw is also a vehicle for Maugham's ideas of the parts played by the state and the individual. Essentially, he sees the state and the free man in opposition to one another and in an unending struggle—the state to impose its will on the individual and the individual to retain his freedom. When Philip returns to England, he considers what he has learned from his experiences in Paris, and the influence of Cronshaw is prominent in his reflections. He conclusions about his position in relation to society and the state are nearly identical to Cronshaw's:

He said to himself that might was right. Society stood on one side, an organism with its own laws of growth and self-preservation, while the individual stood on the other. The actions which were to the advantage of society it termed virtuous and those which were not it called vicious. Good and evil meant nothing more than that. Sin was a prejudice from which the free man should rid himself. Society had three arms in its contest with the individual, laws, public opinion, and conscience: the first two could be met by guile, guile is the only weapon of the weak against the strong: common opinion put the matter well when it stated that sin consisted in being found out; but conscience was the traitor within the gates; it fought in each heart the battle of society, and caused the individual to throw himself, a wanton sacrifice, to the prosperity of his enemy. For it was clear that the two were irreconcilable, the state and the individual conscious of himself. *That* uses the individual for its own ends, trampling upon him if he thwarts it, rewarding him with medals, pensions, honours, when he serves it faithfully; *this*, strong only in his independence, threads his way through the state, for convenience sake, paying in money or service for certain benefits, but with no sense of obligation; and, indifferent to the rewards, asks only to be left alone. He is the independent traveller, who uses Cook's tickets because they save trouble, but looks with good-humoured contempt on the personally conducted parties. The free man can do no wrong. He does everything he likes – if he can. His power is the only measure of his morality. He recognises the laws of the state and he can break them without sense of sin, but if he is punished he accepts the punishment without rancour. Society has the power.[68]

The philosophy of Cronshaw and Philip, and of Maugham himself, owes a great deal to that of Spinoza, and the debt to the philosopher is indicated by the novel's title. Maugham had originally entitled it 'Ashes for Beauty' and then changed it to 'Beauty for Ashes', a phrase taken from Isaiah 61 : 23 :

To appoint unto them that mourn in Zion, to give unto them beauty for ashes, the oil of joy for mourning, the garment of praise for the spirit of heaviness; that they might be called trees of righteousness, the planting of the Lord, that he might be glorified.

There has long been confusion about this original title, and the responsibility for the error must rest with the author himself. In *The Summing Up* Maugham claims that it was 'Beauty from Ashes', and most critics since then have taken him at his word. The title on the manuscript, now in the Library of Congress in Washington, D.C., is nevertheless 'Beauty for Ashes'.

When Maugham discovered that Lady Henry Somerset had used this title in 1913, however, he turned to Spinoza's *Ethics* and borrowed a phrase from the title of the fourth part: 'Of Human Bondage, or the Strength of the Emotions'. His choice of title is appropriate because very much of Philip's story, especially his experiences with Mildred, is a dramatisation of the opening lines of Spinoza's preface:

The impotence of man to govern or restrain the effects I call bondage, for a man who is under their control is not his own master, but is mastered by fortune, in whose power he is, so that he is often forced to follow the worse, although he sees the better before him.[69]

Cronshaw's (and later, Philip's) belief in 'selfishness', that is, 'to follow one's instincts with due regard to the policeman round the corner', and his denial of good and evil, come from the philosopher. Consider the parallel between Maugham's discussion of the state and the individual and Spinoza's proposition that a man who is guided by reason is freer in a state where he lives according to the common laws than he is in solitude, where he obeys himself alone. Spinoza writes:

A man who is guided by reason is not led to obey by fear, but in so far as he endeavours to preserve his being in accordance with the bidding of reason, that is to say, in so far as he endeavours to live in freedom, does he desire to have regard for the common life and the common profit, and consequently he desires to live according to the common laws of the State. A man, therefore, who is guided by reason desires, in order that he may live more freely, to maintain the common rights of the State.[70]

Another important Spinozan concept which Maugham makes an essential part of Philip's developing maturity is the emphasis on acceptance. The free man, for Spinoza, accepts the laws of the state because they ensure self-preservation. More important, acceptance can bring freedom in that it means that the individual can rid himself of enslaving disgusts, jealousies, fears and hatreds. These emotions force the individual into reactions, not positive, freely made choices. By accepting events and the actions of others as part of the course of things, the individual is able to cast off obsessions and hatreds, thus breaking any link with others.

Immediately after his return from Paris, and under the influence of Cronshaw's Spinozan beliefs, Philip formulates a philosophy for living. While this suffices as a set of rules for conduct, it fails to provide him with the answer to the essential question: what is the meaning of life?

The answer to this central question comes to Maugham's protagonist much later—in the hundred and sixth chapter, the climax of the novel. Philip, at this time at the low point in his life when he is working at Lynn and Sedley's, learns that Hayward has been killed in South Africa. Distressed by the news, he goes to the British Museum to seek consolation in its solitude. Here he studies the people and, as in the Bal Bullier, they fill him with disgust; they appear to be weak, stupid, petty and vulgar. Gradually, however, through the art of the ancient Athenian tombstones, he is struck by the tragedy of human suffering. Pity replaces disgust: 'Poor things, poor things.'

Philip considers human life—its suffering, its triviality, its futility—and asks: 'What is the use of it?' There seems to be no logic to the universe; pain, disease and unhappiness overshadow joy, and a happy life appears to be a lucky chance. Then he remembers Cronshaw and his claim that the Persian carpet holds the secret, and, as if he had always known, the answer comes to him: 'The answer was obvious. Life had no meaning.'

Recalling the story of the Eastern king who desired to know the history of man,[71] Philip remembers the answer given to the monarch in a single line:

It was this: he was born, he suffered and he died. There was no meaning in life, and man by living served no end. It was immaterial whether he was born or not born, whether he lived or ceased to live. Life was insignificant and death without consequence.[72]

Philip's realisation of the meaninglessness of human existence is a release, a liberation from the pursuit of the unattainable—a logical and comprehensive design which will account for the state of things. No longer will he need to question cruelty, stupidity, disease, suffering and death; no longer will he need to explain the waste and futility of lives of people such as the Careys, Fanny Price, Miguel Ajuria, Hayward and Cronshaw; no longer will he need to examine the appropriateness of his actions to any eternal plan. Not surprisingly, Philip's revelation comes as a great liberation:

Philip exulted, as he had exulted in his boyhood when the weight of a belief in God was lifted from his shoulders; it seemed to him that the last burden of responsibility was taken from him; and for the first time he was utterly free.[73]

Maugham's recognition of the meaninglessness of human life in any sense beyond the existential has distressed a great many critics. When Philip questions the meaning of life he is expressing the concern of most inquisitive people, and Maugham's answer is uncompromisingly bleak. His logical and scientific outlook forces him to interpret existence to be without metaphysical importance and, however painful, he has come to accept it. Without the capacity for acceptance, however, Maugham's conclusion can be shocking in its pessimism, and many readers recoil from it. To realise that life is insignificant and death without consequence is perhaps the most terrifying vision with which man can be confronted.

For those of religious temperament this interpretation of life is understandably abhorrent. Graham Greene, as might be expected, rejects Maugham's agnosticism because it appears to deny the importance of human activity:

One might trace here the deepest source of his limitations, for creative art seems to remain a function of the religious mind. Mr. Maugham the agnostic is forced to minimise – pain, vice, the importance of his fellow men. He cannot believe in a God who punishes and he cannot therefore believe in the importance of a human action. . . . Rob human beings of their heavenly and their infernal importance, and you rob your characters of their individuality.[74]

Greene's criticism has validity for those who believe in a divinity, but it is a narrow view. Undoubtedly, there is a danger that Maugham's philosophy can lead to irresponsibility of the individual: if there is no eternal importance to one's actions, if good and evil are merely social prejudices, one could act entirely without the discipline of conscience. The good man could therefore be of no greater value than the evil one. Philip, after all, exults in the freedom from the 'burden of responsibility'.

Maugham's seemingly negative interpretation, however, is saved by his emphasis on man's importance to himself and, by implication, to others. The significance of one's actions lies on the humanistic level, and this is no less important than in religious terms. For Maugham, one's conduct is measured, not against dogma, but against its effect on others. Punishment for transgressions will not lead to damnation but it will incur the censure of one's fellows. Thus Maugham merely shifts the element of discipline from the exterior divine source to the interior human one. Philip will not become irresponsible, because he will create his own pattern for living and the significance of his actions will be in relation to this pattern. Moreover, Maugham's claim that each person can make his own life as elaborate and beautiful as a Persian rug gives each character more individuality. His existence is then a manifestation of his personality, rather than a product of a dogmatic belief.

Philip's discovery of man's ability to make his own internal pattern is initiated by his recollection of Cronshaw's Persian rug. Just as the weaver of the rug creates an elaborate and beautiful pattern for no end except his own aesthetic pleasure, man can make his life into a pattern the significance of which is important only to his own sense of satisfaction:

Out of the manifold events of his life, his deeds, his feelings, his thoughts, he might make a design, regular, elaborate, complicated, or beautiful; and though it might be no more than an illusion that he had the power of selection, though it might be no more than a fantastic legerdemain in which appearances were interwoven with moonbeams, that did not matter; it seemed, and so to him it was. In the vast warp of life (a river arising from no spring and flowing endlessly to no sea), with the background to his fancies that there was no meaning and that nothing was important, a man might get a personal satisfaction in selecting the various strands that worked out the pattern. There was one pattern, the most obvious, perfect, and beautiful, in which a man was born, grew to manhood, married, produced children, toiled for his bread and died; but there were others, intricate and wonderful, in which happiness did not enter and in which success was not attempted; and in them might be discovered a more troubling grace.[75]

The acceptance of the meaninglessness of life and the belief in life as a pattern important only to the individual eliminates the necessity of happiness. For Philip, who feels that he has had more suffering than joy, this is the casting off of an illusion. Happiness loses its importance, and is significant, like suffering, only because it is part of the elaborate design of his life. Pain can be tolerated for its contribution to the design, and this Spinozan acceptance means freedom:

Whatever happened to him now would be one more motive to add to the complexity of the pattern, and when the end approached he would rejoice in its completion. It would be a work of art, and it would be none the less beautiful because he alone knew of its existence, and with his death it would at once cease to be.
Philip was happy.[76]

The completion of Philip's philosophical development comes in the penultimate chapter when he is finally able to overcome the obsession about his club-foot. He has previously been able to recognise intellectually that his deformity is a slight disability compared to what others have suffered, but he has never been capable of accepting it emotionally. Now, because he can see that his club-foot is part of the variety of the pattern of his life, he is able almost to welcome it, and with this acceptance of his deformity comes tolerance for those of others and compassion for their suffering:

And thinking over the long pilgrimage of his past he accepted it joyfully. He accepted the deformity which had made life so hard for him; he knew that it had warped his character, but now he saw also that by reason of it he had acquired that power of introspection which had given him so much delight. Without it he would never have had his keen appreciation of beauty, his passion for art and literature, and his interest in the varied spectacle of life. The ridicule and the contempt which had so often been heaped upon him had turned his mind inward and called forth those flowers which he felt would never lose their fragrance. Then he saw that the normal was the rarest thing in the world. Everyone had some defect, of body or of mind: he thought of all the people he had known, (the whole world was like a sick-house, and there was no rhyme or reason in it,) he saw a long procession, deformed in body and warped in mind, some with illness of the flesh, weak hearts or weak lungs, and some with illness of the spirit, languor of will, or a craving for liquor. At this moment he could feel a holy compassion for them all. . . . They could not help themselves. The only reasonable thing was to accept the good of men and be patient with their faults. The words of the dying God crossed his memory:
  Forgive them, for they know not what they do.[77]

The concluding chapters of *Of Human Bondage*, in which Philip abandons his dreams of travel to choose Sally Athelny and the ordinary life of a country doctor, have disturbed many critics. Some argue that the final section is out of tune with the mood of the rest of the novel, and others find it contrived. Maugham himself was aware of the critics' complaints and he provides an interesting explanation of the genesis of Philip's marriage to Sally:

I sought freedom and thought I could find it in marriage. I conceived these notions when I was still at work on *Of Human Bondage*, and turning my wishes into fiction, as writers will, towards the end of it I drew a picture of the marriage I should have liked to make. Readers on the whole have found it the least satisfactory part of my book.[78]

A comment in the manuscript of *The Summing Up*, not included in the published edition, is more specific: 'Women especially have found the girl I there portrayed dull and insipid.'[79]

Opinion about the conclusion to *Of Human Bondage* seems to depend upon the critic's reading of the central theme of the novel. Those who are the most unhappy about Philip's marriage view Maugham's philosophy as pessimistic, morbid and negative. Interpreting the author's vision of life as a gloomy affair, they demand a consistent, and therefore unhappy, ending for the hero.

Surely, however, the ultimate message of *Of Human Bondage* is not pessimistic, morbid or negative. Philip's life, as unhappy and mal-adjusted as it may be, is a progression towards a philosophy which allows him to meet life's disappointments with equanimity. Many critics seem to have fallen into the trap of sharing Maugham's hard, uncompromising portrayal of life but not the redeeming spirit of acceptance. Philip's (and his creator's) conception of life is heavily qualified, but, as Carl and Mark Van Doren point out, it is not depressing:

His conclusion is that life has no meaning which can be set forth in a formula; it is this for one person and that for another, but if one has lived thoroughly one's memories will shape themselves into a pattern as rich though unsymmetrical as those patterns formed by the colours in an oriental rug. It is a wise young man who has learned this at thirty; a generous, intelligent, clear-minded, imaginative, and in no respect morbid human being.[80]

Considering Philip's remarkable philosophical growth, therefore, it should not be surprising that he is able to find a woman with whom he wishes to spend the remainder of his life. The experiences with Miss Wilkinson, Mildred and Norah have taught him a great deal about women and about himself, things which allow him to accept Sally as she is. Sally, after all, is not the perfection of womanhood.

It is an error to describe the marriage of Philip and Sally as 'idyllic' or a perfect relationship. Philip does not, in fact, 'love' Sally (as he has loved Mildred); what he feels toward her is closer to affection or what Maugham calls 'loving-kindness'.

In *The Summing Up*, Maugham distinguishes between two types of love—'love pure and simple, sexual love, namely; and loving-kindness'. Sexual love, he argues, is accompanied by exultation, sense of power and feeling of heightened vitality. The tragedy of it, how-ever, is that it is transitory and very often results in the agony of the situation where there is one who loves and one who lets himself be loved. Sexual love, too, very often means the enslavement of one of the lovers:

The soul of man, struggling to be free, has except for brief moments looked upon the self-surrender that it claims as a fall from grace. The happi-ness it brings may be the greatest of which man is capable, but it is seldom, seldom unalloyed. It writes a story that generally has a sad ending. Many have resented its power and angrily prayed to be delivered from its burden. They have hugged their chains, but knowing they were chains hated them too.[81]

Loving-kindness, on the other hand, does not involve the bondage which is part of sexual passion and it is not as transitory. Closer to affection and friendship, it is more durable. Most important, it is an aspect of goodness:

In loving-kindness the sexual instinct is sublimated, but it lends the emotion something of its own warm and vitalizing energy. Loving-kindness is the better part of goodness. It lends grace to the sterner qualities of which this consists and makes it a little less difficult to practise those minor virtues of self-control and self-restraint, patience, discipline and tolerance, which are the passive and not very exhilarating elements of goodness.[82]

It is clear that, although the sexual element is present, the relationship between Philip and Sally has its basis in 'loving-kindness'. This is not surprising considering that the girl is part of the family which is so strongly characterised by its goodness. Like other Maugham heroines such as Liza, Rosie and Suzanne Rouvier, Sally is warm and maternal, and Philip feels comfortable with her. He is drawn to the idea of marriage to her by thoughts of the pleasures of domesticity— of long evenings together, of shared work, and of children. This may in fact be a form of mature love, but it is not romanticised or idealised; there is no deep spiritual union or boundless passion between them. Maugham, then, does not cheat the reader by contriving the perfect wife for Philip; his hero has achieved a philosophy of modest hopes and Sally seems to fulfil part of them.

The conclusion to *Of Human Bondage* is not false when considered in relation to the central theme of the novel—Philip's search for physical, intellectual and emotional freedom. Maugham creates a situation at the end where his protagonist is faced with a decision which will affect the course of his life, and his choice is made for liberation.

The progression of Philip's life has been a stripping away of many forms of bondage, and he has arrived at the end an almost free man. He has escaped the constraints of environment and of pressures to conform to convention and custom. He has abandoned religious dogma, replacing it with a personal code of ethics. He has found liberation from the desire to find meaning in life and has evolved a philosophy by which he can live. He has freed himself from the warping self-pity about his deformity, and can accept what has been inflicted upon him. Finally, he has escaped from the degrading bondage to a passion which marked the relationship with Mildred.

While Philip is free of his bondage to Mildred, the psychological scars of this affair quite naturally remain with him. On the way to meet Sally to tell her that he wants to marry her, he thinks that he sees Mildred in the street:

Would he never be free from that passion? At the bottom of his heart, notwithstanding everything, he felt that a strange desperate thirst for that vile woman would always linger. That love had caused him so much suffering that he knew he would never, never quite be free of it. Only death could finally assuage his desire.[83]

Maugham here acknowledges that none of the deeply felt experiences of one's formative years are ever entirely forgotten. They may be pushed back in the mind and rendered harmless by rationality, but they are never annihilated. Philip's development has been profoundly affected by his experiences with Mildred and he has been changed by them. Nevertheless, as he has shown in his last encounter with her, he is free from his enslavement.

When Sally informs Philip that she is not pregnant after all, he is faced with the choice between his long-standing dream of travel to exotic foreign countries and his immediate desire for love, a wife and a home. There is, on the one hand, the promise of freedom, mystery and intrigue in travel; on the other, there is the reality of the common, but independent, life of a country doctor. His decision to remain with Sally is a refutation of one of his greatest weaknesses—the tendency to seek an illusion. Instead of being trapped by continuing to seek an imaginary future world, Philip chooses the immediate real one:

What did he care for Spain and its cities, Cordova, Toledo, Leon; what to him were the pagodas of Burmah and the lagoons of South Sea Islands? America was here and now. It seemed to him that all his life he had followed the ideals that other people, by their words or their writings, had instilled into him, and never the desires of his own heart. Always his course had been swayed by what he thought he should do and never by what he wanted with his whole soul to do. He put all that aside now with a gesture of impatience. He had lived always in the future, and the present always, always had slipped through his fingers. His ideals? He thought of his desire to make a design, intricate and beautiful, out of the myriad, meaningless facts of life; had he not seen also that the simplest pattern, that in which a man was born, worked, married, had children, and died, was likewise the most perfect? It might be that to surrender to happiness was to accept defeat, but it was a defeat better than many victories.[84]

By accepting the simplest pattern, Philip achieves the ultimate liberty. Unlike Michael Fane (*Sinister Street*) or Stephen Dedalus (*A Portrait of the Artist as a Young Man*), he chooses an ordinary, unambitious pattern for his life. Freeing himself from his conception of what others would do, he finds liberty in the acceptance of an ordinary life. Those critics who are disturbed because Maugham's protagonist ends with no commitment to a cause or to art overlook his quest throughout the novel—for independence.

The ending of *Of Human Bondage* is significant to the central theme on a more philosophic level. Dean Doner argues that Philip's choice is essential to the author's treatment of Spinoza's concept of free will because it is the first time that Philip is capable of making 'a positive act of will in terms of the entire situation unaffected by prior desire or decision'.[85] His previous choices, according to Doner, have not been made in freedom; they have been influenced by emotions and external pressures. When, for example, Philip gains his 'freedom' in going to Germany, it is not really an act of free will because when he gains his objective he finds that he does not, after all, wish to leave school. Thus his pride forces him to go through with a decision which he now regrets. Similarly, his other choices and actions are dictated by forces which prevent an exercise of free will.

The situation which Maugham contrives in the final chapter, however, is one which allows Philip to make a decision free from inhibitions. When he learns that Sally is pregnant, he must choose between marriage and what appears to be bondage, and Spain and what appears to be freedom. He chooses marriage and 'bondage' in a noble gesture of self-sacrifice and he rationalises this decision by considering the pleasures of domesticity. When, however, he discovers that Sally is not pregnant after all, he is in the position to make a positive act of free will. Since he has discovered that he is willing to abandon his dreams of travel, he is free from bondage to his romantic illusion of foreign exploration and the urge to do what he thinks a young man in his position should. Now that he knows that Sally is not pregnant, there is no need to marry her out of obedience to honour and convention; if he chooses her, it will be from a positive desire, not from a negative act of conscience. Thus Maugham has created what Doner calls the perfect Spinozan situation, and Philip makes a free choice.

Of Human Bondage is Maugham's greatest achievement. It may lack the technical skills and warmth of *Cakes and Ale* or the perfection of many of his short stories, but it is his most serious and complete attempt to deal with the basic questions of human existence. With meticulous care he examines the influences on man of heredity, environment and loss of traditional faiths. He discusses the important question of man's relation to society, and he explores the enigma of the meaning of existence. Finally, he demonstrates the importance to man of truth, beauty and goodness.

What makes *Of Human Bondage* one of the greatest English novels is its credibility. While many other novels of adolescence explore fascinating and complex situations, none is as honest and believable. This particular quality in *Of Human Bondage* is a result of the author's determination to examine his youth with the same scrupulous critical attitude with which he views others. Thus Philip is as severe a self-portrait as can be found in autobiographical fiction. Maugham does not hesitate to reveal his conceit, snobbery, inferiority complex, self-pity, masochism and emotional vulnerability. Many authors have portrayed themselves as weak, but few have been willing to show themselves as being foolish.

The unflinching honesty and self-exposure of Maugham's portrait of Philip is the source of the novel's greatness, and it is this quality which is noticeably lacking in much of his other fiction. The effect is that, although Philip is far from being a universal figure, every reader can see reflected in him a number of his own youthful problems. There are few intelligent and sensitive readers who cannot sympathise with the agony of his struggle to achieve maturity and independence.

Of Human Bondage is Maugham's most complete statement of the importance of physical and spiritual liberty, and in his exploration of this theme he is treating one of the most important issues of twentieth-century life. From the latter part of the nineteenth century onwards, man's progress has been toward more and more essential freedoms. Economically, socially, morally, intellectually and spiritually, there has been a period of great liberation. *Of Human Bondage* reflects its age in treating the effects of these developments on man. Unlike previous youthful heroes such as Tom Jones and David Copperfield, Philip is confronted with many new freedoms, and Maugham's achievement is to show that each one carries with it a corresponding obligation on the individual. Whereas the former protagonists could be confident of certain basic assumptions, Philip, the hero of a new age, must find his own truth. He is in an era of agnosticism and, while this represents intellectual freedom, it also demands that he seek his own vision of man's existence. Similarly, morality has become complex and ambiguous, and Philip must therefore establish his own set of values. In these, and in many other, ways, *Of Human Bondage* attempts to grapple with man's new freedom in the twentieth century.

Maugham, unfortunately, never again reached the heights which he had in this autobiographical novel. Summing up *Of Human Bondage*, Kuner writes that '*Of Human Bondage* is not the beginning, but the end, of Maugham's credo; having said whatever he had to say as simply, as completely, as perfectly as possible, there remained to him either the choice of deepening understanding or of eventual retreat.'[86]

This observation explains a great deal about the disappointment which critics have felt with Maugham's subsequent writing. In no other work does he treat serious themes with such depth and directness. The problem, however, is not so much one of subjects treated as one of the author's attitude or point of view.

The point reached by the autobiographical Philip at the end of the novel is one of emotional balance and detachment. He has been through a great deal of frustration and suffering and has finally achieved independence. Faced with the choice between further exploration and discovery in travel and new experience or contented equilibrium with Sally, he chooses the latter. This decision reflects Maugham's own attitude by the time he had completed *Of Human Bondage*, and his subsequent works are written from a point of view similar to Philip's. The narrator of *The Moon and Sixpence, Cakes and Ale, The Razor's Edge* and many of the short stories is essentially like Philip—interested in observing and recording life, but wary of becoming deeply involved. Therefore the agonies of Strickland, Driffield or Larry Darrell are never revealed with the sincerity and directness of Philip's story. After *Of Human Bondage* Maugham is, as Kuner says, in retreat, and with the exception of some parts of *Cakes and Ale* he never again exposes much of his real self.

V

The Moon and Sixpence and the Artist-Hero Novels

THE GENESIS OF Maugham's next novel, *The Moon and Sixpence*, published in 1919, can be traced back fifteen years earlier to the young writer's days in Paris in that fascinating circle of artists—which included, among others, Gerald Kelly, Clive Bell, Arnold Bennett, Aleister Crowley, Roderic O'Conor, James Wilson Morrice, Paul Bartlett and Penrhyn Stanlaws—who gathered at 'Le Chat Blanc'. This coterie was to provide Maugham with material for *The Magician* (in which Crowley became 'Oliver Haddo', Bartlett became 'Clayson', Morrice became 'Warren' and O'Conor became 'O'Brien') and *Of Human Bondage* (in which Morrice appears as 'Cronshaw', Kelly as 'Lawson', Stanlaws as 'Flanagan' and O'Conor as 'Clutton'), and one member, Roderic O'Conor, contributed to his interest in Paul Gauguin, then known in the art world but not by the general public.

O'Conor, an Irish painter, had encountered Gauguin in Brittany in 1894, after the painter's first voyage to Tahiti, and he became a disciple. At one point, O'Conor had even intended to accompany the master in his return to the South Seas and, although he eventually decided against this, he became an exponent of the artistic and antisocial philosophy of Gauguin. The theorist of 'Le Chat Blanc', he knew more about Gauguin than anybody else in the group, and he was not inclined to hide his opinions.

Maugham was anxious to learn as much as he could about the intriguing Gauguin, but he found O'Conor a belligerent and unco-operative source of information:

The most interesting person in this little group was an Irishman, sullen and bad-tempered, called Roderick O'Conor. He had spent some months in Brittany with Gauguin, painting, and I, already greatly interested in that mysterious, talented man, would have liked to learn from O'Conor what he could tell me about him; but unfortunately he took an immediate dislike to me which he did not hesitate to show. My very presence at the dinner table irritated him and I only had to make a remark for him to attack it.[1]

It is nevertheless clear that, in spite of this antagonism, the young writer learned some of the Gauguin story from O'Conor. In *Of Human Bondage* Clutton, a young painter clearly modelled after O'Conor, tells of finding in Brittany 'a painter whom nobody else had heard of, a queer fellow who had been a stockbroker and taken up painting at middle-age'. Later, in discussing the position of the artist and morality, he describes this stockbroker-painter's rebellion— —his abandonment of income, family and home to go to Tahiti. His brief account of the painter's career is virtually a summary of the plot and theme of *The Moon and Sixpence*.

Although this interest in the Gauguin legend was strong in Maugham as early as 1904, it is perhaps significant that he did not use this material until 1919. The story lay dormant during the interval, while the author turned first to writing for the stage and then to a catharsis in the form of *Of Human Bondage*. During the First World War, however, he visited Tahiti, searched out anyone who had known Gauguin, and even returned with a Gauguin painting on glass. After a mission to Petrograd for the British Secret Service, Maugham was sent to a sanatorium in Scotland to recover from tuberculosis, and in a three-month period at an English seaside resort he wrote *The Moon and Sixpence*.

This new novel was very well received; critics gave the praise they had withheld from *Of Human Bondage*, and the general reading public found it appealing. After having set the Gauguin material aside for fifteen years, Maugham had produced a novel which, in subject and mood, struck a responsive note with the age. The reasons for this timeliness are both public and personal.

The Moon and Sixpence appealed primarily because it was an excellent example in a genre which had become prominent in the early twentieth century—the *Kunstlerroman*, or artist-hero novel. Van Wyck Brooks, looking back to the early decades of this century, writes:

The artist, one might almost say, is the typical hero in contemporary fiction. From *Jean-Christophe* to *Mendel*, from *The Flame of Life* to *The Moon and Sixpence*, and how much further, as one glances over the list of significant novels of the last two decades, one is surprised to find how often the leading character is a painter, a musician or a writer. The artist has always appeared as a character in fiction, but never before, surely, has he so filled the novelist's stage.[2]

Although representations of artists in fiction can be found in earlier novels—for example, Charles Kingsley's *Alton Locke* (1850),

Thackeray's *The Newcomes* (1853) and Dickens's *David Copperfield* (1850)—it was not until the late nineteenth century that the figure of the artist appeared with any frequency, and even then the treatment of the artist-hero tended to be sketchy and stereotyped. Writing in 1894, Katharine de Mattos complained of the unimaginative and shallow portrayals of artists in the literature of her time:

The common method is to huddle together a few of the novelist's "properties", bind them round with certain tricks of speech and manner, push the scarecrow about a bit, and label it a "painter". So long as there are plenty of pipes and pewters, incident and character will matter little.[3]

The artist figures of nineteenth-century fiction tend to fall easily into distinguishable stereotypes—gay bohemians, dilettantes, aesthetes or intellectuals. They are, furthermore, on the whole socially minded characters, with relatively conventional moral outlooks beneath the veneer. Finally, the majority of artist novels of this period deal with the life of the artist rather than with the practice of art, and there is little emphasis on the bearing that one has on the other.

At the turn of the century, however, the artist novel underwent a transformation and there began a period in which the output of this type of novel was immense. Studies of the artist in this era include: Gissing's *The Private Papers of Henry Ryecroft* (1903), Hardy's *The Well-Beloved* (1903), Jack London's *Martin Eden* (1909), Richardson's *Maurice Guest* (1910), Stephen French Whitman's *Predestined* (1910), Mary Austin's *A Woman of Genius* (1912), Lawrence's *Sons and Lovers* (1913), Shaw's *The Doctor's Dilemma* (1913) and *Love Among the Artists* (1914), Frank Norris's *Vandover and the Brute* (1914), Willa Cather's *The Song of the Lark* (1915), Theodore Dreiser's *The Genius* (1915), May Sinclair's *Tasker Jevons* (1916), Joyce's *A Portrait of the Artist as a Young Man* (1916), Gilbert Cannan's *Mendel: A Story of Youth* (1916) and Wyndham Lewis's *Tarr* (1918).

In most of these novels, the artist figure becomes more isolated than his predecessors, and his sensitivity, introspection and artistic temperament demand that he break loose from society. In place of the conventional and relatively harmless bohemianism of the nineteenth-century fictional artists, the new figures rebel in a genuine fashion:

Lacking any defined function within the social framework, the artist feels himself an outcast. The isolation which is an essential part of his work he cultivates by retreating from all public concerns. No longer does he feel that it is encumbent upon him to represent the "collected ideology" of his community. Didacticism in art is supplanted by self-expression and the individual sensibility becomes paramount.[4]

This increase in the social alienation of artists in fiction arose in connection with the development of realism in English literature. It also parallels an attempt by some, but not all, authors to go beyond simply chronicling the artist's life to demonstrating the artistic process and the effect this has on the artist's life. The best example of this type is probably Joyce's *A Portrait of the Artist as a Young Man.*

When examined against the progress of the artist novel, *The Moon and Sixpence* clearly shows the influence of that development. As could be expected from Maugham's early exposure to realism, his novel is one of the best examples of the realistic treatment of the artist. In addition, Strickland shares with so many artist-heroes of his time a revolt against society, duty, convention and anything which constitutes a form of restraint. Finally, although Maugham fails to illuminate the artistic process within his hero in any depth, he is typical of a number of twentieth-century writers in attempting to explain the artistic temperament through his descriptions of the paintings of Strickland.

As well as drawing upon the popularity of the artist novel, *The Moon and Sixpence* benefited from a widespread interest in artists in general—particularly the myth of the genius or superman inspired by Nietzsche at the turn of the century. This concern for the man of genius, together with a fascination for the generation of anti-social artists which came to prominence at the turn of the century, developed near the end of the First World War. People looked back to Verlaine, Van Gogh, Rimbaud and Gauguin, fascinated by their extreme rejection of convention and orthodox social attitudes.

The interest in these artists—in their individuality, creativity and rebellion—was a form of romanticism engendered by the disillusionment of the First World War and by the feeling that increased mechanisation and industrialisation were destroying these instinctual qualities. David Paul describes this phenomenon:

The artist-outcast is a figure of the romantic myths which arose after the advent of industrialism, and because of it. Industrialisation imposes a routine, not based on tradition or any system of beliefs, but simply of the motives of the machine – the saving of time, the non-creative multiplication of production, speed, money. The process of production becomes so sectionalised that all creative sense is lost.[5]

This concern about the destruction of human instincts and natural emotions, a manifestation of which was the philosophy advanced by writers such as D. H. Lawrence, led to the reverence for the genius-artist as a figure who could preserve his essential humanity by denying society and conventional goals. Van Wyck Brooks explains:

Thanks to the universal blocking and checking of instinct that modern industrialism implies for the run of men and even women, the type of life that still, at whatever cost, affords scope for the creative impulses is haloed with an immense desirability. In our age in which everything tends towards a regimentation of character, the average man, presented with no ideal but that of success, finds himself almost obliged to yield up one by one the attributes of a generous humanity. No wonder the artist has come to be the lodestone of so many wishes. He alone seems able to keep open the human right of way, to test and explore the possibilities of life.[6]

It is likely that Maugham was aware of the widespread interest in the artist-hero when he wrote *The Moon and Sixpence*, and it is certain that the artist was a figure who held a great fascination for him. Like the rogue, the criminal and the whore, the artist was attractive because he could be free:

The artist can within certain limits make what he likes of his life. In other callings, in medicine for instance or the law, you are free to choose whether you will adopt them or not, but having chosen, you are free no longer. You are bound by the rules of your profession; a standard of conduct is imposed on you. The pattern is predetermined. It is only the artist, and maybe the criminal, who can make his own.[7]

The Moon and Sixpence was the first of a long line of Maugham studies of the South Seas and the Far East, and, together with *The Trembling of a Leaf* (1921), *On a Chinese Screen* (1922), *The Painted Veil* (1925) and *The Casuarina Tree* (1926), it provided something else that post-war readers longed for—escape. Weary of a bitter war and disillusioned with European civilisation and its problems, people turned for relief to the literature of exotic and unspoiled distant lands. Maugham, having had the misfortune of bringing out *Of Human Bondage* when a world war absorbed the public attention, became the writer with the material appropriate to the mood of the nineteen-twenties.

In this period of his life, Maugham underwent a disenchantment with his own manner of living which paralleled the public cynicism and disillusionment of the 'twenties. After his great success as a dramatist and following years of London parties and literary luncheons, he seems to have become bored with the type of literary life he satirises in *The Moon and Sixpence* and *Cakes and Ale* and tired of the pressures of the role he was supposed to play. Frank Swinnerton claims that this ennui initiated a new period of Maugham's career:

The abandonment of conventionality, or the desire to become what, quoting Hazlitt, he called "the gentleman in the parlour," an anonymous loser of "importunate, tormenting, everlasting personal identity," seemed to offer fascinating new experience. The result of that interest in Gauguin's escape, and the wish to "become the creature of the moment, clear of all ties," was a new birth for Mr. Maugham. Its first literary product was *The Moon and Sixpence*.[8]

Maugham sought freedom, variety and excitement in travel to foreign ports, and his own wish for a pattern of escape matched that of a great many people exhausted, embittered and disenchanted by years of war:

Where Kipling had presented the British Empire in terms of the "White Man's Burden", Maugham presented it as a means of cutting free from the Western "ratrace", from the profitless amassing of possessions that moth and dust were waiting to corrupt. *The Moon and Sixpence, The Casuarina Tree* and "The Fall of Edward Barnard" coloured the outlook of the disillusioned 1920's just as *Ann Veronica* and *Man and Superman* had fired the optimism of the last Edwardians. Maugham was the mouthpiece of that decade.[9]

Although it has been clearly established that *The Moon and Sixpence* was suggested by the Gauguin legend, it would be a serious mistake to treat it as a biography or even a biographical novel. There are, it is true, a number of similarities between the story of Strickland and that of Gauguin: both are stockbrokers who quit their jobs to begin a career of painting; both are unsociable and amoral; both have certain marked physical characteristics; and both find a type of contentment with a native girl before dying a premature death in Tahiti. In addition, Maugham's description of Strickland's style of painting is virtually a verbal representation of Gauguin's art. Finally, both Gauguin and Strickland paint a monumental masterpiece just before their deaths.

Counterbalancing these parallels, however, there are a large number of dissimilarities. Gauguin had painted industriously in his spare time for ten years before losing his job as stockbroker, while Strickland develops his interest in art very suddenly. Gauguin was concerned about his wife and children, and hoped to achieve things for them through his art, even planning that they would eventually join him in Tahiti; Strickland, however, feels nothing for his family. Gauguin continually analysed and discussed his painting, while Strickland is almost inarticulate and unconcerned about artistic theory. Thus, in describing his mother's reaction to Maugham's creation, Pola Gauguin wrote that 'in Somerset Maugham's novel *The Moon and Sixpence* she did not find a single trait of Strickland which had anything in common with her husband'.[10]

What seems to have happened is that Maugham used the basic Gauguin situation and the bits of gossip (with their characteristic aberration) that he accumulated in Paris and Tahiti, and then constructed his novel around these, filling out the picture with imaginative hypotheses about the painter. In *The Razor's Edge* he explained that 'I took a famous painter, Paul Gauguin, and, using the novelist's privilege, devised a number of incidents to illustrate the character I had created on the suggestions afforded me by the scanty facts I knew about the French artist.' Much of the disparity between fact and fiction developed because what Maugham learned of Gauguin were largely the myths which had developed about him—his instantaneous conversion to art, his abandonment of family, his ruthlessness, his idyllic life in Tahiti and his death from leprosy. The misconception that the painter died from leprosy was current for many years and *The Moon and Sixpence* in fact helped to perpetuate the myth. Around these details, Maugham created his portrait of the artist and attempted to illuminate a temperament, and it really is in the area of temperament that his novel has its greatest validity with regard to Gauguin and his contemporaries.

The Moon and Sixpence is written in the first person singular, the first time that Maugham had used this device since *The Making of a Saint* in 1898. The narrator in this case, however, is not the well-developed 'Ashenden' *persona* of *Ashenden*, or the narrator of *Cakes and Ale*, *The Razor's Edge* and the short stories. Whereas the latter is witty, tolerant, and amused by the behaviour of his fellows, the former is youthfully priggish, rather stiff and self-conscious. The ease and mellowness of the later *persona* are not present in *The Moon and Sixpence*.

Maugham seems to identify, not with the narrator of the story, but with Strickland. He once stated that 'I had a lot of sympathy for Gauguin long before I even started work on *The Moon and Sixpence*',[11] and a number of critics have suggested that there is more of the author in the character of Strickland than is commonly recognised. It may be that Strickland is in many ways what Maugham would have liked to have been; in any case, part of the author is undoubtedly represented in the rebel painter:

It may be that in his rogues the writer gratifies instincts deep-rooted in him, which the manners and customs of a civilised world have forced back into the mysterious recesses of the subconscious. In giving the character of his invention flesh and bones he is giving life to that part of himself which finds no other means of expression. His satisfaction is a sense of liberation.[12]

The Moon and Sixpence, then, may have been almost as much a form of catharsis for Maugham as was *Of Human Bondage*. It is quite likely that in Strickland he portrayed the kind of social and artistic rebellion which he would have liked to commit but from which he was inhibited by nature and position. Strickland is in many ways a figure of the id, a projection of that part of the writer which was well hidden by his mask. He has no conscience, no self-discipline, and no recognition that anything is important except his own creativity. The impression of Strickland as a manifestation of the subconscious is encouraged by the emphasis on the image of him as a satyr. Repeatedly, he is presented as brutal, savage and lustful. In this, his character is neatly balanced by that of the narrator, and they represent two poles of the author's personality. The painter is that part of Maugham which would like to ignore society, convention and critical opinion, to find his own idyllic garden where he can achieve artistic liberation. The narrator, on the other hand, represents the part of the author which feels constrained to follow the safer path of moderation and compromise with the dictates of civilisation. The result is that, in many parts, the dialogue between the two sounds very much like a dialogue within the author himself.

The Moon and Sixpence is an examination of freedom in the form of an artist's search for liberty, and the simplest of his bondages—social pressures and conventional ties—are treated at the beginning. In the first chapter, following the technique of Defoe in *Robinson Crusoe* and Swift in *Gulliver's Travels*, Maugham constructs with great detail a picture of the various solid, pedantic studies of the painter, Charles Strickland. With mock gravity he analyses the range of monographs—the discovering critical article, the following book of 'notes', the family apologia and the inevitable caustic realistic dissection. This is established before the story begins, partly to create the impression of verisimilitude, and the novel ends with a return to this atmosphere. The implication, after the reader has known Strickland, is that a vital, powerful and individualistic personality has been encased in academic cement.

The next seven chapters are a brilliant satiric representation of the Edwardian social and literary scene. In a foretaste of what was to come in *Cakes and Ale*, Maugham paints a delicious picture of literary luncheons, lionising society hostesses and commercially oriented authors. In Rose Waterford, Richard Twining, George Road and others, those who knew this period can identify prominent figures. Violet Hunt is supposed to be the original of Rose Waterford and George Street of George Road. In addition, Mrs Strickland bears a considerable resemblance to the prominent social hostess of the time, Lady (Sibyl) Colefax.

With even greater emphasis, Maugham establishes a picture of a dull, pretentious and stifling social scene. Concentrating on the Strickland family, he presents a view of mediocrity and oppressive conformity. Their dining-room, like five hundred others decorated in the same 'good taste of the period', is 'chaste, artistic and dull'. The children are 'clean, healthy and normal', with a father apparently so dull that Mrs Strickland is reluctant to subject the guests at her many dinner parties to his company.[13] These occasions, says Maugham, are attended with indifference and left with relief. The Stricklands are, all in all, well-integrated and normal specimens of their particular class and range:

There was just that shadowiness about them which you find in people whose lives are part of the social organism, so that they exist in it and by it only. They are like cells in the body, essential, but, so long as they remain healthy, engulfed in the momentous whole. The Stricklands were an average family in the middle class. . . . Nothing could be more ordinary.[14]

The purpose of the London social scenes is to create a picture of conventional and mediocre existence which will be contrasted vividly with the vitality and excitement of Strickland's life in Paris and the meaningfulness of his final years in Tahiti. It is not an auto-biographical digression, nor is it a pointless section which is out of tune with the remainder of the novel. It has, like the early social scenes in *Christmas Holiday*, a specific thematic purpose, and Maugham returns to London in the final chapter to reinforce the impression of the life which the painter has escaped.

In his flight from the social milieu and his subsequent refusal to recognise any obligation or duty toward his family, Strickland is typical of twentieth-century artist-heroes. Analysing the artistic achievements of the figures in Joyce's *A Portrait of the Artist as a Young Man* and Proust's *A la Recherche du Temps Perdu*, Maurice Beebe writes:

In both instances, as in many others, the hero attains this state only after he has sloughed off the domestic, social, and religious demands imposed upon him by his environment. Narrative development in the typical artist-novel requires that the hero test and reject the claims of love and life, of God, home and country, until nothing is left but his true self and his consecration as artist. Quest for self is the dominant theme of the artist-novel, and because the self is almost always in conflict with society, a closely related theme is the opposition of art to life. The artist-as-hero is usually therefore the artist-as-exile.[15]

Maugham uses the early Paris chapters of *The Moon and Sixpence* to illustrate the depth of Strickland's denial of family, duty, honour and convention. The narrator, at this point the representative of society and conventional morality, discovers that Strickland genuinely wishes to forget all ties with his former life. He lives a bohemian existence, but even in this there is a detachment; he is as unconcerned with the rules of this life as he is with those he has rejected. Apart from any effect they may have on his art, environment and material comforts mean nothing to him, and fame and recognition have no attraction.

In his rejection of society and convention, Strickland is not very different from many Maugham characters. He is unusual, however, in his total escape from the powerful inward restraint of a conditioned social conscience. When he attempts to appeal to the man's sense of morality, the narrator discovers that this has absolutely no effect:

You might as well ask for a reflection without a mirror. I take it that conscience is the guardian in the individual of the rules which the community has evolved for its own preservation. It is the policeman in all our hearts, set there to watch that we do not break its laws. It is the spy seated in the central stronghold of the ego. Man's desire for the approval of his fellows is so strong, his dread of their censure so violent, that he himself has brought his enemy within his gates; and it keeps watch over him, vigilant always in the interests of its master to crush any half-formed desire to break away from the herd. It will force him to place the good of society before his own. It is the very strong link that attaches the individual to the whole.[16]

Strickland, however, does not possess a conscience, and therefore he is not undermined from within to follow the collective dictates of his fellows. It gives him a liberty that few achieve:

But here was a man who sincerely did not mind what people thought of him, and so convention had no hold on him; he was like a wrestler whose body is oiled; you could not get a grip on him; it gave him a freedom which was an outrage.[17]

Outraged the narrator may be, but there is also obvious admiration.

In the central section of *The Moon and Sixpence* Maugham concentrates on the problem of the artist and morality, and, through the story of Strickland's relations with Dirk and Blanche Stroeve, stretches the problem to its limits. Critics have been distressed by the attention paid to the Stroeves, which occupies almost half of the novel, but it is an essential part of the author's study of the artist.

The question that Maugham poses in this section is that raised by Shaw in *The Doctor's Dilemma*: how much should society tolerate from the anti-social artist in order to benefit from great art? In Shaw's play, the doctor's dilemma is that he must choose to save the life of only one man—a good, but useless, colleague or an unscrupulous, degenerate, but gifted, artist. Through Dr Blenkinsop and Louis Dubedat, Shaw forces the reader to choose the man or the art.

With Dirk Stroeve and Charles Strickland, Maugham presents a similar problem, but he treats it in greater depth and makes the contrast between the two men even greater. Dr Blenkinsop is a minor figure whose goodness is conveyed by reports and conversations. Dirk Stroeve is a well-developed character, and his kindness, generosity and warmth are well-established. Louis Dubedat is unscrupulous, but merely a cheap swindler and social misfit; Strickland is completely amoral and entirely unconcerned as he ruins Stroeve's life and drives Blanche to suicide.

Strickland's actions, on the surface, are cruel, savage and indefensible. His conduct, nevertheless, is given a good deal of justification, and the vehicle for this defence is Stroeve himself. After Blanche's death, Dirk returns to their apartment and discovers a nude portrait that Strickland had painted of her. After an initial impulse to destroy it, he realises that it is a great work of art:

Stroeve tried to talk to me about the picture, but he was incoherent, and I had to guess at what he meant. Strickland had burst the bonds that hitherto had held him. He had found, not himself, as the phrase goes, but a new soul with unsuspected powers.[18]

Thus the suffering of Blanche and the torture of Dirk have led to Strickland's reaching creative heights, and the result is a great work of art. To achieve this end, he has sacrificed not only himself, but also two other people. When the narrator confronts him with his callousness, Strickland asks: 'Do you really care a twopenny damn if Blanche Stroeve is alive or dead?' The narrator, honestly considering the point, is forced to admit to a view that reflects the philosophy of *Of Human Bondage*:

The cruellest thing of all was that in fact it made no great difference. The world went on, and no one was a penny the worse for all that wretchedness . . . and Blanche's life, begun with who knows what bright hopes and what dreams, might just as well have never been lived. It all seemed useless and inane.[19]

The implication of this is that, although the lives of Dirk and Blanche have been futile in themselves, the great art that has come out of their suffering has made it worthwhile. Given the choice between the happiness of a good, but ordinary, man and woman, and the creation of a masterpiece at their sacrifice, Maugham appears to prefer the painting. His argument seems to be that, while the Stroeves live useless and mediocre lives, Strickland, for all his ruthlessness, is able to produce something which transcends his physical existence.

Maugham, of course, oversimplifies the basic dilemma in order to heighten the dramatic effect. A good and generous person is not necessarily a foolish and absurd figure, and a talented artist does not necessarily have to sacrifice his fellows for the sake of his art. It could be argued, furthermore, that as many monumental works of art have grown out of compassion and generosity as out of egotism and selfishness. The choice between life and art as Maugham presents it must ultimately be subjective, and a good argument could be made for the world being better for the presence of Dirk Stroeves rather than Charles Stricklands.

Another important theme which runs through *The Moon and Sixpence* is the relationship between the artistic temperament and love and sex. Strickland is involved with three women in the course of his career and, according to Maxwell Anderson, 'Mrs Strickland and Blanche Stroeve and Ata, the native girl, make up a trio from which we can derive a whole conception of womanhood.'[20] In these female characters and Strickland's reactions to them, the writer expresses a great many of his attitudes toward women.

Mrs Strickland is the socially conscious and convention-bound woman who rarely escapes hard treatment at Maugham's hands. Like the second Mrs Driffield (*Cakes and Ale*), Isabel Longstaffe ('The Fall of Edward Barnard') and Isabel Bradley (*The Razor's Edge*), she represents a threat to the man who desires to preserve his freedom. Charming, intelligent and witty, she is not the kind of woman who tortures her husband by nagging or haranguing. The danger, rather, is that through her he can be assimilated into the mainstream and trapped into a social posture which smothers his individuality.

Blanche Stroeve is an example of the instinctive woman, whose passions are beyond her control and who attempts to bind her men to her through sexual attraction. Like Liza, Kitty (*The Painted Veil*), Rosie (*Cakes and Ale*), Lydia (*Christmas Holiday*) and Suzanne Rouvier (*The Razor's Edge*), she is sensual and emotional, and this often leads to tragedy. Although Blanche is the catalyst which brings about a flowering of Strickland's genius, she is a constant threat to his art.

In his treatment of sex and the artist, Maugham adheres to the widespread tradition in artist novels that a woman can inhibit and destroy the artist. Throughout Strickland's development as a painter, sexual passion and love represent a form of bondage from which, for the sake of his painting, he must remain free. For him, life is not long enough for both love and art:

"I don't want love. I haven't time for it. It's weakness. I am a man, and sometimes I want a woman. When I've satisfied my passion I'm ready for other things. I can't overcome my desire, but I hate it; it imprisons my spirit; I look forward to the time when I shall be free from all desire and can give myself without hindrance to my work."[21]

Strickland is nevertheless attracted to Blanche Stroeve and he takes her. In spite of his hatred of 'the instincts that robbed him of his self-possession', he satisfies his sexual appetites in a brief period with her. Soon, however, she begins to demand a response greater than merely physical advances, and Strickland recognises a danger to his liberty and his art:

"When a woman loves you she's not satisfied until she possesses your soul. Because she's weak she has a rage for domination, and nothing less will satisfy her. . . . The soul of man wanders through the uttermost regions of the universe, and she seeks to imprison it in the circle of her account-book. Do you remember my wife? I saw Blanche little by little trying all her tricks. With infinite patience she prepared to snare me and bind me. She wanted to bring me down to her level; she cared nothing for me, she only wanted me to be hers. She was willing to do everything in the world for me except the one thing I wanted: to leave me alone."[22]

Maugham's argument is essentially that a commitment to a loved one and a commitment to art are incompatible and mutually destructive. The creative man, he writes, can compartmentalise his life, pursuing artistic expression at one time and sexual satisfaction at another. Women, however, resent this dichotomy, and their attempts to invade the man's creative world inhibit and destroy his art.

Maugham's conception of the ideal relationship between love and art is presented in his fairy tale, 'Princess September and the Nightingale', written in 1922. In this story, the princess is befriended by a nightingale which comes to sing for her each day. When her jealous sisters suggest that the bird might leave her someday, she is persuaded to put him in a golden cage. Now, however, the nightingale cannot sing; denied the freedom to fly outdoors and gather inspiration from the outside world, his artistic sense is inhibited. When the princess protests that she loves him and will take him out every day, he replies that it is not the same thing, that the rice fields and the lake and the willow trees look quite different when you see them through the bars of a cage. When the nightingale claims that 'I cannot sing unless I'm free, and if I cannot sing I die', the princess reluctantly gives him his liberty. The story ends with the nightingale free to come and go, returning to sing for the princess when he is so inclined. With no restraints, his artistic temperament thrives.

This idea is reiterated in a letter which, late in his life, Maugham claimed to have written to his wife. In it he argues that she is not compatible with his career as a writer because her presence is a hindrance to the impressions he receives as he examines the world around him. She comes between the world and his artist's sensitive perception of it. His solution to the problem is a demand for the nightingale's freedom.[23]

In *The Moon and Sixpence*, the representative of the type of woman ideal for the artist is the native girl, Ata. Like Sally, Rosie and Suzanne Rouvier, Ata is warm, generous and open. She is both sensual and maternal, but above all she makes few demands of Strickland. Life with her means no deep commitment or spiritual involvement on the part of the man. Asked if he is happy with Ata, Strickland replies: 'She leaves me alone . . . She cooks my food and looks after her babies. She does what I tell her. She gives me what I want from a woman.'

Maugham's analysis of the relationship between art and sex or love has a validity, but only in a limited sense. There can be no disputing that domestic ties, physical and spiritual, can inhibit the artistic temperament, and there is enough authoritative psychological opinion to defend the idea that artistic creativity is the result of the sublimation of the sexual drive. Is it possible, nevertheless, for a man so to compartmentalise his life that he can recognise no connection between living and creating? Moreover, what of the many artists who have not only been sustained by love, but have been inspired to create a work of art out of their experiences or emotions regarding a woman? Indeed, Maugham seems to have included his own contradiction in *The Moon and Sixpence* in that Strickland really finds himself as a painter through his passion for Blanche Stroeve.

In his efforts to free himself from many restrictions—social, familial, physical, sexual and spiritual—Strickland would appear to be like many other characters in Maugham's fiction. He stands apart from the rest, however, because his real bondage is to something different—the passion to paint. His denial of family, home, honour, comfort and love therefore comes not from a voluntary choice but from the force of a stronger obligation. There is within him an obsession, a possessing spirit, which can only be liberated through the medium of paint, and this overshadows all else for him.

The image associated with Strickland throughout the novel is that of an individual possessed by a devil or haunted by a spirit. It is an idea which Maugham uses a number of times, often in an attempt to attach archetypal connotations to the inexplicable actions of his characters. In *Of Human Bondage*, Philip finds the conduct of his fellows irrational, and he wonders if they are possessed by spirits which rob them of self-control. Later, in *Christmas Holiday*, Maugham places a great deal of emphasis on the criminal, Robert

Berger, as a man possessed of a 'devil' which drives him to murder. In the case of Strickland, the possession is a variation of the 'sacred fire', the almost holy inspiration which the romantics attributed to the artistic temperament, but with a slightly insidious and terrifying quality. It is a force which is primitive, awe-inspiring and inescapable. After Strickland's flight to Paris, even before he has developed to any extent as an artist, he confesses:

"I tell you I've got to paint. I can't help myself. When a man falls into the water it doesn't matter how he swims, well or badly; he's got to get out or else he'll drown."

There was a real passion in his voice, and in spite of myself I was impressed. I seemed to feel in him some vehement power that was struggling within him; it gave me the sensation of something very strong, overmastering, that held him, as it were, against his will. I could not understand. He seemed really to be possessed of a devil, and I felt that it might suddenly turn and rend him.[24]

When the narrator returns to England to report his findings to Strickland's wife, he repeats the impression that Strickland is possessed: 'He seems to me to be possessed by some power which is using him for its own ends, and in whose hold he is as helpless as a fly in a spider's web.'

Elsewhere, Maugham compares this obsession to a cancer, and Dirk Stroeve talks of the 'great burden' of the artist, who therefore must be treated with tolerance and patience. Finally, near the end of the novel, even Captain Brunot recognises the nature and strength of Strickland's enslavement:

"Do you know how men can be so obsessed by love that they are deaf and blind to everything else in the world? They are as little their own masters as the slaves chained to the benches of a galley. The passion that held Strickland in bondage was no less tyrannical than love."[25]

Despite the realistic treatment of most aspects of *The Moon and Sixpence*, Maugham's interpretation of the artistic temperament is essentially romantic. Strickland's creative ability is not something which has always been present in him and which has developed over a long period of application and apprenticeship. It is a sudden force which overwhelms him and, because he is by nature inarticulate and uncommunicative, demands expression through painting. The artist, according to Maugham, must create; he cannot do otherwise:

The artist can no more help creating than water can help running down hill. It is a release from the burden on his soul. It is a spiritual exercise which is infinitely pleasurable, and it is accompanied by a sense of power that is in itself delightful. When production fulfils it he enjoys a heavenly sense of liberation. For one delicious moment he rests in a state of equilibrium.[26]

Strickland therefore is not actually free. His revolt from conventional behaviour and love is merely the abandoning of these forms
of bondage in the face of another, more powerful, one. His lack of
concern for his wife, family, duty, the Stroeves, comfort, even fame,
is genuine; blinded by his artistic demon, he is truly unaware of anything else. 'A tormented spirit striving for the release of expression',
Strickland can only communicate through the medium of paint, and
only in this way can he achieve ultimate freedom. The narrator
observes at one point that 'the only thing that seemed clear to me—
and perhaps even this was fanciful—was that he was passionately
striving for liberation from some power that held him'.

In his bondage to the artistic urge, Strickland is similar to Fanny
Price, Miguel Ajuria and Clutton in *Of Human Bondage*, and to
George Bland in 'The Alien Corn'. But where Fanny and George are
destroyed because they cannot achieve artistic expression, where
Miguel Ajuria fails because he is superficial and where Clutton has
only a limited success, Strickland does find his means of artistic
creativity. In Tahiti, in an environment which makes no demands on
him, with a woman who puts no ties on him, he paints his great work.
Dr Coutras discovers the paintings on the walls of Strickland's house
at the painter's death:

From floor to ceiling the walls were covered with a strange and elaborate
composition. It was indescribably wonderful and mysterious. It took his
breath away. It filled him with an emotion which he could not understand
or analyse. He felt the awe and the delight which a man might feel who
watched the beginning of the world. It was tremendous, sensual, passionate; and yet there was something horrible there, too, something which
made him afraid. It was the work of a man who had delved into the hidden
depths of nature and discovered the secrets which were beautiful and
fearful too. It was the work of a man who knew things which it is unholy
for men to know. There was something primeval there and terrible. It was
not human. It brought to his mind vague recollections of black magic. It
was beautiful and obscene.[27]

In this final, monumental work, Strickland has found the means to
communicate his vision and thereby achieve liberation. Maugham is
careful here to make the descriptions of the masterpiece consistent
with the vague illumination he has given of his character's obsession
—huge, sensual, passionate, horrible, primeval, mystical. It is
Strickland's soul in paint, and the demon has been exorcised. With
this last great painting, he assumes an almost heroic stature because,
like Kurtz in Conrad's 'Heart of Darkness', he has had a vision of
man's basic nature and he has found an eloquence to communicate
it. His masterpiece is his expression of 'The horror. The horror.'

In order to emphasise that Strickland's creation is an entirely personal act of catharsis, Maugham adds, almost as a postscript, that this monumental creation was destroyed on the painter's orders. In the end, he is free of everything, from even a wish for justification, fame or posterity; nothing can claim him. Kuner rightly emphasises the symbolism of this act of defiance:

It was a mark of the man's wilful consistency, that, having at last found what he wanted, having created these magnificent portraits, he should be willing to obliterate them as a supreme gesture of contempt for the world's opinion. Here is a study of revolt and ultimate freedom rivalling even the Gidean ideal.[28]

Although both *Of Human Bondage* and *The Moon and Sixpence* are concerned with physical and spiritual freedom, they are remarkably opposed in their approaches to it. Philip abandons his ideas of travel in favour of the rather common life of a country doctor; Strickland gives up what Philip has chosen and seeks freedom away from civilisation and through art. *The Moon and Sixpence* would almost seem to be a refutation of the final chapters of *Of Human Bondage*.

The title of *The Moon and Sixpence* provides a significant commentary on the different solutions in the two novels. In reviewing *Of Human Bondage*, *The Times Literary Supplement* had written that 'like so many young men he (Philip) was so busy yearning for the moon that he never saw the sixpence at his feet'.[29] In the end, however, Philip surrenders the moon in order to grasp the sixpence.

As he was also to do later with *The Mixture as Before*, Maugham adopted a phrase from the review as the title of his next novel. The title has been subjected to a number of interpretations, but the author has himself explained its meaning, in a note which was intended to precede the text, but which did not appear:

Since some readers of this novel have found its title obscure the author ventures upon the following explanation. In his childhood he was urged to make merry over the man who, looking for the moon, missed the sixpence at his feet, but having reached years of maturity he is not so sure that this was so great an absurdity as he was bidden to believe. Let him who will pick up the sixpence, to pursue the moon seems the most amusing diversion.[30]

It would be dangerous to speculate about what developments in Maugham's life between the writing of *Of Human Bondage* and *The Moon and Sixpence* brought about this change of attitude. Certainly, although he would not set Strickland up as a model for others to follow, his admiration for his hero is obvious.

The opposing attitudes of the two novels can perhaps be reconciled in that both Philip and Strickland pursue a life in which they can recognise purpose and satisfaction, and freedom lies in living a life for which one is best suited. In *The Summing Up*, Maugham concludes his discussion of philosophy by writing: 'The beauty of life . . . is nothing but this, that each should act in conformity with his nature and his business.' For Philip, this lies in marriage, domesticity, and an occupation with both independence and interaction with people. For Strickland, however, it means a lonely pursuit of creative expression, defiance of conventional attitudes and exile.

The resolution of the question of what is the best life for a particular individual is provided in *The Moon and Sixpence* in the story of Abraham. This brilliant young physician interrupts a remarkable career in London to take a holiday in the Middle East. In Alexandria, he is suddenly overcome by an 'exultation' and 'a sense of wonderful freedom', and he abandons his career to remain there and live in straitened circumstances in a modest position. Contrasted with him is a wealthy and successful London surgeon, a man who firmly believes that Abraham has made a mess of his life. Maugham disagrees:

Is to do what you most want, to live under the conditions that please you, in peace with yourself, to make a hash of life; and is it a success to be an eminent surgeon with ten thousand a year and a beautiful wife? I suppose it depends on what meaning you attach to life, the claim you acknowledge to society, and the claim of the individual.[31]

This short story, included late in the novel, underlines Strickland's experience in Tahiti, where he finds a way of life and an atmosphere in which his personality has the greatest scope to express itself. In London, and particularly in Paris, he had become increasingly unable to live in a manner consistent with the accepted standards of social behaviour. His personality had become so enlarged in its individuality that he eventually proved to be too anti-social for even the milieu of rogues and criminals in Marseilles. In Tahiti, however, he finds an environment in which eccentricity and sharply defined individuality are accepted, and he is for once able to live in harmony with his surroundings.

To emphasise this point, the book ends with a return to the social scene in England and a re-introduction to the type of life from which Strickland fled. Although the whims of fashion have imposed upon her new colours and designs, his wife is completely unchanged. The bland, average children have reached adulthood in an entirely predictable way, the son being an affable soldier and the daughter the wife of a major in the Gunners. When the narrator meets the family, an American critic is present to discuss Strickland in his tone of 'bloodless frigidity'. When the reader is reminded of the quality of this kind of life as contrasted with the painter's years in Tahiti, he must conclude that Strickland's revolt was, in the end, a success.

The Moon and Sixpence is another example of Maugham's ability to work in a currently popular genre and achieve considerable success. As a portrait of the artist, however, his novel has been subjected to a number of serious criticisms.

Robert M. Lovett reflected the views of a great many critics when he argued that Strickland's conversion to painting is too sudden and unprepared and that this leaves his character too vague. He claimed, therefore, that *The Moon and Sixpence* is full of unexploited possibilities—particularly in the struggle which must have taken place within his mind prior to his revolt:

The one thing interesting above all, we are not allowed to see: through what fiery inner struggle did Strickland break loose to follow his ambition, and what intimate chemistry of soul caused his sudden lapse into the freakish behavior that alone characterises his genius?[32]

Katherine Mansfield criticised not only the lack of explanation at the beginning, but also the absence of any deep probing of the painter's mind throughout the novel. Maugham fails, she claimed, to reveal enough of what makes the artistic temperament, that extraordinary kind of sensitivity or perception which makes the artist a special man: 'We must be shown something of the workings of his mind; we must have some comment of his upon what he feels, fuller and more exhaustive than his perpetual "Go to hell".'[33]

At the heart of the problem of Strickland's characterisation is Maugham's decision to abandon the omniscient author's point of view in favour of the first person singular. This narrative technique automatically absolves the author from the burden of explaining the subtle workings of his characters' minds, and Maugham significantly prefaces the story with the statement: 'It is a riddle which shares with the universe the merit of having no answer.' What he does attempt to present is a picture of a genius as he appears to the ordinary, but perceptive, observer. The result is an external view, with occasional suppositions and hypotheses about Strickland's mental and spiritual condition, and when the artist departs for Tahiti the impression becomes even more vague. Here the use of Conradian techniques of rumour and second- or third-hand accounts places Strickland even further away.

In Maugham's defence, it must be remembered that the creation of a character in fiction who is believable as an artist is rare. The nineteenth century concentrated on the life of the painter, with little

F

emphasis on his work, and the twentieth century, even with an increased interest in the artistic experience, has produced few credible portraits of artists. Shaw's Louis Dubedat, Dreiser's Eugene Witla (in *The Genius*) and Richardson's Maurice Guest do not have their artistic efforts explored. Paul Morel, in Lawrence's *Sons and Lovers*, is treated with sensitivity and perception, but his relationship with his painting is not revealed in any depth. Only Joyce's *A Portrait of the Artist as a Young Man* succeeds at this time in presenting a believable picture of an artistic personality, and even this is limited to the embryonic stage of his development.

Maugham's substitution for analysis in depth of Strickland's mind is an attempt, through facts, rumours, conversations, reactions and artistic criticisms, to create the impression that Strickland must be a great painter. Biographies and academic treatises have been written about him, footnotes locate the famous galleries in which his paintings are hung, Stroeve and Dr Coutras pronounce him a genius, the narrator admits his confused respect, and it is noted that his paintings sell for thousands of dollars. The cumulative effect of this is intended to make the reader believe that Strickland must be a genius, even though the proof is never really given.

Through this technique, Maugham succeeds to a remarkable degree in persuading the reader that he is encountering an artist of great stature. It remains, nevertheless, a method with serious limitations, and the artistic temperament is surely of such complexity as to warrant an examination in greater depth. Maugham's reluctance to use some of the techniques of other writers of this century—particularly the stream-of-consciousness school—perhaps hurts him here. Gully Jimson, in Joyce Cary's *The Horse's Mouth* (1944), for example, through the continual exposure to his thought processes, effectively persuades the reader that he is a true artist with an aesthetic outlook on the world. Cary succeeds, as few other writers have, in placing the reader inside the artist's mind, where he experiences life as it is sensed by the creative consciousness. This intimate understanding of the artistic temperament is not present in *The Moon and Sixpence*.

The second major criticism of Maugham's portrait of Strickland is that his romantic theory of primeval inspiration is not a valid interpretation of genius. Maxwell Anderson doubted the wisdom of making Strickland brutal, sensual and incoherent:

One feels instinctively that genius does not take this guise, and that mastery is gained through understanding rather than through demonic impulses. Maugham consciously discards the modern theories of genius, and returns to the romantic notion of revelation and the hidden flame.[34]

Similarly, Katherine Mansfield argued that artistry does not come out of brutality, animalism and cruelty:

> If to be a great artist were to push over everything that comes in one's way, topple over the table, lunge out right and left like a drunken man in a café and send the pots flying, then Strickland was a great artist. But great artists are not drunken men; they are men who are divinely sober.[35]

These criticisms raise some very serious doubts about the credibility of this portrait of the artist. It is true that Strickland seems to lack sensitivity, and this must, above all others, be an absolute necessity for an artist. Even the most aggressive, unscrupulous and anti-social artist has possessed a sensitivity and a finely developed perception of the world around him. Maugham never succeeds in persuading the reader that Strickland is anything but coarse, sensual and brutal, and for this reason his artist fails to be a representative portrait.

On a limited scale, however, *The Moon and Sixpence* is successful in providing an illuminating picture of a specific generation of painters—that of Gauguin and Van Gogh. Strickland, partly based on the myths surrounding Gauguin and partly on the philosophy of the artist which was dominant at the turn of the century, is, as James M. Wells maintains, the best fictional representative of that school of art:

> Of all the nineteenth and early twentieth century novels which portray the painter, *The Moon and Sixpence* is the only one which succeeds to any extent in creating a character who seems genuine and consistent in his relationship with his time and his art. It manages to distil something of the struggle of the artist in the expression of his personal reactions to the world about him. The great majority of the novels about the artist treat him as a mountebank, as a romantic hero, as a rebel, or an aesthete – but seldom as a person whose characteristics are a natural result of his profession.[36]

VI

Marriage: A Condition of Bondage

THROUGHOUT HIS CAREER, Maugham has frequently displayed the tendency to return to a theme, situation or character which he has previously developed. The themes of unrequited love, man's inexplicable nature, and the destructive power of the emotions, can be found from *Liza of Lambeth* to *Catalina*. Similarly, he often re-introduces, not only type-characters, but actual figures from previous works: Miss Ley appears in *Mrs Craddock*, *The Merry-Go-Round* and 'The Happy Couple' (1908); Frank Hurrell plays a part in *The Merry-Go-Round* and *The Magician*; Canon Spratte of *The Bishop's Apron* appears in *The Explorer*; Rose Waterford can be found in *The Moon and Sixpence* and 'The Creative Impulse'; and Ned Preston plays a part in both 'Episode' and 'The Kite'.

Maugham, furthermore, has frequently transferred whole sections or stories from one source to another: *The Merry-Go-Round* incorporated *A Man of Honour*; *The Bishop's Apron* and *The Explorer* were plays rewritten as novels; *The Bishop's Apron* also absorbed the short story, 'Cupid and the Vicar of Swale' (1900), while *The Explorer* assimilated another story, 'Flirtation' (1904); *Lady Frederick* was an expanded treatment of a situation presented in 'Lady Habart' (1900); *Caesar's Wife* echoed 'Pro Patria' (1903); *The Unknown* was a contemporary re-working of *The Hero*; *The Constant Wife* reflected *Penelope*; *The Circle* used 'Mrs Beamish'; and at least four short stories—'The Mother', 'Cousin Amy', 'A Marriage of Convenience' and 'The Happy Couple'—were revised years after their initial appearance in print.

One of the best examples of Maugham's reluctance to abandon a particular situation is the recurrence of the story first presented in *Mrs Craddock*. In that novel a woman becomes enslaved by her own passionate nature, marries unwisely, discovers that her husband is dull, unresponsive and inadequate, and is finally freed from her intolerable bondage by his death. This situation is in essence repeated in *The Painted Veil* (1925) and *Theatre* (1937), and by reflection in 'The Human Element' (1930). In each of these stories the heroine finds liberation from passion and emotional ties, and in each case the path of escape involves an important concern of the author in the decades from 1919 to 1949. In *The Painted Veil*, Kitty looks for freedom through spiritualism and religious dedication; in *Theatre*, Julia experiences liberation through the creativity of her acting; and in 'The Human Element', Betty cherishes an independence found in escape from the restrictions of social convention.

The Far East setting of *The Painted Veil* is based on observations made by Maugham on a trip to China in 1922; these experiences furnished the material for the sketches in *On a Chinese Screen* (1922) and the background and atmosphere of *The Painted Veil*. These two books, in fact, overlap, and the Mother Superior and the orphanage at Mei-tan-fu in *The Painted Veil* are also described, with equal admiration, in *On a Chinese Screen*.

Although most of *The Painted Veil* takes place in China, English society and its conventions play a prominent part in the course of the story. As he did in *The Moon and Sixpence*, Maugham initially paints a picture of English social life and then contrasts this with an existence in a distant and exotic environment. *The Painted Veil* is an account of the spiritual and moral regeneration of a superficial and silly young woman, and, in a series of flashbacks at the beginning of the novel, Maugham clearly establishes the reason for her superficiality. Kitty Fane is a product of her upper-middle-class background, and the author here attacks conventional English society as enthusiastically as he did in *Mrs Craddock* and *The Moon and Sixpence*.

If there is anything approaching a villain in *The Painted Veil*, it is Kitty's mother, Mrs Garstin. She is a repository for all the narrow and shallow values of the English upper-middle class and, although she is never presented directly, her influence is felt throughout the novel. Ambitious for social success, Mrs Garstin has assimilated all the trappings of convention and decorum, and she is constantly scrutinising and evaluating everything and everybody around her in the light of social advancement. A figure out of Maugham's dramatic comedies, she is in her pretension a beautifully realised character.

Mrs Garstin is the dominant force in Kitty's early life, and the latter, as we first see her, is fully a product of her mother's ambitions. She is brought up in an environment where she is expected to make a brilliant marriage, regardless of whether it is a good one. Kitty 'comes out', but after four 'seasons' she has not married and Mrs Garstin warns her that she will 'miss her market'. When her younger sister, Doris, comes out and becomes engaged in her first season, Kitty, mortified at the humiliation which this means in social circles, panics and marries Walter Fane, a bacteriologist in Hong Kong. She does not in the least love Walter; she marries him to escape the ignominy of being a bridesmaid at Doris's wedding and to be free from her mother's 'bitter tongue'. This decision, dictated by social considerations, is a disaster.

Although Kitty does not, like Bertha Craddock, love her husband when she marries him, the treatment of married life in both novels is similar. Kitty is lively, exuberant and passionate; she likes parties, conversation and games. Walter, however, is restrained, cold and controlled; he is self-conscious, ill-at-ease in groups and unable to respond to his wife's emotional demands.[1] Like Bertha and Julia, Kitty soon reaches a state of equilibrium where she neither loves nor hates her husband, but merely reacts to him with indifference. Inevitably, she has an affair with Charles Townsend, a man who is the antithesis of her husband—handsome, virile and popular.

Kitty, at this point, is not much different from so many of Maugham's English characters in the Far East. She is snobbish, silly and superficial. Committing adultery, she imagines that everything would be perfect if she had the freedom to leave Walter and marry Townsend. Most significantly, she is living in a world of illusion where she cannot recognise the real nature of Townsend's interest in her.

In Mei-tan-fu, the cholera-stricken outpost, the process of re-generation comes about through Kitty's association with the French nuns at the orphanage, and by her contact with the deputy com-missioner, Waddington. In the orphanage, amid the suffering and death, Kitty sees a type of life that she has never known before, and there is an implied contrast between the Mei-tan-fu scenes and the earlier ones in England. The nuns, particularly the Mother Superior, live in simplicity, love and faith. They have sacrificed almost every-thing to work in an alien country, preserving the lives of children rejected by the Chinese themselves. Through all this, they have a compensation which eludes Kitty: an absolute confidence that their lives are not wasted. It is a secret which is beyond Kitty's under-standing, but one which she longs to know.

Waddington is one of Maugham's choruses or *raissoneurs*, and he acts as a kind of catalyst for Kitty's self-discovery. As well as in his discussions of philosophy and Tao, he influences Kitty through his relationship with the aristocratic Manchu woman who lives with him. The Manchu woman has sacrificed home, family, security and honour in order to live with Waddington, and, in spite of the detrimental effect the liaison has had on his career, he loves her very deeply. There is a mystical quality in their relationship, something which is beyond Kitty's reach, and she is impressed.

After Kitty has been assisting the nuns in the orphanage for a while, she begins to feel that in some way she is growing. Exposed to the sacrifice and dedication of the nuns and to the constant threat of death from cholera, she finds her own problems trivial. Her feelings about Walter, however, do not change except to develop into impatience with his obsession with her infidelity:

Why could he not realise, what suddenly had become so clear to her, that beside all the terror of death under whose shadow they lay and beside the awe of the beauty which she had caught a glimpse of that day, their own affairs were trivial? What did it really matter if a silly woman had committed adultery and why should her husband, face to face with the sublime, give it a thought?[2]

Kitty's argument is one which recurs in many forms in Maugham's writings. In 'Virtue', three lives are ruined because a woman cannot overcome her scruples about having an affair, letting her passion exhaust itself, and then returning to her husband. In 'The Back of Beyond', a man discovers that his wife has had a lengthy affair with a man who has just died, and he is advised to be happy with what he has and thus to take back his wife. Similarly, in 'The Colonel's Lady', a man's wife publishes a series of poems about a passionate illicit affair, obviously her own, and his solicitor counsels him to forget the past and to accept his wife as she is. In 'P & O', a woman discovers that her husband is having an affair and she leaves in indignation for England; however, impressed by the pathos of the death of a man aboard ship, she recognises the relative insignificance of her husband's infidelity and she forgives him. In *Cakes and Ale* Rosie, confronted with her promiscuity by a distressed Ashenden, argues that if he is happy when he is with her what does it matter what she does with other men?

There are two important aspects of the thesis presented in these stories. The first, that the pain men cause themselves through their attitudes is foolish in the face of the greater terrors of loneliness and death, is defensible. In *The Painted Veil* Maugham succeeds in persuading the reader that Kitty's affair with Townsend is pale in comparison with the occurrences at Mei-tan-fu.

The second part of Maugham's argument—that infidelity merely involves a sexual drive which can be satisfied without the spirit being influenced—is not, however, so easily defended. While it is true that many relationships are brief and founded solely on sexual attraction, it is a gross over-simplification to claim that a person's spirit remains untouched and unaltered. Whether it is because of his desire to attack society's great error of equating sin with sex or an inherent inability to comprehend fully a deeply committed and subtle spiritual relationship, Maugham fails throughout his writing to present a completely developed love between two people.

As Kitty develops an awareness of suffering and death and a recognition of herself, she imagines that she is free from her bondage to passion. One day, she discovers that she no longer loves Charles Townsend:

Oh, the relief and the sense of liberation! It was strange to look back and remember how passionately she had yearned for him; she thought she would die when he failed her; she thought life thenceforward had nothing to offer but misery. And now already she was laughing. A worthless creature. What a fool she had made of herself! And now, considering him calmly, she wondered what on earth she had seen in him. . . . She was free, free at last, free! She could hardly prevent herself from laughing aloud.[3]

Later, after the death of Walter from cholera, when Kitty leaves Mei-tan-fu to return to England, it is with a similar sense of liberation. She is now free from an unfortunate marriage, free from the cholera-ridden city, and free, so it seems, from her passion for Townsend. She is like a prisoner seeing daylight after a long confinement:

The city of the pestilence was a prison from which she was escaped, and she had never known before how exquisite was the blueness of the sky and what a joy there was in the bamboo copses that leaned with such an adorable grace across the causeway. Freedom! That was the thought that sung in her heart so that even though the future was so dim, it was iridescent like the mist over the river where the morning sun fell upon it. Freedom! Not only freedom from a bond that irked, and a companionship which depressed her; freedom, not only from the death which had threatened, but freedom from the love that had degraded her; freedom from all spiritual ties, the freedom of a disembodied spirit; and with freedom, courage and a valiant unconcern for whatever was to come.[4]

In spite of this exhilaration and optimism, however, Maugham demonstrates that the emotions are not so easily conquered and that freedom is not easily won. When Kitty returns to Hong Kong she is persuaded to stay with the Townsends, and during her visit she is once again seduced by Townsend. With full knowledge of her lover's superficiality and worthlessness, she is unable to prevent herself desiring him. With this episode comes the realisation that she has not been transformed, that she does not completely possess her own person.

This episode has distressed a great many critics. Some argue that, because Kitty repeats her offence after Walter's death, we cannot take her metamorphosis seriously and others find the emphasis on unqualified lust distasteful. Naik, contrasting Bertha Craddock and Kitty, writes:

Both are victims of passion, but Bertha contends with passion, and her struggle is almost heroic. In the snobbish, self-indulgent, weak, and sensual Kitty, there is no struggle but only abject surrender.[5]

Kitty's second fall, nevertheless, is a master stroke. It prevents the novel from becoming a spiritual rags-to-riches story in the worst Hollywood tradition. It emphasises that regeneration is not a simple matter, and that self-examination and contemplation of life are not guarantees of spiritual transformation. Above all, it makes the story more credible; given Kitty's basic nature and her previous relationship with Townsend, her fall is completely believable.

It is also important to recognise that Kitty's surrender is not, as Naik and others have claimed, without struggle. Her self-castigation afterwards is proof that some form of development has taken place within her. This is not the silly and frivolous woman of the beginning of the novel; although she cannot prevent her seduction, she is at least able to recognise what it means, and this realisation influences the determined idealism of her final speeches.

Maugham cheats the reader to some degree at the end because when Kitty returns to her home in England the representative of social interests and conventions, Mrs Garstin, has conveniently died, and he is spared having to resolve the inevitable conflict between Kitty's determinations and her mother's aspirations. Kitty is pregnant, however, and emphatic, not only about finding her own freedom and peace, but about raising her daughter to be independent. Thus, the conflict between the restrictions of social custom and pretence and the liberation that Kitty has found will be resolved in the next generation. Nevertheless, the responsibility for the encouraging of a new sense of awareness in the child lies within the framework of the novel in Kitty. Paul Dottin argues that 'La Kitty régénérée des dernières pages est le porte-parole de la jeune génération qui veut à tout prix se libérer des conceptions mercantiles de la haute bourgeoisie victorienne',[6] an accurate description of her final speech:

"I want a girl because I want to bring her up so that she shan't make the mistakes I've made. When I look back upon the girl I was I hate myself. But I never had a chance. I'm going to bring up my daughter so that she's free and can stand on her own feet. I'm not going to bring a child into the world, and love her, and bring her up, just so that some man may want to sleep with her so much that he's willing to provide her with board and lodging for the rest of her life. . . .

"I want her to be fearless and frank. I want her to be a person independent of others because she is possessed of herself, and I want her to take life like a free man and make a better job of it than I have."[7]

Maugham ends *The Painted Veil* with this enthusiastic speech in which his protagonist declares that she wants to read and learn, enjoy the world, people, music, dancing, the sea, sunrise, sunset and starry nights. She has recognised the pattern, 'an inexhaustible richness, the mystery and the strangeness of everything, compassion and charity, the Way and the Wayfarer, and perhaps in the end— God'.

This rather forced ending was soundly attacked by the majority of critics. Isabel Paterson called the final pages 'rank sentimentality';[8] P. C. Kennedy labelled the ending 'the silliest ever inflicted by a brilliant writer on a brilliant story';[9] and Robert M. Lovett claimed that 'the optimistic yodelling with which she announces her conversion rather suggests the author in search of an ending'.[10]

At some time after the first edition of *The Painted Veil* Maugham himself became dissatisfied with the conclusion, and in the version included in the Heinemann edition of the selected novels, re-issued in 1950, the final paragraph is revised. Instead of ending with a declaration by Kitty, Maugham sets the tone with a description of her thoughts, and Kitty remembers a day of great beauty in China. The reference to 'the Way' and 'the Wayfarer' have been eliminated, and the language is restrained. Kitty, at the end, is seeking 'the path that led to peace'.

The means of liberation portrayed in *The Painted Veil*—through spiritual and mystical regeneration—is the first important manifestation of the interest in spiritual matters which can be found in Maugham in the latter half of his career. Although always restrained by his ingrained scepticism, he shows considerable admiration for genuine religious faith. The culmination of this interest is Larry's mystical pursuit in *The Razor's Edge*, a more subtle and deeper study of Eastern religion.

Theatre, written in 1937, is yet another interpretation of the situation presented in *Mrs Craddock*. Julia Lambert, like Bertha and Kitty, is an intensely passionate woman who finds her husband cold and unresponsive. Like Bertha and Kitty, Julia finds herself a slave to her emotional nature and, like them, she finds freedom at the end. For her, liberation comes, as it does for Charles Strickland, through artistic creativity—in her case, by losing herself in acting.

The parallels between *Theatre* and *Mrs Craddock* are numerous. Like Bertha, Julia develops a fierce love for a man whose appeal is sensual and physical. Michael may be beautiful while Edward is rugged and masculine, but their appeal is basically the same. Julia, like Bertha, is determined to have her man, and she pursues him as relentlessly. Finally, like Edward, Michael calmly and dispassionately agrees to marry Julia.

The course of the Gosselyns' marriage matches that of the Craddocks. Julia expects warm, overt responses from her husband, and finds him restrained and impassive. Although he is involved in a pursuit as imaginative and intellectual as the theatre, Michael is very much a reflection of Edward in his concern for property, profit and loss, and sales of tickets. Just as Edward's primary concern is the material success of Court Leys, Michael's first duty is not to Julia but to the Siddons Theatre. Like Edward, Michael's philosophy in the face of Julia's recriminations about his lack of response is to do nothing and let her emotion exhaust itself:

It infuriated her that when she worked herself up into a passion of tears he should sit there quite calmly, with his hands crossed and a good-humoured smile on his handsome face, as though she were merely making herself ridiculous.[11]

Like Bertha, Julia becomes distressed by her inability to arouse her husband, but, unlike Bertha, she has her acting career to sustain her. Finally, however, she too discovers that she no longer loves her husband. With this realisation comes regret, but also a feeling of relief:

Her heart sank because she knew she had lost something that was infinitely precious to her, and pitying herself she was inclined to cry; but at the same time she was filled with a sense of triumph, it seemed a revenge that she enjoyed for the unhappiness he had caused her; she was free of the bondage in which her senses had held her to him and she exulted. Now she could deal with him on equal terms. She stretched her legs out in bed and sighed with relief.
"By God, it's grand to be one's own mistress."[12]

After this recognition, the Gosselyns' marriage reaches a state of equilibrium; both are absorbed by their careers and they live together in amiable companionship.

Julia's passionate nature, however, becomes reawakened when she is overwhelmed and seduced by a brash young admirer, Tom Fennell. They have an affair, and Julia soon finds herself a prisoner of her love for the young man. Long accustomed to the devotion of a multitude of stagedoor admirers, she is humiliated at the knowledge that she is now dependent upon Tom for her happiness.

Julia's means of escape from her emotional enslavement to Tom is the theatre, and in this novel, as in *The Moon and Sixpence*, an important theme is the relationship between art and love. Like

Strickland, Julia finds love a threat to her creativity, and, like the painter, she finds a liberation in her artistic expression. At one stage in the novel, Julia, jealous and unhappy, returns to London and finds relief in the theatre:

But when she got into the theatre she felt that she shook off the obsession of him like a bad dream from which one awoke; there, in her dressing room, she regained possession of herself and the affairs of the common round of daily life faded to insignificance. Nothing mattered when she had within her grasp this possibility of freedom.[13]

When Julia later visits her relations in St-Malo, she is touched by the contentment and serenity of their lives. Their existence is un-eventful, but free of malice or envy; they have an independence which the actress automatically associates with that which she experiences on the stage.

The liberation which Julia enjoys in the theatre, however, is not simply a cathartic pouring out of her emotions or obsessions through the vehicle of a dramatic character. It is a far more complex release, a form of sublimation in which her emotions are transmuted in a subtle fashion into creativity. In Julia's relationship to her art, Maugham appears to contradict what he has repeatedly stated else-where. In *The Summing Up*, for example, he writes:

The disadvantages and dangers of the author's calling are offset by an advantage so great as to make all its difficulties, disappointments, and maybe hardships, unimportant. It gives him spiritual freedom. To him life is a tragedy and by his gift of creation he enjoys the catharsis, the purging of pity and terror, which Aristotle tells us is the object of art. For his sins and his follies, the unhappiness that befalls him, his unrequited love, his physical defects, illness, privation, his hopes abandoned, his griefs, humilia-tions, everything is transformed by his power into material and by writing he can overcome it. Everything is grist to his mill, from the glimpse of a face in the street to a war that convulses the civilized world, from the scent of a rose to the death of a friend. Nothing befalls him that he cannot trans-mute into a stanza, a song or a story, and having done this be rid of it. The artist is the only free man.[14]

This theory is dramatised in *Cakes and Ale* where the writer, Edward Driffield, utilises a personal agony in a novel. His young daughter dies a prolonged and painful death, and in reaction to this his wife spends the night with another man. Driffield's own form of catharsis is the transfiguration of the event into fiction; the resulting description is harrowing and powerful.

In *Theatre*, however, although Julia's sufferings and frustrations in her affair with Tom provide her with 'grist for the mill', they do not produce a satisfactory artistic experience. When she turns to the stage for solace after the loss of her lover, she throws herself into a

role which parallels her own situation. After a few weeks of performance, she feels that she has never played so magnificently;
Michael, however, an astute judge of acting, tells her that she has
never played so badly. She has, he claims, been over-acting, exag-
gerating emotions and therefore losing credibility. In the theatre,
where everything is by definition artificial and contrived, her sincere
and deeply felt emotion is destructive. She is in the process of feeling
emotions, rather than contemplating them with detachment, and this
inhibits her artistry in portraying them.

Julia's relationship to her art is similar to Charles Strickland's
in that her acting ability is also a form of possession. Her talent is a
force which she cannot control:

Her gift, if you like, was not really herself, not even part of her, but something outside that used her, Julia Lambert the woman, in order to express
itself. It was a strange, immaterial personality that seemed to descend upon
her and it did things through her that she did not know she was capable of
doing. She was an ordinary, prettyish, ageing woman. Her gift had neither
age nor form. It was a spirit that played on her body as the violinist plays
on his violin.[15]

The reason that Julia fails miserably when she attempts to use the
stage as a vehicle for expressing her immediate and personal agony
is that she is attempting to force her 'gift' into a particular purpose.
She is like an author who tries to write to order, without a proper
understanding of his ideas; she is too deeply involved with her
emotions to be able to comprehend their significance with the
necessary objectivity. Reality here impinges upon the world of make-
believe, and its influence is damaging. Significantly, at the end, in the
actress's moment of triumph, she recognises that acting, like poetry,
means emotion recollected in tranquillity.

Julia's liberation through her art comes, not from a form of direct
catharsis, but through a sublimation of her emotions. Her passions
and emotions are given an outlet, but it is not through the expression
of those particular feelings; it comes through the simple act of
creation. In building an imaginary character into the image of a
living person, Julia is able to shut out the frustrations of the real
world and lose herself in the creation of a fictional one:

Thrusting her private emotion into the background and thus getting the
character under control, she managed once more to play with her accustomed virtuosity. Her acting ceased to be a means by which she gave
release to her feelings and was once again the manifestation of her creative
instinct. She got a quiet exhilaration out of thus recovering mastery over
her medium. It gave her a sense of power and of liberation.[16]

Theatre ends, like *Mrs Craddock* and *The Painted Veil*, with the heroine alone and free, physically and spiritually. Julia, long since independent of her husband, frees herself from her sexual attachment to Tom. Testing herself by one last encounter with the young man, she happily finds herself completely detached emotionally. Following this, she proceeds to give a virtuoso acting performance which destroys Avice, the young actress hoping to benefit by appearing with Julia Gosselyn.

The final scene is a masterful touch in an otherwise inauspicious novel. Julia, triumphant in disposing of Avice, in proving herself once more an actress of the first rank, and in discovering that she is no longer tied to Tom, celebrates by going to a fancy restaurant. Here she is divorced from all of her fellow humans, even from the rest of the people in the restaurant. As an act of defiance, she orders what she has denied herself for years—grilled steak and onions, fried potatoes, and a bottle of beer. She has reached, at this point, the independence she has been seeking:

Aloof on her mountain top she considered the innumerable activities of men. She had a wonderful sense of freedom from all earthly ties, and it was such an ecstasy that nothing in comparison with it had any value. She felt like a spirit in heaven.[17]

Maugham provides a serious criticism of Julia's means of escape from the realities of life, within the framework of *Theatre*, but it falls flat because it is in the form of a rather priggish speech by her son, Roger. Having grown up a serious young man, away from the theatre, he revolts against the pretence and make-believe which comprise the world of his parents. He argues that Julia does not confine her acting to the stage, that she is always playing a part, changing chameleon-like as the occasion demands. She lives a protean existence, always avoiding revealing anything of her own soul. Roger, in a scene ironically similar to a stage one—the Hamlet–Gertrude confrontation in *Hamlet*—poses a disconcerting question:

"If one stripped you of your exhibitionism, if one took your technique away from you, if one peeled you as one peels an onion of skin after skin of pretence and insincerity, of tags of old parts and shreds of faked emotions, would one come upon a soul at last?"[18]

After some consideration, Julia counters this accusation by admitting that for her reality is on the stage; ordinary people are only the raw material which she uses to convey truth and beauty. The people, she argues, are only shadows, while the actors and actresses are the symbols and expressions of the significant aspects of life.

Roger's accusation, although hamstrung by his sense of moral outrage, is nevertheless true. The only occasion in the novel that Julia is not acting a role is in her affair with Tom, and in this encounter with sincerity she is hurt. Any time that she has control of a situation and can turn it into an occasion for a tour de force performance, she is safe. In this way, she is able easily to handle Michael's parents by playing the village maiden, Dolly DeVries by playing the faithful confidante, and Charles Tamerley by acting the nobly sacrificing lover. When, however, she abandons playing a role in order to be sincere and honest, as in her relationship with Tom, she loses her mastery and is vulnerable. Therefore, she finds in the theatre a means of retreat, a haven in which she is absolutely sure of her self-possession.

In Julia's psychological dependence upon the theatre Maugham may be defining the relationship of a great many actors and actresses to their profession. Nevertheless, the ultimate position—withdrawal, solitude and insulation from the actual world—is a denial of life as it is being experienced by real people. It is an admission that one can only function in an environment that is well scripted and well directed, and in a setting where people react in a predictable and carefully plotted fashion. The ultimate danger is that one becomes incapable of responding to anything but stage gestures and cues.

Reviewing *Theatre*, Bernard DeVoto wrote that 'it has the speed, smoothness, and entertainment of an expert theatre piece'.[19] The novel does display a number of affinities to a play, and it is quite probable that, had Maugham written the story ten or twenty years earlier, it would have appeared in dramatic form. The superficiality of most of the characters, and the social comedy, touch the same vein as his comic plays. A great many scenes are constructed as if for stage presentation—Julia's meeting with Michael's parents, her tactful handling of Charles Tamerley when she misjudges his intentions, and the final scene in the restaurant. *Theatre* has, in fact, been dramatised a number of times. As early as 1937 it was made into a stage comedy in New York by Helen Jerome; in 1942 Guy Bolton interpreted it for the stage and then re-wrote it as *Larger Than Life* in 1951; in the 1950s a version was written for the French stage by Sauvajon, and it had a run of almost three years in Paris.

Theatre is an excellent example of Maugham's propensity to envisage an idea in a particular genre in which he was interested at the time. After having written *Sheppey* in 1933 he ceased to write plays and no longer conceived his stories in terms of the dramatic form. In 1949 Garson Kanin asked him whether he might yet be struck by an idea for a brilliant play:

"I know," he said, "because I no longer *think* in the category of plays. Moreover, I have never been 'struck', as you put it, by an idea for anything.

It was more a case of . . . mining with me. Mining and refining. When I was interested in the theatre, I would turn up an idea for a play daily. Often two or three. Assuredly, most of them were . . . poor. But they were ideas. When I was interested in short stories, those ideas would . . . come to the surface."[20]

Theatre is only one of the many examples of Maugham's thinking in terms of a particular genre. Had the idea for the story come to him earlier, he would have adapted it for the stage; as it was, he envisaged it in the framework of a novel.

'The Human Element', a short story written in 1930, does not follow the situation of *Mrs Craddock* as closely as do *The Painted Veil* and *Theatre*, but it presents a third way in which a woman preserves her liberty. The central figure, Betty Welldon-Burns, finds her freedom through a method which appears in numerous forms in Maugham's writings of the 'twenties, 'thirties and 'forties—escape.

Betty is a young English woman from an impoverished aristocratic family. She is immensely active—nursing in France during the war, acting in a theatrical tour, holding auctions and selling flags in Piccadilly for charity—and she becomes a national public personality. She excites people and sets fashions, thus incurring the disapproval of the old order—always a compliment in a Maugham story. The most striking thing about Betty, however, is the enthusiasm and intensity with which she pursues life:

And it was vitality that was Betty's most shining characteristic. The urge of life flowed through her with a radiance that dazzled you. . . . She was like a maenad. She danced with an abandon that made you laugh, so obvious was her intense enjoyment of the music and the movement of her young limbs. . . . She was a great beauty, but she had none of the coldness of great beauty. She laughed constantly, and when she was not laughing she smiled and her eyes danced with the joy of living. She was like a milk-maid on the farmstead of the gods.[21]

Because of this vitality and intensity, people are surprised when Betty marries James Welldon-Burns, heir to an industrial baronetcy and a man who is prim, polite and dull—'the most crashing bore'. After the marriage, Betty vanishes from the public eye, and later she and her husband get a separation, with Betty going to live in Rhodes.

When Welldon-Burns dies, an old admirer, Humphrey Carruthers, goes to Rhodes in the hope of persuading Betty to marry him. Distressed to discover that she has found her happiness on the island, Carruthers soon learns to his horror that her chauffeur, Albert, is her lover and has been ever since he was the footman at her aunt's house. Shattered by the revelation that his illusions about Betty are entirely false, he cannot comprehend her 'unspeakable degradation'. Maugham offers an explanation:

"I should have said that Albert was only the instrument, her toll to the solid earth, so to speak, that left her soul at liberty to range the empyrean. Perhaps the mere fact that he was so far below her gave her a sense of freedom in her relations with him that she would have lacked with a man of her own class."[22]

Thus, through escape from society and its conventions, especially the restrictions of marriage, Betty finds perfect freedom. She has a lover who is a satisfactory sexual partner, a man to whom she is not bound by spiritual ties. Her vitality and sensuality are matched by his physical appeal, and their relationship is not restricted by rules and regulations of conduct. Humphrey Carruthers, dull, conventional and restrained, represents the world from which she has escaped, and his reactions to her are those which would convulse society should it learn of her way of life. It is quite understandable, therefore, that he can offer her nothing; she already has all she needs.

Louise Frith, in *The Narrow Corner*, is yet another of the women in Maugham's writings who jealously guards her independence. At her mother's request, she becomes engaged to Erik Christessen, kind, warm and generous, but not a man to inspire intense love. When she gives herself one evening to a handsome young sailor, Fred Blake, Erik discovers them and kills himself. Louise does not feel any remorse at his death because she does not believe that she was responsible; Erik, she argues, killed himself because he had created a vision of her and her infidelity had shattered this illusion. She feels only relief that she has avoided being trapped into living according to a pattern envisaged by Erik and by Fred:

"I tell you he didn't love me. He loved his ideal. My mother's beauty and my mother's qualities in me and those Shakespeare heroines of his and the princesses in Hans Andersen's fairy tales. What right have people to make an image after their own heart and force it on you and be angry if it doesn't fit you? He wanted to imprison me in his ideal. He didn't care who I was. He wouldn't take me as I am. He wanted to possess my soul, and because he felt that there was somewhere in me something that escaped him, he tried to replace that little spark within me which is me by a phantom of his own fancy. I'm unhappy, but I tell you I don't grieve. And Fred in his way was the same. When he lay by my side that night he said he'd like to stay here always, on this island, and marry me and cultivate the plantation, and I don't know what else. He made a picture of his life and I was to fit in it. He wanted, too, to imprison me in his dream. It was a different dream, but it was his dream. But I am I. I don't want to dream anyone else's dream. I want to dream my own. All that's happened is terrible and my heart is heavy, but at the back of my mind I know that it's given me freedom."[23]

In *The Constant Wife* (1926), another woman gains her independence, this time through economic equality with her husband.

The play revolves around the proposition that, as long as men pay the bills, their wives have no justification for claiming any liberties. When, however, the woman is free of the economic obligation, she has the right to demand freedom equal to that of her husband. The heroine, Constance Middleton, is prevented from taking more serious action against her adulterous husband because of her acceptance of what she considers to be the obligations of her marriage contract. As she says to Bernard, her potential lover, the wife in the upper-middle class is nothing but a parasite:

My dear Bernard, have you ever considered what marriage is among well-to-do people? In the working classes a woman cooks her husband's dinner, washes for him and darns his socks. She looks after the children and makes their clothes. She gives good value for the money she costs. But what is a wife in our class? Her house is managed by servants, nurses look after her children, if she has resigned herself to having any, and as soon as they are old enough she packs them off to school. Let us face it, she is no more than the mistress of a man of whose desire she has taken advantage to insist on a legal ceremony that will prevent him from discarding her when his desire has ceased.[24]

To gain economic equality with her husband, Constance goes into partnership in a business with a friend. After a year, she is able to deposit a thousand pounds into her husband's account to pay for her year's keep, and with this economic independence she claims her sexual freedom. She now feels justified in confronting her husband:

I owe you nothing. I am able to keep myself. For the last year I have paid my way. There is only one freedom that is really important and that is economic freedom, for in the long run the man who pays the piper calls the tune. Well, I have that freedom and upon my soul it's the most enjoyable sensation I can remember since I ate my first strawberry ice.[25]

The assumption that financial independence automatically means sexual independence may be a superficial interpretation of the marriage contract suitable only to the light comedy of *The Constant Wife*. Economic freedom nevertheless has an important place in Maugham's hierarchy of values, and within the framework of the play it provides a woman with the means to achieve detachment and personal freedom from all other people.

Maugham's interpretation of marriage has frequently been attacked for being cynical and negative, and he has often been accused of concentrating too much on the lurid, sensational aspects of adultery and divorce. Indeed, when the novels, short stories and plays are examined as a whole, it becomes clear that the plots of over half involve adultery or the destruction of some form of romantic relationship. In story after story, permutations of the marriage contract initiate sacrifice, suicide, conflict and murder.

Despite the obvious popular appeal of adulterous literature, how-ever, the situation of marital infidelity in Maugham's writing is much more than mere sensationalism. The marriage contract is a social institution, evolved with the purpose of maintaining social stability, conformity and continuity. Of all society's institutions, it is that which involves the most people and which affects each person most intimately. For Maugham, therefore, the marriage contract becomes a symbol of society in general, a microcosm in which man's reactions to social restrictions can be epitomised. Just as D. H. Lawrence uses the act of copulation to represent man's natural instincts in the impersonal modern industrial world, Maugham takes marriage to symbolise man's relationship to society. Ronald Barnes explains:

The parties to a marriage contract are partners in a miniature society. The maxims of the miniature society of marriage evolved from the maxims of society. By expressing an attitude toward marriage, Maugham, in a larger sense, was expressing an attitude toward the social order, that is, toward society. By comparing and contrasting the relation of the individual to the marriage contract, Maugham has explored, within the limited scope of the marriage contract, the relation of the individual to society. . . . Man in conflict with the marriage contract is symbolic of man in conflict with his society.[26]

Barnes, in *The Dramatic Comedy of William Somerset Maugham*, provides an astute analysis of the development of Maugham's approach to marriage in his comic plays. He proposes that the comedies revolve around the marriage situation and that marriage always means restriction. The reaction of the characters to this con-dition is either surrender or revolt. Surrender is motivated by romantic attachment, as in the early comedies, or from practical or economic consideration, as in the later plays. Revolt, which becomes more prevalent in the mature comedies, is an attempt to seek sex, romantic love, or a practical objective; in some cases, it is simply an attempt to escape from formalities and restrictions.

Examined as a whole, Maugham's plays are largely superficial and do not warrant extensive thematic analysis. There are nevertheless several comedies of his mature years which provide interesting and serious presentations of the individual's relationship to the marriage situation.

In *The Unattainable* (1916), Caroline Ashley, separated from her husband for ten years, learns of his death. This makes her legally free to marry her lover, Robert Oldham, and their friends, Isabella and Maude, work diligently to bring about the wedding. Both Caroline and Robert are, however, satisfied with the present arrangement because it gives them the benefits of marriage without the restrictions. Caroline tells her maid:

I'm extremely pleased with my own society, Cooper. It's very nice to be alone when one wants to. I like to think it's my own house and nobody can cross my threshold without permission. It's really very pleasant to be one's own mistress.[27]

Robert, similarly, values his liberty:

But I don't mind telling you now that at the first moment the thought of marriage frightened me out of my wits. It meant changing all my habits and forming new ones. It meant giving up my freedom. . . . It's not that I want to be a gay dog, but I want to be able to be a gay dog if I want to.[28]

Although neither Caroline nor Robert wish to marry, the pressure of society in the form of their meddling friends is such that they reluctantly concede defeat. Salvation comes, however, in the final act when Dr Cornish falsely announces that Caroline's husband is actually alive. This deception re-establishes the ideal situation; Caroline, supposedly still married, yet separated, is free from social pressures and is able to continue her relationship with Robert while at the same time preserving her independence. The irony here is that an assumed marriage has provided the heroine with a high degree of flexibility and freedom.

Home and Beauty (1919), a light farce, presents the situation of a husband returning from the war to discover that his wife, having supposed him dead, has remarried. The action of the play seems to start as an attempt to see which husband she should have, but it soon becomes clear that neither husband wishes to remain. Both have found their wife, Victoria, intolerably restricting, and both wish to escape:

Frederick: I confess that sometimes I've thought it hard that when I wanted a thing it was selfishness, and when she wanted it, it was only her due.
William: I don't mind admitting that sometimes I used to wonder why it was only natural of me to sacrifice my inclinations, but in her the proof of a beautiful nature.
Frederick: It has tried me now and then that in every difference of opinion I should always be wrong and she should always be right.
William: Sometimes I couldn't quite understand why my engagements were made to be broken, while nothing in the world must interfere with hers.
Frederick: I have asked myself occasionally why my time was of no importance while hers was so precious.
William: I did sometimes wish I could call my soul my own.[29]

Frederick suggests that it is time that William takes up 'the white man's burden'. The solution, however, comes in the form of a third husband, Mr Leicester Paton, a man whose chief attraction is that he owns a Rolls-Royce. After a comic scene in which a shrewd lawyer devises a way for Victoria to divorce two husbands, the play terminates with William toasting the next husband, adding: 'And for us—liberty.'

The Circle (1921), one of Maugham's finest comedies, concerns the revolt against social convention and the marriage contract by a romantic young wife, Elizabeth Champion-Cheney. Married to a dull, conventional and lifeless member of the English upper class, she falls in love with Teddie Luton, an energetic young man on leave from his post in the Federated Malay States.

The play gets its title from the added complication of the appearance of Elizabeth's mother-in-law, Kitty, who thirty years ago ran away from her husband with Lord Porteous. Elizabeth invites Lady Kitty and Porteous to visit because she is interested in the romance of their past. Far from figures of romance, however, the lovers are old, faded and quarrelsome. Despite this disillusionment, Elizabeth asks her husband, Arnold, for a divorce. He consents, hoping that the spirit of his sacrifice will prevent her from leaving. However, in spite of the example of the old lovers in front of her, Elizabeth elopes with Luton, who has promised her, not happiness, but love.

The conflict in *The Circle* is between the spirit of romance, represented in the past by Kitty and Porteous and in the present by Luton, and conventional social behaviour, represented by Clive and Arnold Champion-Cheney. Elizabeth looks upon her existence as Arnold's wife as imprisonment:

I don't want luxury. You don't know how sick I am of all this beautiful furniture. These over-decorated houses are like a prison in which I can't breathe. When I drive about in a Callot frock and a Rolls-Royce I envy the shop-girl in a coat and skirt whom I see jumping on the tailboard of a bus.[30]

Luton, coming from a colonial environment, is outside the restrictions of this kind of life, and he offers her excitement, love and freedom. When Kitty and Porteous learn of the intended elopement, however, they at first doubt whether the lovers will have the strength to survive social ostracism. Porteous warns that, being a gregarious animal, man is a member of a herd, and 'if we break the herd's laws we suffer for it' and 'we suffer damnably'.

In spite of this warning, Elizabeth and Luton run away, and the audience is left to decide whether they will have the strength to survive the many pressures on their relationship. Porteous concludes that it will depend upon the characters of the lovers.

The Breadwinner (1930) presents the most extreme example of revolt from the marriage contract. Charles Battle, a middle-aged businessmen, discovers one day that he is near to financial ruin, and, rather than enlist aid to enable him to overcome his difficulties, he deliberately allows himself to go bankrupt. When his wife and two children suddenly discover that he intends to abandon them and escape to America, he explains that 'suddenly it seemed to me that for me ruin meant life and liberty—and that tube, with all those people hurrying to catch their train, led to slavery and death'.

The Breadwinner echoes *The Moon and Sixpence* and it anticipates *The Razor's Edge* in its rejection of conventional values. Battle is tired of the social routine, of existing as a drudge in order to provide luxuries for an unfaithful, unloving wife and two silly and thoughtless children. His answer is not accommodation and compromise, but total abdication of his social role.

Barnes has discussed the use of the marriage contract as an image of society in Maugham's dramatic comedies, but the same device can be found in many of the novels and short stories. In the prose fiction, however, the treatment is serious, with far greater consequences to the actions of the characters. The defiance of the restrictions of the marriage contract is based on similar motivation, but the results of infidelity often involve degradation, murder and suicide.

If the marriage contract is symbolic of the social contract in Maugham's writings, it follows that the author's attitude to marriage should mirror his attitude to society in general. His view of the social contract, as presented in *Of Human Bondage* and *A Writer's Notebook*, is that social conventions and institutions should be followed as long as they provide a useful service. Society and the individual are in conflict with each other, with each striving to protect its own entity. The individual finds it suitable to yield much of his independence to the state because the benefits of co-operation make it agreeable. When this situation changes, however, he must revolt.

The marriage contract in Maugham's writing is viewed in a similar utilitarian fashion. Marriages based on deep and enduring romantic attachments are rare; on the other hand, many are made or preserved because of economic advantages, companionship, or even out of apathy. Marriage is always treated as a surrender of one's independence, a worthwhile sacrifice if it brings a desired commodity—security, comfort or companionship. If the marriage state does not fulfil the expectations, however, the sacrifice of personal freedom becomes too high a price and the character rebels. Arthur Little, in *Caesar's Wife*, sums it up when he says 'You didn't know what marriage was and how irksome it must be unless love makes its constraints sweeter than freedom.'

Maugham's view of marriage seems to be that it is a convenience which should not be allowed to interfere with love. He sees the marriage contract as a social document, a legal assurance of certain rights, but not a guarantee of romantic love. Romantic love, which Maugham equates with sexual attraction, exists on a separate plane and if it happens to coincide with marriage the characters are very fortunate. Passion, according to the author, is a natural and uncontrollable drive, and therefore deviations from marital fidelity will occur and are best treated with tolerance.

At the heart of Maugham's treatment of marriage is the choice which faces the individual: commitment or withdrawal. The character can surrender a great deal of his individual and personal entity to become part of a larger organism, or he can retain his detachment by yielding no obligation or fidelity. With Maugham's emphasis always on the individual's independence, there are strikingly few complete relationships in his writings, and this is one of his great weaknesses. It is not the emphasis on adultery or divorce which mars his stories; it is, rather, the glaring lack of a marriage of fulfilment.

VII

Cakes and Ale

CAKES AND ALE, published in 1930, was Maugham's own first choice among his fiction and the book for which he most wanted to be remembered. Writing in the introduction to the Modern Library edition of the novel in 1950, he states:

I am willing enough to agree with common opinion that *Of Human Bondage* is my best work. It is the kind of book that an author can only write once. After all, he has only one life. But the book I like best is *Cakes and Ale*. It was an amusing book to write.[1]

It was also an amusing book to read. Unlike any of his previous works, it had an immediate popular success, and it very quickly assured him a prominent place in the critical estimation of the period. Looking back, Frank Swinnerton suggests that after *Cakes and Ale* 'Maugham's reputation as a novelist had no immediate parallel. Within a few months of its publication all active novel-writers were considerably his juniors.'[2] The novel is indeed a considerable achievement. It remains a delightful book and will be one of the works on which the Maugham reputation will stand.

Cakes and Ale is remarkable because it is one of the very few books in the Maugham canon which does not follow the familiar pattern of being written against the background of a particular literary fashion or genre. It is not the product of any trend; there are no immediate forerunners in which the critic can discern the threads which make up Maugham's novel. The author here, aware of his own capabilities and limitations, strikes out completely on his own and, although the result is not a work of startling innovation, *Cakes and Ale* is original. One looks in vain in its period for a counterpart of approaching quality.

While *Cakes and Ale* does not easily fit into a particular category of the literature of its time, it is nonetheless a literary novel, with close ties to the Georgian literary scene. Much of it is a satire on the social and literary life of the first three decades of the twentieth century, and a number of prominent figures of the period are represented either in fairly direct sketches or in more ambiguous composite portraits. As a result, Maugham's novel instantly became notorious and controversial; for a few months in the latter part of 1930, it was the most discussed, attacked, and defended, of contemporary fiction. The controversy which was initiated by its publication was continued by rumours, accusations and threats of lawsuits, so that for several decades its notoriety was maintained. Thus in 1950, when Maugham wrote a new introduction to *Cakes and Ale* and added some new confessions about his intentions in the novel, the *New York Times* reprinted it in its entirety on the first page of its book review section. The social scandal associated with *Cakes and Ale* may have detracted from a more objective recognition of Maugham's real purpose but, since it is a satire of literary life, it is worth examining that milieu and its reaction to the author's representation.

The first, most obvious, and public, reaction to *Cakes and Ale* was a resentful claim that in the creation of the ageing novelist, Edward Driffield, Maugham was attacking Thomas Hardy. Hardy had died just two years before and the interval had been a period of continued veneration of the last of the great Victorian novelists. In Driffield's life it was easy to discover a number of similarities to that of Hardy. Like Maugham's author, Hardy was born and bred in the country, rubbed brasses in country churches, went through a long period before he achieved recognition, was married twice, received the Order of Merit, and returned to the country to be the Grand Old Man of English Letters. Like Driffield, Hardy wrote about rustic figures with a sturdy straightforward style.

Despite the number of parallels between the careers of Driffield and Hardy, however, there are a great many differences. Hardy, for example, never ran away to sea, never used Kent in his novels, and had none of the boisterous, public-house high-spiritedness of Driffield. The character of neither of his wives bears any relation to that of Rosie or Amy Driffield, and his home, Max Gate, did not resemble Ferne Court. In his late career he needed no such lion-hunter as Mrs Barton Trafford to promote his reputation in English letters. Finally, as Richard Cordell points out, while Hardy was the most notable English poet of his day, Driffield writes only prose.

Instead of neutralising the criticisms of Hardy enthusiasts, however, these differences between the real and the fictional author contributed to their conviction that the great writer was being maligned. Kathleen C. Tomlinson, writing in *The Nation and Athenaeum*, voiced the opinion of this faction:

The formula is simple. Take one of the finest characters and greatest writers of the century; establish by well-known facts the identity of the writer in the mind of the reader – and then invent, but let the invention be belittlement.[3]

In his defence, Maugham claimed repeatedly after the publication of *Cakes and Ale* that he had only met Hardy once, that he could not remember much about this encounter, and that Hardy was not the model for Driffield. The original of his novelist, he argued, was a disreputable and thoroughly unrecognised writer whom he knew as a child in Whitstable. The conception of the Grand Old Man of English Letters in *Cakes and Ale* had, he said, originated years before and was recorded in his notebook:

I am asked to write my reminiscences of a famous novelist, a friend of my boyhood, living at W. with a common wife very unfaithful to him. There he writes his great books. Later he marries his secretary, who guards him and makes him into a figure. My wonder whether even in old age he is not slightly restive at being made into a monument.[4]

It is possible that this formula was suggested by Maugham's encounter with Hardy or that, with this in mind, he saw him as a writer in similar circumstances. His impression of Hardy, recorded many years later, is certainly in a broad sense like his conception of the aged Driffield: 'I took away with me the impression of a small, grey, tired, retiring man who was, though not in the least embarrassed to be at such a grand party as that was, no more intimately concerned with it than if he had been a member of the audience at a play.'[5] This description is not applicable to the inner character of Driffield, but the impression of a man trapped in a social role is the same.

The most sensible answer to the question of the source of the character of Driffield is that he is a composite portrait. Maugham has suggested that comparisons might be made to Tennyson or Meredith. There are, as well, a number of Driffield's qualities which are reminiscent of other prominent writers of the turn of the century. His running away to become a sailor and his later writing about the sea suggest Joseph Conrad. His fondness for bicycling and his use of Kent as a background for his novels are characteristics which could easily have been borrowed from H. G. Wells. Moreover, the portrait of Driffield is diffused by narrative technique; since he is only seen second- or third-hand, there is an ambiguity and haziness about his character which tends to blur the outlines.

In the years since the publication of *Cakes and Ale*, critical opinion has come more and more to the conclusion that Driffield is an imaginary Grand Old Man of English Letters, with a resemblance in some ways to Thomas Hardy but also with affinities to other writers.

This does not, however, alter the fact that in 1930 the literary climate was such that a sensible and perceptive reader could not be blamed for assuming that Maugham had Hardy in mind. As intelligent an observer as J. B. Priestley could write that 'it is impossible to escape the feeling that Driffield is intended as a portrait of Hardy', and he justifiably questioned the wisdom of Maugham's picture: 'If . . . Mr Maugham did not intend his readers to be reminded of Hardy, then he acted with a strange stupidity (and a less stupid man than Somerset Maugham never put pen to paper) when he set out to create the figure of Edward Driffield.'[6]

If Maugham, then, did not intend to attack the reputation of Hardy, the resulting confusion in the minds of the readers was the outcome of an error in technique. Whatever the motivation of the author, the initial reaction of a great many people was to take Driffield for Hardy, and this mistake in identification could only damage the satiric purpose. Instead of emphasising the tendency of the literary world to worship any writer of any period who is prolific and long-lived, the attack became associated with a specific writer at a particular period. Readers therefore delighted or agonised in an author and his circle being pilloried, and felt no necessity to extend the criticisms beyond the limits of that particular circle. Thus there was the danger that the public attention would be absorbed in comparing Hardy to Driffield rather than in seeing how many Driffields there are in the literary world. The result was that in 1930 *Cakes and Ale* became a *roman à clef* for a great many readers, and the excitement of its notoriety tended to overshadow its real literary worth.

The portrait of Driffield disturbed the Hardy enthusiasts, and it was an issue discussed by many reviewers and columnists. In private circles, literary cliques and London clubs, however, *Cakes and Ale* caused far more excitement because of Maugham's supposed crucifixion of Hugh Walpole in the character of Alroy Kear. With even greater intensity than the Driffield–Hardy controversy, the Kear–Walpole sensation became a scandal, and the issue of the ethics of the portrayal took precedence over the validity of the picture of Alroy Kear as an authentic representative of a common type in the literary world.

Walpole's journal records the beginning of what was to be a painful ordeal. He went to a theatre, 'then home and, half-undressed sitting on my bed, picked up idly Maugham's *Cakes and Ale*. Read on with increasing horror. Unmistakable portrait of myself. Never slept.'[7] The next day, Walpole telephoned J. B. Priestley and, brushing aside Priestley's report that Maugham had denied that he had drawn Kear from an original, confessed that 'there are in one conversation the very accents of my voice'.[8] To Francis Brett Young he made similar charges:

Lunching one day at Brackenburn, Hugh spoke of Maugham's *Cakes and Ale*. . . . He said Maugham must have written things down that had been said at a luncheon party in London, and he would neither eat nor drink at his table again. At the same time Eddie [Marsh] wrote from Gray's Inn Road to ask if Francis had read it. "I hear poor Hugh says it has finished him." And Arnold Bennett had tried to put it right by saying that it wasn't in the least a malicious portrait of him but thoroughly just, accurate and benevolent.[9]

In November 1930 Lytton Strachey wrote that *Cakes and Ale* 'is causing some excitement here as it contains a most envenomed portrait of Hugh Walpole, who is out of his mind with agitation and horror'.[10] In his distress, Walpole lashed out at enemies real and imagined. Frank Swinnerton, a longtime friend, claims that an angry and hurt Walpole confronted him in a London club, accusing him of being part of a conspiracy.

Walpole wrote a letter of protest to Maugham, and the reply, containing perhaps more than a touch of irony, was an attempt to be conciliatory:

My dear Hugh,
I am really very unlucky. As you may have seen I have been attacked in the papers because they think my old man is intended to be a portrait of Hardy. It is absurd. The only grounds are that they died old, received the O.M. and were married twice. *You* know that for my story I needed this and that there is nothing of Hardy in my character. Now I have your letter. I cannot say I was surprised to receive it because I had heard from Charlie Evans that Priestley and Clemence Dane had talked to him about it. He told them that it had never occurred to him that there was any resemblance between the Alroy Kear of my novel and you; and when he spoke to me about it I was able very honestly to assure him that nothing had been further from my thoughts than to describe you. I can only repeat this. I do not see any likeness. My man is an athlete and a sportsman, who tries to be as little like a man of letters as he can. Can you really recognise yourself in this? Surely no one is the more complete man of letters than you are and really you cannot think of yourself as a famous golfer and a fervid fox-hunter. Nor is the appearance described anything like yours. Nor so far as I have ever seen do you frequent smart society. Frankau or E. F. Benson might just as well think themselves aimed at and Stephen McKenna much more. The only thing that you can go on is the fact that you also are a lecturer. I admit that if I had thought twice of it I would have omitted this. But after all you are not the only English man of letters who lectures, but only the best known; and it is hard to expect a writer, describing such a character as I have, to leave out such a telling detail. The loud laugh is nothing. All big men with the sort of heartiness I have described have a loud laugh. The conversation you mention in California has entirely slipped

my memory and I cannot place it in the book. Really I should not have been such a fool. I certainly never intended Alroy Kear to be a portrait of you. He is made up of a dozen people and the greater part of him is myself. There is more of me in him than of any writer I know. I suggest that if there is anything in him that you recognise it is because to a greater or less extent we are all the same. Certain characteristics we all have and I gave them to Alroy Kear because I found them in myself. They do not seem to me less absurd because I have them.

I do not think for an instant that there will be any reference to this business in the papers, but if there is I promise you that I will immediately write, protest and vehemently deny that there has ever been in my mind any thought of portraying you.

Yours always,
W. S. Maugham.[11]

Walpole, with his own sense of irony, signed his brief acknowledgement: 'Alroy Maugham Walpole'.

In spite of his unhappiness, Walpole was nevertheless able, late in 1930, to record in his journal that 'of course it was unpleasant for a while to think of all sorts of people going gleefully about laughing at me and it, but that soon wore off'.[12] He was even able to question the validity of Maugham's portrait in relation to his own character. His peace of mind was, however, soon to be shattered again.

Early in 1931, Farrar and Rinehart, the American publishing house, brought out a book called *Gin and Bitters*, written by 'A. Riposte'. The title was an unmistakable parody of *Cakes and Ale* and the central figure, a decadent ageing writer named 'Leverson Hurle', a savage attack on Maugham. The foreword clearly referred to the moral issue associated with *Cakes and Ale*:

The author wishes to make it quite plain that there are no portraits in this book; no attempt at the portraiture of any living or once living person, and for this reason: Upon one side he judges that a biography should be a biography, and a novel a novel: just as a mistress should be a mistress and a wife a wife. Upon the other hand, he makes sure all right-minded persons will agree that there have never been, or could be, such people as the characters shown in this book. . . . After all we are getting on towards the middle of the twentieth century, and civilization is civilization, as we all know.[13]

Gin and Bitters was badly written, with a bludgeoning attack rather than a sharp incisive thrust, and it was far below the calibre needed to bring down someone of Maugham's stature. It nevertheless served to rekindle the Kear–Walpole controversy.

Although Walpole was himself clearly represented in *Gin and Bitters* as an insignificant writer called 'Polehue', he was initially suspected of having been its author. However, he quickly sent a disclaimer to Maugham and then worked to prevent its publication in

England. Heinemann, Maugham's publishers, felt that it was necessary to block the book's appearance in England and, since Maugham's opinion was that it would be best ignored, they enlisted Walpole's aid. After reading *Gin and Bitters*, he wrote Maugham to plead with him to assist Heinemann.

On 5 May Farrar and Rinehart revealed that the author of *Gin and Bitters* was Mrs Elinor Mordaunt (a pseudonym of Evelyn May Clowes), a writer of travel books and contributor to women's magazines. Two days later, the *New York Times* reported that the English edition had been cancelled because of the influence of Maugham's friends, adding that 'Hugh Walpole, one of the prime movers in obtaining the ban, declared that if the edition had appeared here "some one would have suffered".' It is obvious that the 'some one' was Hugh Walpole and that he had suffered considerably already. When Mrs Mordaunt fought against these moves, he wrote: 'Shall I ever be free of the *Cakes and Ale* controversy? I may certainly with my hand on my heart wish that W.M. had never been born.'[14]

The *Gin and Bitters* part of the *Cakes and Ale* controversy terminated in October 1931, when Maugham issued a writ for alleged libel against Elinor Mordaunt, thus forcing Martin Secker to recall the English edition (published in Britain as *Full Circle*). The question of Alroy Kear/Hugh Walpole was ultimately settled in 1950 in Maugham's new introduction to the Modern Library edition of *Cakes and Ale*:

It was true that I had Hugh Walpole in mind when I devised the character to whom I gave the name of Alroy Kear. No author can create a character out of nothing. He must have a model to give him a starting point; but then his imagination goes to work, he builds him up, adding a trait here, a trait there, which his model did not possess, and when he has finished with him the complete character he presents to the reader has little in him of the person who had offered the first suggestion. . . . But the fact remained that I had given Alroy Kear certain traits, certain discreditable foibles which Hugh Walpole too notoriously had, so that few people in the literary world of London failed to see that he had been my model.[15]

Regardless of Maugham's intentions in his portrait of Alroy Kear, the association with Hugh Walpole in the minds of the reading public had a damaging effect on Walpole's stature in English letters. At the time of the publication of *Cakes and Ale*, he had written over thirty books and, although his patrons among the older writers were then dead and his position was being taken by younger writers, he could have expected, in normal circumstances, a consolidation of his reputation. However, the novel that raised Maugham to eminence brought down Walpole. Anthony West explains:

In the ordinary course of British literary events, this situation leads to a period of semi-retirement in which the writer concerned produces a few essays with a golden autumnal tone to them, opens bazaars, sits on cultural committees, and marks time until the crown at last honors him with a knighthood or the Order of Merit and he reemerges on the crest of a wave of Library Editions, Collected Works, and cheap reprints, as a Grand Old Man of the English novel. Maugham, with forty pages and fewer than twelve thousand well-chosen words, twitched this prospect away from Walpole and made what had seemed a certainty an absurdity. The knighthood arrived, in due season, but it was too late; Alroy Kear had simply extinguished Walpole as a serious literary figure.[16]

In the same way that the confusion between Driffield and Hardy tended to confine Maugham's satire to a particular individual, the controversy about Kear and Walpole obscured his attack on self-promoting literary figures in general. Readers concentrated on the similarities between Kear and Walpole rather than recognising the characteristics of Maugham's creation which make him a superb caricature of a common and timeless figure. *Cakes and Ale* has suffered considerably from being treated as a *roman à clef* rather than as a high-spirited, but serious, criticism of the numerous follies of literary social life. Even at present, it is difficult completely to separate the novel from the literary milieu which it satirised and which assimilated it as part of that period's history. Like a good wine of a vintage year, however, it will benefit from ageing.

Technically, *Cakes and Ale* is Maugham's best novel. *Of Human Bondage*, because of the honesty of its presentation of the problems of adolescence and because of the philosophical issues it treats, is probably his most important work, but *Cakes and Ale*, technically and stylistically, is superior. Like its heroine, Rosie, it glows with warmth and life, and it remains one of those rare books that is a joy to read again and again.

The most striking quality of *Cakes and Ale* is the range of the settings and periods which it encompasses. It incorporates Victorian provincial life, Edwardian social and literary manners, and the Georgian scene two decades later. That the reader is transported from one period to another, from one milieu to another, with no sense of disorientation is due to Maugham's consummate mastery of the time-shift. The first person singular, a handicap in many respects, is here the perfect device to facilitate the smooth transference from one point in time to another. Most of the action takes place within Ashenden's memory, and the reader follows his mental wanderings with hardly an awareness of a literary technique.

The best demonstration of Maugham's skill in altering the scene and time without any disruption in tone or atmosphere is the change which takes place between chapters II and III. Ashenden, in Georgian London, returns from his luncheon with Alroy Kear, and he describes the feeling of Half Moon Street. Maugham then ends the chapter with a description of Ashenden's rooms:

The parlour was papered with an old marbled paper and on the walls were water colours of romantic scenes, cavaliers bidding good-bye to their ladies and knights of old banqueting in stately halls; there were large ferns in pots, and the armchairs were covered with faded leather. There was about the room an amusing air of the eighteen eighties, and when I looked out of the window I expected to see a private hansom rather than a Chrysler. The curtains were of a heavy red rep.[17]

Without in any way giving the impression that this is a digression or out of the context of the narrative, Maugham has ended the chapter with an evocation of the atmosphere of the turn of the century. The final image is of the 'heavy red rep' curtains, and this prepares the way for the change of scene in the next chapter, from Georgian London to Victorian village life. Ashenden says that these surroundings have revived old memories; they have also transported the reader.

The pattern which Maugham adopts in *Cakes and Ale* is to create a particular milieu, populate it with characters who represent the beliefs and practices of that society, and to create in each case an environment or characters which provide a significant contrast to that picture. The narrow provincial life of Blackstable is set against that seen in the Driffield household, and the stiff, snobbish townspeople are the antithesis of the relaxed, high-spirited Driffields and Lord George Kemp. The literary life of Edwardian London, populated by 'lion-hunters', parasites, and hypocrites, is cast against the unconscious good nature of Rosie and the simple honest life of Mrs Hudson. The Georgian literary scene, providing a frame at the beginning and the end of the novel, and represented by Alroy Kear and Amy Driffield, is balanced by a final look at Rosie, still exuberant and unpretentious in Yonkers, New York. Rosie is the centre of the novel, one of the most delightful of fictional women, and it is not surprising that she appears as a foil to the figures of all the milieus.

After the initial portrait of Alroy Kear and the introduction of his idea for a biography of the famous novelist, Edward Driffield, the scene shifts, through Ashenden's recollections, to his youth in Blackstable. To those who know Maugham's previous novels, the aspects of the scene are familiar. The prudish, restricted and parochial existence had been exposed in the stifling environment from which Bertha Craddock sought relief. It was demonstrated in the society which finally drove the intellectually and morally liberated James Parsons, in *The Hero*, to suicide. It was part of the surroundings from which Philip Carey, in *Of Human Bondage*, longed for escape. This section of *Cakes and Ale* is in many respects a return to the early part of *Of Human Bondage*; the village is much the same and the narrator is an orphan living with a clergyman uncle and his wife. The treatment in the later novel—mellower and more tolerant—is different and more effective.

The most skilful technique for communicating the snobbish and rigid attitude of mind of the society of Blackstable is the first person narrator. Through an amused recollection of the young snob that he was, Ashenden conveys perfectly the narrow range of tolerance instilled into middle-class youth at the turn of the century. The young boy, for example, encounters his uncle's curate, a man whose rank is not high at the best of times and is especially low at present because he is in the company of a stranger wearing a knickerbocker suit:

Knickerbockers were uncommon then, at least in Blackstable, and being young and fresh from school I immediately set the fellow down as a cad. But while I chatted with the curate he looked at me in a friendly way, with a smile in his pale blue eyes. I felt that for two pins he would have joined in the conversation and I assumed a haughty demeanour. I was not going to run the risk of being spoken to by a chap who wore knickerbockers like a game-keeper and I resented the familiarity of his good-humoured expression. I was myself faultlessly dressed in white flannel trousers, a blue blazer with the arms of my school on the breast pocket, and a black-and-white straw hat with a very wide brim.[18]

Young Ashenden shares the disdain of Blackstable society for the summer visitors from London. It is 'horrid to have all that rag-tag and bobtail' down from the city, but he accepts that it is good for 'the tradespeople'. He reacts in the approved fashion to Lord George Kemp's presumptuous suggestion that he play cricket with the Kemp children: they go to the grammar school at Haversham and of course he cannot possibly have anything to do with them. Throughout his early relationship with the Driffields, he is constantly aware that they are beneath his station, and his visits to their house are therefore always conducted furtively.

The atmosphere of Blackstable society in *Cakes and Ale* is one of narrow and cramped morality, of strict Victorian beliefs, and of restricted individual development. The effect of the confining nature of their lives on the townspeople, says Maugham, was to smother the ease and amiability of their characters.

To emphasise the restricted life of Ashenden's uncle's household and of Blackstable society in general, Maugham provides a glimpse of the bohemian life of the Driffields and Lord George Kemp. None of

G

them pays any attention to social taboos and distinctions; Driffield
and Kemp may be aware of their existence, but Rosie seems totally
oblivious of them. Since the three of them are outside the unwritten
laws which rule Blackstable social life, they exercise certain advantages. Thus, Driffield can introduce himself to Ashenden with no
inhibition, he can overwhelm the Vicar by his cool irreverence, and
Lord George Kemp can upset the household by nonchalantly appearing at the front door. They find the game easier because they recognise
fewer rules:

They seemed to have no sense of the things one could do and the things
one simply couldn't. It never ceased to embarrass me, the way in which
they talked of incidents in their past that I should have thought they would
not dream of mentioning. I do not know that the people I lived among
were pretentious in the sense of making themselves out to be richer or
grander than they really were, but looking back it does seem to me that
they lived a life full of pretences. They dwelt behind a mask of respectability. You never caught them in their shirt sleeves with their feet on the
table. The ladies put on afternoon dresses and were not visible till then;
they lived privately with rigid economy so that you could not drop in for
a casual meal, but when they entertained their tables groaned with food.
Though catastrophe overwhelmed the family, they held their heads high
and ignored it. One of the sons might have married an actress, but they
never referred to the calamity, and though the neighbours said it was
dreadful, they took ostentatious care not to mention the theatre in the
presence of the afflicted. We all knew that the wife of Major Greencourt
who had taken the Three Gables was connected with trade, but neither she
nor the major ever so much as hinted at the discreditable secret; and
though we sniffed at them behind their backs, we were too polite even to
mention crockery (the source of Mrs Greencourt's adequate income) in
their presence. It was still not unheard of for an angry parent to cut off his
son with a shilling or to tell his daughter (who like my own mother had
married a solicitor) never to darken his doors again. I was used to all this
and it seemed to me natural.[19]

Ted Driffield, however, talks casually of being a waiter in Holborn as
though it is the usual course, and he unashamedly reveals that he also
has been a cab driver and a clerk in a booking office. Rosie shocks the
young Ashenden by freely mentioning her jobs as bar-maid in the
Railway Arms and the Feathers.

    Lord George Kemp, a figure of great exuberance and animal
spirits, is yet another example of Maugham drawing upon real life
for his characters. In *Somerset and All the Maughams* Robin Maugham
describes being told of Mr George Holden, usually called 'Gentleman
Holden', who lived in Whitstable when Maugham was a boy:

"You might say he was one of the industrial aristocrats of the town. He
was related to the Gann family – needless to say. A big shipowner, he was,
with luggers, carrying hay and wheat to Tower Bridge, and schooners that

took Kentish coal to Bermuda. Everyone called him 'Gentleman Holden' because of his fine clothes."[20]

Although Robin Maugham does not note the similarities, this is almost certainly the original of Lord George Kemp.

For Maugham's purposes, Lord George is the Sir Toby Belch of *Cakes and Ale*. His loud voice, strident laugh, and forward manner disturb the local people; his natural warmth and unselfconscious cheeriness are considered ill-mannered. His activities in the public good, his donations to worthy causes, and his uninhibited willingness to help someone else, do not in any way break through the barriers of hostility in Blackstable. Ashenden reflects the social attitude at first and reacts with reserve and scrupulous politeness. Lord George, however, seems so totally unconscious of any social differences between them that before long the young man discovers that he has some affection for the rogue. Kemp, he soon realises, is warm, breezy, boisterous and witty. He dresses outrageously and is vulgar and blatant; however, he is a character who, in a setting of dull mediocrity, is a splash of colour.

When the Driffields suddenly leave Blackstable and move to London, the milieu which Maugham treats is completely different. The society is now cosmopolitan, Edwardian literary London. The Driffields and Ashenden, now a medical student, are soon cast against a much different background.

The kind of literary scene which is satirised with delicacy and subtlety in *Cakes and Ale* is one which Maugham had treated before. *The Moon and Sixpence* had contained a number of portraits of prominent literary figures, and the same type of milieu had been exploited in 'The Creative Impulse' (1926). *The Gentleman in the Parlour*, published a few months earlier, contained a whimsical story of an insignificant writer's rise to fame in the eyes of the London literary élite.

The characters of the literary world in *Cakes and Ale* are taken far more definitely than Driffield or Kear from actual figures well-known in the Edwardian literary-social scene. The lion-hunting Mrs Barton Trafford and her husband are undoubtedly thinly disguised representations of Mr and Mrs Sidney Colvin. Jasper Gibbons, the poet who is first championed by Mrs Barton Trafford and then dropped by her when his value as a prize disappears, is clearly the poet Stephen Phillips (1868–1915).[21] Like Gibbons, Phillips rose to prominence very quickly and saw his reputation evaporate equally as fast; he was promoted for a long time by Lady Colvin. The verbose, pompous critic, Allgood Newton, is Maugham's caricature of the critic and man of letters Sir Edmund Gosse. In addition to these satiric figures there are probably more sketches which are recognisable to those familiar with the London literary life of the early twentieth century.

Maugham's account of the lion-hunting career of Mrs Barton Trafford and her circle is incisive, witty, and beautifully realised. Mrs Barton Trafford is characterised as being soft, charming and generous, but there is a definite touch of insidiousness in the impression which Ashenden conveys of her softness:

When you took her hand it was like taking a fillet of sole. Her face, not-withstanding its large features, had something fluid about it. When she sat it was as though she had no backbone and were stuffed, like an expensive cushion, with swansdown.[22]

In spite of this apparent gentleness, Mrs Barton Trafford is hard, predatory and possessive. She has gained her reputation through her friendship with a great Victorian novelist (paralleling Mrs Colvin's association with Robert Louis Stevenson), and her life revolves around her connection with current figures of literary success. She and her husband study the careers of potentially famous writers as avidly as any punter scans the form charts of racehorses. A young artist with promising value as a salon personality is captured, championed and retained as a trophy. Reputations are inflated through carefully timed articles, literary luncheons, and At Homes. When the writer's fame proves impermanent, however, the Barton Traffords nearly always manage to sell their stock before the crash.

Maugham is at his best in his description of the Traffords' experience with the young poet, Jasper Gibbons. After his meteoric rise, Mrs Trafford, through 'miracles of tact', 'tenderness', 'exquisite sympathy' and 'demure blandishments', 'nobbles' Gibbons. She gives luncheons where he meets the right people and At Homes where he recites his poems to the most distinguished persons in England; she arranges commissions for plays, places his poems in the proper periodicals, and deals with publisher's contracts. Her control over his life extends to her demand that he become separated from his wife, to whom he has been happily married for ten years. Domestic ties, she claims, are hindrances to his art.

Gibbons' career, however, crashes. Critical opinion swings against him, he begins to drink heavily, and his writing deteriorates. The critics, annoyed that they had misjudged his talent, tear him to pieces. Finally, Gibbons is arrested for being drunk and disorderly in Piccadilly, and this signals the end for Mrs Barton Trafford. Maugham's irony is never better than in this description of the dropping of Jasper Gibbons:

Mrs. Barton Trafford at this juncture was perfect. She did not repine. No harsh word escaped her lips. She might have been excused if she had felt a certain bitterness because this man for whom she had done so much had let her down. She remained tender, gentle, and sympathetic. She was the woman who understood. She dropped him, but not like a hot brick, or a hot potato. She dropped him with infinite gentleness, as softly as the tear that she doubtless shed when she made up her mind to do something so repugnant to her nature; she dropped him with so much tact, with such sensibility, that Jasper Gibbons perhaps hardly knew he was dropped. But there was no doubt about it. She would say nothing against him, indeed she would not discuss him at all, and when mention was made of him she merely smiled, a little sadly, and sighed. But her smile was the *coup de grâce*, and her sigh buried him deep.[23]

There is in this passage a delicacy, a fineness, which is rarely found in Maugham's writing. The style—smooth-flowing and casual— matches perfectly the ease with which Mrs Barton Trafford casts aside the devalued poet. The imagery of the *coup de grâce* being de- livered by a smile and of the poet being buried by a sigh is reminiscent of the battle scene in Pope's *The Rape of the Lock*.

Maugham treats the literary environment with a good deal of high spirits, and Ashenden admits that he spent many amusing hours at these gatherings. This does not, however, prevent the author from being highly critical of the insincerity and hypocrisy which are a part of this type of existence, and this criticism comes in the form of a con- trast between the life in the salons and that in Mrs Hudson's boarding- house. Mrs Barton Trafford is the perfect foil for Mrs Hudson, just as Amy Driffield is the foil for Rosie.

Maugham prefaces the London section with a chapter describing the boarding-house at which Ashenden lived when he was a medical student, and it is a serious mistake to claim, as many critics have done, that this is a pointless digression from the story. There is rarely an unnecessary passage in a Maugham work. The character of the landlady, Mrs Hudson, and the lives led by the inhabitants of her house establish a standard against which the succeeding description of the literary scene can be measured.

Mrs Hudson's life parallels that of Mrs Barton Trafford in that both, so to speak, have young men in their care—the former through running a boarding-house and the latter through her lion-hunting. Any similarity ends there, however, and the contrast in their treat- ment of people is marked. Physically, the two women are at ex- tremes; whereas Mrs Barton Trafford is soft and spineless, Mrs Hudson is energetic and full of life.

In Mrs Hudson there is an exuberance, vitality, and animal spirits not found in those in the literary environment. She works hard, sings, and gaily quips in her cockney humour. She indulges in a continuous comic feud with a landlady down the street, a fight that has as much amiability about it as rancour. She discusses with enthusiasm the chronic problem of having her teeth out. Everything considered, she is a woman who is close to the basic problems of living, and she is a vivid contrast to the artificial life of the salons.

Where Mrs Barton Trafford's interest in a young writer is entirely self-seeking and parasitic, Mrs Hudson has genuine affection and concern for her boarders. She lights the fires in the morning so that the young men do not have to eat their breakfast in the cold, she worries if they do not get up in time for their lectures, and she takes pleasure in cooking for them. She talks to her lodgers, partly because she likes an audience, but also because she genuinely enjoys their company.

In contrast to Mrs Barton Trafford's intense pursuit of a winning writer, particularly her capture of Ted Driffield, Mrs Hudson's desires are simple. Asked if there is anything she wants, she replies: 'I don't know as there is, now you come to speak of it, except me 'ealth and strength for another twenty years so as I can go on workin'.' Whereas Mrs Barton Trafford only takes what she can, Mrs Hudson gives of herself.

There is a vast difference, as well, in the two worlds in which the young Ashenden lives in London—that of the struggling medical student and that of the frequenter of literary At Homes. At one point, he makes a sentimental return to his old room in Mrs Hudson's house. Here, he thinks of all the people who have lived there, with the complexities of their lives:

Medical students, articled clerks, young fellows making their way in the city, and elderly men retired from the colonies or thrown unexpectedly upon the world by the break up of an old home. The room made me, as Mrs Hudson would have put it, go queer all over. All the hopes that had been cherished there, the bright visions of the future, the flaming passion of youth; the regrets, the disillusion, the weariness, the resignation; so much had been felt in that room, by so many, the whole gamut of human emotion, that it seemed strangely to have acquired a troubling and enig- matic personality of its own.[24]

The 'whole gamut of emotion' had been felt in that room; life had been experienced there in all its intensity. That cannot be said of the existence portrayed in the literary world. It is therefore significant that when Driffield becomes assimilated into Mrs Barton Trafford's circle, away from the raw life that he had known before, his writing deteriorates. Like so many artists, he becomes divorced from the most important source of material for his art—natural human life.

One of the criticisms repeatedly levelled at *Cakes and Ale* is that Maugham writes about the great author without ever providing much real illumination of his greatness. It is frequently argued that Driffield is so pale that the reader finds it difficult to believe that he could have written anything worth reading. It is a serious error, however, to equate *Cakes and Ale* with *The Moon and Sixpence* and to assume that in both novels Maugham is attempting to portray a great artist. The novels are far apart in theme, and Driffield and Strickland bear little resemblance. Driffield is not intended to be a truly great writer; he is a good writer who has written some good novels. Maugham's intention is to reveal how a good writer, through social and public manœuvres, can become a Grand Old Man of Letters. If Driffield were a great novelist, the satiric purpose of the actions of Mrs Barton Trafford, the second Mrs Driffield, and the critics in general, would be lost. It must be remembered that throughout the novel Ashenden points out that, although he recognises that he is going against current critical opinion, he has never considered that Driffield was a great writer. Maugham's point is surely that too many of the Grand Old Men of English Letters have had their literary reputations inflated by non-literary factors.

During his life, Maugham had seen dormant writers whose fame grew with their longevity, a natural source of chagrin for a professional who prided himself on writing every day of his career. Malcolm Muggeridge recalls the kind of writer whose reputation followed the 'Grand Old Man' syndrome: 'I know he [Maugham] sometimes let fall a sigh in the direction of Rapallo along the coast, where Max Beerbohm was growing ever more famous in literary and intellectual circles with every book he did not write.'[25]

To illustrate his theory in *Cakes and Ale* Maugham chronicles Driffield's career, particularly his lionising by Mrs Barton Trafford and his promotion by his diligent second wife. Here, the author argues, is the kind of writer who produces some good things, becomes a host for literary parasites, and then undergoes an apotheosis because he lives to a great age. This transition is most strongly developed in the Edwardian London section and it is continued in the Georgian scenes of Driffield's retirement.

The career of Edward Driffield is illustrated graphically by his position in relation to Alroy Kear. Kear is the complete personification of the public relations aspect of the writing–lecturing–reviewing–publishing world. The perfect critical weather-vane, everything that he thinks, says or does is a reflection of the winds blowing at the time:

Roy has always sincerely believed what everyone else believed at the moment. When he wrote novels about the aristocracy he sincerely believed that its members were dissipated and immoral, and yet had a certain nobility and an innate aptitude for governing the British Empire; and later when he wrote of the middle classes he sincerely believed that they were the backbone of the country.[26]

Because he realises that a wife is considered a nuisance at literary functions, Kear does not marry. He joins the right sort of club, becomes known to prominent reviewers, and lectures in Britain and the United States. Unlike the early Driffield, Kear seems to have no backbone or hard core. He is a type of public chameleon who changes as his surroundings change, and he is the repository for whatever is in vogue at the time.

At the beginning of the novel Kear and Driffield are at opposite ends of the spectrum, but by the end they are, outwardly at least, almost indistinguishable from one another. At the beginning Driffield is exuberant, fun-loving and enthusiastic, while Kear is restrained, inhibited and calculating. As he becomes more and more a public figure, Driffield loses more of his animal spirits and he gradually takes on an artificial role. The final steps in this process take place after his death, when he is re-made according to a pattern by his second wife and when Alroy Kear himself is able to participate in masking him in a suitable image.

Another reason why *Cakes and Ale* does not present a penetrating analysis of Edward Driffield's character is that Maugham wishes to convey the feeling that behind the mask which society has created for him there is a different, living man. As a means of viewing the writer as the world sees him, Maugham uses the device of the first person narrator. Adopting this point of view means that he is committed on the whole to the external view, the figure as seen by Ashenden. Although this does not entirely eliminate the possibilities of exploration of Driffield's personality, it does limit the extent to which his soul can be bared. Despite this, Maugham is able to create, with considerable skill, the impression that there is an enigmatic personality behind the Driffield façade.

Driffield's progress throughout *Cakes and Ale* is one of gradual entrapment and ultimate solidification into conventionality, until he ceases to write at all. With Ted Driffield, Maugham completely reverses the direction which Charles Strickland took, which was toward fewer and fewer encumbrances until he was completely free to express himself. When he moves to London, Driffield becomes absorbed by the literary–social establishment. He joins a literary club, speaks at public dinners, attends luncheons and teas given by lion-hunting ladies, and comes under the influence of Mrs Barton Trafford. The reaction of this basically animal-spirited man is a kind of creeping

schizophrenia; the real Driffield does not change too radi.
his personality becomes increasingly divorced from the outsic
Ashenden senses that the real man is becoming more diffi.
reach:

> But I had a feeling that he was growing more aloof; he was no longer
> jolly, rather vulgar companion that I had known at Blackstable. Perha,
> it was only my increasing sensibility that discerned as it were an invisible
> barrier that existed between him and the people he chaffed and joked with.
> It was as though he lived a life of the imagination that made the life of every
> day a little shadowy.[27]

Shortly after Ashenden makes this observation, Rosie leaves
Driffield to run away with Lord George Kemp, and this escape has
a significance above merely being another example of her promiscuity.
As Driffield becomes more and more an appendage of the literary
community in London, Rosie becomes increasingly isolated from him.
She is too full of high spirits to be comfortable at literary teas and
luncheons, and she recognises that she is considered an unfortunate
hindrance by Driffield's acquaintances. Mrs Barton Trafford treats
her with obvious condescension, and she reacts with indignation. It is
therefore natural that Rosie, who remains constant throughout,
should free herself from Driffield when he becomes estranged from
the kind of life which he had led with her and Kemp.

Rosie's elopement has, of course, a technical purpose; it is necessary that Driffield be separated from her so that he can come completely under the influence of Mrs Barton Trafford and later be
cosseted by his second wife. At Rosie's departure, Driffield becomes
the property of Mrs Barton Trafford and, with her skilful diplomacy,
he soon becomes almost inseparable from her. She arranges every
aspect of his career—his articles, readings, soirées, interviews—and
his reputation flourishes.

When Driffield ceases to write, remarries, and retires to a country
home near Blackstable, his second wife, an energetic, competent and
alert woman, continues the process of creating for him the identity of
the great man of letters. She attempts to break him of undistinguished
habits—wiping his plate clean with his bread, not changing his linen
daily, and not taking regular baths. She redecorates and refurnishes
the house according to her conception of what the home of a distinguished author should be. It means discarding the desk at which
Driffield wrote his novels in favour of a more stylish period-piece, but
this is a price which is paid. She arranges his study and keeps it
scrupulously tidy, and she surrounds it with books which are clean,
neat, and unread. The house becomes a museum and Driffield is the
central museum-piece.

On the only occasion that Ashenden meets the aged writer, Maugham skilfully describes how the luncheon is a performance, a ritual of homage, masterfully stage-managed by Mrs Driffield. Everything is in impeccable good taste—with Chippendale furniture, brightly polished silver, and a smart but not ostentatious menu. It is, says Ashenden, 'the dining room and the lunch and the manner which you felt exactly fitted a literary gent of great celebrity but moderate wealth'.

Driffield is carefully groomed for the occasion. Where he was always bearded before, he is now clean-shaven, and his very white false teeth make his smile seem artificial. His new, well-cut suit, his shirt collar two or three sizes too large, his neat black tie, and his pearl tie pin, make him look like 'a dean in mufti on his summer holiday in Switzerland'. The narrator, recalling the warm, lively extravert whom he knew as a boy, wonders if that personality still exists behind the mask:

Remembering the past, I asked myself curiously what he thought of this grand company, his neatly turned out wife, so competent and discreetly managing, and the elegant surroundings in which he lived. I wondered if he regretted his early days of adventure. I wondered if all this amused him or if the amiable civility of his manner masked a hideous boredom.[28]

Ashenden does discover that, beneath all the trappings of the part he must play, much of the old Ted Driffield is still alive. It appears for only an instant in the form of a casual unexpected gesture, but this conveys a great deal:

He looked at me for what I suppose was no more than a few seconds, but for what seemed to me quite a long time, and then I had a sudden shock; he gave me a little wink. It was so quick that nobody but I could have caught it, and so unexpected in that distinguished old face that I could hardly believe my eyes. In a moment his face was once more composed, intelligently benign and quietly observant. Lunch was announced and we trouped into the dining-room.[29]

Although handicapped by the use of the first person narrator, Maugham manages skilfully to reveal in an instant, as a flash of lightning illuminates a dark sky, the active mind behind the aged writer's mask. He has chosen to examine Driffield from the exterior, supplementing these detailed physical descriptions with suppositions by Ashenden on what might be happening within him. Since this is always done with restraint and moderation, the sudden unexpected physical gesture of the wink takes on considerable import. Through this almost imperceptible action, over in a moment, the elaborate and well-contrived façade is removed and the vital man behind it is revealed. It is an act of communication, unseen—and therefore uncensored—by Mrs Driffield, between the old man and Ashenden, and there is in it a touch of irony, of amused tolerance.

The only other manifestation of the real Ted Driffield in his old age is his necessarily surreptitious visits to the local public house. Here, after a luncheon with prominent figures like Edmund Gosse and Lord Curzon, he can remove the mask and say what he really thinks of them. There is a comfortable lack of restraint at the bar, with his feet on the rail, and the atmosphere is as lively as Ferne Court is moribund. More important, this is a reminder of his early days, a form of contact with real life, which he has lost over the years.

Except for these occasions, the spirit of Edward Driffield remains an enigma. Essentially aloof from the life which the eminence of his position imposes upon him, his real self is rarely touched by those around him. Long after his death, Ashenden accompanies Alroy Kear to Ferne Court to meet Amy Driffield. The house has become even more of a museum and Mrs Driffield is diligently preserving the memory of the man as the world knew him. As they examine the various pictures of Driffield throughout his life, Maugham sums up the course of his career and his retreat within himself:

You saw his face grow thinner and more lined. The stubborn commonplace of the early portraits melted gradually into a weary refinement. You saw the change in him wrought by experience, thought, and achieved ambition. I looked again at the photograph of the young sailorman and fancied that I saw in it already a trace of that aloofness that seemed to me so marked in the older ones and that I had had years before the vague sensation of in the man himself. The face you saw was a mask and the actions he performed without significance. I had an impression that the real man, to his death unknown and lonely, was a wraith that went a silent way unseen between the writer of his books and the fellow who led his life, and smiled with ironical detachment at the two puppets that the world took for Edward Driffield.[30]

Eight years before *Cakes and Ale*, Maugham had written about Charlie Chaplin in much the same manner. The great comic, he thought, was a lively and vivacious cockney who found success a form of bondage:

The celebrity he enjoys, his wealth, imprison him in a way of life in which he finds only constraint. I think he looks back to the freedom of his struggling youth, with its poverty and bitter privation, with a longing which knows it can never be satisfied. To him the streets of southern London are the scene of frolic, gaiety and extravagant adventure. They have to him a reality which the well-kept avenues, bordered with trim houses, in which live the rich, can never possess. I can imagine him going into his own house and wondering what on earth he is doing in this strange man's dwelling.[31]

That Chaplin later rejected this hypothesis in his autobiography indicates that Maugham was superimposing on him a personal concern.

Maugham underlines Driffield's imprisonment in his role by concluding *Cakes and Ale* with a chapter describing Rosie's life in Yonkers, and the contrast of this life with that arranged so meticulously by Amy Driffield is intentional. Rosie, although in her seventies, is essentially unchanged—as vivacious, energetic and enthusiastic as ever. There is no artificial barrier of behaviour between her real self and other people, and Ashenden feels a delightful ease in her company. Unlike Driffield, Rosie has managed to avoid losing contact with life, and the distance between the final glimpses of them is a measure of how much Driffield has been transformed from the man whom Ashenden knew in Blackstable.

In spite of the astringency of Maugham's criticisms of certain segments of the literary world, and despite his caricatures of Mrs Barton Trafford, Alroy Kear, and Allgood Newton, *Cakes and Ale* is a novel of warmth, a rare quality in his works. Although a good many people would dispute this claim, it is a sunny book, and the attitude of the author is far more relaxed and optimistic than in any of his other works.

The source of the warmth of *Cakes and Ale*, and the greatest achievement in it, is the character of Rosie, one of the most memorable women in twentieth-century fiction. Maugham obviously loves his heroine, and this love tends to suffuse the whole book, so that even characters such as Alroy Kear are treated with a degree of affection. Rosie is 'all gold', as Ashenden says, and this colours the rest of the novel.

The character of Rosie Gann is modelled as closely from life as those of Alroy Kear and Mrs Barton Trafford. The original, whose identity has until now remained a mystery, was Ethelwyn Sylvia Jones (1883–1948), the second daughter of the playwright Henry Arthur Jones. Maugham knew her for a number of years between 1902, when she married Montague Vivian Leveaux (a theatrical manager), and 1913, when she remarried, her second husband being Angus McDonnell (1881–1966), the second son of the 6th Earl of Antrim. Although it is difficult to discover exactly the nature of this relationship, a great amount of Maugham's version in 'Looking Back' is certainly true.*

Eventually the full story of the original Rosie will be known, and this will do much to explain part of the enigma of Maugham. The importance to *Cakes and Ale* is that he was largely working from real

* For a more complete account see Appendix A.

life in the case of Rosie and this is nearly always Maugham at his best. In his introduction to the Modern Library edition he called her 'the most engaging heroine I have ever created', and Garson Kanin, commenting on an occasion when his old friend recounted the story of 'Rosie', tells of witnessing an uncharacteristic display of feeling: 'I do not think I have ever seen tears in Maugham's eyes until tonight. But as he comes to the end of this account, there they are.'[32] If Maugham is actually writing about the great heterosexual love of his emotionally scarred life, it provides an excellent opportunity to examine his ideas of a desirable woman.

Maugham has given his novel a double title and it is obvious that 'the skeleton in the cupboard' is Rosie; however, the spirit of the Shakespearian passage alluded to in the other half concerns her equally as much. It is she (aided by Lord George Kemp) who is the counterpart in spirit to Maria, Sir Toby Belch and Sir Andrew Aguecheek and who is the author's way of saying 'Dost thou think, because thou art virtuous, there shall be no more cakes and ale?' to the Malvolios of the novel—Mrs Barton Trafford, Amy Driffield and Alroy Kear. Unlike Ted Driffield, Rosie is never extinguished by the forces of convention, and she remains the symbol of life as opposed to the sterility of the superficial literary society.

Rosie is the most fully realised character in a line of Maugham heroines beginning with Liza, through Bertha Craddock, Sally Athelny, Betty Welldon-Burns ('The Human Element') and Suzanne Rouvier (*The Razor's Edge*). A characteristic common to them all is a fullness of life, an exuberance and energy which flows from them. As soon as Maugham introduces Rosie into the story, he gives Ashenden the comment:

I did not of course realize it then, but I know now that there was a disarming frankness in her manner that put one at one's ease. She talked with a kind of eagerness, like a child bubbling over with the zest of life, and her eyes were lit all the time by her engaging smile.[33]

There is in Rosie a delightful lack of inhibition, an unawareness of restraint or self-consciousness. This gives her a naturalness, an ease which enables her quickly to break through the barriers of conventionality. Even the very young Ashenden, as yet not attracted to her sexually, quickly finds her disarming.

Rosie also shares with the others in this group of heroines a sensuality which gives her otherwise ordinary features a great attractiveness. Her smile, her eyes, her full red lips, and her pale gold hair, combine to communicate a naked and unabashed sexuality. Ashenden describes the painting which awakens in him the realisation of her sensual beauty:

Her nose was a little thick, her eyes were smallish, her mouth was large; but her eyes had the blue of cornflowers, and they smiled with her lips, very red and sensual, and her smile was the gayest, the most friendly, the sweetest thing I ever saw. . . . She had no colour in her face; it was of a very pale brown except under the eyes where it was faintly blue. Her hair was pale gold and it was done in the fashion of the day high on the head with an elaborate fringe. . . . She glowed, but palely, like the moon rather than the sun, or if it was like the sun it was like the sun in the white mist of dawn. . . . She stood like a maiden apt for love offering herself guilelessly, because she was fulfilling the purposes of Nature, to the embraces of a lover.[34]

The most striking quality about Rosie is, of course, her promiscuity. Sexual looseness is certainly not a new factor in Maugham's stories, but in this character he succeeds remarkably in persuading the reader that, in spite of her actions, she is an admirable woman. This, however, is no different from what Maugham has said elsewhere. In 'Virtue' he wrote, 'I prefer a loose woman to a selfish one and a wanton to a fool', and Rosie is the embodiment of that dictum. Maugham uses her to destroy the conventional idea that virtue is a quality which must be measured in the sexual context. To do this, he creates a woman who is unashamedly promiscuous, endows her with warmth, charm, kindness and generosity, and then asks if she is a good woman. Alroy Kear, of course, voices the opinion of society and calls her a nymphomaniac. The narrator replies:

"She was a very simple woman. Her instincts were healthy and ingenuous. She loved to make people happy. She loved love."
    "Do you call that love?"
    "Well, then, the act of love. She was naturally affectionate. When she liked anyone it was quite natural for her to go to bed with him. She never thought twice about it. It was not vice; it wasn't lasciviousness; it was her nature. She gave herself as naturally as the sun gives heat or the flowers their perfume. It was a pleasure to her and she liked to give pleasure to others. It had no effect on her character; she remained sincere, unspoiled, and artless."[35]

With Rosie, the pleasure that she receives from the sex act overflows to the rest of her life. During her affair with Ashenden, for example, she sleeps with him periodically after an evening out and leaves at daybreak, sometimes in warm sunshine, sometimes in cold rain, but always happy. The joy which they experience together makes them look upon the rest of the world with affection, and Rosie is delighted when her lover gives an occasional shilling or two to a homeless beggar. Maugham has always maintained that happiness is a necessary prerequisite for generosity, and the context here has a psychological validity.

Richard Heron Ward[36] has divided the female characters in Maugham's writings into two groups—the 'hetaira' type and the mother figure. The hetairae, more frequent than the mother figures, are the women whose physical beauty excites men's sexual desires and in many cases they lack any spiritual attraction. This category includes Giulia (*The Making of a Saint*), Mildred (*Of Human Bondage*), and Louise Frith (*The Narrow Corner*). The maternal figures, on the other hand, are kindly, humorous women, usually wise, shrewd and ironic. While they often possess sharp tongues, they are generous, and they give the men the contentment and security of a mother. Examples in this category are Miss Ley (*Mrs Craddock* and *The Merry-Go-Round*), Susie Boyd (*The Magician*), and Sally Athelny (*Of Human Bondage*).

Rosie becomes Maugham's most fully realised female character, and his most engaging heroine, because she is a combination of the best qualities of both female types. She has the natural goodness, shrewdness and unselfishness of the mother-figure, and she has the voluptuous physical attraction of the hetaira. The author succeeds in his creation of Rosie because of his skilful fusion of these qualities so that they become inseparable in her character. She is physically attractive because she communicates the charm of her frank tenderness, and she is generous and good-hearted because she enjoys loving. The complexity of her character is never better illuminated than in this passage, one of the most beautiful in all of Maugham's writings, where Rosie is both hetaira and mother to Ashenden:

Rosie raised her hand and softly stroked my face. I do not know why I should have behaved as I then did; it was not at all how I had seen myself behaving on such an occasion. A sob broke from my tight throat. I do not know whether it was because I was shy and lonely (not lonely in the body, for I spent all day at the hospital with all kinds of people, but lonely in the spirit) or because my desire was so great, but I began to cry. I felt terribly ashamed of myself: I tried to control myself, I couldn't; the tears welled up in my eyes and poured down my cheeks. Rosie saw them and gave a little gasp.

"Oh, honey, what is it? What's the matter? Don't. Don't!"

She put her arms round my neck and began to cry too, and she kissed my lips and my eyes and my wet cheeks. She undid her bodice and lowered my head till it rested on her bosom. She stroked my smooth face. She rocked me back and forth as though I were a child in her arms. I kissed her breasts and I kissed the white column of her neck; and she slipped out of her bodice and out of her skirt and her petticoats and I held her for a moment by her corseted waist; then she undid it, holding her breath for an instant to enable her to do so, and stood before me in her shift. When I put my hands on her sides I could feel the ribbing of the skin from the pressure of the corsets.

"Blow out the candle," she whispered.[37]

The strange complex emotion, felt in different ways by each of them, breaks all barriers between them and they experience a rare spiritual and sexual union. In the moderation and restraint of Maugham's style, the emotion of the passage creates a powerful effect.

In spite of Rosie's maternal qualities, she does not share with so many of Maugham's female characters the unpleasant characteristic of possessiveness. She attaches no obligations to her favours and she makes no demands upon her lovers. She accepts any gestures or gifts with gratitude, but expects nothing. As in so many other respects, there is a marked contrast between this unselfishness and the parasitic nature of Mrs Barton Trafford or the manipulatory control of Amy Driffield.

Because Rosie makes no demands on her lovers, she is able to expect the same response from them. When Ashenden discovers that she has been having an affair with an unpleasant Dutch Jew named Kuyper, he chastises her. Her reply is an expression of one of Maugham's most deeply-felt beliefs: 'You must take me as I am, you know.' Rosie has given herself to Ashenden and has been pleased to be able to make him happy; however, she wants to be accepted as she is, not trapped in an illusion of what he would like her to be. She will not be re-made into a different person according to a pattern or conception imposed by someone else. She manages the difficult feat of surrendering herself to her men without ever losing her self-possession, and, although Ashenden becomes intimate with her, she always remains elusive and free.

When all things are considered, Rosie may be the most truly liberated of all of Maugham's characters. She is free from all social pressures to act in what is considered to be an acceptable fashion, and her vitality is not subdued by the restraints of custom. More important, she is free from a puritan conscience which, in spite of the individual's professions and actions, acts as an inhibition.

The most important freedom which Rosie possesses, however, is that which comes with emotional and spiritual self-assuredness. She is, in this respect, the sole Maugham protagonist who is not restricted by self-doubts and rigorous continual introspection. All of the other central figures—Bertha Craddock, Philip Carey, Charles Strickland, Kitty Fane, Dr Saunders, Julia Lambert, and Larry Darrell—are in a constant search for independence and the forms which it may take. In these novels, Maugham illustrates the continual self-analysis and internal dialogue which takes place as the characters grope their way toward their own interpretation of freedom. In *Cakes and Ale* this is not made explicit; Maugham simply creates an entirely free spirit and presents her to the reader in her completed state.

Cakes and Ale is Rosie's story, and the novel ends with a last look at her as a seventy-year-old widow. Maugham, as always, insists upon seeing things as they are, and the contrast between the Rosie he has created and the woman in the final chapter has distressed many critics. She is now fat, has a double chin, wears rubber corsets, and is heavily powdered. Her nails are blood-coloured, her eyebrows plucked, and her hair, once golden and soft, is now white, shingled, and permanently waved.

A number of critics have argued that this last glimpse of Rosie is the cynical side of Maugham's nature breaking out with a vengeance in an otherwise sunny novel. He cannot resist, they claim, giving the readers this shock of disillusionment after he has made them love his heroine, and they are left with a final pessimistic impression of the transitory nature of beauty. Once again, however, the critics seem unable to share Maugham's acceptance of the world as it is and they cannot look on the aged Rosie with the same equanimity as the author. The difference between the young and old woman is great, but the final picture is painted with the same affection as the previous ones. It does not destroy her; the essential Rosie is still there and Ashenden once again falls under her spell. As Desmond MacCarthy rightly maintains, the impression that the reader retains after reading *Cakes and Ale* is of the warm and beautiful woman of the earlier sections:

And when he has created in her softly-glowing charm and delicious honest kindliness, how one respects him for not killing her in order that we should take leave of her in the pathetic and becoming light of early death! The final appearance of Rosie in New York as a game old bridge-playing woman of seventy, still in love with life, was no doubt a shock. But what a salutary shock! Age destroys beauty slowly, death suddenly; it is well to learn that this is the only difference. It is sentimental to wish the "pilgrim soul" in Rosie had been snuffed out in order that we might have escaped seeing her old, fat, pink, made-up, and happy. The beauty that has been, has been – in either case.[38]

Throughout *Cakes and Ale*, the contrast in personalities and out-look between Rosie and Mrs Barton Trafford and Amy Driffield is obvious. The conflict between the women, however, is not confined merely to this level; they are representatives of a confrontation on a higher plane—that of life as opposed to the artificiality of the literary–social milieu. The battle is begun when Ted is assimilated by the literary community and Rosie becomes increasingly estranged from him until she elopes with Kemp. The real conflict, however, takes place after Driffield's death, when Amy Driffield and Alroy Kear, the guardians of the writer's public image, grapple with the problem of the skeleton in the cupboard. They are involved in the process of re-creating a life, manufacturing an artificial, more dignified, version to plaster over the colourful real one. Kear therefore explains Amy Driffield's interpretation of Rosie's part:

"You see, her attitude is that Rose Driffield exerted a most pernicious influence on her husband, and that she did everything possible to ruin him morally, physically, and financially; she was beneath him in every way, at least intellectually and spiritually, and it was only because he was a man of immense force and vitality that he survived."[39]

The truth, which even Kear is perceptive enough to acknowledge, is of course that Driffield wrote his best novels when he was married to Rosie. With her, he had contact with life, life untrammelled by conformity, codes and inhibitions, and this gave energy to his writing. As he became more integrated with the London literary community, his writing deteriorated and after Rosie left him he wrote nothing of value. To underline the importance to Driffield of life through Rosie, Maugham includes an important and lengthy episode at the conclusion of *Cakes and Ale*.

Earlier in the novel, Ashenden had discussed Driffield's book *The Cup of Life*, his most controversial work. Although he is not an admirer of Driffield's writing, the narrator professes a high regard for *The Cup of Life*; it is, he says, original, refreshing, and astringent—the only one of the writer's novels that he would like to have written. It was, however, greeted by universal condemnation, and banned by libraries and railway bookstalls because of its realistic description of a child's death and the immediate infidelity of the bereaved mother.

In the final pages of *Cakes and Ale*, Maugham returns to this epi-sode and reveals the source of its power. The child was the Driffields' six-year-old daughter, who had died a lingering painful death from meningitis, and the infidelity of the mother was Rosie's; life, with all its frustrations and cruelty, had buffeted the writer and he had responded by transmuting it into his art. Driffield reacted in the only way he knew and tried to purge his suffering through his writing; Rosie sought relief in the only way she knew, and spent the night with a theatrical acquaintance. Totally in character, she attempted to escape from pain and death by seeking the living.

This episode is one of the last occasions in Driffield's career that art and life come together in him, and its combination produces his greatest writing. Maugham delights in the irony of the public outrage at this situation taken so directly from raw human experience. Rosie's confession of the background to the events is his rebuttal to the Alroy Kears and Amy Driffields of the world who attempt to divorce the writer and his work from the life that gives them their power.

Cakes and Ale is the high point in Maugham's career. Although he will be remembered for his dramatic comedies, his short stories, and some of his other novels, his reputation may ultimately rest on *Cakes and Ale*. There is about it a sense of perfection that is rare in a novel and a lyrical warmth that is unusual in Maugham's writing. Its success must be attributed to the skilful realisation in it of many intentions—the use of a *persona* appropriate to the atmosphere, the mastery of the time-shift, the memorable caricatures of Mrs Barton Trafford and Alroy Kear, the fully developed character of Rosie, the careful balancing of contrasting social milieus, and the intricate fusion of numerous threads of psychological and philosophical observation and social and literary criticism. Maugham develops these techniques and themes with polished craftsmanship and the ease which comes with the knowledge of one's abilities. Richard Heron Ward captures the feeling of the novel when he writes:

Cakes and Ale is absolutely the expression of an individuality. It owes nothing to any other writer, and it is the work of a man who, at least as far as his work is concerned, has learned to know himself, to know his limitations and to make the best both of what is and what is not limited in him. One reads it with a curious sense of comfort and fitness, almost with joy, it is so complete and satisfying in itself, so assured and direct and finished.[40]

VIII

The Cosmopolitan:
Aspects of the Maugham
Persona

D URING THE FIRST WORLD WAR, Maugham, like so many writers and artists, actively participated in the struggle. While most writers used their professional talents in propaganda agencies, Maugham served in a number of more direct roles. At the outbreak of war, he joined a Red Cross unit in France as a dresser, ambulance driver, and interpreter. After a short while, he was transferred to the Secret Intelligence Service and spent a year in Geneva as a secret agent. Finally, in 1917, he was despatched to Russia with the task of supporting the Provisional Government against the Bolsheviks, who planned to take Russia out of the war.* In the course of his mission, Maugham met prominent figures such as Kerensky, Masaryk, Boris Savinkov (who assassinated both the Grand Duke Sergei and Trepov, the Chief of Police), and Princess Alexandra Kropotkin, daughter of the anarchist Prince Kropotkin. His mission did not succeed, of course, and Kerensky's government fell.

The failure of his mission to Russia strangely haunted Maugham for the rest of his life. In *The Summing Up*, he claims that the revolution might have been prevented if he had arrived six months earlier. Although history has shown that any such mission had little chance of success, he continued to think that the course of international developments would have been different had he been more competent.

Throughout these experiences Maugham recorded his impressions, and *A Writer's Notebook* bears testimony to the sizeable amount of material which he never used in his fiction. An important outcome of his wartime adventures, however, was a collection of short stories, *Ashenden or: The British Agent*, published in 1928. These stories are

* For documentation of Maugham's role in espionage in Russia during World War I, see Appendix B.

based on actual cases and real people, and the central figure, Ashenden, is very much an autobiographical character. For example, 'Sir Herbert Witherspoon', the ambassador in 'His Excellency', is based to some degree on Sir George Buchanan, the British ambassador to Russia; 'Mr Wilbur Schafer' on Francis, the American ambassador; and 'Anastasia Alexandrovna' on Alexandra Kropotkin. And at one point in the book Ashenden's superior officer asks him in exasperation: 'Where have you been living all these years?'. The agent replies: 'At 36 Chesterfield Street, Mayfair'—Maugham's own address in the years before the war.

A graphic example of the factual nature of *Ashenden* can be found in the recollections of Emanuel Voska, a Czechoslovak agent in the service of the British government, for whom Maugham acted as a liaison officer with British Intelligence. He tells this story about his experiences in Russia during the revolution:

We foreigners at the Hotel Europa caught the Russian mood – "Nitchevo" – and went about our business as calmly as the natives. We had only one casualty, and that towards the end. An American banker, whose name escapes me, arrived to conclude a loan to the Kerensky Government. He spoke no Russian, and Koukol, who steered him when he first arrived, found a Russian lady in reduced circumstances to serve as his interpreter. He put his loan through, and returned to his hotel much pleased. It seemed a pity to pour cold water on his enthusiasm, but I felt it my duty.
"The Kerensky Government is probably on the way out", I said. "If it survives your deal is on. If it doesn't you've come to Petrograd for nothing. Staying here will do you no good. I advise you to get out while the going's good, for real hell may pop at any time. The weekly Trans-Siberian leaves to-morrow for Vladivostok. You'd better hop it." After some argument he decided to take my advice. He and the interpreter went to get his washing. Half an hour later I heard firing down the street and paid little attention to it. It stopped. Then the interpreter, considerably agitated, came into the lobby. On the way back from the laundry they had run into a street skirmish. In scurrying to cover they had become separated. Hadn't he come back to the hotel? I ran to the scene of the fight. I found him dead in the gutter, with his bundle of washing under him.[1]

The episode described in this anecdote is undoubtedly the origin of Maugham's story, 'Mr Harrington's Washing'.

Clearly Maugham, an astute observer, found a wealth of raw material during this period. That the *Ashenden* stories did not appear until ten years after his war experiences is yet another example of his ability to gauge the mood of the literary public.

The First World War had a profound effect on a generation of artists, and the shattered idealism which followed in the wake of its destruction is recorded in a great many books. Except for poetry, however, the impact of the war on literature was not immediately felt.

For a number of reasons, some merely practical (the time and the physical conditions of the battlefield being more suitable for the poet), the first interpretations came through poetry, particularly that of Sassoon, Brooke, Rosenberg and Owen. It was a decade before prose writers began in any number to give their impressions of the war. B. Ifor Evans explains:

There seemed a conspiracy of silence about the war as a theme for fiction in the years which immediately followed 1918. The smaller audience which read Sassoon or Owen was prepared to endure again the full tragedy in imaginative retrospect, but the larger audience of fiction demanded in those years immediately after the war any theme rather than that of the conflict itself and its horrors.[2]

Although a few war books—Dos Passos' *Three Soldiers* (1921), E. E. Cummings' *The Enormous Room* (1922), Ford's 'Tietjens' novels (1924–8), and C. E. Montague's *Rough Justice* (1926)—appeared during this time, the public did not seem ready for realistic war studies. By about 1928, however, readers were prepared to re-live the events of 1914–18, and in that year a number of prose accounts were published: Arnold Zweig's *The Case of Sergeant Grischa*, Erich Maria Remarque's *All Quiet on the Western Front*, and Edmund Blunden's *Undertones of War*. These were followed, in 1929, by Richard Aldington's *Death of a Hero*, Hemingway's *A Farewell to Arms*, R. C. Sheriff's *Journey's End*, and Robert Graves' *Goodbye to All That*. The next year saw Frederic Manning's *Her Privates We* and Sassoon's *Memoirs of an Infantry Officer*. Although *Ashenden* is a collection of stories about espionage, rather than about direct war experiences, it must be included in the literature of World War I, and its appearance in 1928 reflected the temper of the times.

There is another motif in *Ashenden* which touched the public interest—Russia. In the first three decades of the twentieth century, Europe became fascinated by that great country, its literature, music, art, religion, and what was called 'the Russian Soul'. The period from 1905 to 1917 saw the captivation at its zenith. Pavlova appeared in London in 1910 and she was followed by Diaghilev, Nijinsky, Karsavina, Fokine, Chaliapin, and Stravinsky. Constance Garnett translated *The Brothers Karamazov* in 1912, rendered seven more of Dostoevsky's novels by 1920, and translated the *Tales of Tchehov* (1916–1922). Between 1914 and 1917 there were English versions published of Tolstoy's *Diaries*, Vladimir Solovyoff's *Three Conversations on War and Progress and the End of History*, Dostoevsky's letters, Gorky's *My Childhood* and *In the World*, a Russian anthology by C. E. Bechhofer, a volume of Russian *Poets and Poems*, and Serge Persky's *Contemporary Russian Novelists*.

Paralleling this outburst in translations of Russian literature, there was a proliferation of studies of Russia by English social historians, critics and novelists. Maurice Baring and Stephen Graham produced a series of Russian books, and numerous critics—Middleton Murry, Sir Edmund Gosse, Havelock Ellis and Rebecca West, for example—analysed Russian literature and its influence on English writers. Hugh Walpole, having lived in Russia during the war, used his experience in two novels—*The Dark Forest* (1916) and *The Secret City* (1919).

In the latter part of *Ashenden*, Maugham describes the enthusiasm for Russia which swept European society and to which he also succumbed:

It was at the time when Europe discovered Russia. Everyone was reading the Russian novelists, the Russian dancers captivated the civilized world, and the Russian composers set shivering the sensibility of persons who were beginning to want a change from Wagner. Russian art seized upon Europe with the virulence of an epidemic of influenza. New phrases became the fashion, new colours, new emotions, and the highbrows described themselves without a moment's hesitation as members of the intelligentsia. It was a difficult word to spell but an easy one to say. Ashenden fell like the rest, changed the cushions of his sitting-room, hung an eikon on the wall, read Chekoff and went to the ballet.[3]

Maugham's tongue-in-cheek description of Ashenden's vision of his Russian mistress catches the attitude toward the Russian spirit of European society:

In her dark melancholy eyes Ashenden saw the boundless steppes of Russia, and the Kremlin with its pealing bells, and the solemn ceremonies of Easter at St. Isaac's, and forests of silver beeches and the Nevsky Prospekt; it was astonishing how much he saw in her eyes.[4]

The events of 1917 in Russia, however, caused a reaction in Europe and, until the mid-nineteen-twenties, there was a great amount of debate about the true nature of Russian culture. Edmund Gosse tempered his enthusiasm for the Russian writers and attacked Dostoevsky, and D. H. Lawrence retained his earlier scepticism. It was not until the middle of the 'twenties that the reaction to the Russian Soul had subsided and Europe could take a more objective view of Russian culture. In 1926 interest was again high enough for three Chekhov plays—*The Cherry Orchard, Uncle Vanya*, and *The Three Sisters*—to be staged in London. It was in this second wave of enthusiasm for Russia that Maugham used his Russian experiences in the form of the later chapters of *Ashenden*.

Despite the appropriate timing of its appearance and the astute use of the author's Russian material, *Ashenden* is a prototype of its genre; it is virtually the first realistic espionage tale. Joseph Conrad's *The*

Secret Agent (1907) was the first novel to treat spying and international conspiracy realistically, but its influence on espionage fiction was not nearly as great as that of *Ashenden*. In the early part of the century spy stories meant romantic tales of heroic adventure and masterful intrigue. The heroes of these stories, faced with countless forms of alien duplicity and treachery, triumphed through their intelligence, courage and integrity.

According to Eric Ambler's introduction to *To Catch a Spy*, the first real espionage novel in English was Erskine Childers' *The Riddle of the Sands*, published in 1903. William Le Queux produced a great many stories, including *Secrets of the Foreign Office* (1903), *The Czar's Spy* (1905), *The Invasion* (1910), *The Mystery of the Green Ray* (1915), and *Donovan of Whitehall* (1917). Together with Edward Phillips Oppenheimer, who wrote *The Great Impersonation* (1920), Le Queux contributed to what Ambler calls the 'early cloak-and-dagger stereotypes—the black-velveted seductress, the British secret-service numbskull hero, the omnipotent spymaster', while Sapper's 'Bulldog Drummond' stories introduced violence in considerable measure. John Buchan's *The Thirty-Nine Steps* (1915), *Greenmantle* (1916), and *Mr Standfast* (1919), were similarly romantic accounts. As late as 1926, when T. E. Lawrence's *Seven Pillars of Wisdom* was published, the spy was still a heroic figure, a British agent of great independence who defied bureaucratic control to achieve his heroic aims.

Ashenden, published just two years later, presented for the first time a totally different picture of the life of a secret agent. Ambler has written, quite rightly, that Maugham's book was 'the first fictional work on the subject by a writer of stature with first-hand knowledge of what he is writing about'. It is the first exposure of what espionage really means—not romance, but boredom, callousness, and dehumanisation.

Ashenden is a collection of short stories, beginning in Geneva and ending in Petrograd during the revolution. These tales are loosely tied together by the presence of the agent, Ashenden, the author's amusing self-portrait and the first of the anti-hero secret agents.

Maugham's version of the secret agent is a vivid contrast to the usual heroic figure in espionage literature. Ashenden does not use an ingenious ploy, make a brilliant deduction, or trick a clever diabolical enemy master mind. He does not perform feats of bravado, recover essential secret documents, or deliver a spy ring to London. On the contrary, he worries about the discomfort of a Swiss jail and the mortification of being conducted to the border. He has a phobia about missing trains and suffers an attack of nerves when a fellow agent is about to murder a Greek spy. Even playing piquet with a

Mexican rogue, he is unable to detect his cheating and is badly beaten.

Unlike previous heroes of spy stories, Ashenden is a well-travelled, slightly world-weary hedonist. Throughout the book, he spends a considerable amount of time contemplating the pleasure of hot baths, *haute cuisine*, reading and train rides. In Geneva, at a time when he is worried about the possibility of imprisonment or deportation, he finds consolation in a hot steaming bath, reflecting that 'really ... there are moments in life when all this to-do that has led from the primeval slime to myself seems almost worth while'.

Ashenden is a cultivated and cultured man, a habitué of the Café Royal who has gone to war, and there is considerable smugness in his self-satisfaction about his tastes. When his duty forces him to have a bottle of beer with a suspected traitor, he feels that he must compensate himself by ordering the best brandy that the tavern can provide. When Grantley Caypor offers him a cheap Swiss cigar, he accepts it, 'making a rueful sacrifice to duty'. When 'R.', Ashenden's superior officer and a man of considerable authority, is embarrassed by the act of tipping and talks too loudly to show that he is really at his ease, Ashenden notes with a smile his 'common-place' background. When 'R.' asks him if he likes macaroni, Ashenden delights in the opportunity of humbling him:

"What do you mean by macaroni?" answered Ashenden. "It is like asking me if I like poetry. I like Keats and Wordsworth and Verlaine and Goethe. When you say macaroni, do you mean *spaghetti, tagliatelli, rigatoni, vermicelli, fettucini, tufali, farfalli*, or just macaroni?"
"Macaroni," replied R., a man of few words.[5]

The most significant and original aspect of Ashenden, and what makes him the prototype of a long progression of anti-hero agents, is his lack of real importance in the espionage system. Only a small part of an intricate network, he knows very little of the purpose of his actions, the background, or the results. He acts as a courier from one point to another without knowing what he is transporting; it is official policy that he often be deliberately uninformed. When, for example, Ashenden is sent to Lucerne to observe the traitor Caypor, he is not told the ultimate objective of his mission. He becomes acquainted with the man, associates with him, and reports on his observations. When Caypor finally asks for a letter of introduction to the censorship department in England (where he will fall into the hands of British Intelligence), Ashenden suddenly realises that 'R.' has been using him as a decoy, gambling on his ignorance of the objective giving his role a greater air of authenticity. He has been merely a tool, a pawn in a large chess game, and he had succeeded in his mission without having had any understanding of its purpose or necessity. Earlier, Ashenden had considered the disparity between the romantic conception of espionage and his own boredom:

It might be, he mused . . . that the great chiefs of the secret service in their London offices, their hands on the throttle of this great machine, led a life full of excitement; they moved their pieces here and there, they saw the pattern woven by the multitudinous threads (Ashenden was lavish with his metaphors), they made a picture out of the various pieces of the jigsaw puzzle; but it must be confessed that for the small fry like himself to be a member of the secret service was not as adventurous an affair as the public thought. Ashenden's official existence was as orderly and mono-tonous as a City clerk's. He saw his spies at stated intervals and paid them their wages; when he could get hold of a new one he engaged him, gave him his instructions and sent him off to Germany; he waited for the information that came through and dispatched it; he went into France once a week to confer with his colleague over the frontier and to receive his orders from London; he visited the market-place on market-day to get any message the old butter-woman had brought him from the other side of the lake; he kept his eyes and ears open; and he wrote long reports which he was convinced no one read till having inadvertently slipped a jest into one of them he received a sharp reproof for his levity. The work he was doing was evidently necessary, but it could not be called anything but monotonous.[6]

Because of the detachment with which Maugham presents the episodes in *Ashenden*, he has frequently been accused of supporting deception, treachery and murder. According to the author's intro-duction to the 1941 edition, Goebbels, in a radio speech during the Second World War, cited *Ashenden* as an example of the cynicism and brutality of the British Secret Service. A recent critic, Richard Cody, argues that Goebbels came close to the truth: 'It is indeed a vulnerable unofficial repository of very orthodox British upper-class values; a vindication through fiction of the whole public school, OHMS, club-land, House of Lords ethos.'[7]

Needless to say, to accuse Maugham of giving unqualified support to the public school, OHMS, House of Lords ethos, the critic must ignore almost everything else that the author has written about these attitudes in his other mature works. These criticisms of *Ashenden* are essentially the same as those levelled at the presentation of slum life in *Liza of Lambeth* and at Maugham's frequent portrayal of the successful adulterer or murderer. This school of criticism demands re-peated and explicit qualifying statements from the author which disassociate his approval from the actions he has chosen to represent. Maugham, however, has often stated that he does not judge his characters and their actions. He presents an accurate picture as he interprets it, and the reader must draw the conclusions for himself.

It is possible to argue, nevertheless, that, just as *Ashenden* exposes the boredom and routine of spying, it contains implicit criticism of the ethics of espionage. This is most apparent in the attitude of Ashenden, an amateur, an ordinary man recruited for war-time service, toward certain aspects of his job. One of the better sections of the book describes the capture and death of an Indian agitator, Chandra Lal. Hostile toward British rule in India, Lal has become a leading political activist. He has fomented rebellions, caused riots in which lives have been lost, and has been involved in bomb outrages which have killed innocent bystanders. Having fallen in love with a dancer, Lal becomes vulnerable, and eventually Ashenden's men capture him. Before they realise what he is doing, however, he commits suicide. Although Ashenden recognises his ruthlessness, and although he has been responsible for the capture of the Indian, he is relieved by the outcome because he is spared having to consider the obscenity of his execution. Unlike 'R.', Ashenden has seen that Lal, while a threat to the Allies, is fighting for his country's freedom, and he admires the courage of a man who will fight the British control of India.

Similarly in 'The Traitor', when Ashenden tricks Caypor into going to England, where he will meet his death, he cannot help visualising the terror of the condemned man and the brutality of the execution. As in the previous situation, the agent recognises that his task is one that must be done, but this does not prevent him from recognising its inherent grotesque violence.

Later Ashenden is faced with the prospect of issuing an order to sabotage munitions factories in Austria, an action which will mean the killing and maiming of a great number of innocent people. Suffering under the responsibility for such a decision, he considers the hypocritical attitude of those in high office:

It was not of course a thing that the big-wigs cared to have anything to do with. Though ready enough to profit by the activities of obscure agents of whom they had never heard, they shut their eyes to dirty work so that they could put their clean hands on their hearts and congratulate themselves that they had never done anything that was unbecoming to men of honour.[8]

In the end, Ashenden is morally unable to make the decision, and the fate of a great many people is decided by the toss of a coin.

The most powerful dramatisation of the callousness of the ethics of espionage is the episode where Ashenden accompanies the "Hairless Mexican', a professional killer, on a mission to prevent an enemy emissary from reaching his contacts in Rome. 'R.' has decided that the Mexican, a rogue with no scruples, will be the one who actually makes contact with the enemy, thus relieving the British agent of an unpleasant task. While Ashenden nervously retreats to his hotel room, the Mexican murders the emissary, but they are unable to find the appropriate documents on him. The mission comes to an abrupt end when a horrified Ashenden receives a message stating that the real agent has been ill and unable to travel:

At first Ashenden could not understand. He read it again. He shook from head to foot. Then, for once robbed of his self-possession, he blurted out, in a hoarse, agitated and furious whisper:
"You bloody fool, you've killed the wrong man."⁹

This episode is typical of Maugham's method. There is no lengthy condemnation of the killing of an innocent man, no ready-made opinions which allow the reader to assume that judgement has been passed on the philosophy of expediency. There are no long passages of rhetoric which blunt the power of the discovery. The author ends the episode, as he does so many of his short stories, with a surprising revelation and lets the shock convey the weight of his argument. There are no nicely quotable opinions, but an attitude toward the spy ethos is present. In this regard, *The Times Literary Supplement* wrote: 'Never before or since has it been so categorically demonstrated that counter-intelligence work consists often of morally indefensible jobs not to be undertaken by the squeamish or the conscience-stricken.'¹⁰

The influence of *Ashenden* on subsequent espionage stories should not be underestimated. Eric Ambler, commenting on *The Times Literary Supplement* review which claimed that his early books were influenced by the Ashenden ethos, replied that they were indeed. 'The breakthrough was entirely Mr Maugham's', he said, adding that 'there is, after all, a lot of Simenon, and a satisfactory quantity of W. R. Burnett, but only one *Ashenden*'. Richard Cody, although finding Maugham's book the 'dreariest of vintage secret service thrillers', is forced to grant it a prominent place in the history of spy fiction:

With the hindsight of thirty years, however, one can now see clearly that the most influential secret service thriller of the 'twenties, so far as the immediate future of the tradition was concerned, was not one of the club-land sort at all, but, ironically enough, Maugham's *Ashenden*. Dreary as it is, that thriller almost completely anticipates the new mannerist stage that the tradition went into when Eric Ambler and Graham Greene began writing in it: the stage of middle-aged, cynical, more or less stateless heroes (often writers by profession) whose inconclusive, semi-documentary adventures in shabby hotels, on slow ships or on uncomfortable continental trains seem to express the *malaise* of the Europe of the time with an anguish – and a selfconsciousness – that the clubland writers never even tried to achieve.¹¹

This school of realistic espionage writers has continued to flourish beyond Ambler and Greene to contemporary writers. When Ian

Fleming's 'James Bond' spy fantasies became widely read in the late 1950s and early 1960s, a number of low-keyed, anti-romantic secret service novels appeared as antidotes. Len Deighton's *The Ipcress File* (1962), *Funeral in Berlin* (1964) and *Billion Dollar Brain* (1966) feature an anti-hero who does not extricate himself from difficulties with the Bond élan. The world of the secret service in these novels is neither glamorous nor ethical, and people are ruthlessly discarded when their usefulness is over.

The best spy novel of the past decade, however, is John Le Carré's *The Spy Who Came in from the Cold* (1963), a book which, although regarded as an innovation in contemporary espionage fiction, is remarkably similar in treatment and purpose to *Ashenden*. It tells the story of Alec Leamas, a middle-aged, spiritually exhausted British Intelligence agent who has lost his ability to carry out his missions successfully. He has one last task to perform before he can 'come in from the cold' to the safety of an office job in London. His orders are to pretend to defect to East Germany and there bring about the downfall of Mundt, an enemy agent who has been too effective in eliminating British spies in Germany. He succeeds in being taken to Intelligence headquarters behind the Iron Curtain, and assists an enemy agent, Fiedler, in bringing Mundt before a tribunal, accused of being in the British service. At the trial, however, Mundt's defence astutely discredits the evidence of Leamas and Fiedler is himself arrested and executed.

At this point, Leamas recognises the true situation: Mundt is, after all, a British agent and British Intelligence have arranged the trial as a means of strengthening Mundt's position and of eliminating a threat in Fiedler. In this manœuvring Leamas has been merely a pawn and he has fulfilled his mission without ever being aware of its true purpose. The enemy has never been visible and recognisable, and the strategy has been devised and projected thousands of miles away in a Whitehall office. The parallel between this situation and the episode in *Ashenden* where Maugham's hero learns that headquarters has been using him to lure Caypor to England is pronounced. The influence of *Ashenden* on *The Spy Who Came in from the Cold* may be devious and indirect, but it is surely there in some manner. Maugham's contribution to this branch of modern fiction is indeed greater than is generally recognised.

A large part of the success of *Ashenden* must be attributed to the skilful creation of the *persona* of the central figure. It is a device which had served Maugham well in *The Moon and Sixpence*, and which he was to use in half of his short stories, *Cakes and Ale*, *The Razor's Edge*, and, in a variation, in *The Gentleman in the Parlour* and *Don Fernando*.

Whether the *persona* is 'Willie Ashenden', the 'I' of the short stories, or merely the character of the writer of the travel books, it is a mask for the author, with the advantages and disadvantages which accompany the use of a mask.

In *The Moon and Sixpence* the narrator serves as a technical device for telling a story which ranges from London to Paris to Marseilles to Tahiti; it is just as important, however, as a means of communicating an ordinary man's view of genius. Moreover, Ashenden acts as a foil for the impetuous, passionate, amoral Strickland, in the same way that the *persona* serves as a contrast to Zorba in Nikos Kazantzakis's *Zorba the Greek*. At one point, for example, Maugham gives Ashenden the line: 'You evidently don't believe in the maxim: Act so that every one of your actions is capable of being made into a universal rule.' Strickland replies that it is 'rotten nonsense', voicing the author's own opinion, as recorded in *A Writer's Notebook*: 'One of the commonest errors of the human intelligence is to insist that a rule should be universally applicable.'

There are really two Ashendens in *The Moon and Sixpence*—the young aspiring writer who encounters genius and the older, more assured author who looks back on his youth with amusement. He is able to view himself as a somewhat priggish and pretentious young man, and he faithfully describes his rhetorical defeats by Strickland and his half-unwilling admiration of the painter. When, for example, Strickland's cheerful amorality negates the young Ashenden's ethical attacks, the narrator is quick to recognise the ridiculous figure he presented:

I glanced at him with surprise. His cordial agreement with all I said cut the ground from under my feet. It made my position complicated, not to say ludicrous. I was prepared to be persuasive, touching, and hortatory, admonitory, and expostulating, if need be vituperative even, indignant and sarcastic; but what the devil does a mentor do when the sinner makes no bones about confessing his sin?[12]

The Ashenden who appears nine years later in *Ashenden or: The British Agent* is the same character, but older, wiser and mellower. He is now an established writer, pleased to use his fame to get a better stateroom or faster service through Customs, but not blind to its disadvantages. Having a greater degree of tolerance, he can see the virtues in an English traitor or an Indian revolutionary. He is not an heroic figure, but a retiring, quiet hedonist more interested in a good meal by the fire than in national secrets.

Cakes and Ale reverts to the narrative technique of *The Moon and Sixpence*; the story is told in the first person singular and the speaker looks back to various stages of his youth. In this novel the character of Ashenden can be seen to develop from the young schoolboy snob in Whitstable to the young man first discovering passion to the middle-aged writer who frequents London clubs. The narrator is a technical device to facilitate the rapid changes in periods, but he becomes as interesting a character as most figures in the story.

Although *Don Fernando* and *The Gentleman in the Parlour* are travel books, written in a straightforward narrative style, the 'I' is as much a *persona* as 'Willie Ashenden'. As a genre, the travel book depends a great deal for its success on the nature of the traveller, and in both the reader is escorted by an intelligent, witty, and charming guide. In *Don Fernando*, he is in the company of a scholar, a man who can discuss the historical, sociological and literary history of Spain without a trace of pedantry or dullness. The result is that, while presented with a lively and thoughtful picture of Spanish culture, the reader is inevitably given an intriguing glimpse into the ideas and philosophy of the narrator. Not surprisingly, much of *Don Fernando* was incorporated three years later into *The Summing Up*.

In *The Gentleman in the Parlour*, Maugham uses a *persona* which is considerably different from that of *Don Fernando*. In this book he is more closely involved with the passing scenes and is less inclined to contemplate artistic and philosophical theories. More relaxed and casual, he draws the reader into his experience along the trail or at an outstation. He is very much a character, viewing himself with amusement and confessing to a number of human weaknesses which he shares with others: he is a bad traveller, over-cautious about nearing a water-buffalo, distressed by the abundance of cockroaches, susceptible to petulance, and beset by obnoxious fellow travellers. He can reproach himself for wasting time playing cards, and he confesses his inability to identify flowers, discuss philosophical matters, or adequately describe the Temples of Angkor. He tries smoking opium and becomes ill, and he falls asleep in his sampan, thus missing the wonderful experience of a glorious Eastern night. A traveller who admits his vulnerability to minor catastrophes, he establishes a rapport with the reader.

The narrator of Maugham's short stories is a technical device, but he is also a meticulously contrived figure, unobtrusive but not invisible. Anthony Burgess[13] considers the *persona* one of Maugham's finest creations; V. S. Pritchett describes him as 'the Great Dry Martini in person';[14] and Raymond Mortimer compares him to 'an absorbingly interesting man in "The Golden Arrow" '.[15] The character of the first person narrator, developed through the cumulative effect of many stories, is very much a part of Maugham's success.

In his introduction to the version of 'Sanatorium' in the omnibus film, 'Trio', Maugham states that 'if you like to take the character of Ashenden as a flattering portrait of the old party who stands before you, you are at perfect liberty to do so'. 'Ashenden' and the 'I' of the short stories are indeed very much representations of Somerset Maugham. Their tastes are the same, their philosophies are similar, and their temperaments match. The *persona*, nevertheless, rather than being a faithful transcript of the author, is a representation of the kind of person he would like to be. Just as Conrad endowed Marlow with many of the traits he would have liked to see in himself, Maugham, despite the self-effacing nature of his narrator, incorporates in him the traits he admires.

The most original quality of the Maugham *persona* is his cosmopolitanism. The geographical and social range of the stories is remarkable, and the ease with which the narrator seems to move in various milieus—the South Seas, the Far East, the Riviera, prison colonies, ocean liners, or Mayfair parties—helps to draw the reader into the stories. In 'Virtue' he is found in London circles, dropping into Sotheby's in Bond Street, going to the Haymarket, and dining at Ciro's. In 'Jane' he attends a party the style of which he has not seen 'since Stafford House was sold'; and in 'A Casual Affair' he describes a party at Claridges at 'the height of the season'. In 'The Pool' the narrator indulges in cocktails in the Hotel Metropole in Apia; in 'Footprints in the Jungle' he describes the club life in Tanah Merah; and in 'The Four Dutchmen' he tells of sitting in the garden of the Van Dorth Hotel, in Singapore, reading the *Straits Times*. 'A Friend in Need' finds him at the British Club in Yokohama; 'The Luncheon', at Foyot's in the Latin Quarter of Paris; and 'The Human Element', in the Hotel Plaza in Rome.

The Maugham *persona*, however, is not restricted to travelling first class, moving only in artistic and aristocratic circles. He is equally comfortable (spiritually, if not physically) travelling by ox-cart in Burma, sailing on tramp steamers in the Pacific, or riding the trans-Siberian railway from Vladivostok to Petrograd. In 'A Man with a Conscience' he is in the penal colony of St Laurent de Maroni; in 'French Joe', on Thursday Island; and in 'The Book-Bag' he is wandering about Malaya, staying with planters or District Officers.

Like the author himself, the *persona* in Maugham's stories moves freely in many circles; he can dine at the Café Royal or at a bohemian restaurant in the Via Sistina in Rome, and he is equally at ease at the 'Countess de Marbella's' parties ('The Romantic Young Lady') or at a tatty English seaside hotel ('The Round Dozen'). Much of the appeal of this kind of narrator is of course escapist in nature. The reader is vicariously the cosmopolitan traveller, sharing cocktails with beachcombers in Tahiti or gossip in a London club. V. S. Pritchett explains: 'Maugham gratified the wish to see oneself as worldly-wise and sagacious, to have impenetrable savoir-faire, to call for that dry Martini and light a sceptical cigar at the end of the day.'[16]

In part, this character of the worldly-wise cosmopolitan is established through the numerous digressions and brief comments about wine, food, cigars, bridge, poker and other cultivated pleasures. These opinions are used to create an atmosphere and to appeal to the reader's wish to imagine himself a connoisseur. 'The Human Element', for example, begins with a lengthy description of the Hotel Plaza in Rome, its food and its wine. In 'Jane' the narrator complains that the food is execrable and he claims to dislike champagne at lunch. He likes Mrs Albert Forrester (in 'The Creative Impulse'), however, because she gives you 'uncommonly good food, excellent wine, and a first-rate cigar'. In 'The Man With the Scar' he applauds the dry martinis concocted in the Palace Hotel in Guatemala City, compares the merits of his hotel in Seville to the Hotel de Madrid in 'The Romantic Young Lady', and in *Cakes and Ale* he ruefully scans the pedestrian menu at Alroy Kear's club. In *Ashenden* he describes to 'R.' the 'simple' things that he likes—boiled eggs, oysters, caviare, *truite au bleu*, grilled salmon, roast lamb, and cold grouse; and in *The Gentleman in the Parlour* he devotes a chapter to a discussion of the pleasures of food and the problems of finding a good cook. 'The Book-Bag' sees him playing cards and drinking gin pahits in Malaya, 'The Portrait of a Gentleman' reveals his inclination to bet on straight flushes, and 'The Escape' includes the peculiar agony of the bridge player who has his aces trumped.

The best illustration of Maugham's use of the man-of-the-world narrator is the opening paragraphs of 'Virtue'. He writes:

There are few things better than a good Havana. When I was young and very poor and smoked a cigar only when somebody gave me one, I determined that if ever I had money I would smoke a cigar every day after luncheon and after dinner. This is the only resolution of my youth that I have kept. It is the only ambition I have achieved that has never been embittered by disillusion. I like a cigar that is mild, but full-flavoured, neither so small that it is finished before you have become aware of it nor so large as to be irksome, rolled so that it draws without consciousness of effort on your part, with a leaf so firm that it doesn't become messy on your lips and in such a condition that it keeps its savour to the end.[17]

The speaker then proceeds from this specific discussion of the merits of a good cigar to a contemplation of the complicated organisation and numerous lives that have been involved in giving him this half hour of pleasure. He compares this to eating a dozen oysters (with, he is careful to specify, a half bottle of white wine) and a lamb cutlet, and

H

he considers the progress of fate which has led these creatures to the plate of crushed ice or the silver grill. From thoughts of their fate, it is a smooth transition to consideration of the lives of humans, and this introduces his story.

This is a skilful opening because, in addition to facilitating the introduction of the story, it tells the reader a great deal about the kind of person in whose company he is. The narrator is a man of experience—knowledgeable, philosophic and contemplative. He is likely to tell a fascinating tale.

The cosmopolitanism of the Maugham narrator is an engaging quality, and in most respects it is a sincere reflection of the author's personality. Its failing, however, is also that of the author himself: that is, that frequently its worldliness and *savoir-faire* tend to be clever and glib, rather than deeply understood and fully experienced. Just as Ian Fleming later invested James Bond with worldly knowledge and cultivated tastes in order to give him a superhuman charisma, Maugham makes his *persona* a seemingly cultured and experienced man. He is, of course, much more subtle and skilful in this technique than Fleming, but there is a similarity of purpose. The effect is that, while the narrator succeeds initially in convincing many readers of his knowledge and catholic tastes, he rarely convinces them that he is deeply proficient in any matter. The nagging feeling remains that Maugham collected many scraps of information which his professional eye recognised as valuable material for building the credibility of his teller and his tales. It too often seems that, although an adventurous traveller, he skimmed along the surface of experience, rather than fully exploring anything in real depth.

Another notable characteristic of the Maugham *persona* is his self-deprecating humility. Although he is worldly-wise and intelligent, the narrator is prepared to tell a story against himself and to see the ridiculous side of his own behaviour. In *The Moon and Sixpence* he laughs at his inability to match Strickland's arguments; in *Ashenden* he teases himself about his playing the role of detective; and in *Cakes and Ale* he describes the narrow-minded snobbishness of his adolescence. In 'The Alien Corn' he expresses mock annoyance at being included by the pianist Lea Makart in her claim that 'you are only our raw material'. 'The Poet', in which he wrongly takes a bristle-merchant for a Spanish poet, and 'Raw Material', in which he mistakes two prominent businessmen for card sharks, are both wry jokes at his own expense. Both 'The End of the Flight' and 'A Man From Glasgow' end with the speaker confessing his nervous fear after being told chilling gothic tales.

More significant, however, than the *persona*'s self-effacing humour is the catholic nature of his interests. Of his attitude, Richard Aldington writes:

It is so entirely free of any trace of condescension, pretentiousness and superciliousness – the besetting sins of the highbrow. It is not merely a question of good manners, but of an attitude to life which is far superior to the limited interests and prejudices of intellectualist cliques. Maugham is a pretty good bridge-player and does not hesitate to reveal the fact in his writings. If he had such an accomplishment, the average littérateur would not dare reveal it – unless of course Maugham's example has now made it fashionable.[18]

Not only does the Maugham *persona* play bridge, he enjoys a game of poker, a round of golf, and Nick Carter stories. Although he can discuss the writings of Christian saints and the mysticism of the East, he readily confesses to being incapable of adequately discussing philosophy. When forced by circumstances in 'The Portrait of a Gentleman' to choose between reading treatises on the Old Testament or a book about poker, he chooses the latter.

It would be a mistake to conclude, after recognising the worldly, hedonistic traits of the Maugham *persona*, that the author is writing down to the public. If the speaker confesses an inclination toward certain physical or unintellectual pursuits, it does not negate the many perceptive and carefully considered observations that he advances. Maugham has deliberately created a character with whom the reader can identify, and this gives his writing a greater impact. Referring to the uniqueness of this first person narrator, Anthony Burgess is right when he says:

Here again was something that English fiction needed – the dispassionate commentator, the "raisonneur", the man at home in Paris and Vienna but also in Seoul and Djakarta, convivial and clubbable, as ready for a game of poker as for a discussion on the Racine alexandrine, the antithesis of the slippered bookman.[19]

The tone of the stories in which Maugham uses a *persona* is that of a congenial gentleman telling a tale in front of the fireplace over cigars and port. In this respect, he shares the point of view of the writers of the eighteenth and nineteenth centuries who told their stories as a raconteur would over dinner, with digressions, inter-jections, and hypotheses about the actions of the characters. In all of Maugham's writings in which he uses the first person singular there is a repeated use of 'you'. 'You' wonder at Rosie Gann's beauty, suffer the hardships of travel in Burma, and feel the defects of Spanish literature. The 'I' and the 'you', the teller and the listener, become intimate during the course of the story, and a great attraction lies in the shared reflection or common observation. In many places, particularly where Maugham discusses literature, art, or philosophy, he establishes a feeling of 'we' and 'they'—'they' being the supposedly pompous and pretentious intellectuals who infuriate 'us', 'we' who view matters with balance and common sense. His stance is that of the man of common sense, and this attitude appeals to a great many readers who find the excesses of intellectual snobbery intolerable.

Maugham's stories are always conversational in tone, and he has frequently been criticised for his liberal use of colloquialisms and clichés. It is not true, however, that Maugham uses colloquial expressions indiscriminately. An extensive analysis of his writing would show that, while he does frequently use common words to achieve lucidity, his use of clichés is on the whole restricted to dialogue and to the stories told by the first person narrator. It should not be forgotten that these novels and short stories are being told by a particular character, carefully created and developed. It is to maintain atmosphere and verisimilitude that colloquialisms such as 'nineteen to the dozen', 'slap-up dinner', 'cut-up' and 'brown study' appear. In his other writing, Maugham noticeably uses fewer popular expressions or clichés.

If 'Ashenden' and the 'I' of the short stories is a picture of the author as he would like to be, it reveals a great deal about Maugham, particularly about his attitude toward his relationship with his fellows. The position of the narrator with regard to the stories he tells and the degree of his involvement with the characters is consistent with the author's respect for independence. The *persona* is a manifestation of Maugham's search for emotional and physical liberty, and is as much a study in freedom as the other major figures of his writings. It is a mask, providing the psychological and literary advantages which have always appealed to writers. In *The Gentleman in the Parlour* Maugham quotes Hazlitt to explain the attraction of the mask:

Oh! it is great to shake off the trammels of the world and of public opinion – to lose our importunate, tormenting, everlasting personal identity in the elements of nature, and become the creature of the moment, clear of all ties – to hold to the universe only by a dish of sweet-breads, and to owe nothing but the score of the evening – and no longer seeking for applause and meeting with contempt, to be known by no other title than *The Gentleman in the Parlour*![20]

The narrator in Maugham's stories occupies an interesting position within the action and yet detached from it. He moves within the circle of characters, often being present when the conflict occurs, but he rarely ever influences the course of events in any appreciable way. Jealously guarding his independence and mobility, he protects himself emotionally by his attitude of clinical interest in, and amused tolerance of, his fellow men. Reviewing *Cakes and Ale, The Saturday Review* blamed the novel's weaknesses on the detachment of Ashenden:

It is not cheap cynicism which one feels to be the defect in the narrator's character, preventing those tenuous outlines from being filled in with the illuminating candour of a really creative novelist, but a sort of defensiveness of spirit, masked behind his irony and reserve.[21]

The Maugham *persona* indeed frequently adopts this defensive attitude, and he often views the other characters as agents of some form of oppression. In 'Mr Know-All', for example, he is forced to take whatever liner accommodation is available, and he is relieved to be given a cabin with only two berths. The thought of sharing his cabin with anyone for fourteen days nevertheless fills him with dismay. This turns to agony when he discovers that his fellow traveller is aggressively familiar, insisting on telling him how to play his game of patience. The narrator's only defence is to hope that his tormentor will recognise that he is 'frigidly indifferent' to his presence.

In 'A String of Beads' the speaker begins with an expression of his disappointment at being trapped at the dinner table into hearing a story from a friend who feels she has some valuable raw material for him. 'The Luncheon' is constructed around the anguish of the storyteller as he takes a friend to lunch and cannot escape from her extravagant expenditures at his cost. 'The Social Sense' begins with a description of the narrator's dislike of long-standing engagements. They are a nuisance because they are restrictions on his freedom of action:

You accept, and for a month the engagement hangs over you with gloomy menace. It interferes with your cherished plans. It disorganises your life. There is really only one way to cope with the situation and that is to put yourself off at the last moment.[22]

When he does attend the dinner party, it is in fear that he will be 'laboriously making conversation through a long dinner with two total strangers'. In *The Moon and Sixpence*, when attending literary evenings, he wants to be able to stand aside and remain unnoticed so that he can observe people at his ease.

The best illustration of the *persona*'s defensive nature is the relationship between Ashenden and Alroy Kear, Mrs Barton Trafford and Amy Driffield in *Cakes and Ale*. The latter are the representatives of censorial literary and social convention, and they are aggressive—albeit subtle, flattering and slick—in imposing their wills on others. In one respect Ashenden spends most of the novel defending the characters and philosophy of Driffield, Rosie, Kemp and himself from the sanctions of the trio. He also has to guard his own flexibility against their devices. *Cakes and Ale* begins brilliantly, with Ashenden immediately on the defensive, suspicious of the urgency of a telephone call:

I have noticed that when someone asks for you on the telephone and, finding you out, leaves a message begging you to call him up the moment you come in, as it's important, the matter is more often important to him than to you. When it comes to making you a present or doing you a favour most people are able to hold their patience within reasonable bounds.[23]

When Ashenden discovers that the caller is Alroy Kear, he becomes suspicious and he remains guarded throughout his encounters with him. At Alroy's club he wonders what the imposition will be and he amuses himself by watching his friend's manœuvring to approach the matter. Later, when Kear interrupts Ashenden's recollections of his Blackstable days, it is as an intruder on an intensely private scene:

He came in, big, bluff, and hearty; his vitality shattered with a simple gesture the frail construction I had been building out of the vanishing past. He brought in with him, like a blustering wind in March, the aggressive and inescapable present.[24]

As Kear attempts tactfully to introduce his proposition, Ashenden dons a mask of incomprehension and delights in remaining elusive. Ultimately, however, he cannot avoid the issue, and he reluctantly is persuaded to contribute his remembrance of Driffield to Kear's research.

The Maugham *persona* protects himself from involvement with other people on a much more important level than that of mere physical contact. He allows himself a very restricted amount of emotional commitment toward the people whose story he tells. He admires their goodness, tolerates their badness, and pities their suffering, but the course of their lives rarely affects his mental equilibrium. In fact, the narrator frequently attempts to prevent any real spiritual communication between himself and another character.

In 'Virtue', although he knows all of the individuals involved in the tragedy, he confesses that his sympathies are not deeply engaged and that he only observed the action out of curiosity. In *The Moon and Sixpence*, after the horrible suicide of Blanche Stroeve, Ashenden confesses that he was getting bored with the affair, that it 'did not really concern me'. In 'A Man With a Conscience' the narrator prefaces his tale by saying: 'All this has nothing to do with me. It is vain to torment oneself over sufferings that one cannot alleviate.' In *Ashenden* his ability to keep his emotions in check and to remain detached from the feelings of others make him a capable agent. 'R.' recognises these advantages when he assigns Ashenden the case of Giulia Lazzari:

Her grief was real, but there was something theatrical in the expression of it that prevented it from being peculiarly moving to Ashenden. He felt his relation to her as impersonal as a doctor's in the presence of a pain that he cannot alleviate. He saw now why R. had given him this peculiar task; it needed a cool head and an emotion well under control.[25]

Although the narrator in Maugham's writings travels around the world to collect stories and to hear people tell their tales, he reacts defensively when someone reveals his innermost self. The baring of the soul seems too intimate a gesture, one which demands an emotional response or commitment which the *persona* is not willing to give. The frank revelation of personal and hidden truths alters the situation of observer and observed, tending to involvement rather than detachment. The speaker, uncomfortable and nonplussed, retreats.

In *Ashenden*, for example, the narrator dines with Sir Herbert Witherspoon, who proceeds to relate the most important and intimate relationship of his life:

It was quite plain now that the story he was telling was about himself and Ashenden felt a certain indelicacy in the man's stripping his soul before him so nakedly. He did not desire this confidence to be forced upon him.[26]

And Ashenden once more wished that he would stop, it made him shy and nervous to see the man's naked soul: no one has the right to show himself to another in that destitute state.[27]

A similar, but more graphic, illustration of this reluctance to be drawn into a person's private griefs occurs in 'The Human Element', where the distressed Carruthers suddenly blurts out: 'I'm so desperately unhappy.' This sudden abandonment of social role and revelation of soul creates a considerable shock to the narrator:

It was amazing that a man so self-controlled, so urbane, accustomed to the usages of polite society should break in upon a stranger with such a confession. I am naturally reticent. I should be ashamed, whatever I was suffering, to disclose my pain to another. I shivered. His weakness outraged me. For a moment I was filled with a passion of anger. How dared he thrust the anguish of his soul on me. I very nearly cried:
"What the hell do I care?"[28]

The narrator does not prevent Carruthers from telling his story, but his confession is treated as an imposition, a claim for an emotional support that he is reluctant to give. In 'Masterson', on the other hand, when the *persona* encounters, in the course of his travels, a character whom he will never meet again, he is more willing to allow the man to reveal himself. In the freedom of travel, these revelations require fewer obligations from the listener. He can observe with pity and tolerance, but, being on the road the next day, there are fewer demands on his responsibility.

As has been noted previously, the Maugham *persona* is very often closely associated with the action of the story, but almost never influences the course of events in any way.[29] In 'The Round Dozen', for example, he observes the bigamist and his potential prey, but he is unable to do anything to prevent the elopement. In 'The Alien Corn' he knows the major characters, moves in their circle, observes them and conveys their messages, but he takes no part in the action. In 'Sanatorium' he is present as a tuberculosis patient, but his only function is to provide a stable point of view. It is not he who is threatened by the disease; the real drama of love, hate, and death, is played out by the other figures.

The persistent tendency of the Maugham *persona* toward non-involvement with events around him explains a great deal about Maugham's presentation of the anti-hero spy in *Ashenden*. Here, although he is a man who has specific tasks to perform, the agent is totally consistent with the *persona* of the other works. It is the intention of British Intelligence that he should not know any more than is necessary for his missions, but this coincides with his own wishes. Throughout, he demonstrates a real indifference to his occupation, often being more interested in his writing or in material comforts. When faced with the decision whether to order the sabotage of the factories, which will result in the deaths of many people, he chooses to relinquish his responsibility and the choice is made by the toss of a coin.

The 'Willie Ashenden' of *The Moon and Sixpence* and *Cakes and Ale* has no more real effect on the action than he does in *Ashenden*. In the former novel he is persuaded to go to Paris to bring Strickland back, but he does this with misgiving. He indulges in arguments with the painter and offers some assistance, but his presence in no way alters the progress of the artist's career. Although he knows the Stroeves and Strickland very well, he does not in the slightest alter the course of their tragedy. When the Stroeves quarrel about their caring for the desperately ill Strickland, Ashenden is embarrassed and he stands apart. He is present after Blanche's death only to comfort Stroeve.

Ashenden's position in *Cakes and Ale* epitomises the *persona* in Maugham's writing. Although he loves Rosie and she becomes his mistress, there is no analysis at length of their relationship, and the effect on him of her elopement is quickly dismissed. Ashenden is involved in both the high-spirited, lively world of the early Ted Driffield, Rosie and Kemp, and in the literary–social milieu of the Barton Traffords, Alroy Kear and Amy Driffield, but he is really not part of either life. He stands, not somewhere between the two worlds, but to one side, apart from both. From here he can observe his fellows with interest and pleasure, but he does very little which alters them in any way. Here, as in so many of Maugham's stories, the *persona* moves among people, studies them, considers the meaning, or lack of meaning, in their lives, but he only slightly becomes a factor in the progress of events.

The *persona* in Maugham's stories is as much a study in freedom as Philip Carey, Charles Strickland, Kitty Fane, Rosie Gann or Julia Lambert. His freedom is that of the cosmopolitan, the traveller who finds himself at home wherever his wanderlust takes him. He is fascinated by the people he encounters, but he has few ties with any other person and he carefully guards this independence. He enjoys the human spectacle, but likes to keep it at one remove from himself.

The detached, uncommitted nature of the Maugham narrator has a significant effect on the way in which the reader reacts to his stories. The actions are filtered through the interpretation of the speaker, and the reader's point of view becomes that of the story-teller. When the Maugham *persona* maintains a physical and emotional distance between himself and the characters involved, this results in a distance between the reader and the feelings and actions of the participants. The reader, as John Brophy notes, experiences, not the emotions of the people whose story is told, but the ironic and tolerant gaze of the narrator:

It is because so much attention is directed to the narration, rather than to the matter narrated, that this is more a talker's than a writer's story. Maugham's verisimilitude does not aim at making the reader experience, as directly as possible, the emotions of the characters. . . . The dominant reality belongs to the narrator. The reader identifies himself not with any of the characters but with the audience.[30]

The pleasures of these Maugham stories are of observation and contemplation, rather than of involvement and participation. Like the speaker, the reader can feel affection, admiration, annoyance, disgust, pity or tolerance for the characters, but he does not re-live their experiences. When the narrator confesses, as he frequently does, that he does not understand the workings of a character's mind, the reader is left with the exterior view. When the narrator treats a situation clinically, rather than with involvement, the reader shares his detachment. In his explanation of the story told in the first person singular in *Ten Novels and Their Authors*, Maugham states that 'the narrator begets in the reader the same sort of familiarity with the creatures of his invention as he has himself'. Clearly, this familiarity is restricted and inhibited, and thus the reader remains a distant, rather than an intimate, observer.

This type of narration has an obvious attraction. The point of view of the sensible, balanced, sceptical ordinary man appeals to a wide spectrum of readers. Moreover, his distrust of emotion and his moderate temperament provide a relief from the involvement and lack of restraint of a great deal of twentieth-century writing. Exhausted by the emotional demands of the stream-of-consciousness school, the intricacies of symbolism, and the obscurities of mysticism, the reader can appreciate the detached realism of Maugham's stories. In a socio-historical sense, the popularity of his writing in the 1920s may owe much to the style of the detached observer. Just as emotionally drained people after the First World War turned for relief to the escapism of exotic foreign stories, they responded to the restrained, low-keyed approach. Weary of idealism and the pain of disillusion-ment, readers found a great attraction in the point of view of amused tolerance.

For a great many readers, however, this approach to fiction is inadequate. For them literature means involvement with the emotions of the characters, an absorption into the narrative. Maugham's de-tached, professional and clinical treatment does not permit the reader to undergo the experiences he describes; the character of the narrator interprets everything and he stands, admittedly in a subtle fashion, between the reader and the story. This technique does not reveal its disadvantages as much in the short stories as it does in the novels since, by its nature, the short story does not often draw the reader in and submerge him totally in the action. In the novel, how-ever, the reader can be made to experience in depth the emotions and conflicts of the characters, and it is in this form that Maugham's approach most hampers him. Through his point of view, he abdicates the responsibility of plumbing the depths of a character's soul, and this results in the kind of criticism frequently made that the characters of Charles Strickland and Edward Driffield are inadequate portraits of artists, that Larry Darrell is a shallow picture of a seeker. In *Of Human Bondage*, on the other hand, there is no intermediary between Philip's story and the reader, and the involvement with the novel is, for most people, intense.

It may be ultimately that the short stories and novels in which Maugham uses a *persona* fall short of excellence because of this detachment and non-involvement. It could be argued, nevertheless, that the reader's understanding is increased as much through

Maugham's technique as through the experiments of the twentieth-century schools which seek totally to absorb the soul of the reader. There is much to be said in favour of his carefully considered interpretation of life, presented in his moderate tone of voice. In any case, it has its place in the spectrum of perceptive serious literature.

Through his travels and his cosmopolitan narrator Maugham has matched the achievement of the most prominent authors—the creation of an imaginary world which is universally identified with him. For him it is the world of plantations, seedy Pacific hotels, colonial administrators, isolated outposts and human derelicts. Although this world may not be entirely authentic, and although it is now certainly significant only as a part of the social history of twentieth-century colonialism, it is a milieu which retains many attractions and is a microcosm in which Maugham is able to reveal a number of significant truths about human nature. As Cyril Connolly says, it is unique:

But, if all else perish, there will remain a story-teller's world from Singapore to the Marquesas that is exclusively and forever Maugham, a world of verandah and prahu which we enter, as we do that of Conan Doyle's Baker Street, with a sense of happy and eternal homecoming.[31]

IX

The Razor's Edge
and the New Vedanta

THE NOVELS of the final period of Maugham's career—
Christmas Holiday (1939), *Up at the Villa* (1941), *The Hour
Before the Dawn* (1942), *The Razor's Edge* (1944), *Then and
Now* (1946), and *Catalina* (1948)—are a varied collection. Written late
in life and revealing the decline of his artistic ability, they nevertheless
sparkle with the occasional master stroke.

Except for some of his early novels, *The Hour Before the Dawn* is
perhaps the worst thing that Maugham has written; it is reputed to
be the work with which he was most dissatisfied. He referred to it in
A Writer's Notebook as 'a war novel that I wrote as part of the war
work I was asked to do in America and which I found a weariness to
do', and it was never part of the pattern which he had visualised for
the closing stages of his career. Produced at the request of the British
Ministry of Information, at a time when Maugham was living in the
United States, it was intended to demonstrate to the Americans the
effect of the war on a typical British family. His response was a picture
of the landed gentry, in no way typical of the average British household, and their adventures were scarcely representative of the actual
experiences of the ordinary person. This novel, which the author
never allowed to be published in England, is proof that Maugham was
not simply a commercial writer capable of turning out stories to
order.

The novelette *Up at the Villa* was written under similar circumstances and is little better than *The Hour Before the Dawn*. It was the
result of a suggestion by the editor of a woman's magazine, and was
to be published serially. According to Maugham, the completed
version proved too frank for the tastes of the magazine's readers, and
it was rejected. It is a trivial piece, and he makes no claim that it
provides anything more than an hour's diversion.

Christmas Holiday, Then and Now and *Catalina*, more than anything else that Maugham has written, reflect the political climate of the time. The questions of totalitarianism and political freedom, so pertinent in the pre-war and post-war periods, are given expression through allegorical and historical fiction.

Christmas Holiday, published in the political watershed of 1939, is very much a reflection of the political ferment of the 'thirties. It is the story of an upper-middle-class English youth's discovery of the social upheavals taking place in Europe, and it is a warning to the complacent, insular middle class in Britain.

In his essay 'Somerset Maugham and Posterity' Glenway Wescott develops an extremely interesting interpretation of *Christmas Holiday*. It had, he claims, greater social significance than any other comparable novel in 1939:

Maugham in this slight volume, less than a hundred thousand words long, with his air of having nothing on his mind except his eight characters – how they came together and what happened and what they said and how they felt – explains more of the human basis of fascism and nazism and communism than anyone else has done: the self-fascinated, intoxicated, insensible character of all that new leadership in Europe; the womanish passivity of the unhappy masses dependent on it and devoted to it; the Anglo-Saxon bewilderment in the matter, which still generally prevails; and the seeds of historic evil yet to come, not at all extirpated in World War II but rather multiplied and flung with greater profusion in no less receptive soil farther afield, even beyond Europe. Europe the starting point, the womb and the cradle, as in fact it has been for milleniums.[1]

In Wescott's analysis, *Christmas Holiday* is a political allegory. Young Charlie Mason is a representative of the prosperous liberal middle class, the predominant ruling caste in Europe between the wars. Robert Berger, the murderer, is a member of the 'new dictating' class which grew out of the First World War, while the embryonic revolutionary, Simon, is his intellectual apologist and propagandist. Finally, the Russian émigrée prostitute, Lydia, tortured by the need to expiate the sins of Berger, is a symbol of the mass of gullible common people.

Although most of *Christmas Holiday* is concerned with Charlie's experience with Lydia and the revelation of her life with Berger, some of the most interesting passages are those which treat the radical Simon. In this character Maugham attempts to examine the early development of a dictator, and the relevance to the totalitarian régimes of the 'thirties is obvious. Like so many of Maugham's characters, Simon is an outsider, driven forward by a force within him and searching for the freedom to achieve his ends. Accordingly, with an almost religious austerity, he attempts to purge himself of all human ties, to become completely detached from basic human demands. Only when he is entirely independent of emotion will he be capable of establishing a totalitarianism which will be able to ignore decent human sympathies. Therefore, just as he struggles to destroy his friendship with Charlie, he strives to purge himself of romantic attachments:

"I've got to be free. I daren't let another person get a hold over me. That's why I turned out the little sempstress. She was the most dangerous of the lot. She was gentle and affectionate. She had the meekness of the poor who have never dreamt that life can be other than hard. I could never have loved her, but I knew that her gratitude, her adoration, her desire to please, her innocent cheerfulness, were dangerous. I could see that she might easily become a habit of which I couldn't break myself. Nothing in the world is so insidious as a woman's flattery; our need for it is so enormous that we become her slave. I must be as impervious to flattery as I am indifferent to abuse. There's nothing that binds one to a woman like the benefits one confers on her. She would have owed me everything, that girl, I should never have been able to escape from her."[2]

Christmas Holiday reflects the end of an era of quiet complacency for a large segment of society; *Then and Now*, written seven years later, is an attempt to underline some of the lessons learned in the years between 1939 and 1946. The latter is Maugham's second historical novel and, as the title suggests, it draws parallels between the past and the present. An indication of Maugham's intentions can be found in an entry in *A Writer's Notebook* in 1941:

People should read history. The people of the Italian republics thought they could maintain their liberty by buying off with hard cash the enemies who threatened them, and with mercenaries defend their frontiers. Their history proves that unless the citizens of a state are prepared to fight, unless they are willing to spend their money to provide sufficient armaments, they will lose their freedom. It is a trite statement that no one can enjoy freedom unless he is willing to surrender some part of it. It is always forgotten.[3]

To ensure that this dictum is not forgotten, Maugham turns to the example of the historical period of Niccolo Machiavelli and Cesare Borgia. Here he finds material enough to demonstrate that the axioms of power politics which Machiavelli formulated in *The Prince* have validity both then and now. The duplicity and machinations of the *condottieri*, and the diplomatic intrigue of Cesare Borgia and Machiavelli, provide a historical parallel to the events in Europe in the nineteen-thirties and nineteen-forties. The conclusion to *Then and Now*, echoing the passage in *A Writer's Notebook*, is an address to the present:

"You say that Caesar Borgia suffered the just punishment of his crimes. He was destroyed not by his misdeeds, but by circumstances over which he had no control. His wickedness was an irrelevant accident. In this world of sin and sorrow if virtue triumphs over vice, it is not because it is virtuous, but because it has better and bigger guns; if honesty prevails over double-dealing, it is not because it is honest, but because it has a stronger army more ably led; and if good overcomes evil, it is not because it is good, but because it has a well-lined purse. It is well to have right on our side, but it is madness to forget that unless we have might as well it will avail us nothing. We must believe that God loves men of good will, but there is no evidence to show that He will save fools from the result of their folly."[4]

In spite of the seriousness of Maugham's intentions, this novel is very dull reading. Like *The Making of a Saint*, it relies too much on historical detail, and it rarely comes to life. With the exception of the tale of Machiavelli's pursuit of Monna Aurelia, and the subsequent manner in which he fashions it into a play, *Then and Now* is second-rate Maugham.

Maugham's final novel, *Catalina*, is a mellow, romantic celebration of Spain. It contains some characteristic portraits, but on the whole there is a lack of the tautness of his mature writing. Despite the historical setting and the general warmth of the treatment, it is nevertheless possible to detect the influence of contemporary events. Much of the novel deals with the Inquisition and, as in *Christmas Holiday*, the relevance to the practices of modern totalitarian states is inescapable. The section in which the Bishop, as Inquisitor, is compelled to torture his old intellectual companion is, for example, representative of the dehumanising effect of state censorship of opinion. In this respect, Laurence Brander argues:

The story of the Greek is a hand mirror of part of the European story. The totalitarianism of church or state breaks down the common decencies between men. *Catalina* is a study of power stresses, of the absolute and insolent exertion of power by people who had no enlightened conception of human values or human dignity. It is a picture of an Establishment twisted and deformed by an excess of zeal and power. In terms of Maugham's own ethic, it is simple goodness at the mercy of a human organisation. It is the humane at the mercy of organised bigotry.[5]

Catalina, like *The Hour Before the Dawn, Up at the Villa* and *Then and Now*, adds nothing to Maugham's reputation. Only *Christmas Holiday*, in many respects his most underrated novel, contains enough good writing to survive. The others in this group will be forgotten.

In his advanced years, however, Maugham produced a novel—*The Razor's Edge*—which contains some of his best writing. Unlike the other late novels, it is the culmination of years of thought and consideration, and it is the author's final exposition of a serious and profound theme. Garson Kanin, describing Maugham in California, where he had gone in 1945 to fashion the screenplay for *The Razor's Edge*, writes:

This work means a great deal to him, more than any of us suspected. He thinks of it as being, perhaps, his last major work. No matter what the critics or the public thought of its philosophical content, it is profound and meaningful to him.[6]

To many observers Maugham's interest in mysticism and saintliness came as a surprise and signified an important change of attitude. It seemed that the man who for so long had professed to see no meaning in the world except for the pattern the individual imposes on it had begun to feel the need to find a viable spiritual belief. Writing to Louis Wilkinson in 1947, John Cowper Powys discussed Maugham's apparent conversion:

What you say about S.M. arrested our deepest philosophical & psychological attention. My view is based on his book "The Razor's Edge" – a *very* bad & *in*appropriate title – and it is, as it wd. be with a bookworm like me, *and* a *University Extended* bookworm! – a bookish view. I think he's gone and "got religion". He's got it in *his way*, and his rough and tumble Saint Larry or whatever his name was, wasn't the kind that wd. suit Aldous Huxley or Graham Greene or Rex Warner, but nevertheless for an ex-man-of-the-world and ex-virtuoso in Brandy this Piccolo Santo will serve... To my taste the best of all S.M.'s inventions is that arch-snob-social-man-of-the-world and snob-artistic called Temple or Templeton – or summat like that – and my own fancy tells me that in this fine gent he pictured with happy exaggeration, as if in a Cartoon or Caricature, himself as he was when you knew him in those earlier days. Yes, I think this admirable craftsman and most honest cod has seriously "got religion" & thus naturally doesn't like what he liked (either in men or books) in his primrose days.[7]

The truth is, however, that examined closely *The Razor's Edge* reveals that Maugham had not 'got religion'. It does show an interest in goodness and in Indian philosophy, but these are subjects which had clearly fascinated him for a great many years. As early as 1899 he had treated the role of the good man in modern society, in the short story 'A Bad Example'. Dirk Stroeve, in *The Moon and Sixpence*, is, despite the foolish appearance he makes in the world, a good and generous man. 'Salvatore', written in 1924, attempted to portray a young man who possesses 'goodness, just goodness'. *The Narrow Corner* presented Erik Christessen, who, as his name indicates, is the personification of idealistic goodness. In *Sheppey*, Maugham's last play, there is a return to the theme of 'A Bad Example'; here the author develops his argument that a Christ-like figure will not be accepted by modern society. Maugham's interest in goodness was so apparent in the 'twenties and 'thirties that Ward, writing in 1937, could make this astute prediction:

Potentially, he is something more than he is in, say, *Cakes and Ale*; he is capable, excellent agent that he has become, of being used by a greater force of inspiration; he is, like anyone else or anything else, capable of development and change while yet remaining the same. And this development must come. Sheppey and others have hinted at it, and it is already on its way, embodied in Erik Christessen in the next novel, *The Narrow Corner*.[8]

Similarly, Maugham's interest in mysticism and Eastern philosophy is not a sudden development of his later life. Although his early questioning of Christianity culminated in the atheism represented in Philip Carey, he continued his examination of the religions of the East and his enquiries into mysticism. 'Faith', a short story published in 1899, considered sympathetically the dilemma of a young monk who loses his ability to believe in God. *The Painted Veil* treated, in however superficial a manner, the serenity of the belief in 'The Way'. In *The Gentleman in the Parlour* Maugham discussed the philosophy of Buddha, and he confessed to finding considerable attraction in the belief in the transmigration of souls. In *Don Fernando* he wrote at length about Catholic mysticism, particularly the asceticism and meditations of St Ignatius. The severity of these practices characteristically struck him as being the means by which 'the spirit was enslaved and cowed', but he was willing to admit that 'if the mystical experience is a liberating sense of community with what for a want of a better word we name reality', then at some time we are all in some degree mystics.

Because of the impact which *The Razor's Edge* made in 1944, it has generally been overlooked that in *The Narrow Corner* Maugham had already treated in considerable depth the philosophy of Indian religion. In this underrated serious novel there is extensive discussion of Buddhism, and the progress of the story is a movement in the direction of that belief by the central figure. It is possible, furthermore, to argue that in *The Narrow Corner* the tenets of Indian philosophy are more skilfully integrated with the story than they are in *The Razor's Edge*.

The Narrow Corner is constructed around the travels in the Pacific of Dr Saunders, an Englishman who has been struck from the Register for unethical practice. Having settled in China, he has a successful practice among the native population. He is an outsider, and a bit of a rogue, and Maugham gives him so much of his own philosophy that Cordell considers this almost an autobiographical novel. In many respects, the doctor's point of view represents the author's vision of life carefully developed over fifty years.

Throughout the novel Saunders is interested in the mystical experience and he becomes increasingly drawn to Buddhism. At the beginning this manifests itself in his indulgence in opium. The drug, which has become a habit, is a means of escaping bodily ties, and he undergoes a kind of mystical experience:

In this condition of freedom his soul could look down upon his flesh with the affectionate tolerance with which you might regard a friend who bored you but whose love was grateful to you. His mind was extraordinarily alert, but in its activity there was no restlessness and no anxiety; it moved with an assurance of power, as you might imagine a great physicist might move among his symbols, and his lucidity had the absolute delight of pure beauty. It was an end in itself. He was lord of space and time. There was no problem that he could not solve if he chose; everything was clear, everything was exquisitely simple.[9]

Maugham introduces the philosophy of Buddhism in the episode of the death of the Japanese pearl diver. Saunders considers Karma, the actions of the many lives the Japanese is believed to have experienced, and the transmigration of souls, reaching the same conclusion that Maugham did in *The Gentleman in the Parlour* and *The Summing Up*: 'A reasonable belief but an incredible'.

The really explicit treatment of Buddhism, however, comes later in the form of Frith, the dreamer-scholar on Kanda-Meira. Examining his library, Saunders notes two shelves of works on Indian philosophy and religion. There are translations of the *Rig-Veda* and some of the *Upanishads*, as well as studies of Indian religious texts. Prompted by Saunders' interest, Frith discusses, in simple terms, the basic aspects of Buddhist belief.[10] In the light of Maugham's treatment of Indian religion in *The Razor's Edge*, it is interesting that Frith dismisses the practice of Yoga as 'inane'.

In addition to Frith's direct pronouncements on Buddhism, Maugham reveals the man's belief in it in more subtle ways. On one occasion, for example, Erik describes how the old man, Swan, once destroyed the manuscript of Frith's translation of *The Lusiad*. The loss of the result of a year's laborious work touches Frith only slightly, and he reacts with Buddhist acceptance:

" 'Never mind, old man,' he said, 'you've only torn up a few dozen sheets of paper; they were merely an illusion and it would be foolish to give them a second thought; the reality remains, for the reality is indestructible.' "[11]

Later, in a moment of great beauty outside Louise Frith's bedroom, Erik recollects Frith's philosophy and, like the above passage, this belief is an essential part of Buddhism:

At that moment Erik understood what Frith meant when he said that the Primal Spirit, whom you can call God if you will, was not apart from the world but in it. That great spirit was in the stone on the mountain side, in the beast of the field, in man and in the thunder that rolled down the vault of heaven.[12]

Finally, Saunders, too, accepts some of the basic beliefs of Indian thought. The novel terminates with him sitting on the terrace of the Van Dyke Hotel in Singapore, and the last sentence is a Buddhist tenet: 'He sighed a little, for whatever it was, if the richest dreams the imagination offered came true, in the end it remained nothing but illusion.'

Dr Saunders' role in *The Narrow Corner* is primarily as a chorus or *raissoneur*, an observer of the ironies of human life. He is detached and watches with aloofness the roguery of Captain Nichols, the self-destruction of Fred Blake, the romantic illusions of Erik Christessen, the philosophic musings of Frith, and the elusiveness of Louise. Nevertheless, he undergoes a psychological change through what he witnesses, and, without the use of opium, he is able to recognise his essential freedom. All the other figures have been revealed to be prisoners of their personalities. They have been unable freely to determine the course of their own lives, and some have died with tragic inevitability. Only Saunders, through his philosophy, has been able to remain aloof from the events, and his detachment, although reached by different means, approaches that of the Eastern mystics:

He was glad he had made the journey. It had taken him out of the rut that he had been in so long. It had liberated him from the bonds of unprofitable habits, and, relaxed as never before from all earthly ties, he rejoiced in a heavenly sense of spiritual independence. It was an exquisite pleasure to him to know that there was no one in the world who was essential to his peace of mind. He had reached, though by a very different path, the immunity from the concerns of this world which is the aim of the ascetic.[13]

Despite the surface story of passion, disillusionment and murder, *The Narrow Corner* is very much a philosophical novel. Like Philip Carey before him, and Larry Darrell after, Dr Saunders is in search of meaning, of a suitable pattern. This search involves a careful examination of Buddhism, and his conclusion—that the world is only an illusion—is Buddhist.

As Maugham's last novel of magnitude, *The Razor's Edge* provides the most complete example of the author's ability to rework material from earlier writing. Despite the contemporaneity of the theme, *The Razor's Edge* incorporates a number of the characters and situations which had interested Maugham for many years. Garson Kanin tells this revealing anecdote:

At that party in the Plaza in 1949, a silly fat woman we all know pressed close to him, spilled some of her Bloody Mary on to his lapel, and blew smoke into his face as she gushed, "Do you know what my favorite is? The one about Isherwood. Christopher Isherwood? What's it called? Wait a second. Don't tell me. *Razor* something. *A Razor Edge*! What a book. How long did it take you to write it?"

W.S.M., unperturbed, replies, "Sixty years."[14]

In the same way that the basic situation in *Mrs Craddock* reappears in *The Painted Veil* and *Theatre*, one aspect of *The Razor's Edge* can be traced back to *The Unknown* (1920) and its earlier version, *The Hero* (1901). The action in each of these three works is initiated by the similar device of the soldier returning from shattering war experiences unable to readjust to his former way of life.

When Maugham rewrote *The Hero* as a play, *The Unknown*, in 1920, the treatment of alienation was tailored to a different age. John Wharton returns from action in the First World War, and the author is explicit about the experience which transforms his character. Explaining the reason for his loss of Christian faith, John describes how his best friend, Robbie Harrison, a young man full of life, kindness and goodness, was killed. This leads to a psychological trauma in the young man:

And I suppose Robbie's death was the last straw. It seemed so unjust. I don't know that it was grief so much that I felt as indignation. I was revolted by all the horror and pain and suffering.[15]

This use of the war experience as a catalyst for character development is continued in *The Razor's Edge*, and although Maugham chose to set his story at the end of the First World War, it was easy in 1944 to see Larry's problems in terms of the Second World War. Much of the novel's popularity resulted from its presentation of a widespread and common war experience. Larry Darrell, an average young American, returns to Chicago a deeply altered and troubled person. The cause of this change, an echo of that in *The Unknown*, is the death of a close friend, a pilot who has saved Larry's life, and his death in this manner instils in the young man's conscience the burden of being worthy of his sacrifice. It is interesting that, while the experiences in *The Hero* and *The Unknown* lead the central figures to disillusionment and loss of faith, Larry's emotional upheaval leads to a quest for faith.

The Razor's Edge assimilated characters and setting from the short story, 'The Fall of Edward Barnard', written in 1921. The background for this story is Chicago, and there are prototypes of characters who appear in the novel. Edward Barnard, the young man who rejects a business career, social life, and marriage to a beautiful woman, is an early sketch of Larry. The compactness of the story prevents an extensive development of his character, but his denial of what the others consider to be the important values in life parallels Larry's. The young woman, although not nearly as well-developed as her counterpart in *The Razor's Edge*, is essentially the same character, and it is significant that both are named 'Isabel'. Bateman Hunter, the conventional, socially integrated young man who cannot understand Edward's 'fall', is a version of Gray Maturin.

There are, nevertheless, important differences between 'The Fall of Edward Barnard' and *The Razor's Edge* and, as might be expected, these reflect the differences in the times in which they were written. The atmosphere of the 'twenties was remote from the tensions of the Second World War, and the actions of the central figure in each story are in keeping with the spirit of the times. Alec Waugh explains:

For whereas Edward Barnard made an escapist's choice, living on in Tahiti, idly, with a pretty Polynesian, the hero of *The Razor's Edge* refused the conventional pattern out of a discovery in himself of a sense of purpose, a working towards the life of a mystic and ascetic. It was a theme appropriate to the hour. Escapism is sympathetic to a decade of disenchanted lassitude, but it is not sympathetic to an hour of strain and action.[16]

Maugham's interest in escape as a path to personal freedom is expressed in various ways. In addition to 'The Human Element' and *The Breadwinner* discussed earlier, there are numerous works which develop this theme. In 'Mayhew', a short story written in 1923, he traces the life of a lawyer from Detroit who abandons a lucrative practice to live in Capri studying Roman history. Mayhew is interesting because he has managed to escape the pattern which the circumstances of his birth and environment should have imposed upon him, and so Maugham writes: 'I am fascinated by the men, few enough in all conscience, who take life in their own hands and seem to mould it to their own liking.'

Similarly, in 'The Lotus Eater' (1935), which tells of a London bank manager who turns his back on the conventional life to enjoy freedom and contentment in Capri, the central figure attracts the author because he has thrown off the determined course of his life:

Most people, the vast majority in fact, lead the lives that circumstances have thrust upon them, and though some repine, looking upon themselves as round pegs in square holes, and think that if things had been different they might have made a much better showing, the greater part accept their lot, if not with serenity, at all events with resignation. They are like tramcars travelling for ever on the self-same rails. They go backwards and forwards, backwards and forwards, inevitably, till they can go no longer and then are sold as scrap-iron. It is not often that you find a man who has boldly taken the course of his life into his own hands. When you do, it is worth while having a good look at him.[17]

The early work which has the closest affinities with *The Razor's Edge* is an unproduced and unpublished play, 'The Road Uphill'.[18] Maugham wrote it about 1924, and when no one showed any interest he destroyed all the copies he could find. Just as 'The Artistic Temperament of Stephen Carey' reappeared years later as *Of Human Bondage*, this material was allowed to lie dormant, to come to fruition years later in a much more artistic form.

'The Road Uphill' opens in Chicago in 1919, at the home of Mrs Cornelius Sheridan. Her two sons, Joe and Ford, have returned from the war, both unsettled by the experience. Ford has taken to writing a play, and Joe has done nothing. Mrs Sheridan's brother, Broderick Madden, visiting from Paris, is a dilettante who lives for his Louis XV apartment, clothes, and dogs. Both boys have girlfriends, Joe being engaged to Ruth Latimer. To contrast the unsettled nature of the brothers, Maugham introduces Howard Green, a business success and prospective multi-millionaire.

Early in the play, Ford abandons playwriting to go into the bond business, but Joe cannot adjust. He decides to go to Paris for two years to learn to paint. He wants Ruth to marry him but, since she cannot leave an invalid mother, she promises to wait. In Act II, when the scene is two years later and in Paris, Joe announces that, since an expert has told him that he will never be anything more than a gifted amateur, he has abandoned painting. Ruth then attempts to make him see that he must settle down and do 'a man's work'. The young man nevertheless maintains that he must continue his search for 'the unknown lands of the soul', so Ruth returns his engagement ring and decides to marry Howard Green.

In Act III, three years later, Joe returns to the United States, having now written a book. Ruth and Howard have married and have a child, but it soon becomes clear that Ruth still loves Joe. It is revealed that Howard has been hit by financial ruin and, having been speculating with other people's money, he can be imprisoned. Before anyone realises what he is doing, he takes off in his private plane, and the play ends with his suicide.

It should be obvious, even from this skeletal summary, that this is indeed an early version of *The Razor's Edge*. The setting—from Chicago to Paris—is the same, and most of the characters have counterparts. Mrs Sheridan is Mrs Bradley, Broderick Madden is an undeveloped Elliott Templeton, Howard Green is Gray Maturin, and Joe Sheridan resembles Larry. Even a minor comic figure such as Gregory Brabazon in *The Razor's Edge* finds a parallel in Charles Stuart Willoughby, the interior decorator in 'The Road Uphill'. For

Isabel Bradley, however, it seems that Maugham went back to Isabel Longstaffe in 'The Fall of Edward Barnard'.

Between 'The Road Uphill' and *The Razor's Edge* lies 'The Alien Corn', a short story which is directly connected to this unpublished play. This story expands and explores the idea of the young man who leaves for Europe for two years to become an artist and who learns that he can never be anything more than a talented amateur. The young man, George Bland, finds the pretentious life of a wealthy Jewish family intolerable, and he goes to Germany to become a pianist. When he returns after two years and is told by a famous pianist that he will never be a great artist, he cannot face the future and he kills himself. As in *The Razor's Edge*, the hero is surrounded by a social environment which attempts to impose its demands on him. Unlike Larry, however, George Bland does not have the regenerative spark which will enable him to find a suitable pattern for realising himself.

In many respects, Ferdy Rabenstein of 'The Alien Corn' is the counterpart to Elliott Templeton in *The Razor's Edge*. Like Templeton, he is a foreigner who as a young man made a quick rise in English society. He, too, is a snob, but he has a number of useful and admirable qualities. Like Templeton, Rabenstein serves as a foil for the aspirations of the central figure.

Elliott Templeton is one of Maugham's most delightful creations and has, in the years since the novel's appearance, become the most memorable figure in the story. There has been speculation about the original for Templeton, and it has been argued that, in the character of the man who spurns America for the social milieu of Europe, Maugham was suggesting Henry James. Considering his opinions of James as a man and as a writer, it would not be surprising to find him using this opportunity to draw a caricature. The truth, however, lies elsewhere.

The man who was undoubtedly the basis for most of Elliott Templeton was Sir Henry ('Chips') Channon (1897–1958). Channon, an American, spent most of his life in England, became a naturalised Englishman, and for three decades was a prominent social figure. It should be noted, however, that, as with all of Maugham's characters, Channon's career and personality only suggested many aspects of Templeton; Maugham's character has a specific fictional purpose and is not intended to be a direct portrait of Channon.

A number of parallels are immediately obvious between the lives of Channon and Templeton. Channon was born in Chicago and went to Europe as a young man; Templeton is a Virginian (the American scenes, however, are set in Chicago) who becomes a social success in Paris and London. 'Chips' lived in Paris before the First World War, and returned to that city with the American Red Cross in 1917; Templeton joins the ambulance corps in the war, and later takes a position with the Red Cross in Paris. Channon became fascinated by the Abbé Mugnier (1853–1944), a favourite of the aristocracy ('Chips' noted that 'there is always a queue of princesses waiting to see him'[19]), and he quickly became converted from Protestantism to Roman Catholicism. Templeton, writes Maugham, meets an abbé who specialises in ministering to the rich and aristocratic, and he is converted from being Episcopalian to Roman Catholic. That Maugham is here describing the Abbé Mugnier becomes obvious when one notes the many similarities between his description of the abbé in *The Razor's Edge* and the picture he gives of Abbé Mugnier in *Points of View*.

After the war Channon spent four years at Oxford, during which time he had a meteoric rise in English society. He soon included among his friends Lord and Lady Curzon, Lady Elizabeth Bowes-Lyon (the future Duchess of York, now Queen Mother), the Prince of Wales (later the Duke of Windsor), and the future Duchess of Kent. Supported by a generous settlement from his father and a large inheritance from his grandfather, Channon lived luxuriously in London. Elliott Templeton rises equally quickly in European circles and becomes the companion of royalty and aristocracy. Although Maugham explains his wealth as being the result of his dabbling in art, Templeton lives comfortably without really working.

Although there are necessarily many discrepancies between the careers of 'Chips' Channon and Elliott Templeton, their characters are remarkably alike. 'Chips', enchanted by the gentility and romance of European society, intensely disliked the United States and the American way of life. Templeton never disguises his disdain for the Chicago surroundings of his sister's home, and his attitude to his American relatives is always patronising. Channon's diaries reveal that he was an inveterate (and, to his credit, self-confessed) snob, concerned, like Templeton, with the idea of gentility and blood lines. His candid assessment of himself could have been written by Elliott Templeton:

Sometimes I think I have an unusual character – able but trivial; I have flair, intuition, great good taste but only second rate ambition: I am far too susceptible to flattery; I hate and am uninterested in all the things most men like such as sport, business, statistics, debates, speeches, war and the weather; but I am rivetted by lust, furniture, glamour and society and jewels. I am an excellent organiser and have a will of iron; I can only be appealed to through my vanity.[20]

When *The Razor's Edge* was published, Channon recognised himself in Templeton, and his diary records a confrontation with the author in New York in 1944:

I saw much of Somerset Maugham, who never before was a friend. He has put me into a book, "The Razor's Edge" and when I dined with him, I asked him why he had done it, and he explained, with some embarrassment, that he had split me into three characters, and then written a book about all three. So I am Elliott Templeton, Larry, himself the hero of the book, and another: however I am flattered, and the book is a masterpiece.[21]

This is a remarkable entry, particularly for what it tells that Channon does not realise. It is easy to see that Maugham, caught unexpectedly, extricated himself with the preposterous explanation that Channon provided the raw material for all three characters. Had he not been guilty of using him for Templeton, it would have been much easier to simply deny everything. As it is, this fabrication, as ironic in its way as Maugham's letter to Walpole in similar circumstances, seems ample proof that Channon was right. It must have caused Maugham a great deal of amusement to witness Channon visualising himself as the unworldly, unmaterialistic Larry.

The portrait of Elliott Templeton, however, is not a vicious one; the author takes great pains to explain that, in addition to his foibles, he is kind, generous and cultivated. From contemporary accounts, 'Chips' Channon shared these good qualities. What Maugham probably saw in him was a man who superbly epitomised everything that established European society represents. Needing a character to contrast the spiritual quest of Larry and the American ambition of Gray Maturin, Maugham found a perfect model in the man who so completely embraced English social institutions.

When Maugham converted the story of 'The Road Uphill' to *The Razor's Edge* in 1942, the most significant addition that he made was the extensive material about Indian mysticism and Vedanta. The presence of this element absolutely reflects the spirit of the times, and reviewers were quick to note the contemporary appeal of the theme. Edward Weeks wrote in *The Atlantic Monthly* that 'even at this distance, Mr Maugham is right in his perception of a new quest for faith that is abroad',[22] and Orville Prescott noted that 'it has the religious theme so popular at present'.[23]

The wave of interest in religious subjects developed as a natural reaction to the Second World War. As a result of the cumulative effect of anguish, suffering and death, people became increasingly interested in spiritual matters, both as an escape and as a means of hope. Religious novels—*The Keys of the Kingdom, The Song of Bernadette*, and *The Robe*—were best-selling books in America in 1941, 1942, and 1943. In 1944, religious themes dominated the motion picture industry in such films as 'The Song of Bernadette', 'The Robe', 'The Miracle', 'The Keys of the Kingdom', 'The Church of the Good Thief', 'The Hoodlum Priest', 'Till We Meet Again', 'Between Two Worlds', 'The Rosary', 'The Sign of the Cross' and 'Quo Vadis'.

There is, nevertheless, little direct connection between this kind of religious story and Maugham's novel, except that both reflect the interest of the public in matters of the soul. The manner of Larry's quest is much more closely allied to a relatively new literary development—the treatment of Indian religion. Reviewing *The Razor's Edge*, Cyril Connolly immediately noted the association:

The novel is a considerable addition to the literature of non-attachment, and ranks with Huxley's *Grey Eminence* and Heard's *Man the Master* as powerful propaganda for the new faith or, rather, new version of an old faith, which is called by various names – neo-Brahmanism, or the Vedanta of the West – and which has made its home in somewhat macabre proximity to Hollywood.[24]

The movement to which Connolly refers was a development of the late 'thirties and early 'forties, a surprisingly recent assimilation of an old religion. Indeed, the history of the influence of Indian philosophy and religion on English literature is puzzling because of the delayed nature of its impact. The nineteenth century saw a great flood of translations of Indian classics and studies of Indian thought, and the bibliography of translations of Indian books and analyses of Indian thought in the twentieth century is so lengthy that it would take a separate study to outline it properly.

Despite this considerable influx of books dealing with Indian thought, however, a real movement to Vedanta in English literature is a relatively recent development. Earlier philosophers such as Schlegel, Hegel and Emerson were interested in Hinduism, but it did not become explicit to any degree in their writing. W. B. Yeats, having read *Esoteric Buddhism* (1883), a study by Madame Blavatsky's apostle, A. P. Sinnett, became interested in Oriental philosophy and occultism. In his final years he renewed his interest in Hinduism and, after the development of his friendship with the yogi Shri Purohit, in 1931, he celebrated it with poems in *The King of the Great Clock Tower* (1934). Subsequently, he wrote an essay on the 'Mandookya Upanishad' for the *Criterion*, and with Purohit translated *The Ten Principal Upanishads* (1937).

The real assimilation of Vedanta into English literature, however, occurred in the writings of Gerald Heard, Aldous Huxley and Christopher Isherwood. Heard, the fountainhead of this movement, wrote a series of studies of religion and the modern world, and his ideas are strongly flavoured with Indian philosophy. In 1931 his *The Social Substance of Religion* stated that the chaos of the world could only be cured by religion. *The Third Morality* (1937) advocated a vegetable diet and yoga training of the mind and body. *Pain, Sex and Time* (1939) suggested the formation of small independent groups of people who could explore the range of psychological experience free from the influence of social institutions. Heard continued to formulate his ideas in *The Creed of Christ* (1941), *Training for the Life of the Spirit* (1941), *Man the Master* (1942), *A Decalogue in the Desert* (1942), and *The Code of Christ* (1943).

The most important figure in this movement, however, is Aldous Huxley. Having met Heard some time in 1930, he soon became a disciple. *Eyeless in Gaza* (1936), an autobiographical novel, reveals the influence of Heard through the character of James Miller, a proponent of peace and meditation. He claims that there is a connection between posture and personality, and advocates a special diet—no butcher's meat, no milk, one heavy meal a day—for a proper spiritual life. *Eyeless in Gaza* ends with the Buddhist tenet that there is a unity in all things in the universe.

Ends and Means (1937), a companion piece to Heard's *The Third Morality*, presents a formula for reorganising the structure of society. It discusses the use of yoga and mysticism, and it argues the need for men of charity, courage, intelligence, generosity and disinterestedness. Above all, it calls for the detachment of the Eastern philosophies:

The ideal man is the non-attached man. Non-attached to his bodily sensations and lusts. Non-attached to his craving for power and possessions. Non-attached to the objects of these various desires. Non-attached to his anger and hatred; non-attached to his exclusive loves. Non-attached to wealth, fame, social position. Non-attached even to science, art, speculation, philanthropy. Yes, non-attached even to these.[25]

In 1937 Huxley left England and joined Heard in California. There Huxley produced a fictional counterpart to *Pain, Sex and Time* in *After Many a Summer* (1939). This novel repeated Heard's idea of independent communities, and he is represented in the character of William Propter, a mystic presiding over a colony of meditators. Propter advocates withdrawal from large-scale, organised society into smaller groups where the individual can find 'liberation from time. . . .

Liberation from craving and revulsions. Liberation from personality.'[26]

There is a large element of Buddhism in *Grey Eminence* (1941), Huxley's study of the relationship between religious and political involvement. At one point, he expresses the opinion that, had the teachings of Buddha made a greater impression on Catholicism, that religious establishment would have been less preoccupied with superstitious rites, torture and death. Later, when he argues that lasting personality change can only come through mysticism, he looks for salvation in the 'theocentric saint':

Society can never be greatly improved until such time as most of its members choose to become theocentric saints. Meanwhile, the few theocentric saints who exist at any given moment are able in some slight measure to qualify and mitigate the poisons which society generates within itself by its political and economic activities. In the gospel phrase, theocentric saints are the salt which preserves the social world from breaking down into irremediable decay.[27]

This passage is of particular interest because of its remarkable similarity to that in *The Razor's Edge* where Larry explains what he hopes to achieve in his life:

"When a man becomes pure and perfect the influence of his character spreads so that they who seek the truth are naturally drawn to him. It may be that if I lead the life I've planned for myself it may affect others; the effect may be no greater than the ripple caused by a stone thrown in a pond, but one ripple causes another and that one a third; it's just possible that a few people will see that my way of life offers happiness and peace, and that they in their turn will teach what they have learnt to others."[28]

Some time around 1940 Huxley became influenced by Swami Prabhavananda of the Ramakrishna Mission, located, ironically, in Hollywood. He began writing for *Vedanta and the West*, a periodical begun in 1938 by Swami Prabhavananda and Swami Ashokananda of San Francisco. In 1942 Huxley wrote a foreword to Swami Nikhilananda's *Gospel of Sri Ramakrishna*, and in 1944 he contributed an introduction to a new translation by Swami Prabhavananda and Christopher Isherwood of the *Bhagavad-Gita*. Very quickly his association with what were called the 'Californian gurus' became widely known, drawing the scorn of Edmund Wilson:

He has succumbed to one of the impostures with which the Golden State deludes her victims: the Burbankized West Coast religion; and Mr. Huxley and his ally, Mr. Gerald Heard, will be lucky if they do not wake up some morning to find themselves transformed into Yogis and installed in one of those Wizard-of-Oz temples that puff out their bubble-like domes among the snack bars and the lion ranches.[29]

Heard and Huxley, nevertheless, were joined in 1939 by Christopher Isherwood, who was to become one of the leading Western exponents of Vedanta. Having gone to California as an atheist, he found himself unable to disbelieve the belief of Swami Prabhavananda in God, and he became converted. He became an editor of *Vedanta and the West*, and he collaborated with the swami on a translation of the *Bhagavad-Gita* (1944), *Shankara's Crest-Jewel of Discrimination* (1947), and *How to Know God: The Yogi Aphorisms of Patanjali* (1953). In addition, Isherwood edited *Vedanta for Modern Man* (1951), and wrote *Ramakrishna and his Disciples* (1965). He is at present a member of the Vedanta Society of Southern California in Hollywood.

At one time it was conjectured that in Larry Darrell Maugham was portraying Isherwood. The earlier counterparts of the young man in 'The Road Uphill' and as Edward Barnard make this unlikely. Nevertheless, it is possible that Isherwood, whom the author knew at the time of the writing of *The Razor's Edge*, provided some aspects of Larry's character, particularly his faith in his guru.

It is with this movement that *The Razor's Edge* has its closest associations. One can only guess at the degree to which these writers exerted a direct influence, but Maugham's friendship with them is known. He lived in a rented house in Beverley Hills in the early 1940s, and in a letter to Christopher Hassall in July 1941 Edward Marsh describes Maugham in California:

I've heard at last from Willie Maugham at Los Angeles. . . . He says he wants next winter to sit down to a long and serious novel, but he is completely tied up in propaganda, which he finds duller and duller and is sick to death of. Aldous and Gerald Heard are godsends to him. Christopher Isherwood has retired from the world and is living in a Quaker camp! "G. Heard, terribly emaciated, with a long beard and a very red nose, is spreading the Word with diligence, striking success, and a certain incoherence."[30]

It is difficult to imagine that Maugham could find relief from the boredom of his task with Huxley, Heard and Isherwood without being influenced to some degree. It is likely that, although he did not necessarily share the beliefs of this group, Maugham was made aware of the popularity and appeal of their exploration into Indian mysticism. Larry Darrell's quest for spiritual liberation resembles their aims too closely to be mere coincidence.

When *The Razor's Edge* is compared to *The Narrow Corner*, it is easy to see that there is a different treatment of Indian religion in the later novel. The earlier work concentrates on the philosophy of Buddhism—on meditation, meaning and existence. These same elements are examined in *The Razor's Edge*, but there is a new and considerable emphasis on Yoga. Here, the treatment is more explicit and there is more dogma, and this new approach may very well have come from Maugham's association with Huxley, Heard and Isherwood.

Very likely Maugham's impressions of the Californian Vedantists provided him with a theme around which to use Indian material he already possessed. He had travelled to India in 1938, where he had made many observations, a large number of which are recorded in *A Writer's Notebook*. Discovering much that excited his imagination, Maugham intended to return to India in the winter of 1939–40 to finish gathering material for a novel. International developments, however, prevented this journey, and thus the Indian section of *The Razor's Edge* is not as extensive as he had originally planned. He had to be content with the notes he already had, and he was careful to take them with him when he fled from France in 1940.

The Indian section of *A Writer's Notebook* offers considerable evidence that these observations provided much of the background for *The Razor's Edge*. His description of a 'Major C.', who lives in an 'ashrama' and wishes to remain there until he achieves enlightenment or until his yogi dies, becomes Larry's attitude. The similarity of the following passages from the notebook and the novel is even more striking:

A Yogi wanted to cross a river and had not the penny to pay the ferryman, so he walked across the river on his feet. Another Yogi hearing of this said the miracle was only worth the penny it would have cost to cross by ferry.[31]

"I remember one of them telling me of a Yogi who came to the bank of a river; he hadn't the money to pay the ferryman to take him across and the ferryman refused to take him for nothing, so he stepped on the water and walked upon its surface to the other side. The Yogi who told me shrugged his shoulders rather scornfully. 'A miracle like that', he said, 'is worth no more than the penny it would have cost to go on the ferry-boat.' "[32]

In *A Writer's Notebook*, Maugham describes 'The Yogi', the holy man who in 'The Saint' (*Points of View*) he identifies as the Maharshi Venkataraman. He was, according to the author, fond of saying: 'Silence also is conversation.' This experience with the yogi provided the inspiration for Larry's guru, Shri Ganesha. Many of the descriptive passages are similar, and Larry reports that 'Shri Ganesha used to say that silence also is conversation.'

In addition to the Indian material which was the fruit of his personal experiences, Maugham made considerable use of academic studies. It has been said that his research for *The Razor's Edge* amounted to at least forty volumes. Certainly, that portion of Maugham's library which he gave to King's School, Canterbury, contains a number of books about Indian or Chinese religion, some of which are heavily annotated. These annotations cannot be dated with any certainty, and it is very likely that some are the result of Maugham's research for his essay 'The Saint' in 1958. Nevertheless, it can also be assumed that a number of these books, known to be in the author's possession before the writing of *The Razor's Edge*, gave him some of the information for the discussions of theology and mysticism in the novel. They show that, although the discussion of Vedanta is simplified to suit the character of Larry, the author approached the subject with a great deal of consideration of all it entails.

Although *The Razor's Edge* is constructed around a new framework appropriate to the spirit of the middle of the twentieth century, it is essentially yet another manifestation of a lifelong preoccupation with freedom. In a great many ways, it is *Of Human Bondage* as it would be written in the 'forties, and Larry is the Philip of a new generation. Philip's problems are those of the young at the turn of the century and his search for a viable independence follows the pattern of the times; Larry is motivated by the same desire for liberating truth, and his quest takes the form, not particularly of his time, but characteristic of the age in which the novel was written. *The Razor's Edge* is thus further evidence of Maugham's ability to recognise the changing forms of this timeless theme.

This novel is set against an American background (even the Paris scenes revolve around an American colony), and the central figures are American. Maugham is careful to emphasise at the beginning that the ethos which he treats is particularly American, although it is likely to become more widespread as the influence of the United States increases. The characters, products of their environment, are manifestations of this new social philosophy. To the hypothetical question of why he could not have made his characters English he replies at the beginning of the novel: 'The answer is simple: I couldn't. They would not then have been the people they are.' The United States has become the most wealthy and powerful nation, and its material growth is prodigious, therefore Maugham turns to examine new pressures and restrictions on the individual. The New World offers unlimited scope for ambition, energy and dedication, but the goals of a developing country are necessarily materialistic. Accordingly the social climate is one which demands the participation of its members in the accumulation of capital in all its forms, and this becomes a form of social imposition. It is Larry's rejection of a life dedicated to the attaining of these material ends which struck a responsive nerve in young American readers in the post-war years.

To provide a milieu in which Larry's spiritual quest will stand out vividly, Maugham has created a number of characters who epitomise the values he has rejected and who are foils which illuminate his achievement. The best of these creations is Elliott Templeton, a delightful portrait of the man of the world. Having the intense enthusiasm of a convert, Elliott represents all the restrictions of the European social structure. Existing totally in relation to all the more superficial aspects of gentility, he spends his entire life in pursuit of clothes, jewels, appearances, aristocracy and 'the season'; these are his values, his realities. The important point about his world, however, is that it is the most demanding of all in its conventions and codes of conduct, yet it is quick to forget those who fall. Having been *'serviable'* for most of his life, Elliott finds at the end that he is inescapably bound by its values. In some of Maugham's most superbly bitter-comic writing, he describes the dying snob's anguish at the thought of not being invited to one of the season's big parties. The pathos of his distress about such a superficial matter is underlined by his simultaneous interest in having the proper rites of the Church. His death moves the narrator, both for the loss of a friend and for the waste of a life:

An old, kind friend. It made me sad to think how silly, useless and trivial his life had been. It mattered very little now that he had gone to so many parties and had hobnobbed with all those princes, dukes and counts. They had forgotten him already.[33]

American commercial enterprise and ambition is quite obviously represented by Gray Maturin, and the contrast with Larry is clear and intentional. He is good-natured and likeable, but narrowly motivated toward concrete, easily recognisable goals. His hopes are for the conventional dream of property, family and wealth. His name—'Gray'— suits his character, and Larry stands out brilliantly beside him. It should be noted, however, that Maugham is careful, even with such a relatively minor figure, to avoid making him one-dimensional. Gray and his father, for all their competitive business philosophy, do attempt to serve their investors with honour.

Maugham provides temptations for his hero-saint in the form of three women, and characteristically they are the greatest threat to his detachment. His fiancée, Isabel Bradley, is a marvellous character, a well-drawn picture of American womanhood seen through the eyes of a European. As a young girl she is charming, vivacious and sensitive.

Conditioned by the mores of American middle-class life, however, she can be seen developing into a beautiful, but ruthless, woman.

For Larry, Isabel's most dangerous characteristic is her desperate need to possess and dominate. In this regard, there is an interesting and pertinent entry in *A Writer's Notebook* in 1941: 'In America when a man marries his wife engulfs him. She demands his undivided attention and she makes his home his prison.' This quality, it will be recalled, has always been one which Maugham has given to his astringent female portraits, beginning with Mary Clibborn in *The Hero*. With Isabel the possessiveness becomes more obvious as Larry becomes more elusive. Before his war experiences, it seems that he was content to be part of the group, and Isabel later boasts that 'I could always do anything I wanted with him. I could turn him round my little finger.' When Larry goes to Paris to 'loaf' for two years, Isabel is content that she is still in control of the situation and she fully expects ultimately to have her way. When Larry refuses to return to a conventional life in the United States, however, she marries Gray Maturin, whose attractions are his money, position, sexuality and complete dependence on her. Discussing her marriage with the narrator, she invests it with poetry and romance, but Maugham is quick to dispel this illusion:

> "Has it ever struck you that you're a very possessive woman? You've told me that Gray has a deep strain of poetic feeling and you've told me that he's an ardent lover; and I can well believe that both mean a lot to you; but you haven't told me what means much more to you than both of them put together – your feeling that you hold him in the hollow of that beautiful but not so small hand of yours. Larry would always have escaped you. D'you remember that Ode of Keats's? 'Bold Lover, never, never canst thou kiss, though winning near the goal'?"[34]

Isabel, however, never abandons her attempts to trap Larry, and she becomes ruthless in her actions. His habit of disappearing for months to reappear when he wants and his practice of keeping his address secret are a constant vexation. More than this, the thoughts of the women Larry may have had and of those who might claim him inflame her jealousy. This latter obsession leads to Isabel's most insidious act—the destruction of Sophie MacDonald.

In one respect, Sophie MacDonald is a foil for Larry. She is essentially a kindred spirit with him, but she represents the type of spiritual sensitivity which cannot stand up to the realities of life. As an adolescent, she displayed a quiet spiritual beauty, a love of poetry, and a desire to see human suffering eliminated. She had, says Larry, a delicate ear, a sense of rhythm and a feeling for the forms of natural life around her.

I

Sophie's sensitive nature, however, is not durable enough to survive the shocks of the world. Whereas Larry's spiritual search leads him to a detached goodness, she becomes too closely bound up in her dreams, her husband and her baby. When one of those inexplicable and undeserved accidents occurs, and they are killed, the emotional maelstrom destroys her and she degenerates to drunken promiscuity. Few scenes in *The Razor's Edge* are more poignant than Maugham's final picture of Sophie, in Toulon, when he gives her a copy of his latest novel, with the inscription: 'Mignonne, allons voir si la rose. . . .'

As well as reflecting Larry's spiritual sensitivity, Sophie poses the most powerful threat to his detachment. When he sees her in the Paris nightclub and remembers the girl she once was, he falls prey to one of man's greatest desires—that of sacrifice. Like Michael Fane's chivalric mission to save Lily Haden in Compton Mackenzie's *Sinister Street*, Larry's intention is to rehabilitate the fallen woman, and much to Isabel's chagrin he decides to marry Sophie. Larry, the prospective saint, thus succumbs to the most subtly alluring of temptations. Maugham explains:

"I only wanted to suggest to you that self-sacrifice is a passion so overwhelming that beside it even lust and hunger are trifling. It whirls its victim to destruction in the highest affirmation of his personality. The object doesn't matter; it may be worth while or it may be worthless. No wine is so intoxicating, no love so shattering, no vice so compelling. When he sacrifices himself man for a moment is greater than God, for how can God, infinite and omnipotent, sacrifice himself? At best he can only sacrifice his only begotten son."[35]

Furthermore, the author suggests, the young man will fail to save Sophie's soul and, with his acute sensibility, he will torture himself. The ruthlessness that even saints must have is beyond him.

It is perhaps a serious weakness of *The Razor's Edge* that Maugham avoids resolving the issue of Larry's sacrifice to Sophie by the device of letting Isabel prove to Sophie that she cannot live up to his expectations. One might argue that Isabel only precipitates the inevitable, but more significance could have been invested in the hero's ultimate non-attachment had Maugham shown him faced with the unalterable reality of Sophie's spiritual condition. As it is, Larry's reaction to Sophie's surrender is given very little illumination.

The third woman, Suzanne Rouvier, is a female character of a type familiar to readers of Maugham. Like Sally Athelny and Rosie Driffield, she is warm, generous and maternal, and her promiscuity is amoral rather than immoral. Charming, sensible and kind, her purpose is to provide a contrast to the insatiable selfishness of Isabel. She is also, however, the vehicle by which Larry is confronted with the temptations of the flesh. In this regard, he differs from other Maugham heroes such as Philip Carey and Charles Strickland in that he becomes totally detached in sexual matters. Suzanne describes her weeks of living with Larry and how he became her lover—'very sweet, affectionate and even tender, virile without being passionate'. The young man, however, remains as elusive for Suzanne as he is for Isabel: 'You might as well fall in love with a reflection in the water or a ray of sunshine or a cloud in the sky.' Later, Larry explains the nature of sexual gratification for him:

"I am in the fortunate position that sexual indulgence with me has been a pleasure rather than a need. I know by personal experience that in nothing are the wise men of India more dead right than in their contention that chastity intensely enhances the power of the spirit."[36]

Despite the temptations of the ways of life represented by Elliott, Isabel, Sophie and Suzanne, Larry finds his own truth. It comes, after a search which takes him from Paris to Germany, from coal mines to monasteries, through his experiences in India. His years there profoundly influence his character, and there he finds the spiritual serenity for which he has been searching. It is interesting that Maugham chooses to make India the source of Larry's revelation, and what he finds to be the core of Indian religious belief is significant. Characteristically, the aspect of Vedanta which attracts Larry, and which is emphasised by the author, is spiritual liberation. (In this regard, the annotations in the studies of Indian religion in the Maugham Library at King's School are heavily concerned with those tenets which deal with the liberation of the spirit.)

Maugham presents his interpretation of Indian religious belief very skilfully in the key chapter late in the novel, in the form of a dialogue between the narrator and Larry. In effect, this is a discussion of two interpretations of freedom. For the first time in his career Maugham uses a narrator who is entirely a portrait of himself, and accordingly he uses his own name. Thus, we are presented with two characters who have sought truth and liberty, one being the man who recorded his formative years in the story of Philip Carey and his mature age as Dr Saunders, and the other being the youthful bohemian finding his answers in a different place in a different time. Chapter VI therefore becomes an interesting exercise in critical self-examination, and an honest attempt to see the new movement without necessarily embracing it.

In Chapter VI Larry sets out to explain what Vedanta means to him and what he expects to achieve through it. If his discussion seems over-simplified, it should be remembered that Maugham never uses fiction for didactic purposes, and his concern here is to give his character a rhetoric appropriate to him. There is considerable description of holy men and temples, and then Larry turns to the actual belief, beginning with the transmigration of souls. At this point the narrator confronts him with one of the author's long-held opinions—that the individual is in bondage to the physical entity of his body. Can the soul develop independently of the physiology of the body?

"But you see, I'm not only my spirit but my body, and who can decide how much I, my individual self, am conditioned by the accident of my body? Would Byron have been Byron but for his club foot, or Dostoyevski Dostoyevski without his epilepsy?"[37]

Larry's answer is that the body's imperfections are the punishment for the imperfections of the soul in previous lives. According to his understanding, transmigration means the experiencing of a series of lives until the soul is purified enough to achieve, as he says, 'liberation from the bondage of rebirth'. It then returns to the infinitude, the Absolute, what the Indians call the Brahman: 'It is truth and freedom.' It is 'that state when you have at last burst the bonds of ignorance, and know with a certainty there is no disputing that you and the Absolute are one'. Similarly, the language which Maugham gives Larry to describe the teachings of Shri Ganesha betrays the author's lifelong concern:

"He sought to wean them from the slavery of selfhood, passion and sense and told them that they could acquire liberation by tranquility, restraint, renunciation, resignation, by steadfastness of mind and by an ardent desire for freedom. . . . He taught that we are all greater than we know and that wisdom is the means to freedom."[38]

"When I asked how, if the world was a manifestation of the nature of a perfect being, it should be so hateful that the only reasonable aim man can set before him is to liberate himself from its bondage, Shri Ganesha answered that the satisfactions of the world are transitory and that only the Infinite gives enduring happiness."[39]

The attraction, then, of Vedanta is its orientation toward the liberation of the spirit. Larry has previously experienced a feeling of sublime freedom when flying during the war, but the practices of Yoga have taken him far beyond this to the reaches of meditation. This is, Maugham is saying, the new means of escape. The time when one could preserve one's independence through artistic isolation or distant travel is past; the world no longer allows solitude and anonymity. The new movement is spiritual; while physically bound to the common existence, one can escape inwards into the depths of self. Thus Larry is capable of submerging himself into the life of New York, the epitome of American materialism and industry, without surrendering his essential liberty. He is, beneath the exterior, the typical Maugham hero, in the company of James Parsons, Philip Carey, Charles Strickland, John Wharton, Edward Barnard and George Bland, but his revolt is that of a new era. David Paul explains:

Larry, the happy and beautiful hero of the novel, is the new Parsifal. He is pure ideal, and does not, like the artist hero, embody the scapegoat as well. He cannot realise our dreams for us by escaping to the South Seas. The South Seas are now better known as a zone of the Pacific, and have other associations. The weight of mechanised civilization has now become so heavy and widespread that escape in place is no longer possible. He can only escape by a process of spiritual levitation or non-attachment.[40]

Through the dialogue between the narrator and Larry, Maugham illustrates the differences between the pattern he has sought and that adopted by Larry. This is best demonstrated by their discussion of the relationship of money to their conception of the best way to fulfil themselves. To the narrator's claim that 'the only thing that may make the kind of life you propose possible is financial independence', Larry replies: 'On the contrary, financial independence would make the life I propose meaningless.'

The Razor's Edge is Maugham's last major work written in the first person singular, and the character of the narrator is much the same as that developed through his previous works. He is mellower and warmer, but the same qualities of caution, restraint and guarded independence are clearly visible. It is a candid and transparent self-portrait, and in many respects a summing-up of the author's life. He frequently refers to his early career, his experiences among the bohemians in Paris, and his later literary success. In addition, a great many of his observations are those which he has expressed previously in prose or drama.

The narrator's opinion of Larry's plan to surrender his private income is therefore an expression of Maugham's lifelong concern with financial independence. To Larry's claim that the narrator attaches more importance to money than he does, Maugham replies:

"I can well believe it. . . . You see, you've always had it and I haven't. It's given me what I valued almost more than anything else in life – independence. You can't think what a comfort it's been to me to think that if I wanted to I could tell anyone in the world to go to hell."[41]

This is the argument of the author who saw the greatest advantage of his success as a dramatist in 1908 as being the freedom gained through the elimination of financial worries. It is the theory, put forward in *The Merry-Go-Round*, that poverty is a more exacting task-master than all the conventions of society. It is the root of the idea, dramatised in *Of Human Bondage*, that economic deprivation degrades the human character. It is the basis of Leslie Ardsley's hope, in *For Services Rendered*, that through Wilfred Cedar's wealth she will win 'freedom and opportunity'. It is the justification for Constance Middleton's demand, in *The Constant Wife*, for equality of independence with her husband.

It has always been a cherished belief of Maugham that a healthy bank balance ensures the escape from at least one form of bondage, and he does not abandon this opinion in *The Razor's Edge*. He is nevertheless capable of recognising that, in the new creeds of the young, independence may take a new form and be defined in a new way. To the narrator's argument, Larry counters: 'You see, money to you means freedom; to me it means bondage.' Maugham is not very clear in explaining precisely why a private income entails bondage for Larry, but, in the light of the subsequent growth of the Beat Generation in the 'fifties and its counterpart in the 'sixties, it is an accurate reflection of the beliefs of the rebellious young.

When we see Larry for the last time, he is about to leave for the United States. He has given up his income, and he leaves with the conviction that 'I've never been happier or felt more independent in my life.' Maugham is left with a deep admiration for his sincerity and goodness, and with a sympathy for, and understanding of, his belief that ultimate happiness lies in the life of the spirit. Nevertheless, the dichotomy between the author's own position and that of the new Vedanta is emphasised at the end. Maugham readily confesses his inability to go the way of the spirit:

I am of the earth, earthy; I can only admire the radiance of such a rare creature, I cannot step into his shoes and enter into his inmost heart as I sometimes think I can do with persons more nearly allied to the common run of men.[42]

There is a great temptation among critics to use Maugham's considerable interest in mysticism, the Buddhist element in *The Narrow Corner*, and the Vedanta material in *The Razor's Edge*, to prove that he was moving toward a conversion to some kind of faith. However, the writer who consistently detested the dogma of Christianity is not likely to be any more comfortable in the dogma of Hinduism, despite its more flexible nature, and Larry's belief, like that of the Californian neobrahmins, is based heavily on Yoga practices and Hindu doctrines such as the transmigration of souls.

More significantly, the Vedanta movement has at its core the assumption that truth can be apprehended, not through the intellect, but through emotional engagement. In this respect, it has affinities with romanticism, and Maugham is always the realist. Could the man whose writing is filled with wretched characters who are destroyed by their emotions, whose human bondage can only be thrown off by the restraint of a rational mind, ever embrace a philosophy centred on emotional intuition? There can be little doubt that Maugham occasionally looked longingly at Christianity, and that he found considerable appeal in Hinduism. However, in the same year that *The Razor's Edge* was published, he wrote:

For a while I was attracted to the Hindu conception of that mysterious neuter which is existence, knowledge and bliss, without beginning, without end, and I should be more inclined to believe in that than in any other God that human wishes have devised. But I think it no more than an impressive fantasy. It is impossible logically to deduce the multiplicity of the world from the ultimate cause.[43]

Despite his sympathetic understanding of Vedanta in *The Razor's Edge*, Maugham's commitment to reason was, in intention at least, absolute.

The Razor's Edge is a considerable achievement for a writer approaching seventy years of age, and it is one of his novels which will not be weeded out by time. Nevertheless, as a portrait of a modern saint it has a number of serious flaws, the most damaging being that Larry, around whom the novel turns, is the weakest of the characters. Maugham, of course, encounters the problem that has faced so many theological writers—that the sinner is a more fascinating figure than the saint—and it is inevitable that the reader's attention wanders. Thus the most interesting figure in *The Razor's Edge* is Elliott Templeton, and the response to his silly, snobbish life becomes more sympathetic than it should be. Larry, on the other hand, remains on the level of the ideal—a symbol or abstract representation of the potential of the spirit.

The common criticism of *The Razor's Edge* is essentially that which is levelled at *The Moon and Sixpence* and *Cakes and Ale*, that is, that Maugham fails to explore adequately the character of his central figure. Larry's progress from a conventional young man to a student of Vedanta is never examined in depth. We are told that he has undergone a traumatic experience during the war, but the remainder of his path unwinds too smoothly. He encounters inexplicable facts of human existence and he frequently does not know the direction his search is taking him, but he rarely seems racked by the real torture—self-doubt. Owing to the novel's construction, his experiences are only seen in retrospect, through second- or third-hand accounts. The effect is that the reader does not experience the inevitable intellectual problems which beset the spiritual pilgrim. Christopher Isherwood, who finds much to admire in Maugham's treatment, regrets this lack of illumination:

Surely the mishaps and setbacks which beset the path of spiritual progress can be recounted with some of the humor which invests one's failures in cookery or falls in learning to ski? Maugham, I believe, would agree with me here. There is nothing gloomy about Larry's career. Unfortunately, however, his creator has gone to the other extreme, and one gets the impression that becoming a saint is just no trouble at all.[44]

Naik carries the criticism further, arguing that Maugham's use of the detached observer and his reluctance to use a lyrical style to communicate spiritual states of mind fails to make the necessary impression: 'It does no good to tell the reader, "No words can tell the ecstasy of my bliss." The reader must feel this ecstasy along with the hero, which, one must confess, does not happen here.'[45]

These criticisms, both valid, explain why *The Razor's Edge* falls below excellence. Nevertheless, although it fails to reach the heights it is a very good novel of its type because Maugham has recognised his limitations. He has set out to portray the progression of a modern saint as viewed by those he is leaving behind, and Larry is always observed from the point of view of another. Furthermore, Maugham is always conscious of the need to communicate with his audience, and conveying the subtleties of the mystical experience with lucidity is a very difficult task. There have been many attempts to treat spiritual development in literature, but few have also been artistic successes. Maugham has achieved at least a degree of success, as indicated by the inscription in the copy of Paramhansa Yogananda's *The Autobiography of a Yogi* in the Maugham Library:

To Somerset Maugham, author of "The Razor's Edge", which has done so much good in the world by spreading the seed of India's teachings. With the sincere good wishes of Yogananda and Self-Realization Fellowship of India and America. March 21, 1947. Encinitas, California.

It is difficult to find a better fictional presentation of Vedanta than *The Razor's Edge*. Those which are written in what Arthur Koestler calls 'the Yogi-journalese of the Gerald Heard type'[46] have lacked clarity and sustaining interest. Huxley has written the most perceptive studies of spiritual regeneration and Vedanta, but the artistic merit of his fiction declined as he became more personally involved with his subject. Growing more dogmatic and didactic, his characters developed into mouthpieces and his situations became less plausible. Similarly, it might be expected that Christopher Isherwood, so deeply committed to Vedanta, would write the great novel of spiritual pilgrimage. However, despite his numerous contributions to *Vedanta and the West* and his efforts in translating Indian books, he has not yet produced an illuminating fictional study. Even now, when the movement toward Vedanta has proliferated, the definitive work has not yet arrived.

X

Conclusion

WHEN MAUGHAM'S LITERARY CAREER is examined in its entirety, it becomes clear that his essential convictions changed only imperceptibly during the course of his life. The themes and ideas expressed in *Liza of Lambeth* and the other early novels are essentially little different from those presented in his mature work. The youthful observations of *A Writer's Notebook* may be less tolerant and more pretentious than the later entries, but the ideas do not differ appreciably. When Maugham's work is analysed, it is not often that the critic can trace the evolution of an idea, revealing a changing and developing conception. Without doubt, his attitudes became more complex and subtle as he matured, but they rarely altered in the face of new experience or insight. Most writers possess ingrained ideas and obsessions which recur throughout their work, but few are as markedly static.

Despite this pronounced continuity of ideas, Maugham managed to remain contemporary for almost five decades, an achievement unmatched by other writers. The source of this remarkable ability lay in his attitude toward writing as a profession. By establishing a strict daily output of work, observing what his fellow authors were producing, keeping his finger on the public pulse, and forcing his ideas into acceptable forms, he was able to reach a high degree of consistency in the appeal of his books. His professional attitude made him reluctant to discard anything that he had written, and therefore with great frequency he would re-fashion old material for new forms and new eras. Thus, when one scans his complete work, there is very often the feeling that one is going over the same ground. Characters reappear, pronouncements are re-phrased, and situations are re-shaped.

It has been shown that the central concern of Maugham's life, and the continuing theme in all his writing, was physical and spiritual independence. He wrote about the importance of money, the dangers of emotion, the snares of passion, the handicaps of heredity and environment, and the narrowness of conformity, but he was really working out his own ideas about individual freedom. His achievement was the success with which this basic concern was adapted for many situations and many ages from the turn of the century to the 1940s.

It may be, however, that the dexterity which enabled Maugham to attract a wide readership for a number of generations is also the reason that most critics have nearly always sensed that he somehow lacks the quality of greatness. It may well be that the writer who can easily adapt his ideas and his style to new demands and new vogues lacks, in his writing at least, a distinct original personality. It is possible to argue that writers such as Galsworthy, Wells, and Shaw became anachronistic because their personalities were so original that they could not re-shape themselves for a new generation of readers. Although they eventually became relegated to social history, they nevertheless represented and influenced their times. In Maugham's case, however, there is the danger that he rode along the surface of contemporary thought and style, rather than exploring in true depth the interests of each age.

Although Maugham rarely treated matters of politics and although he infrequently proselytised, it must be admitted that he is representative of the twentieth century in his examination of the manifestations of freedom and bondage. His life spanned a period in which in many ways there was a great readjustment of man's freedom and dependence. Nineteenth-century economic growth meant that many more people were freed from the narrow struggle to live. Christianity had lost some of its influence, and it was easier for the individual to discover his own faith and life-pattern. Education had become more universal, and a great many minds were liberated. In matters of public morality, Victorianism began to lose force, and attitudes became more liberal. Travel and communication became more highly developed and accessible, and this acted as a liberating influence on those who were able to enjoy their benefits.

With these new forms of freedom, however, there were a corresponding number of new responsibilities, and these presented the perceptive individual with new demands. He might be freed from adhering to religious dogma, but he was then forced to discover a personal belief in existence. The Victorian codes of conduct might be relaxed, but this demanded a self-discipline of the person concerned with living a satisfying and responsible life. The expanding knowledge of the mind and its complex functions brought about new attitudes toward human behaviour, but it also forced upon the sensitive individual a rigid and constant introspection.

This period of transformation in freedoms and bondages influenced many of the novels of adolescence at the turn of the century, but none is more representative than *Of Human Bondage*. Reflecting the author, Philip Carey is, despite his idiosyncrasies, very much a product of his age. Just as Tom Jones, David Copperfield and Holden Caulfield are shaped by their societies and their times, Philip is composed from the concerns of the early twentieth century. In response to the new freedoms afforded the individual, he feels the compulsion from an early age to develop his own philosophy, and it is a long, nervous, tortuous struggle before he is finally able to discover a suitable pattern for his life. Like much of twentieth-century society, Philip is the hero who has lost his assurance, becoming as a result nervous, alienated and unhappy.

Although none of Maugham's other writing is as important as *Of Human Bondage*, almost all of his protagonists are studies of freedom and bondage. Liza Kemp, James Parsons, Bertha Craddock, Basil Kent, Alec MacKenzie, Charles Strickland, Kitty Fane, Rosie Driffield, Willie Ashenden, Dr Saunders, Louise Frith, Betty Welldon-Burns, Julia Lambert, Larry Darrell and many others, all seek liberation in some form. The direction of their search varies with the age and the setting of their story, but their progress is essentially similar.

The most significant aspect of Maugham's treatment of his central characters is that nearly all of them come in the end to be completely detached from other people. Liza, like James Parsons and George Bland, is defeated in her rebellion and dies. Bertha Craddock, relieved at the death of her burdensome husband, is determined to live a life of independence and solitude. Charles Strickland divests himself of all ties and obligations, and lives his final years in freedom in Tahiti with a woman who demands nothing of his spirit. Kitty Fane, when her husband's death ends an unhappy marriage, returns to England determined to dedicate her life to her as yet unborn child. Rosie Driffield lives with her husband until he becomes absorbed by the literary establishment, and then she flees to America where the last glimpse of her is as an old, lively widow. Louise Frith feels no remorse at Erik Christessen's suicide over her infidelity, and she is relieved that Fred Blake is leaving, preferring her spiritual freedom to living out their dreams of her. Dr Saunders finds philosophical truth on his voyage, and at the end of the novel he feels immensely pleased that he is totally divorced from others. Julia Lambert becomes reconciled to a marriage of convenience, is then relieved at freeing herself from a passionate enslavement, and finally luxuriates in her independence, absolutely alone. Betty Welldon-Burns retreats from conventional society to live with her chauffeur in Rhodes—an arrangement which leaves her spirit free to rise above the physical world. Larry Darrell, in one of Maugham's most important studies in freedom, arrives finally at a position of complete detachment from others and intends to submerge himself in the anonymity of New York. Finally, Willie Ashenden and the first person narrator of Maugham's stories are always figures of detachment—onlookers but never participants in human affairs.

In addition to these central characters who embark on quests for various forms of liberation, there are the many figures in Maugham's writing who demonstrate the restrictions that man faces and the narrow range of freedoms he can achieve. These are the people who leave England for America, Africa, the South Seas and the Far East, and they are the multitude of pathetic figures who can never rise above their circumstances. Maugham's writing is filled with characters whose lives seem futile because they have no control of their directions—people who grasp at the smallest chance or symbol of freedom in some form.

Maugham's explorations of the forms of restrictions which surround the individual and of the difficulties he faces in finding true liberation of spirit are a valuable contribution to twentieth-century writing. The literature of rebellion and alienation no doubt has more powerful and complete expression than that of Maugham, but his attempt to find a compromise between the demands of society and the needs of the individual warrants consideration. When this theme is more widely recognised as central to his writing, his importance to the literature of his time will be more accurately assessed.

There can be no doubt that the detachment and eventual retreat of most of Maugham's protagonists are a projection of the author's own desire for uninvolvement. It is also arguable that this alienation can be found beneath the veneer of most human relationships, even perhaps that it is a desirable condition for many people. Nevertheless, if Maugham is to be measured against the greatest writers, the consistency with which his central figures seek to separate themselves from others must be considered. It would seem to indicate a limited outlook on human relations and a lack of total understanding of life.

When Maugham's protagonists are examined collectively, the course of their actions is striking in its negativity. Retreat from the pressures of social conformity, superficial and meaningless relationships and painful emotional affairs is justifiable, and most literary heroes divest themselves of many of these restraints. In Maugham's writing, however, the retreat goes far beyond this level to a point where the characters strive to divorce themselves from any intimate human contact. The Maugham protagonist interacts with others, but he never allows this to reach the level of any real involvement of his personality.

In a number of respects, the actions and the beliefs of the central characters in Maugham's works lack maturity. Maturity is, of course, a relative term open to many interpretations. It remains, however, that the outlook and attitude toward the self of many of Maugham's protagonists resembles that of the child. The individual is nearly always egocentric, measuring other people and events entirely in relation to how much they affect his own life. When Maugham argues that most people do not fit the cosy picture of selflessness that is expounded by sentimentalists, he is correct. But is he really any more accurate with his own creation of characters who are incapable of adjusting to the personalities of others and who cannot merge their own ego with that of another? It would be foolish to demand that his characters express a commitment to causes or people, but the repeated pattern of the figure who sacrifices communication and contact for the freedom to indulge his own tastes can hardly stand as a complete picture of humanity.

Maugham's exposition of freedom found in retreat from human relationships is an authentic aspect of human affairs, but there is nevertheless a sense of incompleteness in it. In most of his stories, the rebellion and liberation of the characters does not lead to a constructive end: Charles Strickland isolates himself to paint, but his art is not intended to reach others; Julia Lambert guards her art against the intrusions of life, but it is for personal sublimation, not for better communication with others; and Larry Darrell professes to hope to influence others, yet he remains elusive and detached from his friends, finally losing himself in New York. There is in all these cases a sensation of denial of life, of retreat from the important areas of human communication. The Maugham characters seem to create barriers between themselves and others, not for a higher purpose, but as an end in itself. This would not be detrimental in a consideration of Maugham as an important writer if he also presented scenes of intimacy and commitment, but one looks in vain for many portrayals of this aspect of human life.

The real inadequacy of Maugham's writing—his lack of true warmth and intimacy—is a natural extension of his own life. Reacting to the unhappiness of his childhood, to what he felt were physical handicaps, and to unfortunate experiences with others as a young man, he sought protection in freedom and detachment. The wall which he created between his essential self and those he met could not help influencing the tone of his writings, and as a result most of his writings lack the willingness to expose the soul which is in some form the mark of all great writers. In *Of Human Bondage* Maugham unashamedly bared his innermost obsessions and fears for the scrutiny of all readers, and thus it has a sincerity and credibility which appears infrequently in his other writing.

Of Human Bondage was an act of catharsis, however, and afterwards Maugham retreated to the position of the tolerant detached observer, and he revealed little of himself, even indirectly, through his fiction. This is somewhat surprising since in other respects he is one of the least pretentious and devious of writers. His sincerity in recognising his limitations and in professing few illusions about the role of the writer in society is not simply a professional stance. Nevertheless, this refreshing honesty and humility should not deceive readers into believing that Maugham very often ever completely exposed himself. After *Of Human Bondage*, he revealed only what he wished, and this was a carefully edited version of W. Somerset Maugham. His homosexual tendencies, for example, are never even hinted at in the millions of words he wrote. In 1900 the young author had written in his notebook: 'Am I a minor poet that I should expose my bleeding vitals to the vulgar crowd?' The answer should surely be: yes. The truly great writers have always bared their souls, albeit in devious and conventionalised ways, to the gaze of their readers. This true intimacy between the reader and the author is a quality which one unmistakably senses in the greatest literature, and it is not an element which can be artificially created.

Maugham's own concern for detachment and reluctance to expose himself is largely responsible for his failure to create many well-developed characters. His belief, developed from his medical studies, that there is no such thing as the normal, that each person is a mixture of warped and noble elements, makes it difficult for him to draw characters with a universal quality. His conviction that each person is essentially unable ever to understand fully or communicate with his fellows leads to his treating his characters as unfathomable mysteries. Thus some of his most important protagonists—for example, Charles Strickland, Rosie Driffield and Larry Darrell—are always viewed externally. The complexities of their minds are never developed and revealed, and they remain fascinating, but remote, characters. Unlike the protagonists of the greatest writers, these figures never remain in one's memory as people one has actually known and understood.

Maugham was never able, for all his professional skill, to overcome his own emotionally warped nature. It is not true, as Sir Noël Coward claims, that Maugham never believed in human goodness; his admiration for this quality is expressed in many places. He was, however, chronically incapable of comprehending a truly intimate, fully-committed relationship. He developed his belief that love meant either physical, sexual attraction or loving-kindness, which was based on need, companionship and comfort. He could not visualise a relationship in which two people genuinely shared emotions, hopes, fears and joys. Nowhere in his hundreds of stories, novels, plays and essays does there appear a well-developed, truly intimate love. It cannot be disputed that a great many relationships are based on sexual attraction, economic consideration, comfort or companionship, and it is not the presence of these kinds of affairs which mars Maugham's work. It is, rather, the glaring absence of deeper personal relationships which leaves an unmistakable void in his writing.

Maugham has always presented a disturbing problem for literary critics, and they have yet to reach a proper assessment of his importance. While other writers have been elevated to greatness or relegated to the second-rate, he has remained in a kind of limbo, not yet given a proper estimation. Throughout his career he displayed a great many obvious literary skills, yet a lack of something essential to great writing has always left the critics with an uneasy feeling that he falls short of what he could be. This bafflement with Maugham's real literary worth led Malcolm Cowley finally to label it 'The Maugham Enigma'.[1]

Some of the critics' complaints are not, of course, justifiable. Maugham was remarkably successful in four areas—novels, short stories, plays, and travel books—and critics have always been suspicious of versatility. The writer of superficial dramatic comedies could not, they argue, create serious and important prose fiction. Moreover, Maugham made a great deal of money through his consistent popularity over many years, and many critics have been unable to accept that a living writer can be both popularly successful and a creator of serious literature. His stories appeared in *Cosmopolitan*, *Hearst's International Magazine*, and *Nash's Magazine*, and many could not believe that good literature could be found in such common settings. In addition, a certain amount of antipathy to Maugham must be attributed to personal antagonism. Many found it hard to forgive his ruthless use of people he met or his attacks on the follies and vices of the middle and upper classes. This may explain why he is far less appreciated in England than in most other countries. The French accepted him as a serious writer of magnitude in the 'twenties, and many academic studies of his writing have come out of the United States, Japan, Mexico, Germany and other countries. In England, however, he is almost completely ignored as a writer worthy of serious consideration.

The criticisms of a large segment of academics and critics are best expressed in Edmund Wilson's article, 'The Apotheosis of Somerset Maugham', written in 1946. Wilson begins:

It has happened to me from time to time to run into some person of taste who tells me that I ought to take Somerset Maugham seriously, yet I have never been able to convince myself that he was anything but second-rate. His swelling reputation in America . . . seems to me a conspicuous sign of the general decline of our standards.[2]

Wilson bases his judgement on a reading of *Then and Now* and on Maugham's remarks in his *Introduction to Modern English and American Literature*. From this limited reading, he argues that Maugham's language is always banal and that he lacks an interesting rhythm. Maugham is invidious when talking of his contemporaries and he cannot understand writers such as Joyce, Yeats and James because of his limited intellect. In conclusion, says Wilson, he is nothing more than a literary hack:

Mr. Maugham makes play with more serious themes, but his work is full of bogus motivations, that are needed to turn the monthly trick. He is for our day, I suppose, what Bulwer-Lytton was for Dickens's: a half-trashy novelist, who writes badly, but is patronized by half-serious readers, who do not care much about writing.[3]

Maugham, however, has been admired by Desmond MacCarthy, Frank Swinnerton, Cyril Connolly, Glenway Wescott, Paul Dottin, Theodore Dreiser, William Rose Benet, Carl and Mark Van Doren, Christopher Isherwood, St John Ervine, Richard Aldington, George Orwell and S. N. Behrman, and these writers can scarcely be called 'half-serious readers, who do not care much about writing'.

Despite the deficiencies in his writing, Maugham deserves much greater critical attention than he is now being accorded. While no one would rank him with the greatest English writers, he is much better than most of those in the second rank. He has produced much more of lasting value than Wells, Bennett, Galsworthy, Mackenzie and Waugh—all of whom are treated with more academic respect.

One of the significant factors in assessing the importance of Maugham is what reader and what criteria a writer should be measured by. In an age when literary criticism almost completely concerns itself with experiments in form, Maugham will occupy no space in literary surveys. His readership, however, despite the claims of his severest critics, is not composed of indiscriminate readers whose tastes are formed by a diet of Frank Yerby, Thomas Costain, Harold Robbins and Mickey Spillane. Maugham is read by those who are baffled by the complexities of Joyce, Woolf, Yeats and Eliot, but he is also enjoyed by many whose critical sensibilities are highly developed.

More than most contemporary writers, Maugham has a respect for his readers and, like Bertrand Russell, he is always concerned with communicating with them. He was, for example, gratified to receive many letters from American soldiers who had enjoyed *The Razor's Edge*, most of whom had probably never before read a serious book. What Maugham's wide readership has given him is an ability to reach a great many more people than most serious authors ever do in their lifetime. Some would argue that he has gained the readership by writing nothing profound, but this is surely ignoring the issues that he treats in his better works.

Predicting a writer's stature with future generations is always a hazardous undertaking, but it can be argued that Maugham has an excellent chance of being read as a serious writer long after some of the giants of twentieth-century English literature have been relegated to academic preserves. He has produced a massive amount of written work, more than enough to avoid becoming, like Bennett, remembered for one excellent novel. Most of his writing will be rightfully forgotten, as much is already, and time will reveal what will be remembered. *Liza of Lambeth*, *Of Human Bondage*, *The Moon and Sixpence*, *Cakes and Ale*, and possibly *The Razor's Edge*, should survive among the novels. *The Constant Wife* and *The Circle* will become part of that company of social comedies which delight audiences in revival. *The Summing Up* has already almost reached the stature of a classic philosophical autobiography, and it will survive for its style and its lucid discussions of the writer's art. Finally, Maugham's reputation may ultimately rest on the hundred or so short stories which, as a collection, are unmatched in English literature.

Maugham will survive to be read by future generations because he is, as he always claimed, basically the story-teller, having his affinities with the tellers of tales around campfires ages ago. His use of colloquial expressions and clichés will harm him for future readers, but he has the advantage that little of his prose writing depends on references to the political or social upheavals of his time. His themes of love, hate, murder, suicide, belief and doubt are timeless, and his treatment of man's search for liberation may become more significant as humanity becomes more controlled by technology and circumstance.

Since Maugham's death there have been only two serious critical surveys published—Naik's *W. Somerset Maugham* and Brown's *W. Somerset Maugham*. Three biographical works—Nichols' *A Case of Human Bondage*, Robin Maugham's *Somerset and All the Maughams*, and Kanin's *Remembering Mr Maugham*—have appeared, but they do not analyse Maugham's writing. Now that he has departed the scene, it is the task of critics and students seriously to examine his body of work to determine what is valuable and what is worthless. During his life Maugham was ignored by most critics and then, much like his own creation—Edward Driffield—he slipped into becoming 'the Grand Old Man of English Letters' or, as he was known in France, 'Cher Maître'. Thus a proper and concrete evaluation of his writings has never been made. Now, with personal jealousies, inhibitions and grudges soon to disappear, new objective criticism should be able to give a well-considered judgement of this prolific and popular writer's true place in English literary history.

Appendices

Appendices

Appendix A

'Rosie'

Soon after its publication in 1930 *Cakes and Ale* became a sensation because of the similarities of Edward Driffield to Thomas Hardy and Alroy Kear to Hugh Walpole. Amidst all the controversy about the two literary figures, however, no one attempted to discover the original of the central character in the novel—Rosie Driffield. It was assumed that Rosie, Maugham's most delightful female creation, was a product of the author's imagination. When Maugham talked freely to Allen B. Brown in 1951[1] about the literary figures in *Cakes and Ale*, he remained silent about Rosie. Even though he ultimately admitted that she was based on a young woman he had once loved, her identity has until now remained a mystery.

Maugham first revealed that there was an original of Rosie in his introduction to the Modern Library edition of *Cakes and Ale* published in 1950. After refuting the allegation that Driffield was based on Hardy and confessing that Kear was a thinly disguised Walpole, he proceeded to explain that his real purpose in writing the novel was to capture in fiction the character of a beautiful woman he had known:

In my youth I had been closely connected with the young woman whom in this book I have called Rosie. She had grave and maddening faults, but she was beautiful and honest. The connection came to an end as such connections do, but the memory of her lingered on in my mind year after year. I knew that one day I should bring her into a novel.[2]

Seeing the opportunity to use this woman as the first wife of Edward Driffield, Maugham created what he always considered his most engaging heroine. She could never have recognised herself in the novel, he claimed, because she was dead by the time he wrote it. 'Rosie', however, was very much alive in 1930.

In 1962 Maugham revealed a great deal more about the woman behind Rosie. As a young writer, he said, he was frequently invited to Merton Abbey, the home of a prominent social figure at the turn of the century, Mrs G. W. Steevens. At one of these afternoon parties he was introduced to a very pretty young woman with pale golden hair and blue eyes. Though more delicate, her lovely figure was reminiscent of a Renoir nude; but it was her beautiful smile that made her unforgettable.[3]

His description, written very late in life, is particularly interesting because of the light it casts on two entries in *A Writer's Notebook* for 1904. There can be little doubt that they describe the same woman:

She had something of the florid colouring of Helena Fourment, the second wife of Rubens, that blonde radiancy, with eyes blue as the sea at mid-summer and hair like corn under the August sun, but a greater delicacy withal. And she hadn't Helena's unhappy leaning to obesity.[4]

She was a woman of ripe and abundant charms, rosy of cheek and fair of hair, with eyes blue as the summer sea, with rounded lines and full breasts. She leaned somewhat to the overblown. She belonged to that type of woman that Rubens has set down for ever in the ravishing person of Helena Fourment.[5]

According to Maugham's account in 'Looking Back', the woman was an actress and unhappily married. They soon became lovers and the affair lasted eight years. 'Rosie' divorced her husband and continued as an actress, taking parts (some in Maugham's own plays) as an understudy or in the provinces. She clearly would have liked to marry him, but he was reluctant because of her promiscuity, which he is careful to point out was simple and artless amorality.

Maugham decided nevertheless that, although he was not in love with the young woman, he would like to marry. Being in the United States on business, he met 'Rosie' in Chicago, where she had a good part in a new play. He confidently proposed to her and she rejected him. Stunned by her adamant refusal, he left for New York and soon returned to England. A few weeks later, he read that Rosie had been married in Chicago to the son of an earl. He claims that he never saw her again; however, Garson Kanin[6] writes that Maugham once told him that 'many, many years later' she told him that what had happened was that, when he finally proposed to her, she had just learned that she was pregnant by another man. In spite of his subterfuge in the 1950 preface about her death, he now wrote of having seen her obituary in *The Times* a few years before, and recalled with constant tenderness her beautiful smile and essentially good and sweet nature.[7]

In 1961, the year before 'Looking Back' was published, Richard Cordell told this story from a different point of view, in his monograph *Somerset Maugham: A Biographical and Critical Study*, and he brought to light a number of interesting, though veiled, details. The

woman, whom he calls 'Nan', was the daughter of a prominent figure
in London life, married first to a theatrical producer and then to the
younger son of a nobleman. Her second husband, he says, later distinguished himself in politics, and he was still living in 1960. 'Nan' was
apparently well-educated, but not an intellectual. She was intelligent,
and Maugham was attracted by 'her warmth of heart, her invariable
good humour, her good sense, her expertness at bridge . . . and her
great beauty. Compared with most of the professional hostesses of
Mayfair and Belgravia who sought the company of the successful
young author, Nan was simple, artless, generous in her affection.'[8]
She died, says Cordell, eighteen years after the publication of *Cakes
and Ale* (1930), after spending her last years in a beautiful English
country house.

These accounts were all that was generally known of the woman
who was 'Rosie' until a conversation the author had with the late Sir
Gerald Kelly in September 1969 uncovered the fascinating story. Sir
Gerald, then the only person alive who had known Maugham intimately during the early years of the century, revealed that the
mysterious woman was Ethelwyn Sylvia Jones, the second daughter
of the playwright, Henry Arthur Jones.

Ethelwyn, always called 'Sue' (not, as Cordell says, 'Nan'), was
born at Lothian Lodge, New Hampton, in 1883. She began acting at
the age of fourteen, under the direction of Frederick Harrison, as
'Pamela' in Jones' *The Manœuvres of Jane*. After gaining experience
in the provinces (and being complimented by George Bernard Shaw
in a letter to Jones), she returned to London and appeared in *The
Chevalier* and *The Third Degree* at the Garrick Theatre, *The Princess'
Hose* at the Duke of York's, and *The Heart of the Firm* at the Vaudeville. She also played under Sir Herbert Beerbohm Tree as Calpurnia
in *Julius Caesar*, Charmian in *Antony and Cleopatra* and Patience in
Henry the Eighth. One role which is of great interest is her part as
'Peyton' in the first production of Maugham's *Penelope* at the
Comedy in 1909. J. T. Grein (*Sunday Times and Special*, 10 January
1909) wrote of 'the stoic and impeccable maid of Miss Ethelwynn
[*sic*] Arthur Jones, who "buttled" as well as the most time-honoured
butler'.

Ethelwyn married Montague Vivian Leveaux in 1902, and this
marriage was dissolved a few years later. It is likely that, as Maugham
claimed, she met him (Maugham) at Merton Abbey. In 1932
Maugham wrote a preface for *What a Life!* (London, Jarrolds, 1932),
the autobiography of Ethelwyn's sister, Doris, and in it he states that
he first met Doris at the home of Mrs G. W. Steevens, Merton
Abbey. Considering that Henry Arthur Jones was a regular visitor to

Merton Abbey and that his daughters were accustomed to associating with writers, actors and actresses, and social figures, it is probable that Maugham also met 'Sue' there.

Circumstances make it difficult to discover the veracity of Maugham's account of the affair, but his version of the denouement would seem to be true. On 14 September 1913 the *Chicago Sunday Tribune* (Part II, p. 1) stated that 'among those who will assist Miss Doris Keane in the coming performance of 'Romance' at the Princess is Miss Ethel Jones'. Edward Sheldon's *Romance* had played for a year in New York and opened on 29 September in Chicago. Surprisingly, Ethelwyn is not listed in the cast for the opening night, but the *Chicago Sunday Tribune* announced on 19 October (Part III, p. 3) that she was playing in *Romance*. The play's run ended on 3 January 1914. Maugham, at this time, was in the United States working on a new play.

On 13 December 1913 Ethelwyn married Angus McDonnell (1881–1966), the second son of the 6th Earl of Antrim. He had gone to North America a few years earlier and was managing a construction company. In fact in January and February of 1914 he was in Vancouver and Ottawa to secure a contract for work on the harbour at Victoria, British Columbia. He served in the First World War and was awarded the C.B. and C.M.G. From 1924 to 1929 he held the parliamentary seat of Dartford for the Conservative Party. In the Second World War he served in Washington as an honorary attaché, helping the ambassador to present the British cause to the American public (which, coincidentally, was what Maugham was doing in the United States at the same time).

In England, the McDonnells lived at Five Ashes, a village south of Tunbridge Wells in Kent, and it was here on 3 April 1948 that Ethelwyn died. Her husband lived until April 1966.

Any doubts that Ethelwyn Sylvia Jones was the original of Rosie were dispelled when Sir Gerald Kelly revealed that he was the artist who painted the picture which Maugham describes in such detail in Chapter XIV of *Cakes and Ale*. From his carefully arranged collection of prints he produced a great many photographs of paintings which he had done of 'Sue' and one, which at the time of his death in 1972 he still possessed,—'Mrs L. [Leveaux] in White 1907'—is without doubt the portrait of 'Rosie'. She is, as Maugham describes, in the white silk dress, with the black velvet bow in her hair. Her position and stance correspond exactly; she is in the middle of the canvas, with her head thrown back 'like an actress taking a call'. The only disparity is that, in Kelly's picture, 'Sue' has her palms facing behind her, rather than forward as in Maugham's description. Either

Maugham felt that his version better emphasised the gesture of giving of herself which he saw in Rosie, or there is possibly another, slightly different, painting. In any case, as Sir Gerald says, the portrait enchanted Maugham:

She posed beautifully for the picture, so patiently, and both of us did our best, and I think Willie loved the portrait. I did several portraits of her – all, I felt, quite good. The picture was painted when I myself was very much under the influence of the great Whistler: but it really was like dear Sue.[9]

The discovery of the identity of the woman who was 'Rosie' opens the way to a greater understanding of one of the most important events in Maugham's life. According to Garson Kanin, Maugham claimed that this was the only time that he ever proposed marriage, and the rejection inevitably altered the course of his life: 'I often wonder what course my life might have taken had it not been for that . . . freakish happenstance.'[10] Any future biography will have to examine this bitter-sweet love affair very carefully, and it may be that it will have to be treated as the turning-point in Maugham's adult life.

The truth about this relationship is important also because it refutes the frequently voiced claim that, because of his homosexual nature, Maugham could not have loved a woman. Beverley Nichols, for example, relates how he once infuriated Maugham by telling him that Hugh Walpole had stated that the only character in *Cakes and Ale* who is obviously fictional is 'Rosie'. Walpole's reason, says Nichols, was that 'there'd never been a Rosie in your life and never would be'.[11] Even without being aware of the background, the character of 'Rosie' is so well-developed and credible that it should be hard for one to doubt her existence. The revelation of the real woman behind the fictional character, however, should finally discredit the argument that there could have been no woman in Maugham's life.

Finally, the facts of Maugham's affair with 'Sue' provide some significant insights into certain developments in his writing. Since it is now known that the relationship must have ended in 1913 and that, according to Maugham, it lasted for eight years, their affair must have begun around 1904 or 1905. The notebook descriptions quoted earlier are dated 1904, and so it is likely that this marked the beginning.

The dates of this relationship are significant in regard to a fairly common hypothesis—that the originals of 'Rosie' and 'Mildred' in *Of Human Bondage* were the same person, interpreted much differently by the author in two stages of his career. Allen B. Brown represents the opinions of many when he suggests that the prototype of both female characters is probably revealed in this passage in *The Summing Up*:

I was at the time much taken with a young person of extravagant tastes and the gratification of my desires was frustrated by the attention of more opulent admirers who were able to provide the luxuries that her frivolous soul hankered after. I had nothing much to offer but a serious disposition and a sense of humour. I determined to write a book that would enable me to earn three or four hundred pounds with which I could hold my own with my rivals.[12]

In the preface to the collected edition of *Liza of Lambeth* (1934), however, Maugham revealed that the book in question was *The Bishop's Apron* (1906) and that, by the time it was printed and he had received the money, 'I was no longer in the least interested in the young person and wished neither to take her out to supper nor to spend a romantic day with her on the river'. The young woman may have been the original of Mildred, but, since Maugham's affair with Sue lasted until 1913, it is hardly likely that they are the same person.

In addition, it is significant that the affair began around 1904 because by that time Maugham had already written extensively about the bitterness of unrequited love. In *The Making of a Saint* (1898), the situation between the narrator and Giulia is an embryonic version of the Philip–Mildred relationship in *Of Human Bondage*. In the same year, *A Man of Honour* developed the same theme in the tragic affair of Basil Kent and Jenny Bush. Finally, by examining the manuscript of 'The Artistic Temperament of Stephen Carey', it can be established beyond doubt that Maugham had already encountered the woman he described as 'Mildred' when he met Sue. In this early version of *Of Human Bondage* written in 1897, the same young woman appears as 'Rose Cameron' and Stephen's unhappy experiences with her are basically the same as Philip's with Mildred. There can now be no doubt that the originals of 'Mildred' and 'Rosie' were different women. The former was probably a girl the author knew as a medical student, as Philip does in *Of Human Bondage*; the latter was 'Sue' Jones, whom he encountered in his early days as a writer.

Appendix B

Maugham's Role in Allied Espionage in Russia in 1917

The following material is from the Private Papers of Sir William Wiseman, in the E.M. House Collection, Yale University Library, New Haven, Connecticut. Wiseman was officially head of the British Purchasing Commission in the United States during the First World War, but he was in fact the head of M.I. 1.C. (later known as M.I.6) in the United States, and he controlled all its agents there.

These hitherto unpublished documents[1] are a fascinating revelation of the magnitude of Maugham's role in the espionage in Russia in 1917. Until now, little has been known of the degree of Maugham's participation, the only evidence being his own account. From these letters and reports, however, it is clear that he was in fact Wiseman's chief agent in Russia between July and November of 1917 and that he played a major role in the unsuccessful attempt to influence the course of the revolution.

[Wiseman Mss. File 91–112]

Maidstone Inn,
East Hampton, L.I.

July 7.
My dear Wiseman

(i) I saw Dr. Wise yesterday & he is arranging for me to meet two important Russian Jews when he next comes up to New York.

I suggested that I desired to make the acquaintance of the Jewish circles which are opposed to the Jewish socialists, & he is going to give me letters which will facilitate this. My idea is that there must be Jews of fortune & position whose views are diametrically opposed to their Socialist co-religionaries; & it should be possible to get them to work against the latter. They would have more efficacious ways of dealing with them than we could possibly have.

(ii) Voska[2] has arranged to find me a Bohemian servant & will communicate with you on the subject. I might interview the applicant next time I come up to New York. I suggest that Voska should go to Petrograd as soon as possible, since I do not see how the part of the work he is connected with can proceed in his absence.

(iii) I find the Empress of Russia sails from Vancouver on August 2. That apparently is the first boat that does, & subject to your approval I propose to take it.

If I send my pass-port to you would you very kindly see that I get the necessary *visés*.

Having so short a time before me I do not want to come up to New York more often than I can help. I have wired to Mr. Crowley saying that unless Monday is the only day he can see me I should prefer to postpone the luncheon to some future date. In point of fact all my business with him can be arranged in five minutes.

Of course when you want me to come to Washington I am ready at any time; likewise if there is need I can always travel up to New York, but the journey is three & a half hours each way & I should like to get in as much as possible each time I come.

(iv) I do not know whether it is intended that I should have any salary for the work I am undertaking. I will not pretend that I actually need one, but in Switzerland I refused to accept anything and found afterwards that I was the only man working in the organization for nothing and that I was regarded not as patriotic or generous but merely as damned foolish. If the job carries a salary I think it would be more satisfactory to have it; but if not I am not unwilling to go without. I leave the matter in your hands.

Yours sincerely
W. S. Maugham [signed]

[Wiseman Mss. File 91–112]

July 12, 1917.

RUSSIAN MATTERS

VOSKA will write a letter to the Secretary of State, announcing his departure in the Company of other members of the Committee of American citizens of Slav origin to Petrograd for the purpose of studying conditions in Russia. In his letter he will offer the services of his Committee, as American citizens, to the State Department. The State Department should reply to Voska's letter in the following sense:

Approving the Committee's Mission and wishing it all success and stating that it is desirous of benefiting by any useful knowledge which the Mission may acquire, asking, for this purpose, that it shall be furnished with copies of all reports which the Mission may submit to its fellow members of the Committee of American citizens of Slav origin (or to the Bohemian National Alliance).

Take up with proper authorities the matter of passports for V. and his fellow travellers. The applications will be forwarded to Washington on Monday.

Take up with the proper person the perfecting of arrangements for the forwarding of M's reports and cables through the U.S. Embassy. Everything that M sends to be addressed to, say, Auchinloss. The arrangements should, of course, provide for these reports and cables to reach us as quickly as possible and not be held up either in Washington or NEW YORK.

Emanuel V. Voska	Secretary of Bohemian National Alliance and Director of Slav Press Bureau, New York, N.Y.
Ven Svarc	Assistant City Attorney of City of Cleveland, Ohio.
A. B. Koukol	President of Slavonic Emigration Institute, 437 West 23rd Street, New York, N.Y.
Joseph Martinek	Editor of Socialist paper, Delnicke Listy, 4130 Broadway, Cleveland, Ohio.

[Wiseman Mss. File 91–112]

Maidstone Inn
East Hampton, L.I.

July 14

My dear Wiseman

I shall be in town at 9.30 on Wednesday morning & if it suits you will come straight to your office.

For convenience I add a list of the matters which I think should be settled.

(i) To whom I am to address reports & cables.
(ii) What is my address in Petrograd.
    This should be given to Voska. For safety's sake I think it would be well for me to have an address of his in Petrograd.
(iii) Letter of recommendation to the U.S. ambassador.
(iv) What arrangements have been made for funds. Funds for journey.
    I agree with Voska that it is waste of money to take a servant

or secretary here when he can find me some one reliable in Russia.

(v) Passport. One of your clerks with an official word can get the *visés* more expeditiously & conveniently than I.

With regard to my interview with Commandant Stefanik, he has arranged that Voska should put me in communication with the Vice-president of the society of which he himself is president, & guarantees that every possible help will be given me.

Prof Shatsky is going to Russia in August. If I do not see him on the journey he has asked me to see him in Petrograd. His relations with the British Ambassador are very intimate, & he spoke of him so much that I thought it wiser to say that my connections were with the U.S. government. I fancy it will be prudent not to have more dealings with the Professor than I can help. I should judge him to be rather a fishy customer.

Yours sincerely
W. S. Maugham [signed]

[Wiseman Mss. File 91–112]

Maidstone Inn,
East Hampton, L.I.

July 16

My Dear Thwaites[3]

Would you very kindly give the enclosed passport to one of the clerks in the office & tell him to get the *visé* at the Japanese & Russian consulates. If he is asked what is the purpose of my journey he should say I am going to Russia for literary purposes—to write for American publications—but I have always found that when the passport is taken by an official clerk no questions are asked.

I shall be in town on Wednesday & could get the passport at the office.

Will you let W. know that not having been able to get a berth on the 2nd I am taking a slow boat on the 28th & must start from New York on Monday next.

Yours sincerely,
W. S. Maugham [signed]

[Wiseman Mss. 91–112]

July 18, 1917.

RECEIVED the sum of Twenty-one thousand Dollars.

W. Somerset Maugham [signed]

$21,000.00.

[Wiseman Mss. File 91–112]

July 19, 1917.

W. M. Wilson	– Weston	Wise	– Richards
W. S. M. Somerset			
Maugham	– Somerville[4]	F.P.	– Harper
E. V. Voska	– Victor	U.S. Govt.	– Curtis Co.
Ven Svarc	– Arnold	Brit. Il. Att.	– Black
A. B. Koukol	– Bennett	Francis	– Dodd
Joseph Martinek	– Snaith	Tscheidze	– Mead
Masaryk	– Marcus	Brit. Govt.	– Eyre & Co.
Stefanik	– Long	Buchanan	– Dewar
Kerensky	– Lane	Hall	– Lobb
Milyukoff	– Locke	Lenin	– Davis
Workmen's &			
Soldiers' Council	– Dent & Co.	Trotzky	– Cole
Maximalists	– Dutton & Co.	Russian Govt.	– Waring & Co.
Boris Bakmehtieff	– Fisher	Lvoff	– Bird
Shatsky	– Unwin	Tseretelli	– Hodder
Gottheil	– Grant		
Grand Duke			
Nicholas	– Norris		
Ukraine	– Brown		
Poles	– Jones		

Should V have occasion to wire about W.S.M., he will call him
IVAN.
Password: Friend of Mr. King of New York.

[Wiseman Mss. File 90–42]

MEMORANDUM

August 22, 1917.

FOR SIR ERIC DRUMMOND:[5]

Can you send a message to this effect to Consul-General or
Ambassador, Petrograd:

Mr. W. Somerset Maugham is in Russia on a confidential
mission with a view to putting certain phases of the Russian
situation before the public in United States. Please give him
facilities for cabling his principals through British Consul-General,
New York. Please cable if he has presented himself at the Embassy
yet.

K

[Wiseman Mss. File 91–112]

C.

September 3–16.

3

It will be known to you that the situation in Finland is very disquieting. Even if there is no truth in the suggestion that a secret agreement has been entered into between Sweden and Finland for these countries to join the Central Powers in the event of the Germans taking Petrograd, it is pretty generally allowed that if Reval falls no reliance whatever can be placed on the Finns. Neither the British nor the American Intelligence Departments have agents in Finland, and there is no accurate knowledge of conditions there. I have made arrangements for Kokol, one of the agents who came out with Voska, to go to Finland to enquire first as to the state of things generally, and secondly as to which points it would be desirable to station agents at. These will be provided by Vs organization and will remain as long as it is thought desirable. In this manner a reliable amount of information should be quickly obtained. It will then be possible to judge also whether it would pay to conduct any systematic propaganda in Finland. So far as I can learn no attention has been paid to Finland. The same conditions appear to prevail in the Ukraine, and V. is going down there himself to make inquiries. But in this case there is the advantage that throughout this district members of V's organization are already settled; and it will be very easily possible to give them instructions and put them in touch with the central office. I will send further reports on these two matters as soon as the information comes in.

Propaganda. So far as I can see this may be divided into two parts, that which is done by word of mouth, and that which is done by the dissemination of literature, included in which of course are films, post-cards, etc. With regard to the former, Professor Masaryk is of opinion that the Russians have grown tired of the lectures and speeches to which they listened avidly three months ago. He does not think it would be worth while to engage speakers to give lectures, but suggests that it would pay to get men to join in the discussion which generally takes place after the lectures and so have the allied cause represented. The Germans have men who mingle with the crowds in the bread lines, and it might be worth while to engage people to counteract their efforts. I am assured that lectures and speeches are still profitable in the provinces, but expect to be able to give you further information on this point when V. returns from his trip. I understand the British have a certain number of agents working in these directions and hope through the intervention of the Ambassador in due course to be given access to information on this subject. Any agents we need for this sort of work can be found by V's organization, and they would not be expensive.

With regard to the second point, there is no doubt in the mind of anyone whom I have consulted about the desirability of greatly extending propaganda by way of literature. There is a great need for postcards and posters, not so much pro-Ally as anti-German. There is a great need for films, showing what Great Britain and the U.S. have done for Russia; for films showing the conditions of work both in the towns and in the country. If stories could be found, preferably of an emotional character, they would be very popular. Any reading matter that is provided should be copiously illustrated. It is important to notice that reading matter manufactured in England or America is not likely to be of great use; a large amount brought out by the American Red Cross has had to be scrapped as entirely unsuited to the Russian temperament; the most economical plan would be to provide material and illustrations and engage Russian writers to furnish the reading matter. I believe that a little work of this sort is being done, but I cannot yet tell you how much and how efficiently.

Naturally I have not yet been able to do much. I have instructed Kokol to make a report on the chief papers, their tendencies, power and circulation. He will endeavor to find out also which of them it would be possible or advisable to influence. I hope in my next report to be able to give you facts and suggestions. Further, I have instructed V. to get artists in his association to make designs for postcards and posters; if any of them seem to me suitable I will inquire what the cost of production would be and what one could count on getting back by the sale of postcards. I may point out to you that we have at our disposal an extremely efficient means of distribution entirely free of charge. The organization has 1200 agencies throughout Russia. I think it is very desirable that the Allied Propaganda Bureaux should be persuaded to avail themselves of these means of distribution.

S[6]

[House Mss. File 20–45]

SUMMARY OF REPORTS RECEIVED FROM AGENT
IN PETROGRAD,

UNDER DATE OF SEPTEMBER 11, 1917

The CZECH organization, which has been established throughout Russia for many years, has 1,200 branches and a membership of

70,000 men admirably disciplined and organized. The whereabouts and activities of each member is controlled by a card system.

The members of this organization are mostly of the better-educated workmen, mechanics, and shop-keeping class, and their leaders are writers, University men, and journalists.

PROPAGANDA:

This may be divided into two parts: (a) that which can be done by word of mouth; (b) that which is done by the dissemination of literature, including films, posters, postcards, etc.

Under (a) there would be a system of lecturers at workmen's meetings, and speakers at informal gatherings at factories, among the soldiers, in the breadlines, etc.; also speakers to attend enemy meetings, and engage in the discussions which generally take place after the lecture. The Germans have men who mingle with the crowd on all important occasions, and are stationed in the bread-lines. This would apply not only in Petrograd, but to perhaps a dozen chief centres.

With regard to (b), there is a great need for a standing propaganda by way of literature. There is great need for postcards and posters, not so much pro-Ally as anti-German. Films could play a most important part as all classes of Russians eagerly attend moving pictures. These could show what the Allies and the United States are doing for Russia; could show the life of the working-classes of America, pictures of Washington and New York; and some pictures of German militarism and what that means. Of course, nothing is of too sensational or emotional a character to be popular with the Russians.

It is important to note that reading-matter manufactured in England or America is practically useless. A great deal brought out by the American Red Cross has had to be scrapped as unsuitable. The most economical plan would be to provide material and illustrations, and engage Russian writers to furnish the reading-matter.

It should be remembered that we have access to organizations which have, in all, more than 4,000 branches throughout Russia, and this provides an extraordinarily efficient and economical voluntary agency for distribution.

The following is a summary of some of the most important notes of our agent:—

1. The mass of Russians feel that their Radical views are not received sympathetically by the Allies or the States. They feel that the Ambassadors and the Press are supporting the reactionary party. To this is due much of the unpopularity from which the Allies are now suffering.

2. Our agent, mingling with the crowd, found the general wish that

KORNILOV should succeed, because it was thought that he could solve the food difficulty. Our agent believes that the Kornilov attempt was the result of a plan arranged between KERENSKY and KORNILOV whereby it was hoped to get rid of the SOVIET, but the plan miscarried. He says there is written proof of this.

3. The situation in FINLAND is very disquieting. There is a secret understanding between certain of the leaders in SWEDEN and FINLAND to induce this country to join the Central powers if the Germans take Petrograd. The Allies appear to be paying no attention to conditions in Finland or Ukrania, where the German agents are having it all their own way.

4. Our agent reports relations somewhat strained between the British and American Ambassadors—faults probably on both sides.[7] He was able to do something to remedy this owing to his friendship with the British First-Secretary and the good offices of the new American Consul, Tredwell, whom he describes as 'very able and energetic'.

Professor Harper is described as having known Russia well before the war, and being more or less intimately acquainted with many foreign political men. Our agent doubts whether Harper has been able to keep up to date with political moves. Is rather too sure of his information, which he gains from sources which were once reliable but now out of touch with current politics.

5. The chief German agent in Russia is MAX WARBURG, of Hamburg, brother of Paul Warburg. Wolf von Igel has been located in Finland, and is supposed to be going to Petrograd with a Swedish passport.

6. The following is a report of an interview with Professor Mazaryk, who, of course, knows Russian politics very intimately, and is MILUKOFF'S closest friend. His views, however must be taken as those of the Cadet party:—

The condition of things is much more serious than appears on the surface. Nothing can be awaited from Russia except that she will not make a separate peace, and will continue to hold a certain number of German troops on the Eastern front. There is no danger of a separate peace, because Russia realizes that she can get nothing from Germany except a certain amount of money. She can get neither railways nor the bread which at the moment she chiefly lacks; and peace with the Central Powers would leave her internal conditions unchanged. But notwithstanding, it is to the Allies' advantage to give her such help as they can; but so far as financial help is concerned, in moderation and only on explicit conditions. Professor Mazaryk insisted on the need of a definite *quid pro quo* for all money advanced. 'If you give them all they ask without conditions,' he said, 'they will spend it like children, and you will get nothing in return.' If it were possible to send a Japanese army of at least 300,000 men, these would serve to restore the morale of the Russian troops. Professor Mazaryk suggests that Japanese intervention might be paid for, if money would not be accepted, by the cession of a part of Manchuria, which in fact is already under Japanese influence; and he thinks that Russia would be willing to cede to China some part of Central Asia; faced with the alternative of losing a part of Asia, and falling into complete political and economic dependence upon Germany, Russia could be induced to choose the former. But nothing of this sort can save the situation unless it is done quickly. Professor Mazaryk insisted repeatedly on the fact that now the war could be won only by victories on the Western front, and urged the necessity of a large American army being placed in the field with as little delay as possible.

The internal and external weakening of Russia means *eo ipso* the strengthening of the Central Powers, which makes it the more necessary to form independent Bohemian, Polish, and South-Slav states as a natural barrier against Pan-Germanism. The dismemberment of Austrian-Hungary [sic] is the real object of the war; Germany must be prevented from using Austria–Hungary with its population of 51 millions for her imperialistic aims. Austria–Hungary is the Prussian bridge to the nearer and to the farther East.

Professor Mazaryk made the valuable suggestion that further propaganda should be conducted in Sweden; he asserts that the German agents have spent a great deal of money on the influencing of public opinion through the press; and the dispatches of Russian correspondents in Sweden, which are given much space in the Russian papers, are very largely colored by this opinion. He insists that Allied opinion is very little represented. Sweden has been occupied by the Germans because the Allies did not work in that country.

[Wiseman Mss. File 90–42]
CABLEGRAM
Out

No. CX159   Date: Septr. 24, 1917.

Following for Sir Eric Drummond in private cipher:—
  I am receiving interesting cables from Maugham, Petrograd:—
  (A) He is sending agent to Stockholm for promised information,

and also to Finland. He has reports of secret understanding for
Sweden and Finland to join Germany on capture of Petrograd.

(B) Government change their mind daily about moving to
Moscow to avoid Maximalists. He hopes to get agent into Maxi-
malist meetings.

(C) KERENSKY is losing popularity, and it is doubtful if he can
last.

(D) Murder of officers continues freely. Cossacks are planning a
revolt.

(E) There will be no separate peace, but chaos and passive resistance on Russian front.

(F) Maugham asks if he can work with British intelligence officer
at Petrograd, thereby benefitting both and avoiding confusion. I see
no objection providing he does not disclose his connection with
officials at Washington. If D.M.I. agrees, I suggest he be put in touch
with KNOX, but positively not under him.

(G) I think Maugham ought to keep his ciphers and papers at
Embassy for security. He is very discreet and would not compromise
them, and may be useful as I believe he will soon have good organization there. Anyway I will cable you anything interesting he sends me.

[House Mss. File 20–46]

October 21, 1917.

Our chief agent in RUSSIA has cabled from Petrograd, under date
of October 16th, submitting a scheme for a Propaganda and Secret
Service organization in Russia to combat German influence.

You will remember that we sent him to Russia from here in July
for this purpose. We also sent at about the same time representatives
of Polish, Jugo-Slav, and Czech Societies in the United States. These
men—for the most part American citizens—are of undoubted loyalty
and have had considerable experience and success in defeating German plots in the United States. They went to Russia to get into touch
with similar organizations in Russia, and confer on the best method of
defeating the enormous and powerful German propaganda and Secret
Service in Russia. In the present unsettled state of Russia, the greatest
menace we have to face is the unseen German influence at work in
every phase of Russian political life. The Germans have got a great
start on us, and have no doubt a very complete organization. We may
never be able to equal them in efficiency. This should not deter us
from making the attempt, and we have found by experience that
German Secret Service methods can even be defeated by the more

honest, though possibly less efficient, means which we adopt. In any case it seems that we ought not to let them have a free field. We can at least hamper them, and may be in a position at the right moment to exercise considerable influence.

After careful investigation of the possibilities of an organization in Russia, our Chief Agent (who meantime has been sending us very accurate information regarding the political situation in Russia) reports as follows:—

He proposes, with the help of the above-mentioned leaders whom he brought from America, to make use of all and any societies and organizations in Russia which are anti-German in character. These will be dealt with separately and used for their own particular purpose. No one but the Chief Agent will know that they are all working under one direction; and even the Chief Agent himself does not know the people who are providing the necessary funds.

It is proposed, in the first place, to form a Slav Press Bureau, which will do legitimate propaganda business and serve as a centre and cover for other activities. Part of the expense of this orga nization wil be taken care of by the existing societies in Russia, and part should be paid by us.

Three departments will be formed under independent and competent leaders:

Department No. 1. will issue and distribute widely through various societies popular literature, well illustrated, in the chief languages used in Russia, together with certain news items from time to time received from the United States or Allied countries.

Department No. 2. will send speakers to all political meetings, to Church services, and throughout the army. It will also organize its own meetings wherever possible.

Department No. 3. will support the moderate Socialist party known as the MENSHEVICS. This party is opposed to the BOLSHEVICS, or extremists, and favors reorganization of the army, and energetic continuation of the war. It is, however, entirely Liberal and even Socialist in character, but its outstanding feature is anti-Prussian. This department will start a newspaper at the Front for distribution amongst the soldiers to counteract the very dangerous BOLSHEVIC newspaper which is now being published there.

Other friendly newspapers are prepared to assist, and a sort of anti-German Press Agency could be organized.

A second branch of the organization will concern Poles in Russia, and be run entirely by them, but supervised by our Chief Agent and partly financed by us. It will run on similar lines to the one above-described, but will naturally be chiefly Polish in character and sentiments. It can, however, be safely said that its activities will be entirely anti-German.

In addition to the above, special Secret organizations will be used, working separately and recruited from Poles, Czechs, and Cossacks. This organization will have as its chief object the unmasking of German plots and propaganda in Russia. It will be under the direction of the man who has been responsible for the unmasking of a great deal of the German and Austrian activities in the United States. Their agents should be everywhere in the pro-German pacifist societies— both in order to actually discover information which can be exposed by the patriotic party, and also to instil a feeling of fear and distrust among the German workers in Russia.

Our Chief Agent estimates that the total cost of all the above activities will be $500,000 per annum, but this is naturally an approximate calculation as it is very difficult to say where these activities will lead. I suggest that we should be prepared to finance same to the extent of half-a-million dollars a year, and judge by the results which he can show from time to time as to whether we consider it worth while to increase this subsidy, or to warn him to close down his organization.

I feel sure that the time will come when we shall want to get an organized movement among the Bohemian and Czech troops in Austria and the Polish troops in Germany; and I think this organization ought to provide the channel through which we can reach them. If the Polish Army which is being raised in the United States could appear on the Western Front with the Polish national flag, and simultaneously with their appearance a mutiny should occur among all the Polish soldiers serving in the German army, one can see that the effect might be absolutely disastrous to the German forces. If this could be made to synchronize with a rising of the Bohemians and Czechs in Austria, it should be overwhelming in effect. These things naturally take a good many months to organize, and there does not seem to be any better way of reaching these people than by the organization which we now have started in Russia. Our agent reports that communication with the enemy is comparatively easy through the Roumanian frontier, and such communication reaches both the Poles and the Czechs.

In conclusion, I would point out that the advantages of this movement would not only be the actual results which we could show, but the moral effect that it would have on the German military organization. If we could achieve only partial success it would shake their confidence, and be of considerable advantage to the Liberal Party in Germany, who are at heart in sympathy with the aspirations of the Polish and Bohemian people.

Appendix B

[Wiseman Mss. File 91–113]

January 19, 1918.

INTELLIGENCE & PROPAGANDA WORK IN RUSSIA
JULY TO DECEMBER 1917

In July 1917 it was decided to start an Intelligence and Propaganda service in Russia. The objects in view were to obtain accurate information as to the political situation and ascertain whether it was possible to support the more responsible elements in Russia. No attempt was to be made to support any reactionary movement, but it was thought it might be possible, to some extent, to 'guide the storm', and to expose the German political intrigues in Russia.

The difficulties under which this work started were tremendous. The Germans were before us in the field with a vast well-organized Secret Service, covering all chief Russian centres. The period over which our operations extended (July to December 1917) coincided with some of the greatest political changes in Russia.

In July last it appeared the best thing was to endeavour to induce all the moderate elements in the country to support the KERENSKY Government. We endeavoured to organize the Poles and Cossacks with this object. Early in October we organized a POLISH deputation which called on Kerensky to endeavour to persuade him to agree to the formation of an absolutely independent State under the guarantee of the Allies, with the capital at MINSK to be defended by Polish troops. Kerensky favoured the plan, but was too weak to put it into operation although the Poles themselves began to concentrate their forces at Minsk from that time on.

Similarly, our agents worked with KORNILOV and other COSSACK leaders to try and form a strong Cossack combination to support any Government which took a strong line about the War. This also failed owing to the hasty action of Kornilov and internal dissensions among Cossack groups.

One of our agents from America is a well-known international Socialist, & he was at once accepted by the BOLSHEVICS and admitted to their conferences. He challenged TROTZKY to a public discussion of the situation, which was accepted and the discussion took place in Petrograd at the beginning of November.

We took advantage of the presence of the AMERICAN MISSION in Europe to recall one of our chief agents to meet us in London for a conference. He left Petrograd 48 hours before the fall of Kerensky's Government—bringing with him messages from Kerensky to Lloyd George.[8]

Our agent reported the situation in Russia was entirely out of hand, and that no propaganda or organized support undertaken by the Allies could possibly stem the rising tide of Bolshevism. In the opinion of our agent it was by that time entirely too late to hope for any results from propaganda. Something he thought might still be done by supporting the Cossacks in their continuance of the war against Germany. After much discussion this plan was abandoned for military reasons.

We decided, therefore, in view of the state of affairs in Russia to withdraw our agents, and await a more favourable opportunity for action. It was by this time extremely difficult to communicate with all our agents, and the work of disbanding even the small organization created is not yet finished.

Attached are copies of various reports and suggestions for work in Russia which were submitted by our agents from time to time. These, however, must all be considered as out of date owing to changed conditions.

The question for decision now is: What should be our future policy? Our experience in the past seems to indicate that we ought to concentrate on some special object rather than attempt general political propaganda.

Attached is a memorandum on the new proposals.

[Wiseman Mss. File 91–105]

CABLEGRAM

N.G. —C.

Out

No. CXP. 524   Date: February 5, 1918.

Following for SIR ERIC DRUMMOND from W.W.:—

No. 50. STATE DEPARTMENT inform me that POLISH NATIONAL COMMITTEE have asked for 60,000 dollars a month subsidy for propaganda and intelligence work. ADRAMYTI has agreed to provide 30,000 dollars for a minimum of siz [sic] months if KONIA will do the same. Suggestion is that KNIA [sic] and HADEMKENI shall each appoint one unofficial representative to keep in touch with POLISH NATIONAL COMMITTEE to receive reports and give them questionaires. Will you please consult D.M.I. who knows about scheme and let me know if KONIA wish to co-operate. If you do I suggest SOMERSET MAUGHAM as a suitable man to go between London and Paris and keep in touch with ST. MIHIEL and other Poles.

The following material is a transcript of the interview which Maugham had with Kerensky in October 1917.[9] According to Maugham, the Russian leader's message was so secret that he would not put it in writing and he requested the author to deliver it to Lloyd George personally. Afraid that his stammer might ruin his delivery, Maugham wrote this report, and many years later he blamed himself for the Prime Minister's lack of response to Kerensky's requests.

Whatever Maugham's feelings about Lloyd George's indifference, the Bolshevik seizure of power shortly afterward made his report obsolete. Sir Eric Drummond's comment, written on the outside of the document on 18 November, aptly described the situation: 'I fear this of only historical interest now.'

Transcripts of documents in the Public Record Office appear by permission of the Controller of Her Majesty's Stationery Office.

[Public Record Office, Private Secretary Archives,
1917–1924, A. J. Balfour, FO 800/205]

I saw Kerensky on this evening of October 18th, O.S. He took me into a private room and made the following observations:—

(i). I wrote to Llord [sic] George about a fortnight ago and added a few lines with my own hand. I want you to repeat to him what I said.

I must make the Russian soldiers understand what they are fighting for. We haven't got boots or warm clothes or food. They have been fighting a year longer than England. They are tired out. We must give them something which will give them new heart and courage to go on. The Germans have made three offers of peace and we have refused them all. We ought to make our offer now. If we offer peace without annexations or compensations the Germans will refuse. The mass of population in Germany think they are winning. They will never give up the three islands in the Baltic. Our diplomacy is bad. We must be better diplomats. When the Germans refuse then I can go to my soldiers and say: 'You see, they don't want peace.' Then they will fight. They will fight to defend their country, but they won't fight to give Alsace-Lorraine to France. If we can have something like that in three months we shall have a good army, smaller than now, but with the help of the Allies adequately equipped. If something of this sort is not done, when the cold weather comes, I don't think I shall be able to keep the army in the trenches. I don't see how we can go on. Of course, I don't say that to the people. I always say that we shall continue whatever happens, but unless I have something to tell my army it's impossible.

(ii). The Allies must help us with guns and ammunition. When I go down to the front the generals say to me: 'What are the Allies doing for us? They send us nothing.' In the advance in March we had to stop because the Allies had not sent us the ammunition we wanted. They send us a little, and there they stop, and then they send us a little more. What we want is regular supplies that we can count on.

(iii). It is very important that the newspapers should treat Russia's affairs sympathetically. They have nothing but criticism. Why does the *Times* let a man like Hilton represent it? He has only done harm to Russia. By writing the things they do the correspondents only help the Bolsheviks. They have done a great deal to persuade the people that the Allies are thinking of making peace at the expense of Russia. It would be a good thing if you could see the editors of papers and tell them of the difficulties of the government, and say to them that if they will support Russia, they will sow their own interests. Russia wants sympathy and confidence and a little money.

(iv). The environment of the Ambassador does not seem able to get into sympathetic relations with the new conditions, and the information that reaches the ambassador through these channels is prejudiced. It would be a good thing if this environment could be changed. I have the highest opinion of the Ambassador, and he is a perfectly honest man. He tries very hard to judge things for himself. He has a great prestige with the government, but if they could send someone of the type of M. Thomas it would be good for Russia and good for England. The Ambassador is identified with the old regime. It would be better if we had someone who was more sympathetic to present conditions. The military advisers of the Ambassador, though certainly well acquainted with the technical side of their business, have no understanding of present circumstances. They understand nothing of the political situation.

Appendix C

Five Fictional Portraits of
Somerset Maugham

Somerset Maugham's practice of borrowing from life to create fictional characters is well-known. At various times, he sketched the Sidney Colvins, Sir Edmund Gosse, Stephen Phillips, Maxine Elliott, Violet Hunt and Hugh Walpole, as well as countless people who were not among the famous. Maugham's notoriety about portraying those he encountered was such that Edgar Lustgarten, commenting about a job in Singapore, could quip: 'I'm not applying—there's nothing to do at Singapore except sit on your backside and wait three or four years for Somerset Maugham to turn up and write a short story about you.'[1] The portraits could be affectionate, satiric, or cruel, but the author never doubted the justification of drawing upon the personalities of real people.

It is not generally known, however, that on a number of occasions Maugham has himself been portrayed in works of fiction: Ada Leverson's *The Limit* (1911), Elinor Mordaunt's *Gin and Bitters* (1931), Hugh Walpole's *John Cornelius* (1937), S. N. Behrman's *Jane* (1952), and Noël Coward's *A Song at Twilight* (1966). These impressions vary in depth and directness, but all bar one are fairly accurate pictures. They are worthy of consideration because, as long as it is remembered that they are placed in a fictional setting, they provide interesting speculations on Maugham's character. They represent the author as seen at various stages of his life by perceptive fellow writers, and, despite the idiosyncrasies of each viewpoint, they contribute to an understanding of him.

Ada Leverson met the young Maugham in the early years of this century, and they became good friends (Yale University possesses thirty-eight letters written to her by Maugham between 1908 and 1910). She had already been an admirer of *Liza of Lambeth* and she later considered *Of Human Bondage* to be a masterpiece. Struck by the shy, dark-eyed young man who had four plays running simultaneously in London, she saw the opportunity of sketching him in her novel, *The Limit*, as 'Gilbert Hereford Vaughan', known to a few intimate friends as 'Gillie'.

The portrait is accurate. 'Hereford Vaughan' is thirty-four, quiet, reserved and modest in spite of his amazing success as a dramatist. His opinion of play-writing is flippant: 'It's perfectly easy really . . . it's just a knack.' He is willing to forgive anything, as long as it 'amuses' him. He is 'rather secretive and mysterious than blatant or dashing', and this makes him more interesting to women. Leverson's description of Vaughan at a party is remarkably similar to the Maugham *persona*'s description of himself at literary parties in *The Moon and Sixpence*:

Hereford Vaughan, who was an object of considerable curiosity to several of the guests on account of his phenomenal success in having eleven plays at the same time being performed in London, New York, Berlin, Paris, and every other European city, was, to those who did not know him before, an agreeable surprise. Heaven knows what exactly people expected of him; perhaps the men feared "side" and the women that he would be over-powering after so many triumphs, but he was merely a rather pale, dark, and rather handsome young man. He behaved like anybody else, except that perhaps his manner was a little quieter than the average. Unless one was very observant (which one isn't), or unless one listened to what he said, he did not at first appear to be alarmingly clever. He had one or two characteristics which must have at times led to misunderstandings. One was that whatever or whoever he looked at, his dark opaque eyes were so full of vivid expression that women often mistook for admiration what was often merely observation. For instance, when he glanced at Lady Walmer she at once became quite confused and intensely flattered, nearly blushed and asked him to dinner. While, if she had but known, behind that dark glance was merely the thought, "So that's the woman that Royalty. . . . What extraordinary taste!"[2]

Vaughan's bachelorhood leads to a great deal of speculation that he has had a tragic love affair or that he is secretly married. Leverson, however, reveals that he often leaves his flat in Belgravia and drives up to a pub, 'The Bald-Faced Stag in Edgeware', where he enjoys the company of the publican's daughter, Gladys. He eventually proposes to her, but she rejects him because she is engaged to the son of another publican. Alluding to Maugham's theory that the unattainable is the most desired, Leverson adds: 'This ungratified wish was, in all his full life with its brilliant success, perhaps his greatest real pleasure.'

There is a temptation to see this encounter with an illiterate daughter of an inn-keeper as a reflection of an episode in Maugham's life. It is much more probable, however, that Leverson was enjoying a joke on her friend. He had shown a propensity to write about attractive lower-class girls—in *Liza of Lambeth*, *A Man of Honour*, and *The Merry-Go-Round*—and this part of *The Limit* may have been a burlesque of this tendency. In most other respects, however, Leverson's portrait is accurate, and it gives an interesting picture of the author at the time of his sudden popularity as a dramatist.

Gin and Bitters, written by Elinor Mordaunt in 1931 under the pseudonym of 'A. Riposte', was intended to be a reply in kind to *Cakes and Ale*. It is vitriolic, clumsy and inaccurate, and it fails entirely to expose Maugham as an unscrupulous literary hack. Its attack lacks subtlety and wit, and the language too often becomes melodramatic:

> Leverson Hurle was a small dark man, proud of his smallness; rather sallow; showing, even then, yellow pouches under his dark eyes: eyes as sad and disillusioned as those of a sick monkey.[3]

> He was very young and far less yellow than he was in later days, when there were people who said that he secreted bile, as snakes secrete poison in their fangs: the bile of sheer venom. His eyes were very black, like currants in an under-baked bun, or tea cake.[4]

Unlike Ada Leverson, Elinor Mordaunt did not know Maugham personally, and *Gin and Bitters* is therefore a fabrication on a few scraps of literary gossip. The story parallels Maugham's, but frequently strays far from plausibility. The author, 'Leverson Hurle', has an affair with an illiterate cockney girl, 'Lizzie', whom he uses in his first book, published during the Boer War. When this relationship dissolves, he marries a divorcée with whom he has been having an affair, 'Mrs Cynthia Stoddard' (presumably meant to be Syrie Wellcome). Bored with London society, Hurle sets out for the South Seas, stopping first in Paris and then Marseilles to 'collect local colour' for his new book (clearly *The Moon and Sixpence*). Mordaunt emphasises that Hurle's only talent lies in recording what he has seen:

> He used people without any sort of scruple: accepted their hospitality and kindness, and put them bodily – their most private affairs, their loves and hates and sorrows – into his books. For though he was acclaimed as a great writer he was quite unable to work without someone actual to work upon.[5]

After completing his book in Tahiti, Hurle moves on to Singapore, where his observation of a casual affair between a high government official and the wife of a junior administrator is turned to good use as a novel (*The Painted Veil*). Mordaunt explains that Hurle's wife's dog destroyed the first three chapters, 'and that, and that alone, is the reason why this particular book begins, as it does begin, in the very thick of things'. Hurle and his wife finally separate and, after years of using people and becoming more alienated as a result, he dies unlamented by those who knew him.

Gin and Bitters is an undistinguished novel, and it would be forgotten if it were not for the sensation which surrounded its appearance in the United States and the attempts to publish it in Britain. It is too feeble to exist apart from its satiric purpose, and that satire is blunt and exaggerated. The author clearly tries to pillory Maugham, but her portrait of Hurle has not the skill of a caricature. Satiric representations depend upon the recognition of the follies and vices, albeit exaggerated, of the subject, and there is little of Maugham's real character in Hurle.

Hugh Walpole, made wretched by Maugham's portrait of him as 'Alroy Kear' in *Cakes and Ale*, in turn drew Maugham in *John Cornelius: His Life and Adventures* (1937). Maugham is here represented as 'Archie Bertrand', a writer who has had great success in the theatre. He is a cynic who constantly expresses disbelief in men's virtues—their love, loyalty and sincerity. Walpole writes:

He is, both in his outward self and in his books, a cynic, a pessimist, a man who sees things exactly as they are. He is apparently a modest man who writes as he can a simple English style and tells the truth about the little bit of life that he has seen.

But within, Bertrand is, I think, self-assured, rather arrogant and deeply sentimental. He is, in fact, the man whom Rose tries to be in his writings, while Bertrand's writings have the cynicism that is in reality deeply embedded in Rose's character.

Bertrand, in his plays, his novels, his stories, his books of travel, has every gift but genius. Genius is something that is greater and more accountable than its possessor. But Bertrand has complete command of his gifts and can write only of what he has personally encountered. He has a fine narrative gift, humour, drama and a philosophy that is neither as original nor as true as he thinks it is. He is more delightful to read than any of his contemporaries, but he does not give joy in retrospect. Joy and loving compassion are elements in life altogether omitted from his work.[6]

If there is any passage which is a reference to Maugham's portrait of Walpole in *Cakes and Ale*, it is where Walpole describes Bertrand's tendency to draw from real life. 'Rose', who seems to be a self-portrait, has been talking to Bertrand, and this brings a warning from the narrator:

"I'm afraid you're for it," I cried.
"How?" asked Rose.
"You'll be in Bertrand's next novel. I always know when Bertrand is taking notes."
"I don't care. Bertrand and I are the greatest friends."
"That makes no difference."[7]

John Cornelius, however, was not intended to be Walpole's revenge for *Cakes and Ale*. 'Archie Bertrand', although definitely incorporating a number of Maugham's characteristics, is only part of the

L

literary background of the novel, and he is not set apart as a special
target.

When S. N. Behrman adapted Maugham's short story 'Jane' for
the stage (it was first produced in 1946) he converted the first person
narrator into a character, 'Willie Tower', who is clearly a representation of Maugham. Tower is a cynical, well-travelled English writer,
with a daughter and a marriage that has failed. His daughter,
describing him as 'opaque', calls him 'my fascinating, remote father',
and his wife complains that 'you retire behind that mask'. Like
Maugham, Tower claims: 'I do not have to wait for old age to know
loneliness. I have known it since I was a child.' Behrman has given
his character many other Maugham qualities—his lack of faith that
people will be better than they are, his detachment, his belief that his
career has been the victory of character over circumstances, and his
faith that 'there are very few calamities in life in which the possession
of money is not a mitigation'.

In many places, Behrman touches upon intimate matters of
Maugham's life which were not yet public knowledge. In one remarkable passage Mrs Tower says: 'my daughter—yes, and your daughter
too, Willie—though you won't acknowledge it—'. Referring to his
marriage, Tower anticipates what Maugham was to claim later:

I have made very serious mistakes in my life, Jane. Many of them have
come from my abnormal inability to cause other people pain. The truth is,
my marriage with Millicent was no good the moment it occurred – even
before.[8]

Jane is remarkable because of the intimate nature of a number of
the characteristics of Willie Tower, and in retrospect it is amazing
that it did not create a greater stir. Even though Basil Rathbone
played Tower as a Maugham impersonation, the critics seem not to
have noticed the hints at Maugham's own problems. In the light of
Maugham's public revelations sixteen years later, it seems likely that
Behrman created his portrait in *Jane* out of what the author had told
him privately years before.

Sir Noël Coward has created several characters who are to a large
degree based on Maugham. *South Sea Bubble* (1956) contains John
Blair-Kennedy, 'a novelist of some repute' whose novels are 'awfully
cynical . . . and none of his characters seem to believe in anything.
They're amusing . . . in a flippant way.'

Earlier, in *Point Valaine* (1935), which is dedicated to Maugham,
Coward had painted a more precise portrait. Mortimer Quinn, an
eminent writer, has 'a certain dry aloofness in his manner but in spite
of his enviable detachment he is quite amiable and polite'. His

preference in writing is for subtle drama, 'strange little twists in psychology—small unaccountable happenings in people's minds'. Like Blair-Kennedy (and, interestingly, like Maugham's own literary *persona*), Quinn is really only present as an observer and commentator. His description of his role could almost equally apply to Maugham:

You see I always affect to despise human nature. My role in life is so clearly marked. Cynical, detached, unscrupulous, an ironic observer and recorder of other people's passions. It is a nice façade to sit behind, but a trifle bleak. Perhaps I am misunderstood. I often toy with that idea. Perhaps I have suffered a great deal and am really a very lonely, loving spirit.[9]

This final observation is developed at considerable length in *A Song at Twilight* (1966), the first attempt since Maugham's death to treat the conflicts and paradoxes in his life. Although there are a number of dissimilarities—the ageing writer, unlike Maugham, has been knighted and is married—much of the story is unmistakably Maugham's. Coward himself played the part of the author, and he was deliberately made up to look like the 'Old Party'.

Coward, an observant, long-standing friend of Maugham, uses many of the old man's habits and obsessions. 'Sir Hugo Latymer' is a distinguished man of seventy, in transition from the author of many best-sellers to 'the Grand Old Man of Letters'. His studied calmness irritates those around him, and it seems that he has made 'a private vow to remain Captain of his Soul no matter what emotional hurricanes he might encounter'. Like Maugham, Latymer responds to trivial annoyances by adopting the role of the enfeebled and deliberately ancient man. Like Maugham, Latymer professes to be merely an observer, not a judge:

I prefer to see people as they are rather than as more sentimental minds would wish them to be. However, I am a commentator, not a moralist. I state no preferences.[10]

At one point, another character voices a criticism of Latymer which is Coward's own opinion of Maugham:

I would never suspect you of missing a trick. Except perhaps the most important of all. . . . The knack of discovering the best in people's characters instead of the worst.[11]

This is echoed in what Coward wrote of Maugham in his introduction to Kanin's *Remembering Mr Maugham* in 1966: 'He believed—rather proudly, I think—that he had no illusions about people, but in fact he had one major one and that was that they were no good.'

A Song at Twilight is a problem comedy in which a figure from the past threatens to reveal that the aged distinguished author has all his life been a homosexual. It shows that the conflict in Latymer between his natural inclinations and the dictates of society has made him emotionally crabbed and unable to respond with genuine feeling.

The play opens as Latymer receives a visit from 'Carlotta Gray', a woman with whom he has had an affair in the past. It seems here that Coward based her on Maugham's account in 'Looking Back' of the woman who was the original of 'Rosie'. Carlotta comes to seek Latymer's permission to publish his letters to her, and when he refuses she blackmails him with the threat that she will publish his love letters to his deceased former secretary—'the only true love of your life'. The secretary, 'Perry Sheldon', described as 'foolish, conceited, dishonest and self-indulgent', is clearly Gerald Haxton, Maugham's former secretary, and his death from alcoholism matches the real situation. It is difficult to establish how much truth there is in Coward's version of the secretary's final years, but his description of Latymer's shame-fully brief tribute to his secretary in his autobiography is almost identical to Maugham's references to Haxton. Carlotta claims:

He loved you, looked after you and waited on you hand and foot. For years he travelled the wide world with you. And yet in your book you dismiss him in a few lines as an "adequate secretary".[12]

Maugham's description of Haxton was that he was 'a very useful companion'.[13]

There are further references to Maugham's notorious auto-biography, particularly in regard to its protestations of many healthy heterosexual relationships. Carlotta questions this suspicious emphasis in Latymer's autobiography:

But why the constant implications of heterosexual ardour? Why those self-conscious, almost lascivious references to laughing-eyed damsels with scarlet lips and pointed breasts?[14]

The play is a progression of attacks on Latymer, and he is ultimately revealed as a bankrupt soul. He is accused of moral cowardice in his lifelong denial of his homosexuality. He points out that homosexual conduct at this time is still a penal offence in England (and Maugham's memories of the Wilde trial may have left him with a fear of imprisonment on these grounds), and then he argues that even the removal of this law will not eliminate the stigma that the public attaches to homosexuality.

Carlotta also accuses him of complacent cruelty, of exploiting people:

You used me. You used me and betrayed me as you've always used and betrayed every human being who has ever shown you the slightest sign of true affection.

Hugo. In what way did I use you any more than you used me?
Carlotta. You waved me like a flag to prove a fallacy.
Hugo. What fallacy?
Carlotta. That you were normal, that your morals were orderly, that you were, in fact, a "regular guy".[15]

Finally, Coward makes it clear that Latymer has himself paid the greatest price for his hypocrisy. The constant strain of having to live up to an image implanted in the public mind has destroyed his capacity for intimacy and genuine feeling. Unable to come to terms with his own nature, he has become a spiritual wreck, totally isolated behind his professional façade. Carlotta again speaks of his incapacity:

He has never taken into account the value of kindness and the importance of compassion. He has never had the courage or the humility to face the fact that it was not whom he loved in his life that really mattered but his own capacity for loving.[16]

Of all these attempts to render Maugham into fiction, *A Song at Twilight* perhaps gives the greatest real insight into his personality. While the other writers are in varying degrees successful in capturing the surface appearance, Coward attempts sympathetically to explain some of the most ingrained conflicts and obsessions in Maugham's enigmatic life. Were Coward inclined to literary biography, these theories would likely have formed the basis of a valuable study. In its own way, and with the obvious limitations of its form, *A Song at Twilight* provides worthwhile observations of Maugham by one who knew him for nearly fifty years.

Appendix D

Images of Bondage and Freedom

Examined in their entirety, Maugham's works contain over three hundred images concerned with liberty or enslavement. These can be classified into seven or eight fairly well-defined groups, and some of these occur with great frequency. The adoption of certain images for particular kinds of bondage explains something of the author's attitudes to various manifestations of imprisonment.

The most common type of image found in Maugham's writing is that of the figure in chains, fetters, or shackles. The picture here is of the character who, through ignorance, conventionality or passion, finds himself chained or bound, like a prisoner in jail or in the stocks. The language used to convey this is liberally sprinkled with 'fetters', 'bonds', 'ties', 'manacles' and 'shackles'. There are many instances: 'You can't imagine what are the chains that bind us in England' (*The Hero*); 'there are some chains that having broken you can never weld together; and no fetters are so intolerable as the fetters of love' (*Mrs Craddock*); 'He remembered very vividly the violence of the emotions which had possessed him and his inability, as if he were tied down to the ground with ropes, to react against it' (*Of Human Bondage*). In some cases, the image of the character bound is invested with the sensation of pain: 'they [ties] burn the wrist like fetters of fire' (*The Hero*); or 'I feel as though chains were eating into my flesh, and I want to get free' (*The Merry-Go-Round*).

The second most common type of image is that which evokes the picture of a prison or jail. Here the figure is placed in circumstances where he is restricted from exercising his independence or where he is cut off from contact with the rest of the world. His means of imprisonment may be environment, oppression, social pressures, or emotional obsession: 'Why are you so eager to detain me when my soul yearns to escape from the prison in which it has dwelt for so long?' (*Catalina*); 'the ten commandments hedged one round with the menace of hellfire and eternal damnation, a dungeon more terrible because it had not walls, nor bars and bolts' (*Mrs Craddock*); 'His love became a prison from which he longed to escape, but he had not the strength to merely open the door—that was all it needed—and walk out into the open air' ('Red'). A related device is the metaphor or simile evoking a picture of a trapped animal—a rat, a hare, and most frequently a bird: 'I'm like a trapped hare' (*Catalina*); 'I felt like a bird struggling in the net' (*Don Fernando*); or 'James was indeed a bird beating himself against the imprisoning cage' (*The Hero*).

Maugham often uses an image of the character being confined, oppressed, or smothered. This usually suggests a form of physical oppression, the figure developing claustrophobic feelings about a particular social environment or suffering a physiological reaction to an imagined constraint: 'his home affected him like a hot-house' (*The Hero*); 'the air was close with servitude' (*The Hero*); 'and the dull stupidity of it just chokes me, so that I pant for the fresh air' (*The Merry-Go-Round*).

The picture of slavery, of the master and the servant, occurs in Maugham's writings with considerable frequency. Most often, it is used in connection with romantic or sexual infatuation, but it can also be found to describe such relationships as Strickland's to his art and James Parsons' to village life: 'They are as little their own masters as the slaves chained to the benches of a galley' (*The Moon and Sixpence*); and 'He had looked forward to a sensation of freedom such as a man might feel when he had escaped from some tyrannous servitude' (*The Hero*).

Maugham seems to have been particularly fond of another image of human bondage—that of the puppet or automaton which is totally at the mercy of stronger powers. This device is used effectively to convey the feeling of the character's lack of free will, of having his life controlled by forces beyond him: 'he found himself powerless in the hands of a greater might, and Fate, for once grown ghastly visible, directed each step as though he were a puppet' (*The Merry-Go-Round*); or 'they wished him to always dance to their piping—a marionette of which they pulled the strings' (*The Hero*).

Maugham also uses the image of a disease, madness, or spiritual possession which dominates the individual. This is often used to illustrate the power of love or sexual attraction, and it also communicates the impression of subjection to control by sinister forces: 'This love has been a loathesome cancer in my heart' (*East of Suez*); and 'I asked myself whether there was not in his soul some deep-rooted instinct of creation ... which grew relentlessly, as a cancer may grow in the living tissues, till at last it took possession of his whole being and forced him irresistibly to action' (*The Moon and Sixpence*).

In addition to these groups of images, there are numerous others which do not lend themselves to easy classification. In several instances, for example, Maugham uses the figure of the policeman to represent the restraints of conventional society. On occasion, he draws upon a picture of birds in flight to represent a soul at liberty. Also, throughout his writing, the sea is used both as a means of escape and as a symbol of spiritual freedom.

In general, Maugham's use of figurative language is neither original nor successful. Examined as a whole, it is obvious that he returned with great frequency to a few favourite images, so much so that they become clichés to which it was all too easy to turn, and with some themes and situations there is too much predictability about the language which he will use. In some cases a well-worn image is made to carry the weight of communicating a state of mind or atmosphere which warrants more subtle treatment. Here the cliché, rather than extending the reader's understanding, tends to eliminate further imaginative exploration.

With his usual candour, of course, Maugham recognised his limitations regarding figurative language; he readily admitted that any strength he had lay elsewhere, and it appears that he consciously laboured to avoid exposing his weakness. Viewed chronologically, a pattern definitely emerges which reveals a move away from the use of superficial imagery. The greatest concentration of figurative language clearly lies in the writing which appeared between 1897 and 1915. *The Hero*, *Mrs Craddock*, and *The Merry-Go-Round* are especially luxuriant, and this is understandable considering that this was the period in which Maugham was attempting to write in the style of the aesthetes. With *Of Human Bondage*, however, this kind of imagery begins to become less noticeable and, with some exceptions, the progression from here is toward more subtle language. *Cakes and Ale*, for example, contains almost no imagery of the type analysed here, yet it is very much concerned with the theme of liberty and repression. Maugham here achieves his most effective form of expression, and it is one which is free of attempts at apt metaphors and similes.

Notes

Note: References to Maugham's works are to the Heinemann (London) editions. Reference to the Doubleday (New York) editions follow in brackets.

Chapter I. Biographical Introduction

1 As quoted by Leslie Rees, 'Remembrance of Things Past: A Meeting With Somerset Maugham', *Meanjin Quarterly*, Vol. XXVI, No. 4, Summer Number, 1967, p. 453.
2 Robin Maugham to R. L. Calder, 27 September, 1969.
3 *The Traveller's Library*, Doubleday, Doran, 1933, p. 6.
4 *Somerset and All the Maughams*, London, Longmans–Heinemann, 1966, p. 105.
5 *Ibid.*, p. 120.
6 *A Writer's Notebook*, Heinemann, 1949, p. 261. (Doubleday, 1949, p. 274.)
7 As quoted by Robin Maugham, *Somerset and All the Maughams*, p. 121.
8 'Some Novelists I Have Known', *The Vagrant Mood*, Heinemann, 1952, pp. 232–233. (Doubleday, 1953, pp. 241–242.)
9 Lord Clark to R. L. Calder, 15 September, 1969.
10 'Looking Back', *Show*, Vol. II, No. 6, June, 1962, p. 64.
11 As quoted by Robin Maugham, *Somerset and All the Maughams*, p. 117.
12 *A Writer's Notebook*, p. xv. (p. xv.)
13 *The Land of the Blessed Virgin: Sketches and Impressions in Andalusia*, Heinemann, 1905, p. 51.
14 Preface to the revised edition of *Mrs Craddock*, Heinemann, 1955, p. xi.
15 *A Writer's Notebook*, pp. 84–85. (p. 89.)
16 *Somerset Maugham: A Biographical and Critical Study*, London, Heinemann, 1961, p. 24.
17 *Remembering Mr Maugham*, New York, Atheneum, 1966, pp. 272–273.
18 *The Summing Up*, Heinemann, 1938, p. 177. (Doubleday, Doran, 1938, p. 173.)
19 As quoted by Hamilton Basso, 'Very Old Party', *New Yorker*, 30 December, 1944, p. 26.

20 As quoted by Klaus W. Jonas, 'The Gentleman From Cap Ferrat', in *The World of Somerset Maugham*, ed. K. W. Jonas, London, Peter Owen, 1959, p. 34.

21 *Chronicles of Barabbas – 1884–1934*, Toronto, George J. MacLeod, 1935, p. 153.

22 'Maugham: Compassionate Cynic', *Sunday Times*, 19 December, 1965, p. 35.

23 'Somerset Maugham', *The Observer*, 19 December, 1965, p. 22.

24 *The Summing Up*, pp. 99–100. (p. 97.)

25 *A Case of Human Bondage*, London, Secker and Warburg, 1966, p. 103.

26 Lord Clark to R. L. Calder, 15 September, 1969.

27 As quoted by Hamilton Basso, 'Very Old Party', *New Yorker*, 30 December, 1944, p. 24.

28 *Ibid.*, p. 24.

29 *Afterthoughts*, London, Constable, 1931, p. 31. This copy is now in the Maugham Library in King's School, Canterbury.

30 Sir Gerald Kelly to R. L. Calder, 9 September, 1969.

31 As quoted by Kelly, 'Old Friends', *Sunday Times*, 24 January, 1954, p. 6.

32 As quoted by Kanin, *Remembering Mr Maugham*, p. 182.

33 Library of Congress, Washington, D.C., Rare Book Collection, Portfolio 306, No. 5a.

34 Harold Acton, in Sir Julian Hall's 'Somerset Maugham in the Theatre', a talk on BBC Radio 3, 2 October, 1969.

35 *Swinnerton: An Autobiography*, New York, Doubleday, Doran, 1936, p. 270.

36 The British Museum, Add. Ms. 46465, p. 129.

37 Frederick Herbert Maugham, 1st Viscount Maugham of Hartfield (1866–1958).

38 Robin Maugham to R. L. Calder, 27 September, 1969.

39 'Somerset Maugham', *The Observer*, 19 December, 1965, p. 22.

40 *The Summing Up*, p. 80. (p. 78.)

41 'Looking Back', *Show*, July, 1962, p. 98.

42 *The Two Worlds of Somerset Maugham*, Los Angeles, Sherbourne Press, 1965, p. 169.

43 According to Compton Mackenzie (*My Life and Times: Octave Four*, London, Chatto and Windus, 1965, p. 233), Brooks, Benson and Maugham each paid a share of the Villa Cercola on Capri, which had become the refuge for many homosexuals after the Wilde case, and Maugham went there regularly in the summer.

44 *A Case of Human Bondage*, p. 19.

45 *The Infirm Glory*, London, Michael Joseph, 1967, p. 263.

46 *Ibid.*, p. 264.

47 *A Case of Human Bondage*, pp. 144–145.

48 *Somerset and All the Maughams*, p. 201.

49 'Maugham the Merrier', *Sunday Times*, 30 August, 1970, p. 9.

50 *A Writer's Notebook*, p. 245. (p. 258.)

51 *The Summing Up*, pp. 297–298. (pp. 290–291.)

52 *A Writer's Notebook*, p. 337. (pp. 353–354.)
53 *Strictly Personal*, Heinemann, 1942, p. 154. (Doubleday, Doran, 1941, p. 216.)
54 'Looking Back on Eighty Years: We are Freer', *The Reporter*, Vol. X, 25 May, 1954, p. 34.
55 *The Partial View*, Heinemann, 1954, pp. ix–x.
56 As quoted by Sheridan Morley, *A Talent to Amuse*, London, Heinemann, 1969, p. 302.
57 'Looking Back', *Show*, August, 1962, p. 100.
58 As quoted by F. A. Beaumont, 'Luck in Authorship', *John O'London's Weekly*, Vol. XXX, No. 756, 7 October, 1933, p. 4.
59 As quoted by John Cruesemann, 'Some New Short Stories by Somerset Maugham', *Daily Express*, 4 October, 1958, p. 4.
60 'Somerset Maugham Sums Up', *Daily Express*, 20 January, 1958, p. 3.
61 *The Summing Up*, p. 308. (pp. 300–301.)
62 *Ibid.*, p. 316. (p. 309.)
63 *A Writer's Notebook*, p. 153. (p. 160.)
64 *Portraits and Self-Portraits*, ed. George Schreiber, Boston, Houghton Mifflin, 1936, p. 97.
65 'Somerset Maugham', *The New Statesman*, Vol. XV, No. 383, 14 August, 1920, p. 525.
66 'Maugham and the Two Myths', in *The Maugham Enigma*, ed. K. W. Jonas, London, Peter Owen, 1954, p. 158.
67 *Years in a Mirror*, London, The Bodley Head, 1965, pp. 178–179.
68 *The Summing Up*, p. 180. (pp. 175–176.)

Chapter II. *Liza of Lambeth* and the Novels of Misery

1 Preface to *Liza of Lambeth*, Collected Edition, Heinemann, 1934, pp. vii–viii.
2 The British Museum, Add. Ms. 46465, p. 262.
3 'The Record of Badalia Herodsfoot', in *Many Inventions*, London, Macmillan and Company, 1913, p. 316.
4 *A Child of the Jago*, London, Nelson and Sons, 1894, p. 93.
5 'The Record of Badalia Herodsfoot', p. 308.
6 *Liza of Lambeth*, p. 165. (Doran, 1921, p. 213.)
7 *L'Influence du Naturalism Française sur les Romanciers Anglais de 1885 à 1900*, Paris, Marcel Giard, 1925, pp. 185–186.
8 As quoted by Jocelyn Bell, 'A Study of Arthur Morrison', in *Essays and Studies for the English Association*, London, John Murray, 1952, p. 18.
9 Morrison, 'What is a Realist?', *The New Review*, Vol. XVI, 1897, p. 330.
10 *The Bookman*, Vol. XIV, October, 1897, p. 23.
11 *Of Human Bondage*, Heinemann, 1915, p. 606. (Doran, 1915, p. 606.)
12 *Liza of Lambeth*, pp. 2–3. (pp. 8–9.)
13 Francis Hackett, *The New Republic*, Vol. XXVIII, No. 359, 19 October, 1921, p. 221.

14 This idea was developed in an unpublished paper on Maugham and Morrison by R. D. Chambers, Department of English Literature, Trent University, Peterborough, Ontario, Canada.
15 *Liza of Lambeth*, p. 59. (p. 78.)
16 *Ibid.*, p. 101. (p. 131.)
17 *Ibid.*, p. 6. (p. 13.)
18 *Ibid.*, p. 8. (p. 15.)
19 *Ibid.*, p. 109. (p. 142.)
20 *Ibid.*, pp. 134–135. (p. 176.)
21 *Ibid.*, p. 153. (p. 199.)

Chapter III. Seven Early Novels: Experiments and Potboilers

1 Preface to *Liza of Lambeth*, p. xviii.
2 Cordell, *Somerset Maugham*, p. 116.
3 Robin Maugham, *Somerset and All the Maughams*, p. 138.
4 *The Making of a Saint*, London, T. Fisher Unwin, 1898, p. 167.
5 *The Development of William Somerset Maugham*, Columbia University doctoral dissertation, 1953, Ann Arbor, Michigan, University Microfilms, publication 6651.
6 *The Hero*, London, Hutchinson, 1901, p. 46.
7 *Ibid.*, p. 96.
8 *Ibid.*, p. 207.
9 *Ibid.*, pp. 247–248.
10 *Ibid.*, pp. 238–239.
11 *Ibid.*, p. 240.
12 *Ibid.*, p. 335.
13 *Ibid.*, pp. 249–250.
14 *Ibid.*, p. 335. Psychologically and spiritually, *The Hero* is fairly closely autobiographical, James' attitude to life in Little Primpton reflecting the young Maugham's view of the life he knew in Kent. These pastoral descriptions, for example, are echoed in *A Writer's Notebook* (pp. 44–46).
15 'Mr. W. S. Maugham's New Novel', *The Bookman*, Vol. XXIII, No. 135, December, 1902, p. 108.
16 'William Somerset Maugham', in his *Gods of Modern Grub Street*, Toronto, Musson Book Company, 1904, p. 213.
17 'W. Somerset Maugham, Playwright and Novelist', *The Bookman*, Vol. LVII, No. 337, October, 1919, p. 12.
18 *Somerset Maugham*, p. 117.
19 *Mrs Craddock*, Heinemann, 1902, pp. 13–14. (Doran, n.d., p. 19.)
20 *Ibid.*, p. 60. (pp. 62–63.)
21 *Ibid.*, p. 129. (p. 146.)
22 *Ibid.*, p. 227. (p. 266.)
23 For 'Court Leys' Maugham drew upon his boyhood experience and described 'Court Lees', an estate a few miles south of Whitstable.

24 Maugham has frequently expressed his admiration for Jonathan Swift and has admitted the influence on his style. This passage, 'The Idyll of Corydon and Phyllis', with its strong eighteenth-century flavour, may owe its inspiration to Swift's pastoral burlesques, particularly the astringent 'unprintable' poems.

25 Preface to *Liza of Lambeth*, p. xxiii.

26 *Somerset Maugham: A Guide*, London, Oliver and Boyd, 1965, p. 18.

27 *The Merry-Go-Round*, Heinemann, 1904, p. 73.

28 *Ibid.*, p. 92.

29 *Ibid.*, pp. 387–388.

30 *Ibid.*, p. 103.

31 *Ibid.*, p. 394.

32 *Athenaeum*, No. 4093, 7 April, 1906, p. 417.

33 *The Bookman*, Vol. XXX, April, 1906, p. 36.

34 *Somerset Maugham: A Guide*, p. 22.

35 Preface to *Liza of Lambeth*, p. xv.

36 *Somerset Maugham: A Bibliography*, London, Nicholas Vane, 1956, p. 126.

37 *Novels of Empire*, New York, Columbia University Press, 1949, p. 8.

38 Although *The Explorer* is so very unlike 'Heart of Darkness', there is an echo of Conrad's theme in Maugham's description of what happens to lesser men than MacKenzie:

Alec had seen so many men lose their heads under the influence of that climate. The feeling of an authority that seemed so limited, over a race that was manifestly inferior, the subtle magic of the hot sunshine, the vastness, the remoteness from civilisation, were very apt to throw a man off his balance. The French had coined a name for the distemper and called it *folie d'Afrique*. Men seemed to go mad from a sense of power, to lose all the restraints which had kept them in the way of righteousness. (*The Explorer*, Heinemann, 1908, p. 180. Doran, n.d., p. 180.)

39 *Athenaeum*, No. 4184, 4 January, 1908, p. 9.

40 *The Saturday Review*, Vol. CV, No. 2729, 15 February, 1908, p. 209.

41 *Novels of Empire*, p. 24.

42 *The Explorer*, p. 45. (p. 45.)

43 *The Explorer*, p. 277. (p. 277.)

44 'Somerset Maugham', *The New Statesman and Nation*, Vol. XIX, No. 486, 15 June, 1940, p. 750.

45 *The Nation*, Vol. LXXXVIII, No. 2280, 11 March, 1909, p. 255.

46 *The Saturday Review*, Vol. CVI, No. 2774, 26 December, 1908, p. 798.

47 *Athenaeum*, No. 4232, 5 December, 1908, p. 715.

48 *The Development of William Somerset Maugham.*

49 Edward Alexander Crowley (1875–1947).

50 'A Fragment of Autobiography', in *The Magician*, Heinemann, 1956, pp. viii–ix. (Doubleday, 1957, p. xi.)

51 *The Nation*, Vol. LXXXVIII, No. 2280, 11 March, 1909, p. 255.

52 *A Number of People: A Book of Reminiscences*, London, Heinemann, 1939, p. 328.

53 'A Fragment of Autobiography', p. x. (p. xii.)

54 *The Confessions of Aleister Crowley: An Autohagiography*, ed. John Symonds and Kenneth Grant, London, Cape, 1969, pp. 570–571.
55 'How to Write a Novel! After W. S. Maugham', *Vanity Fair*, 30 December, 1908, pp. 838–840.
56 Preface to *Liza of Lambeth*, p. xxv.
57 'W. Somerset Maugham: Theme and Variations', *College English*, Vol. VIII, No. 3, December, 1946, p. 115.
58 *The Magician*, p. 110. (p. 115.)
59 *Ibid.*, pp. 110–111. (p. 116.)
60 *Ibid.*, p. 118. (p. 123.)
61 *The Summing Up*, p. 121. (pp. 117–118.)

Chapter IV. *Of Human Bondage* and the Novels of Apprenticeship

1 *The Summing Up*, pp. 194–195. (p. 190.)
2 *Ivory Towers and Sacred Founts: The Artist as Hero in Fiction from Goethe to Joyce*, New York, New York University Press, 1964, p. 30.
3 *Forces in Modern British Literature 1885–1956*, New York, Vintage Books, 1956, p. 146.
4 *Remembering Mr Maugham*, p. 177.
5 Library of Congress, Washington, D.C., 'The Artistic Temperament of Stephen Carey', unpublished manuscript, p. 258.
6 *Wilhelm Meister and His English Kinsmen*, New York, Columbia University Press, 1930, p. 4.
7 *Ibid.*, pp. 5–6.
8 As quoted by Kanin, *Remembering Mr Maugham*, pp. 74–75.
9 As quoted by F. A. Beaumont, 'Luck in Authorship', p. 4.
10 Introduction to *Of Human Bondage*, New York, Pocket Books Incorporated, 1950, p. vi.
11 *The Vagrant Mood*, pp. 226–227. (p. 235.)
12 *Ibid.*, pp. 229–230. (p. 239.)
13 'Possible Influences of George Gissing's *Workers in the Dawn* on Maugham's *Of Human Bondage*', *Modern Language Quarterly*, Vol. VII, No. 3, 1946, p. 315.
14 As quoted by Burton Rascoe, 'A Chat with Somerset Maugham', in his *A Bookman's Daybook*, New York, Liveright, 1929, p. 153.
15 As quoted by F. A. Beaumont, 'Luck in Authorship', p. 4.
16 'Mr. Maugham's Notions', *Spectator*, No. 6941, 7 July, 1961, p. 24.
17 *Somerset and All the Maughams*, p. 163.
18 *Of Human Bondage*, pp. 12–13. (pp. 12–13.)
19 'An Interview With Somerset Maugham', *The New York Times Book Review*, 21 April, 1946, p. 3.
20 *Of Human Bondage*, p. 32. (p. 32.)
21 *Ibid.*, p. 126. (p. 126.)
22 *Ibid.*, p. 34. (p. 34.)
23 *Ibid.*, p. 42. (p. 42.)
24 *Ibid.*, p. 43. (p. 43.)

25 *A Writer's Notebook*, p. 345. (p. 362.)
26 Robin Maugham (*Somerset and All the Maughams*, p. 151) quotes James Robert Smith, who knew Maugham as a young schoolboy: 'I don't think he liked school much, and *he* probably wanted to be free and living at home the same as I was.'
27 *Of Human Bondage*, p. 79. (p. 79.)
28 *Ibid.*, p. 84. (p. 84.)
29 *Ibid.*, pp. 97–98. (pp. 97–98.)
30 *Ibid.*, pp. 103–104. (pp. 103–104.)
31 *Ibid.*, pp. 121–122. (pp. 121–122.)
32 *Ibid.*, pp. 122–123. (pp. 122–123.)
33 *Ibid.*, p. 148. (p. 148.)
34 *Ibid.*, p. 156. (p. 156.)
35 *Ibid.*, p. 145. (p. 145.)
36 Cordell (*Somerset Maugham*, p. 76) states that the character of Cronshaw was suggested by the original of Oliver Haddo in *The Magician*, Aleister Crowley. Although there are some similarities between Crowley and Cronshaw, it is more likely that the original model was (as has been suggested by Donald W. Buchanan in his *James Wilson Morrice: A Biography*, Toronto, Ryerson Press, 1936) a Canadian painter whom Maugham knew in Paris, James Wilson Morrice.
37 *Of Human Bondage*, p. 211. (p. 211.)
38 *Ibid.*, p. 246. (p. 246.)
39 *Ibid.*, p. 198. (p. 198.)
40 *Ibid.*, p. 251. (p. 251.)
41 *Ibid.*, p. 252. (p. 252.)
42 *Ibid.*, p. 259. (p. 259.)
43 *Ibid.*, p. 327. (p. 327.)
44 *Ibid.*, p. 329. (p. 329.)
45 *Ibid.*, p. 465. (p. 465.)
46 *Ibid.*, p. 286. (p. 286.)
47 *Ibid.*, p. 307. (p. 307.)
48 *Ibid.*, p. 294. (p. 294.)
49 *Ibid.*, p. 237. (p. 237.)
50 *Ibid.*, p. 317. (p. 317.)
51 *Ibid.*, p. 408. (p. 408.)
52 *Ibid.*, p. 511. (p. 511.)
53 *Somerset Maugham: A Guide*, p. 34.
54 *The Development of William Somerset Maugham*, p. 163.
55 *Of Human Bondage*, p. 496. (p. 496.)
56 Preface to Louis Marlow, *Two Made Their Bed*, London, Gollancz, 1929, p. 9.
57 *The Merry-Go-Round*, pp. 249–250.
58 *Of Human Bondage*, p. 261. (p. 261.)
59 *Ibid.*, p. 570. (p. 570.)
60 *Ibid.*, p. 612. (p. 612.)
61 *Ibid.*, p. 445. (p. 445.)

62 *Ibid.*, p. 558. (p. 558.)
63 *Ibid.*, p. 251. (p. 251.)
64 *Ibid.*, p. 445. (p. 445.)
65 *Ibid.*, p. 520. (p. 520.)
66 *Ibid.*, pp. 219–220. (pp. 219–220.)
67 *The Summing Up*, p. 288. (p. 281.)
68 *Of Human Bondage*, pp. 273–274. (pp. 273–274.)
69 *Ethics*, trans. W. Hale White and Amelia Hutchinson, London, Fisher Unwin, 1894, p. 176.
70 *Ibid.*, Part Four, Proposition LXXIII, p. 239.
71 In *The Summing Up*, pp. 258–259 (pp. 251–252), Maugham attributes this story to Anatole France's *La Vie Littéraire*.
72 *Of Human Bondage*, p. 559. (p. 559.)
73 *Ibid.*, p. 559. (p. 559.)
74 'Mr. Maugham's Pattern', *Spectator*, No. 5716, 14 January, 1938, p. 59.
75 *Of Human Bondage*, pp. 559–560. (pp. 559–560.)
76 *Ibid.*, p. 560.
77 *Ibid.*, pp. 643–644.
78 *The Summing Up*, p. 198. (pp. 193–194.)
79 The British Museum, Add. Ms. 46465, p. 306.
80 *American and British Literature Since 1890*, New York, Century, 1925, p. 208.
81 *The Summing Up*, p. 314. (p. 306.)
82 *Ibid.*, pp. 314–315. (p. 307.)
83 *Of Human Bondage*, p. 645. (p. 645.)
84 *Ibid.*, p. 647. (p. 647.)
85 'Spinoza's *Ethics* and Maugham', *University of Kansas City Review*, Vol. XXI, p. 263.
86 *The Development of William Somerset Maugham*, p. 178.

Chapter V. *The Moon and Sixpence* and the Artist-Hero Novels

1 Maugham, *Purely For My Pleasure*, Heinemann, 1962, pp. 7–8. (Double-day, 1963, p. 22.) Aleister Crowley (*The Spirit of Solitude: An Auto-hagiography*, Vol. II, London, The Mandrake Press, 1929, p. 243) writes with typical hyperbole of the relations between Maugham and O'Conor: 'To O'Conor, Maugham was not even funny. He was like a bed-bug, on which a sensitive man refuses to stamp because of the smell and the squashiness.'
2 'The Hero as Artist', in his *Sketches in Criticism*, New York, Dutton, 1932, p. 93.
3 'The Artist in Fiction', *The Magazine of Art*, Vol. VII, 1884, p. 159.
4 Gerald Jay Goldberg, 'The Artist-Hero Novel in Transition', *English Fiction in Transition*, Vol. IV, No. 3, 1961, pp. 21–22.
5 'Maugham and the Two Myths', p. 159.
6 'The Hero as Artist', pp. 93–94.
7 Maugham, *The Summing Up*, p. 51. (p. 50.)

39 *Cakes and Ale*, p. 139. (p. 158.)
40 *William Somerset Maugham*, pp. 151–152.

Chapter VIII. The Cosmopolitan: Aspects of the Maugham *Persona*

1 *Spy and Counter-Spy*, London, Harrap, 1941, p. 201.
2 *English Literature Between the Wars*, London, Methuen, 1949, pp. 104–105.
3 *Ashenden: or The British Agent*, Heinemann, 1928, p. 273. (Doubleday, Doran, 1928, p. 273.)
4 *Ibid.*, p. 274. (p. 274.)
5 *Ibid.*, p. 48. (p. 48.)
6 *Ibid.*, p. 101. (p. 101.)
7 'Secret Service Fiction', *The Graduate Student of English*, Vol. III, No. 4, Summer, 1960, p. 8.
8 *Ashenden*, p. 244. (p. 244.)
9 *Ibid.*, p. 98. (p. 98.)
10 As quoted by Ambler, *To Catch a Spy*, London, The Bodley Head, 1964, p. 19.
11 'Secret Service Fiction', p. 10.
12 *The Moon and Sixpence*, p. 49. (pp. 64–65.)
13 'W. Somerset Maugham: 1874–1965', *The Listener*, Vol. LXXIV, No. 1917, 23 December, 1965, p. 1033.
14 'Man of the World', *The New Statesman*, Vol. LXX, No. 1815, 24 December, 1965, p. 1008.
15 *The Nation and Athenaeum*, Vol. XLIII, No. 1, 7 April, p. 19.
16 'Man of the World', p. 1008.
17 'Virtue', *The Complete Short Stories*, Vol. II, p. 599. (Vol. I, p. 705.)
18 *W. Somerset Maugham: An Appreciation*, New York, Doubleday, Doran, 1939, pp. 11–12.
19 'W. Somerset Maugham: 1874–1965', p. 1033.
20 *The Gentleman in the Parlour*, Heinemann, 1930, p. 6. (Doubleday, Doran, 1930, p. 6.)
21 *The Saturday Review*, Vol. CL, No. 3910, 4 October, 1930, p. 409.
22 'The Social Sense', *The Complete Short Stories*, Vol. II, p. 931. (Vol. II, p. 579.)
23 *Cakes and Ale*, p. 1. (p. 1.)
24 *Ibid.*, pp. 127–128. (p. 145.)
25 *Ashenden*, p. 132. (p. 132.)
26 *Ibid.*, pp. 232–233. (pp. 232–233.)
27 *Ibid.*, p. 236. (p. 236.)
28 'The Human Element', *The Complete Short Stories*, Vol. II, p. 998. (Vol. I, p. 678.)
29 Maugham, an enthusiastic bridge player, maintained that the card table is an excellent arena for the demonstration of character. If this is true, it is interesting to analyse the kind of card player he makes his *persona*. In *Ashenden*, p. 34 (p. 34), he writes:

8 'Somerset Maugham as a Writer', *John O'London's Weekly*, Vol. LXIII, No. 1, 541, 22 January, 1954, p. 77.
9 Alec Waugh, 'Maugham at Eighty', *Encounter*, Vol. II, No. 1, January, 1954, p. 40.
10 *My Father Paul Gauguin*, trans. Arthur C. Chater, London, Cassell, 1937, p. ix.
11 As quoted by Menard, *The Two Worlds of Somerset Maugham*, p. 187.
12 Maugham, *The Moon and Sixpence*, Heinemann, 1919, p. 167. (Doran, 1919, p. 203.)
13 Maugham here uses a variation of his own experience. Godfrey Winn (*The Infirm Glory*, p. 258) quotes Maugham: 'I used to write all day in my house in Chesterfield Street, and come down to dinner dead tired and not knowing one of the guests in my own house, eating my expensive food. They had all been invited by my wife.'
14 *The Moon and Sixpence*, p. 27. (p. 38.)
15 *Ivory Towers and Sacred Founts*, p. 6.
16 *The Moon and Sixpence*, p. 62. (p. 80.)
17 *Ibid.*, p. 61. (p. 79.)
18 *Ibid.*, pp. 160–161. (p. 196.)
19 *Ibid.*, p. 173. (p. 210.)
20 'In Vishnu-Land What Avatar?', *The Dial*, 29 November, 1919, p. 478.
21 *The Moon and Sixpence*, p. 171. (p. 207.)
22 *Ibid.*, p. 172. (pp. 208–209.)
23 'Looking Back', *Show*, July, 1962, p. 98.
24 *The Moon and Sixpence*, pp. 54–55. (p. 70–71.)
25 *Ibid.*, p. 235. (p. 283.)
26 *Don Fernando: or Variations on Some Spanish Themes*, Heinemann, 1935, p. 217. (Doubleday, Doran, 1935, p. 249.)
27 *The Moon and Sixpence*, pp. 249–250. (pp. 299–300.)
28 *The Development of William Somerset Maugham*, p. 195.
29 *The Times Literary Supplement*, No. 708, 12 August, 1915, p. 269.
30 Published in *A Comprehensive Exhibition of the Writings of W. Somerset Maugham*, Stanford, Stanford University Press, 1958.
31 *The Moon and Sixpence*, p. 220. (p. 265.)
32 *The New Republic*, Vol. XXI, No. 262, 10 December, 1919, p. 57.
33 'Inarticulations', *Athenaeum*, No. 4645, 9 May, 1919, p. 302.
34 'In Vishnu-Land What Avatar?', p. 478.
35 'Inarticulations', p. 302.
36 'The Artist in the English Novel, 1850–1919', *Philological Studies*, West Virginia University, Vol. IV, September, 1943, p. 80.

Chapter VI. Marriage: A Condition of Bondage

1 Many critics have pointed out the numerous similarities between Walter Fane and the author. Maugham, however, wrote to R. F. V. Heuston (*Lives of the Lord Chancellors 1885–1940*, Oxford, Clarendon

Press, 1964, p. 571) in 1959 to explain: 'I don't suppose you have ever read a novel of mine called "The Painted Veil". I used my brother as a model for the doctor in that story.'

2 *The Painted Veil*, Heinemann, 1925, p. 156. (Doran, 1925, p. 156.)
3 *Ibid.*, p. 174. (p. 174.)
4 *Ibid.*, p. 248. (p. 248.)
5 *W. Somerset Maugham*, Norman, University of Oklahoma Press, 1966, p. 64.
6 *W. Somerset Maugham et ses Romans*, Paris, Perrin et Cie, 1928, pp. 206–207.
7 *The Painted Veil*, pp. 288–289. (pp. 288–289.)
8 *New York Herald Tribune Books*, 12 April, 1925, p. 5.
9 *The New Statesman*, Vol. XXV, No. 628, 9 May, 1925, p. 107.
10 *The New Republic*, Vol. XLII, No. 542, 22 April, 1925, p. 243.
11 *Theatre*, Heinemann, 1937, p. 55. (Doubleday, Doran, 1937, pp. 54–55.)
12 *Ibid.*, p. 60. (pp. 59–60.)
13 *Ibid.*, p. 142. (p. 141.)
14 *The Summing Up*, p. 193. (pp. 188–189.)
15 *Theatre*, p. 178. (p. 177.)
16 *Ibid.*, p. 218. (p. 216.)
17 *Ibid.*, p. 293. (p. 292.)
18 *Ibid.*, p. 264. (p. 262.)
19 *The Saturday Review of Literature*, Vol. XV, No. 19, 6 March, 1937, p. 3.
20 *Remembering Mr Maugham*, p. 60.
21 'The Human Element', *The Complete Short Stories of W. Somerset Maugham*, Vol. II, Heinemann, 1951, p. 1000. (Vol. I, Doubleday, 1952, pp. 680–681.)
22 *Ibid.*, p. 1023. (p. 704.)
23 *The Narrow Corner*, Heinemann, 1932, p. 284. (Doubleday, Doran, 1932, pp. 304–305.)
24 *The Constant Wife, The Collected Plays of W. Somerset Maugham*, Vol. II, Heinemann, 1931, p. 160.
25 *Ibid.*, p. 181.
26 *The Dramatic Comedy of William Somerset Maugham*, The Hague, Mouton, 1968, p. 65.
27 *The Unattainable, The Collected Plays*, Vol. II, p. 157.
28 *Ibid.*, p. 188.
29 *Home and Beauty, The Collected Plays*, Vol. II, p. 288.
30 *The Circle, The Collected Plays*, Vol. II, p. 74.

Chapter VII. *Cakes and Ale*

1 Introduction to *Cakes and Ale*, New York, Modern Library, 1950, pp. xi–xii.
2 *Figures in the Foreground*, London, Hutchinson, 1963, p. 92.

3 *The Nation and Athenaeum*, Vol. XLVIII, No. 4, 25 October, 1930, p. 140.
4 Preface to *The Selected Novels of W. Somerset Maugham*, Vol. I, Heinemann, 1953, p. viii.
5 Introduction to the Modern Library edition, p. vi.
6 'A Letter From England', *The Saturday Review of Literature*, Vol. VII, No. 15, 1 November, 1930, p. 299.
7 As quoted by Rupert Hart-Davis, *Hugh Walpole: A Biography*, London, Macmillan, 1952, p. 316.
8 *Ibid.*, p. 316.
9 Jessica Brett Young, *Francis Brett Young: A Biography*, London, Heinemann, 1962, p. 172.
10 Michael Holroyd, *Lytton Strachey: A Critical Biography*, Vol. II, London, Heinemann, 1968, p. 680.
11 As quoted by Hart-Davis, *Hugh Walpole: A Biography*, pp. 316–317.
12 *Ibid.*, p. 318.
13 *Gin and Bitters*, New York, Farrar and Rinehart, 1931.
14 As quoted by Hart-Davis, *Hugh Walpole: A Biography*, p. 326.
15 Introduction to the Modern Library edition, pp. ix–x.
16 'Waiting For Mr. Right', *New Yorker*, Vol. XXVIII, 23 August, 1952, p. 73.
17 *Cakes and Ale: or The Skeleton in the Cupboard*, Heinemann, 1930, p. 35. (Doubleday, Doran, 1930, p. 39.)
18 *Ibid.*, p. 41. (pp. 45–46.)
19 *Ibid.*, pp. 83–84. (pp. 94–95.)
20 *Somerset and All the Maughams*, p. 154.
21 Allen B. Brown ('Substance and Shadow: The Originals of the Characters in *Cakes and Ale*', *Papers of the Michigan Academy of Science, Arts, and Letters*, Vol. XLV, 1960, p. 444) claims, however, that John Drinkwater considered Gibbons a cruel caricature of himself.
22 *Cakes and Ale*, p. 163. (pp. 187–188.)
23 *Ibid.*, p. 169. (pp. 193–194.)
24 *Ibid.*, p. 152. (p. 173.)
25 'Somerset Maugham', *The Observer*, 19 December, 1965, p. 22.
26 *Cakes and Ale*, p. 14. (p. 16.)
27 *Ibid.*, p. 203. (pp. 232–233.)
28 *Ibid.*, p. 55. (p. 61.)
29 *Ibid.*, p. 53. (p. 59.)
30 *Ibid.*, pp. 246–247. (p. 282.)
31 *A Writer's Notebook*, pp. 189–190. (p. 199.)
32 *Remembering Mr Maugham*, p. 132.
33 *Cakes and Ale*, p. 65. (p. 73.)
34 *Ibid.*, pp. 177–178. (pp. 202–204.)
35 *Ibid.*, p. 249. (pp. 284–285.)
36 *William Somerset Maugham*, London, Geoffrey Bles, 1937, p. 157.
37 *Cakes and Ale*, pp. 189–190. (pp. 217–218.)
38 'Somerset Maugham', in his *Memories*, London, MacGibbon and Kee, 1953, p. 65.

He had (he flattered himself) few illusions about himself, and so far as bridge was concerned none. He knew that he was a good player of the second class, but he had played often enough with the best players in the world to know that he was not in the same street with them.

In 'Sanatorium', the final struggle between the two irascible Scots is fought at the bridge table. The bidding is adventurous and extravagant, but Ashenden is non-committal, and hardly a factor in the game. Similarly, in 'The Pool', the narrator joins in a poker game, but plays 'modestly, neither wishing to win nor anxious to lose'. As a card player, the Maugham *persona* reflects his place in the stories – present and interested, but not an influencing factor.

30 *Somerset Maugham*, p. 28.
31 'Maugham: Compassionate Cynic', *Sunday Times*, 19 December, 1965, p. 35.

Chapter IX. *The Razor's Edge* and the New Vedanta

1 *Images of Truth*, London, Hamish Hamilton, 1963, pp. 71–72.
2 *Christmas Holiday*, Heinemann, 1939, p. 45. (Doubleday, Doran, 1939, pp. 48–49.)
3 *A Writer's Notebook*, p. 328. (pp. 344–345.)
4 *Then and Now*, Heinemann, 1946, p. 229. (Doubleday, 1946, pp. 277–278.)
5 *Somerset Maugham: A Guide*, p. 195.
6 *Remembering Mr Maugham*, p. 113.
7 *Letters of John Cowper Powys to Louis Wilkinson*, London, MacDonald, 1958, pp. 222–223.
8 *William Somerset Maugham*, p. 155.
9 *The Narrow Corner*, pp. 41–42. (pp. 44–45.)
10 It cannot be conclusively proved, but it is likely that Maugham found the material for this passage in S. Radhakrishnan's two-volume *Indian Philosophy*, published in 1929 and 1931. The copies in the Maugham Library at King's School are heavily annotated, and the following passages show a remarkable similarity. Frith says:

'And when you ask those wise men of the East why the supreme spirit should have sent forth this phantasmagory they will tell you it was for his diversion. For being complete and perfect, he could not be actuated by aims or motive. Aim and motive imply desire and he that is perfect and complete needs neither change nor addition. Therefore the activity of the eternal spirit has no purpose, but like the frolic of princes or the play of children, is spontaneous and exultant.' (*The Narrow Corner*, p. 162; p. 174.)

Maugham notes in *Indian Philosophy*:

So it is said that 'the activity of the Lord may be supposed to be mere sport (lila) proceeding from his own nature, without reference to any purpose' . . . The act of creation is not motivated by any selfish interest. It is the spontaneous overflow of God's nature (svabhava), even as it is the nature of man to breathe in and out. God cannot help creating. The work of the world is not the result of chance or thoughtlessness, but is simply the outcome of God's nature. (*Indian Philosophy*, Vol. II, London, George Allen and Unwin, 1931, pp. 550–551).

11 *The Narrow Corner*, p. 187. (p. 201.)
12 *Ibid.*, pp. 218–219. (pp. 234–235.)
13 *Ibid.*, p. 288. (p. 309.)
14 *Remembering Mr Maugham*, p. 107.
15 *The Unknown, The Collected Plays*, Vol. III, pp. 58–59.
16 *My Brother Evelyn and Other Profiles*, London, Cassell, 1967, p. 288.
17 'The Lotus Eater', *The Complete Short Stories*, Vol. III, p. 1279. (Vol. II, p. 248.)
18 The manuscript for this play was discovered by Raymond Mander and Joe Mitchenson. For a more extensive synopsis and commentary, see their *Theatrical Companion to Maugham*, London, Rockcliff, 1955, pp. 195–199.
19 *Chips: The Diaries of Sir Henry Channon*, ed. Robert R. James, London, Weidenfeld and Nicolson, 1967, p. 5.
20 *Ibid.*, p. 38.
21 *Ibid.*, p. 392.
22 *The Atlantic Monthly*, Vol. CLXXIII, No. 5, May, 1944, p. 127.
23 *The Yale Review*, Vol. XXXIII, No. 4, June, 1944, p. 765.
24 'The Art of Being Good', in his *The Condemned Playground*, New York, Macmillan, 1946, p. 250.
25 Huxley, *Ends and Means*, London, Chatto and Windus, 1937, pp. 3–4.
26 *After Many a Summer*, London, Chatto and Windus, 1962, p. 109.
27 *Grey Eminence*, London, Chatto and Windus, 1956, p. 296.
28 *The Razor's Edge*, p. 254. (p. 307.)
29 'Facing the Pacific', in his *Classics and Commercials*, New York, Farrar, Straus, 1958, p. 48.
30 *Ambrosia and Small Beer*, London, Longmans, 1964, pp. 163–164.
31 *A Writer's Notebook*, p. 271. (p. 284.)
32 *The Razor's Edge*, p. 136. (p. 165.)
33 *Ibid.*, p. 217. (p. 261.)
34 *Ibid.*, p. 149. (p. 180.)
35 *Ibid.*, p. 188. (p. 227.)
36 *Ibid.*, p. 253. (p. 306.)
37 *Ibid.*, p. 238. (p. 288.)
38 *Ibid.*, p. 247. (p. 298.)
39 *Ibid.*, p. 251. (p. 303.)
40 David Paul, 'Maugham and the Two Myths', p. 160.
41 *The Razor's Edge*, p. 257. (p. 310.)
42 *Ibid.*, p. 284. (p. 343.)
43 *A Writer's Notebook*, pp. 343–344. (p. 361.)
44 'The Problem of the Religious Novel', *Vedanta For Modern Man*, New York, Harper and Brothers, 1951, p. 250.
45 *W. Somerset Maugham*, p. 97.
46 *The Yogi and the Commissar*, London, Cape, 1945, p. 18.

Chapter X. Conclusion

1 'The Maugham Enigma', *The New Republic*, 30 March, 1938.
2 'The Apotheosis of Somerset Maugham', in his *Classics and Commercials*, p. 319. Maugham seems to have been somewhat of an obsession for Wilson. John Lehmann (*I Am My Brother*, London, Longmans, 1960, p. 288) tells of Wilson's vehemence on the subject of Maugham during the war, and Garson Kanin (*Remembering Mr Maugham*, pp. 262–264) describes a similar attack by Wilson on Maugham in 1960.
3 *Ibid.*, p. 326.

Appendix A. 'Rosie'

1 'Substance and Shadow: The Originals of the Characters in *Cakes and Ale*'.
2 Introduction to the Modern Library edition, p. xi.
3 'Looking Back', *Show*, June, 1962, p. 67.
4 *A Writer's Notebook*, p. 80. (p. 84.)
5 *Ibid.*, p. 80. (pp. 84–85.)
6 *Remembering Mr Maugham*, p. 132.
7 'Looking Back', p. 111.
8 *Somerset Maugham*, p. 98.
9 Sir Gerald Kelly to R. L. Calder, 4 February, 1970.
10 *Remembering Mr Maugham*, p. 133.
11 *A Case of Human Bondage*, p. 86.
12 *The Summing Up*, p. 171. (p. 167.)

Appendix B. Maugham's Role in Allied Espionage in Russia in 1917

1 Maugham's part in Allied espionage in Russia has been discussed in W. B. Fowler's *British–American Relations: 1917–1918: The Role of Sir William Wiseman*, Princeton, Princeton University Press, 1969 pp. 114–118.
2 Emanuel Voska, Secretary of the Bohemian National Alliance and Director of the Slav Press Bureau in New York.
3 Major Norman Thwaites, M.C., a military attaché who was Wiseman's assistant in Washington.
4 Maugham uses the code name 'Somerville' several times in *Ashenden* as the agent's pseudonym.
5 Private secretary for the Secretary of State for the British Foreign Office.
6 The author of this report is almost certainly Maugham. The style is his, and the 'S' would represent his code name, 'Somerville'.
7 Maugham was later to use this episode in *Ashenden* in 'Behind the Scenes', and he recounted it in detail in 'Looking Back', *Show*, July, 1962, p. 49.

8 Maugham describes the circumstances of his meeting with Lloyd George and his conveying of the message from Kerensky in 'Looking Back', *Show*, July, 1962, p. 95.

9 Sir Eric Drummond wrote across the top of the report: 'Communicated by Sir W. Wiseman who had received document from Mr. Maugham who has just returned from Petrograd. E.D. 18–11–17.' (Public Record Office, Private Secretary Archives, 1917–1924, A. J. Balfour, FO 800/205, p. 215.)

Appendix C. Five Fictional Portraits of Somerset Maugham

1 As quoted by James Agate, *Ego* 5, London, Harrap, 1942, p. 113.
2 *The Limit*, London, Grant Richards, 1911, pp. 51–52.
3 *Gin and Bitters*, p. 5.
4 *Ibid.*, p. 32.
5 *Ibid.*, pp. 44–45.
6 *John Cornelius: His Life and Adventures*, London, Macmillan, 1937, pp. 287–288.
7 *Ibid.*, p. 341.
8 *Jane: A Comedy in Three Acts*, London, Samuel French, 1953, p. 99.
9 *Point Valaine*, London, Heinemann, 1935, p. 97.
10 *A Song at Twilight*, London, Samuel French, 1966, p. 15.
11 *Ibid.*, p. 15.
12 *Ibid.*, p. 41.
13 'Looking Back', *Show*, July, 1962, p. 49.
14 *A Song at Twilight*, p. 41.
15 *Ibid.*, p. 44.
16 *Ibid.*, p. 52.

A Select Bibliography

Bibliographies

Bason, Frederick T. *A Bibliography of the Writings of William Somerset Maugham*. London (1931).

Stott, Raymond T. *Maughamiana: The Writings of W. Somerset Maugham*. London (1950, revised 1956 with suppl. 1964).

Jonas, Klaus W. *Bibliography of the Writings of W. Somerset Maugham*. South Hadley, Mass. (1950).

Novels

Liza of Lambeth (1897).
The Making of a Saint (1898).
The Hero (1901).
Mrs Craddock (1902, revised 1928).
The Merry-Go-Round (1904).
The Bishop's Apron (1906).
The Explorer (1908).
The Magician (1908).
Of Human Bondage (1915).
The Moon and Sixpence (1919).
The Painted Veil (1925).
Cakes and Ale (1930).
The Narrow Corner (1932).
Theatre (1937).
Christmas Holiday (1939).
Up at the Villa (1941).
The Hour Before the Dawn (1942).
The Razor's Edge (1944).
Then and Now (1946).
Catalina (1948).

Short Stories

Orientations (1899).
The Trembling of a Leaf (1921).
The Casuarina Tree (1926).
Ashenden: or The British Agent (1928).
Six Stories Written in the First Person Singular (1931).
Ah King (1933).

Cosmopolitans (1936).
The Mixture as Before (1940).
Creatures of Circumstance (1947).
Seventeen Lost Short Stories (1969).

Plays

Schiffbruechig (Marriages are Made in Heaven).
A Man of Honour (1903).
Lady Frederick (1911).
Jack Straw (1911).
Mrs Dot (1912).
The Explorer (1912).
Penelope (1912).
The Tenth Man (1913).
Landed Gentry (1913).
Smith (1913).
The Land of Promise (1913).
The Unknown (1920).
The Circle (1921).
East of Suez (1922).
Caesar's Wife (1922).
Our Betters (1923).
Home and Beauty (1923).
The Unattainable (Caroline) (1923).
Loaves and Fishes (1924).
The Letter (1927).
The Constant Wife (1927).
The Sacred Flame (1928).
The Breadwinner (1930).
For Services Rendered (1932).
Sheppey (1933).

Non-Fiction

The Land of the Blessed Virgin: Sketches and Impressions in Andalusia (1905).
On a Chinese Screen (1922).
The Gentleman in the Parlour (1930).
Don Fernando: or Variations on Some Spanish Themes (1935, revised 1950).
The Summing Up (1938).
France at War (1940).
Books and You (1940).
Strictly Personal (1941).
Great Novelists and Their Novels (1948, revised and published as *Ten Novels and Their Authors* in 1954).
A Writer's Notebook (1949).
The Writer's Point of View (1951).
The Vagrant Mood (1952).

Points of View (1958).
Purely For My Pleasure (1962).
'Looking Back' (*Show*, June–August, 1962).

Collected Editions
The Collected Plays (6 vols., 1931–34; 3 vols., 1952).
The Somerset Maugham Sampler (1943).
The Maugham Reader (1950).
The Complete Short Stories (Heinemann, 3 vols., 1951; Doubleday, 2 vols., 1952).
The Selected Novels (1953).
The Partial View (1954).
Mr Maugham Himself (1954).
The Travel Books (1955).
Selected Prefaces and Introductions (1964).

Biographical and Critical Studies
a. Books
Towne, C. H. and others. *W. Somerset Maugham*. New York (1925).
Dottin, Paul. *W. Somerset Maugham et ses Romans*. Paris (1928).
Guéry, Suzanne. *La Philosophie de Somerset Maugham*. Paris (1933).
MacCarthy, Desmond. *W. Somerset Maugham: The English Maupassant*. London (1934).
McIver, Claude Searcy. *William Somerset Maugham: A Study of Technique and Literary Sources*. Philadelphia (1936).
Cordell, Richard A. *William Somerset Maugham*. New York (1937).
Dottin, Paul. *Le Theatre de W. Somerset Maugham*. Paris (1937).
Ward, Richard Heron. *W. Somerset Maugham*. London (1937).
Aldington, Richard. *W. Somerset Maugham: An Appreciation*. New York (1939).
Brophy, John. *Somerset Maugham*. London (1952).
William Somerset Maugham. Aetat 80. London (1954).
Jonas, Klaus W. (ed.). *The Maugham Enigma*. London (1954).
Mander, Raymond and Mitchenson, Joe. *Theatrical Companion to Maugham*. London (1955).
Jensen, Sven Arnold. *William Somerset Maugham: Some Aspects of the Man and His Work*. Oslo (1957).
Pfeiffer, Karl. *Somerset Maugham: A Candid Portrait*. New York (1958).
Jonas, Klaus W. (ed.). *The World of Somerset Maugham*. New York (1959).
Cordell, Richard A. *Somerset Maugham: A Biographical and Critical Study*. London (1961, revised 1969).
Brander, Laurence. *Somerset Maugham: A Guide*. London (1963).
Menard, Wilmon. *The Two Worlds of Somerset Maugham*. Los Angeles (1965).
W. Somerset Maugham: An Appreciation. New York (1965).
Kanin, Garson. *Remembering Mr Maugham*. New York (1966).

Maugham, Robin. *Somerset and All the Maughams*. London (1966).
Naik, M. K. *W. Somerset Maugham*. Norman, Oklahoma (1966).
Nichols, Beverley. *A Case of Human Bondage*. London (1966).
Barnes, Ronald E. *The Dramatic Comedy of William Somerset Maugham*. The Hague (1968).
Brown, Ivor. *W. Somerset Maugham*. London (1970).

b. Articles, Parts of Books.

Note: Readers wishing to examine extensive Maugham criticism will find the annotated secondary bibliography of *W. Somerset Maugham*, edited by Charles Sanders, DeKalb, Illinois, 1970, very useful. The references below are to important Maugham material which is not included in the Sanders bibliography.

Crowley, Edward Alexander ('Oliver Haddo'). 'How to Write a Novel! After W. S. Maugham', *Vanity Fair*, 30 Dec., 1908, pp. 838–840.

Mencken, H. L. 'Point of View', *Smart Set*, 1919. Reprinted in *Smart Set Criticism*. Ithaca (1968), pp. 45–48.

Walpole, Hugh. 'William Somerset Maugham: A Pen Portrait by a Friendly Hand', *Vanity Fair* (U.S.), 1920. Reprinted in *Vanity Fair: A Cavalcade of the 1920's and 1930's*. New York (1960), pp. 40–41.

Lawrence, D. H. *Vogue* (London), 20 July, 1928. Reprinted in *Selected Literary Criticism*. London (1955), pp. 144–145.

Rascoe, Burton. 'A Chat With Somerset Maugham', *A Bookman's Daybook*. New York (1929), pp. 148–153.

Stokes, Sewell. 'Maugham is Stranger Than Fiction', *Pilloried!* New York (1929), pp. 38–53.

Bason, Frederick T. *Gallery Unreserved*. London (1931).

MacCarthy, Desmond. 'The Skirmishers', *Life and Letters*, Feb. 1931.

Doran, George H. *Chronicles of Barabbas – 1884–1934*. Toronto (1935).

Nichols, Beverley. *Twenty-five*. London (1935).

Buchanan, Donald W. *James Wilson Morrice: A Biography*. Toronto (1936).

Wells, James M. 'The Artist in the English Novel, 1850–1919', *Philological Studies*, Vol. IV, Sept., 1943, pp. 77–80.

Isherwood, Christopher. 'The Problem of the Religious Novel', *Vedanta For Modern Man*. New York (1951).

Hart-Davis, Rupert. *Hugh Walpole: A Biography*. London (1952).

Marlow, Louis. 'William Somerset Maugham', *Seven Friends*. London (1953), pp. 142–170.

John O'London's Weekly, Jan. 22, 1954.

Kelly, Sir Gerald. 'Old Friends', *Sunday Times*, Jan. 24, 1954, p. 6.

Hassall, Christopher. *Edward Marsh: Patron of the Arts*. London (1959).

Ambler, Eric. *To Catch a Spy*. London (1964).

Reed, John R. *Old School Ties: The Public Schools in British Literature*. Syracuse (1964).

Connolly, Cyril. 'Maugham: Compassionate Cynic', *Sunday Times*, Dec. 19, 1965, p. 35.

Muggeridge, Malcolm. 'Somerset Maugham', *The Observer*, Dec. 19, 1965, p. 22.

Pritchett, V. S. 'Man of the World', *The New Statesman*, Vol. LXX, No. 1815, Dec. 24, 1965, p. 1008.

Bason, Frederick T. 'Postscript to Maugham', *The Saturday Book*. London (1966), pp. 185–188.

Pearson, John. *The Life of Ian Fleming*. London (1966).

Pittman, R. N. 'The Maugham Library', *The Cantuarian*, Vol. XXXI, No. 4, Dec. 1966, pp. 282–284.

Waugh, Alec. *My Brother Evelyn and Other Profiles*. London (1967).

Winn, Godfrey. *The Infirm Glory*. London (1967).

Crowley, Edward Alexander. *The Confessions of Aleister Crowley: An Autohagiography*. London (1969).

Acton, Harold. *More Memoirs of an Aesthete*. London (1970).

Daubeny, Peter. *My World of Theatre*. London (1971).

Gordon, Ruth. *Myself Among Others*. New York (1971).

Index

Titles refer to works of Maugham unless otherwise specified.

A la Recherche du Temps Perdu (Proust), 139
Acton, Harold, 18
adaptations for other media, 36f
Adcock, St John, 60, 61
After Many a Summer (Huxley), 239f
Aldington, Richard, 215
'Alien Corn, The', 146, 235
Ambler, Eric, 204, 208
Amis, Kingsley, 92f
Anderson, Maxwell, 142, 150
apprentice novels, 83f
Apprenticeship of Wilhelm Meister, The (Goethe), 83f
art and morality, 140ff
artist-hero novels, 83, 132ff, 149ff
artistic creation, as bondage, 105f, 144ff; as catharsis, 29ff, 146f, 160f, 198
'Artistic Temperament of Stephen Carey, The', 30, 79ff, 272
Ashenden, 77, 200ff, 219, 220

'Bad Example, A', 40, 53, 228
Barnes, Ronald, 167
beauty, 31, 106
Beebe, Maurice, 78
Beerbohm, Sir Max, 187
Behrman, S. N., 290, 294
Bennett, Arnold, 6, 85, 87f
Bishop's Apron, The, 52, 68f, 152
body and soul, 97
Brander, Laurence, 69, 112, 227
Breadwinner, The, 170
Brooks, Van Wyck, 132, 134f
Brophy, John, 221
Brown, Allen B., 271f
Buchan, John, 204
Buchanan, Sir George, 201
Buddhism, 229ff, 237ff
Burgess, Anthony, 211, 215
Butler, Samuel, 85ff

Caesar's Wife, 152
Cakes and Ale, 77, 155, 160, 172–99, 210f, 217f, 220f, 268ff
Californian Vedantists, 239ff
Cannan, Gilbert, 85, 89
Cary, Joyce, 150
Casuarina Tree, The, 135
Catalina, 31, 36, 77, 224f, 227
Channon, Sir Henry ('Chips'), 235ff
Chaplin, Charlie, 191f
Child of the Jago, A (Morrison), 39, 41ff
Childers, Erskine, 204
China, Maugham on, 18, 153
Christmas Holiday, 144f, 224ff
Circle, The, 152, 169
Clark, Lord, 6, 14
Clayhanger (Bennett), 85, 87f
clichés, 216, 300
Clowes, Evelyn May, *see* Mordaunt, Elinor

cockney speech, 40, 43f
Cody, Richard, 206, 208
Colefax, Lady (Sibyl), 138
Collins, J. P., 61
colloquialisms, 216
'Colonel's Lady, The', 155
Colton, John, 14
Colvin, Mr & Mrs Sidney, 183, 184
commercialism, 52f, 68ff
Connolly, Cyril, 12, 223, 238
Conrad, Joseph, 70, 146, 203f, 212
Constant Wife, The, 114, 152, 165f
contemporaneity of Maugham's writing, 26ff, 35ff, 255f
convention, Maugham's abhorrence of, 19
Cordell, Richard, 10, 54, 61f, 229, 268f
cosmopolitanism of Maugham *persona*, 212ff
'Cousin Amy', 152
Coward, Sir Noel, 14, 28, 259, 290, 294ff
Cowley, Malcolm, 260
'Creative Impulse, The', 152, 183
criticisms of Maugham's writing, 122, 129f, 149ff, 158, 166, 187ff, 197, 206, 217, 222, 251f, 261
Crowley, Aleister, 73ff, 307
'Cupid and the Vicar of Swale', 152

'Daisy', 53
Deighton, Len, 209
De Mattos, Katharine, 133
detachment in Maugham's writing, 17ff, 41, 130, 257ff
determinism, 32, 59, 67f, 117ff, 128
DeVoto, Bernard, 163
Diana of the Crossways (Meredith), 61
Doctor's Dilemma, The (Shaw), 140f, 150
Don Fernando, 211, 229
Doner, Dean, 128
Doran, George H., 11
Dottin, Paul, 157
Dreiser, Theodore, 150
Drinkwater, John, 311
Drummond, Sir Eric, 227, 282f, 288

economic independence, importance of, 10ff, 113ff, 166, 249f
Ends and Means (Huxley), 239
environment, influence of, 42, 46, 50, 56f, 66f, 92ff
'Episode', 152
Esther Waters (Moore), 39, 41
Ethics (Spinoza), 20, 120f
Evans, B. Ifor, 202
experimentation, literary, 37f, 65
Explorer, The, 9, 52, 69ff, 77, 152
Eyeless in Gaza (Huxley), 239

'Faith', 229
'Fall of Edward Barnard, The', 232f
female characters in Maugham, 3f, 89ff, 195f 244ff

First World War, literature of, 201f
Flaubert, Gustave, 39, 60
Fleming, Ian, 208f, 214
'Flirtation, The', 152
France at War, 27
free will, *see* determinism
French Naturalism, 39, 41, 88
Frierson, William C., 44
Frohman, Charles, 11
Full Circle, see Gin and Bitters

Gauguin, Paul, 105f, 131f, 136f, 151
Gauguin, Pola, 136
Genius, The (Dreiser), 150
Gentleman in the Parlour, The, 183, 211, 216, 229
Gielgud, Val, 37
Gin and Bitters (Mordaunt), 177f, 290, 292f
Gissing, George, 39, 41, 42, 45, 89f
Goebbels, Josef, 206
Goethe, 78, 83f
goodness, 32, 107, 112ff, 228f
Gosse, Sir Edmund, 183, 203
Greene, Graham, 122
Grey Eminence (Huxley), 240

'Happy Couple, The', 152
Hart, Moss, 16
Hardy, Thomas, 173ff
Haxton, Gerald, 13f, 23ff, 238, 239ff, 296
Hazlitt, William, 216
'Heart of Darkness' (Conrad), 70, 146
Hero, The, 52f, 55ff, 77, 152, 232
historical novels, 53f
Holden, George, 182f
Hole in the Wall, A (Morrison), 39
Hollywood, Maugham in, 11
Home and Beauty, 168f
homosexuality, Maugham's, 23ff, 296
Horse's Mouth, The (Cary), 150
Hour Before the Dawn, The, 77, 224
Howe, Sir Ronald, 7
Howe, Susanne, 70, 71, 83f
'Human Element, The', 153, 164f, 219
Hunt, Violet, 138
Huxley, Aldous, 238, 239ff, 252
Huysmans, Joris Karl, 39, 73

illusion and reality, 95, 103ff, 109
imperialistic fiction, 69ff
Indian mysticism, 229ff, 237ff
Isherwood, Christopher, 239ff, 252f

Jack Straw, 9
Jane (Behrman), 290, 294
Jean-Christophe (Rolland), 83, 85, 89
John Cornelius (Walpole), 290, 293f
Jones, Doris, 269
Jones, Ethelwyn Sylvia, 192, 269ff
Jones, Henry Arthur, 44, 192, 269f
Joyce, James, 83, 127, 134, 139, 150
'Judgement Seat, The', 66f
Julius Caesar (Shakespeare), 54

Kanin, Garson, 10, 82, 163f, 193, 227f, 231f, 268, 271
Kant, Immanuel, 31
Kelly, Sir Gerald, 10, 12, 16, 74f, 87, 269ff, 271
Kelly, Rose, 75
Kennedy, P. C., 158
Kerensky, A. F., 200, 277, 281, 283, 286, 288f
King's School, Canterbury, 7, 15, 20
Kipling, Rudyard, 39, 41ff, 69, 70
'Kite, The', 152

Koestler, Arthur, 252
Kornilov, 281, 286
Kropotkin, Princess Alexandra, 200, 201
Kuner, Mildred C., 55, 73, 113, 129, 147
Kunstlerroman, see artist-hero novels

Lady Frederick, 9, 152
'Lady Habart', 152
Land of Promise, The, 11
Lang, Andrew, 53f
Larger than Life (Bolton), 163
Lawrence, D. H., 60, 134, 150, 167, 203
Lawrence, T. E., 204
'Le Chat Blanc' (restaurant), 73, 74, 77, 131
Le Carré, John, 209
Le Queux, William, 204
Leveaux, Montague Vivian, 192, 269
Leverson, Ada, 290ff
Limit, The (Leverson), 290ff
literary experimentation, 37f, 65
Liza of Lambeth, 9, 39–51, 76f
Lloyd George, David, 286, 288
Loaves and Fishes, 68
'Looking Back', 22, 34, 192, 268
'Lotus Eater, The', 233
love, sexual, 98, 142ff, 155f, 171, 195f; and loving-kindness, 125f, 260
Lovett, Robert M., 149, 158, 291
Lustgarten, Edgar, 291

MacCarthy, Desmond, 36, 197
McDonnell, Angus, 192, 270
Mackenzie, Compton, 83, 90, 127, 246, 302
Magician, The, 52, 72ff, 77, 131, 152
Making of a Saint, The, 52, 53ff, 272
Man of Honour, A, 53, 66, 152, 272
Mansfield, Katherine, 149, 151
Marlow, Louis, 113
marriage as bondage, 21ff, 61ff, 152–71
'Marriage of Convenience, A', 152
Marriages Are Made in Heaven, 53
Marsh, Edward, 73f, 241
Masaryk, 200, 277, 278, 281f
Maugham, Edith, 3
Maugham, Frederick, 19
Maugham, Henry MacDonald, 4f, 86, 93
Maugham, Henry Neville, 9
Maugham, Liza, 19
Maugham, Robert Ormond, 4
Maugham, Robin, 2, 3, 5, 19, 24, 25, 93, 182f
Maugham, Syrie, *see* Wellcome, Syrie
Maupassant, Guy de, 41
Maurice Guest (Richardson), 85, 88f, 150
'Mayhew', 233
meaninglessness of life, 116ff, 121ff
Menard, Wilmon, 22f
Meredith, George, 61
Merry-Go-Round, The, 40, 52f, 65ff, 77, 152
Mixture as Before, The, 35f
money and independence, *see* economic independence
Moon and Sixpence, The, 77, 131–51, 152, 210, 220, 228
Moore, George, 39, 41, 42
Mordaunt, Elinor, 177f, 290, 292f
Morrice, James Wilson, 307
Morrison, Arthur, 39, 41ff
Mortimer, Raymond, 211
'Mother, The', 152
'Mr Harrington's Washing', 201
'Mrs Beamish', 152
Mrs Craddock, 52f, 60ff, 77, 152f, 158f
Mrs Dot, 9
Muggeridge, Malcolm, 12, 20, 187

Mugnier, Abbé, 236
mysticism, 158, 229ff, 237ff

Naik, M. K., 157, 252
narrators, *see persona*
Narrow Corner, The, 77, 165, 228, 229ff, 241f
Naturalism, French, 39, 41, 88
Nichols, Beverley, 14, 23, 24f, 271

occultism, 73ff
O'Conor, Roderic, 131f
Of Human Bondage, 30, 40, 45, 77, 78–130, 131, 146, 147, 271f
old and middle age, Maugham on, 26f
Old Wives' Tale, The (Bennett), 85, 87f
On a Chinese Screen, 18, 135, 153
Oppenheimer, E. Phillips, 204

'P & O', 155
Painted Veil, The, 77, 135, 153ff, 229
Paramhansa Yogananda, 252
Paterson, Isabel, 158
Paul, David, 36, 134, 249
Penelope, 114, 152
persona of narrator, 41, 209–23, 249; in short stories, 211ff; in travel books, 211; in *Ashenden*, 204ff, 209ff, 220; in *Cakes and Ale*, 181, 210f, 217f, 220ff; in *The Moon and Sixpence*, 220; in *The Razor's Edge*, 247ff
Phillips, Stephen, 183
Point Valaine (Coward), 294f
Points of View, 31
politics in Maugham's writing, 54f, 225ff
Portrait of the Artist as a Young Man, A (Joyce), 83, 127, 134, 139, 150
Powys, John Cowper, 228
Prescott, Orville, 237
Priestley, J. B., 175
'Princess September and the Nightingale', 143
Pritchett, V. S., 72, 211, 213
'Pro Patria', 152
professionalism of Maugham, 35ff, 255f
Proust, Marcel, 139

Razor's Edge, The, 224, 227–53
'Record of Badalia Herodsfoot, The' (Kipling), 39, 41ff
rejuvenation treatment, Maugham's, 28
religious belief, 100f, 227ff
religious novels, 237ff
Richardson, Henry Handel, 85, 88f, 150
Riddle of the Sands, The (Childers), 204
'Riposte, A.' (pseudonym), *see* Mordaunt, Elinor
'Road Uphill, The', 234f, 237
Rolland, Romain, 83, 85, 89
Ross, Woodburn O., 75
Russia, European fascination with, 202f; Maugham as agent in, 200, 274–89

'Saint, The', 242, 243
St Thomas's Hospital, 40
'Salvatore', 228
'Sanatorium', 211f
Schiffbruechig, 53
Searle, Alan, 29
Secret Agent, The (Conrad), 203f
Seven Pillars of Wisdom, The (T. E. Lawrence), 204
Shaw, G. B., 140f, 150
Sheppey, 228
short stories, Maugham *persona* in, 211ff
Sinister Street (Mackenzie), 83, 90, 127, 246

slum novels, 39ff
snobbery, 19f, 112, 181ff
Song at Twilight, A (Coward), 290, 295ff
Sons and Lovers (D. H. Lawrence), 83, 85, 150
Sorrows of Young Werther, The (Goethe), 78
South Sea Bubble (Coward), 294
Spain, Maugham on, 9
Spinoza, 20, 119ff
spy stories, 203ff
Spy Who Came in from the Cold, The (Le Carré), 209
Stanley, H. M., 70
state and individual, 119ff
Steevens, Mrs G. W., 268, 269f
Stott, Raymond Toole, 70
Strachey, Lytton, 176
Street, George, 138
Strictly Personal, 27
success, Maugham and, 12f, 135f
Summing Up, The, 30, 31
Swinnerton, Frank, 18, 135f, 172

Tales of Mean Streets (Morrison), 39, 41, 42
theatre, Maugham on, 30, 76
Theatre, 77, 153, 158ff
Then and Now, 31, 77, 224f, 226f
Tindall, William York, 79
Tomlinson, Kathleen C., 173f
Tono-Bungay (Wells), 90
Towne, Charles Hanson, 11
travel, Maugham and, 13f, 17f
Trembling of a Leaf, The, 135
'Trio' (film), 212
Two Made Their Bed (Marlow), 113

Up at the Villa, 77, 114f, 224
Unattainable, The, 167f
Unknown, The, 152, 232
Unwin, Fisher, 40, 79

Van Doren, Carl & Mark, 125
Van Gelder, Robert, 94
Vedanta, 237ff
Vedanta and the West (periodical), 240, 241
Venkataraman, Maharishi, 242
Venture, The (periodical), 53
Villa Mauresque, 12
'Virtue', 66f, 155, 213f
Voska, Emanuel, 201, 274ff

Walpole, Hugh, 175ff, 203, 271, 290, 293f
Ward, Richard Heron, 195, 199, 228f
Waugh, Alec, 136, 233
Way of All Flesh, The (Butler), 85ff
Webster, H. T., 89f
Weeks, Edward, 237
Wellcome, Henry, 22
Wellcome, Syrie, 21f
Wells, H. G., 90
Wells, James M., 151
Wescott, Glenway, 225
West, Anthony, 178f
Wilson, Edmund, 240, 261
Winn, Godfrey, 24, 309
Wiseman, Sir William, 274ff
women, Maugham and, 20ff. *See also* female characters
Workers in the Dawn (Gissing), 39, 89f
Wrong People, The (Robin Maugham), 25

Yeats, W. B., 238
Young, Francis Brett, 176

Zola, Emile, 39, 40